ORGANIZATIONAL BEHAVIOUR

ORGANIZATIONAL BEHAVIOUR

Dr. V G KONDALKAR
Professor
People's Institute of Management & Research
People's University
Bhopal, MP

NEW AGE
MANAGEMENT

An Imprint of

NEW AGE INTERNATIONAL (P) LIMITED, PUBLISHERS
LONDON • NEW DELHI • NAIROBI
Bangalore • Chennai • Cochin • Guwahati • Hyderabad • Kolkata • Lucknow • Mumbai
Visit us at **www.newagepublishers.com**

Published by New Age International (P) Ltd., Publishers
First Edition: 2007
Reprint: 2018

GLOBAL OFFICES

- **New Delhi** **NEW AGE INTERNATIONAL (P) LIMITED, PUBLISHERS**
7/30 A, Daryaganj, New Delhi-110002, (INDIA)
Tel.: (011) 23253771, 23253472, **Telefax:** 23267437, 43551305
E-mail: contactus@newagepublishers.com • Visit us at www.newagepublishers.com
- **London** **NEW AGE INTERNATIONAL (UK) LTD.**
27 Old Gloucester Street, London, WC1N 3AX, UK
E-mail: info@newacademicscience.co.uk • Visit us at www.newacademicscience.co.uk
- **Nairobi** **NEW AGE GOLDEN (EAST AFRICA) LTD.**
Ground Floor, Westlands Arcade, Chiromo Road (Next to Naivas Supermarket)
Westlands, Nairobi, KENYA, **Tel.:** 00-254-713848772, 00-254-725700286
E-mail: kenya@newagepublishers.com

BRANCHES

- **Bangalore** 37/10, 8th Cross (Near Hanuman Temple), Azad Nagar, Chamarajpet, Bangalore- 560 018
Tel.: (080) 26756823, **Telefax:** 26756820, **E-mail: bangalore@newagepublishers.com**
- **Chennai** 26, Damodaran Street, T. Nagar, Chennai-600 017, **Tel.:** (044) 24353401, **Telefax:** 24351463
E-mail: chennai@newagepublishers.com
- **Cochin** CC-39/1016, Carrier Station Road, Ernakulam South, Cochin-682 016, **Tel.:** (0484) 2377303, **Telefax:** 4051304
E-mail: cochin@newagepublishers.com
- **Guwahati** Hemsen Complex, Mohd. Shah Road, Paltan Bazar, Near Starline Hotel, Guwahati-781 008,
Tel.: (0361) 2513881, **Telefax:** 2543669, **E-mail: guwahati@newagepublishers.com**
- **Hyderabad** 105, 1st Floor, Madhiray Kaveri Tower, 3-2-19, Azam Jahi Road, Near Kumar Theater, Nimboliadda Kachiguda, Hyderabad-500 027, **Tel.:** (040) 24652456, **Telefax:** 24652457
E-mail: hyderabad@newagepublishers.com
- **Kolkata** RDB Chambers (Formerly Lotus Cinema) 106A, 1st Floor, S N Banerjee Road, Kolkata-700 014
Tel.: (033) 22273773, **Telefax:** 22275247, **E-mail: kolkata@newagepublishers.com**
- **Lucknow** 16-A, Jopling Road, Lucknow-226 001, **Tel.:** (0522) 2209578, 4045297, **Telefax:** 2204098
E-mail: lucknow@newagepublishers.com
- **Mumbai** 142C, Victor House, Ground Floor, N.M. Joshi Marg, Lower Parel, Mumbai-400 013
Tel.: (022) 24927869, **Telefax:** 24915415, **E-mail: mumbai@newagepublishers.com**
- **New Delhi** 22, Golden House, Daryaganj, New Delhi-110 002, **Tel.:** (011) 23262368, 23262370, **Telefax:** 43551305
E-mail: sales@newagepublishers.com

ISBN: 978-81-224-2011-1
C-17-08-10719

Printed in India at Saras Graphics, Rai, Haryana.
Typeset at Pagitek Graphics, New Delhi.

NEW AGE INTERNATIONAL (P) LIMITED, PUBLISHERS
7/30 A, Daryaganj, New Delhi-110002
Visit us at **www.newagepublishers.com**
(CIN: U74899DL1966PTC004618)

In fond memory of

My Parents

Shri Gopalrao and Gayabai Kondalkar

Preface

Globalisation, technology advancement, open market system and desire of human beings to excel in the field one works has increased competitiveness and resultant work stress. Management of human behaviour and chanalizing it into correct direction has become important. Application of motivational theories, art of leadership and skill of redesigning jobs and modification to organisational structure is an on going process that facilitates positive work environment leading to increased job satisfaction of employees, greater productivity and organizational growth. Due to scientific advancement managing human resources is more challenging. It has been observed that everybody wants to catch up with next higher strata of life style. Social obligations have increased and so has increased the purchasing power, thanks to financial institutions who are doing a tremendous business of financing individuals. This situation has led to designing an appropriate situational model of managing human behaviour in varying conditions. There is no specific model for this purpose. There are however standard models of behaviour that can be modified depending upon the situation and applied in work settings. The traditional ways of managing organizations infact have fast diminished. New ways have emerged. The work is now being accomplished by work teams and work groups. Participative decision making, delegation, empowerment, TQM, flexible work time and many more such concepts have emerged. Redesigning of work and organizational structure, regrouping, mergers have become the order of the day. This has led to employees undergoing more stress. The book has attempted to solve issues mentioned above in a systematic manner. An attempt has been made to include various chapters that form the curricula of various universities across the country. The book is written in a simple language supported by case at the end of the chapter and various exercises on behavioural skills.

The book has been thoroughly prepared in terms of contents and its application. New concepts of human behaviour have been included in the book. The book is intended for a wider readership. It is not only useful to students of MBA but also to the students of MA (psychology), students who have taken OB as one of the subjects for competitive examination, practicing HR executives and for common person who would like to implement behaviour modification. The book is also recommended for Defence Services Organizations with particular requirement of junior leaders to manage soldiers.

Organisation of the book

The book has been divided into four parts. Part one titled "Introduction to Organizatiional

Behaviour" contains two chapters. Chapter 1 – Organizational Behviour, that deals with introducing the subject, and studying various behavioural models for organizational efficiency. Chapter 2 – deals with Evolution of Management Concepts. The aim of the this chapter has been to make readers aware of the evolution of human behaviour. Individual dimentions of organizational behaviour have been included in Part 2. It contains total of six chapters. Chapter 3 – Individual dimentions of organizations behaviour covers various factors that have direct impact on human behaviour. Special attention has been paid to the topic of emotional competence and its impact on individual performance. Chapter 4 – deals with personality. Apart from normal features of personality, traits of Indian managers find its place. Chapter 5 – covers various models of learning. Value, attitude and job satisfaction has been covered in Chapter 6. Chapter 7 – exclusively deals with various motivational theories. Perception and individual decision making is included in Chapter 8.

Part three contains seven chapters. Chapter 9 deals with group behaviour. Transactional analysis has been covered in chapter number 10. Management of conflict in chapter number 11 and Stress management in chapter number 12. Dynamics of communications in chapter number 13. Power and politics and Leadership have been covered in chapter numbers 14 and 15 respectively. Part four relates to dynamics of organization. Organizational structure has been covered in chapter 16. Job design and Management of change have been covered in chapters 17 and 18 respectively. Organizational development, Organizational culture and climate have been covered in chapters 19 and 20. I have tried to write the book in simple language so that it is interesting to read. Concepts have been explained with the help of flow charts. Most of the chapters have case study at the end and skill development exercises have been given wherever it is desired. Text questions at the end of the chapters have been aimed at assimilation by the reader.

In the process of writing the book I have consulted many books, papers and cases of various eminent and distinguish writers. Without their literature, the book would not have seen the light of the day. I have tried to acknowledge their contribution wherever possible. Notwithstanding the above, I would like to convey my deep gratitude to each one of them including those whose names do not appear. I am personally grateful to Dr. Upinder Dhar and Dr. M.L. Bhasin for I could include few of their valuable cases in the book. Author wishes to acknowledge the support and guidance rendered by Shri Sanjay Pande, Chairman, VNS Group of Educational Institutes, Bhopal and Prof. P.K. Chopra, Director, VNS Institute of Management. I am thankful to Dr. V.D. Garde, Colonel N.P. Dixit, Prof. H.N. Dhabalia, Prof. S.K. Yadav, Dr. Rajesh Tripathi and Dr. Kalpana Dixit for encouraging me to complete the project. I am grateful to all my colleagues namely Prof. Archana Nema, Dr. Abhaya Swarup, Dr. Neeraj Singh, Prof. C. Rama Gopal, Prof. Akhilesh Mittal, Prof. Sameer Sharma and Prof. Sumit Kishore Mathur, Hema Chhura, Krati Misra and Neha Patel, who have been the source of inspiration and have helped me in correcting the script. I am also thankful to Shri Vikas Varshney who has assisted me in typing. Mrs. Rashmi Mishra, the librarian of the institute and Shri Leeladhar have been of great help to me.

I have received valuable suggestions from my daughter Ujwala who is working as Editor, Hindustan Times, Bhopal and my Son-in-law, Shri Sudeep. My Son, Major Rahul and daughter–in–law Captain Anuradha enriched the script by valuable tips which are distinctly visible in the book. Last but not the least my wife Kranti has bear the most, right from the inception of the book till its publication. She has been a source of inspiration, a guide, and a silent spectator in her "Wheel Chair" while I would write or be engaged elsewhere. She would push me to expedite the progress all though. I am thankful to Shri. Saumya Gupta, Managing Director and all the staff of New Age International Publications, New Delhi who have taken great pains to print a very attractive book in record time. I am sure they will continue to give the same support in future too.

I hope the book will meet the requirement of students, academicians, professionals and a common person who has interest in the study of behaviour science. Any suggestions or modification to the script is welcome.

V.G. KONDALKAR
Email : vgkondalkar@rediffmail.com

"DOGRA HOUSE"
C-89, Sarvadharma Colony
Kolar Road
Bhopal (MP) 462042

Contents

Part Two: Individual Dimensions of Organizational Behaviour

PART ONE

Introduction to Organizational Behaviour

CHAPTER 1

Study of Organizational Behaviour

INTRODUCTION

The study of Organizational Behaviour (OB) is very interesting and challenging too. It is related to individuals, group of people working together in teams. The study becomes more challenging when situational factors interact. The study of organizational behaviour relates to the expected behaviour of an individual in the organization. No two individuals are likely to behave in the same manner in a particular work situation. It is the predictability of a manager about the expected behaviour of an individual. There are no absolutes in human behaviour. It is the human factor that is contributory to the productivity hence the study of human behaviour is important. Great importance therefore must be attached to the study. Researchers, management practitioners, psychologists, and social scientists must understand the very credentials of an individual, his background, social framework, educational update, impact of social groups and other situational factors on behaviour. Managers under whom an individual is working should be able to explain, predict, evaluate and modify human behaviour that will largely depend upon knowledge, skill and experience of the manager in handling large group of people in diverse situations. Preemptive actions need to be taken for human behaviour forecasting. The value system, emotional intelligence, organizational culture, job design and the work environment are important causal agents in determining human behaviour. Cause and effect relationship plays an important role in how an individual is likely to behave in a particular situation and its impact on productivity. An appropriate organizational culture can modify individual behaviour. Recent trends exist in laying greater stress on organizational development and imbibing a favourable organizational culture in each individual. It also involves fostering a team spirit and motivation so that the organizational objectives are achieved. There is a need for commitment on the part of the management that should be continuous and incremental in nature. The scope of the organizational behaviour is as under:

(*a*) Impact of personality on performance
(*b*) Employee motivation
(*c*) Leadership
(*d*) How to create effective teams and groups

(*e*) Study of different organizational structures
(*f*) Individual behaviour, attitude and learning
(*g*) Perception
(*h*) Design and development of effective organization
(*i*) Job design
(*j*) Impact of culture on organizational behaviour
(*k*) Management of change
(*l*) Management of conflict and stress
(*m*) Organizational development
(*n*) Organizational culture
(*o*) Transactional analysis
(*p*) Group behaviour, power and politics
(*q*) Job design
(*r*) Study of emotions

The field of the organizational behaviour does not depend upon deductions based on gut feelings but attempts to gather information regarding an issue in a scientific manner under controlled conditions. It uses information and interprets the findings so that the behaviour of an individual and group can be canalized as desired. Large number of psychologists, social scientists and academicians have carried out research on various issues related to organization behaviour. Employee performance and job satisfaction are determinants of accomplishment of individual and organizational goals.

Organizations have been set up to fulfill needs of the people. In today's competitive world, the organizations have to be growth-oriented. This is possible when productivity is ensured with respect to quantity of product to be produced with zero error quality. Employee absenteeism and turnover has a negative impact on productivity. Employee who absents frequently cannot contribute towards productivity and growth of the organization. In the same manner, employee turnover causes increased cost of production. Job satisfaction is a major factor to analyse performance of an individual towards his work. Satisfied workers are productive workers who contribute towards building an appropriate work culture in an organization. Organizations are composed of number of individuals working independently or collectively in teams, and number of such teams makes a department and number of such departments make an organization. It is a formal structure and all departments have to function in a coordinated manner to achieve the organizational objective. It is therefore important for all employees to possess a positive attitude towards work. They need to function in congenial atmosphere and accomplish assigned goals. It is also important for managers to develop an appropriate work culture. Use of authority, delegation of certain powers to subordinates, division of labour, efficient communication, benchmarking, re-engineering, job re-design and empowerment are some of the important factors so that an organization can function as well-oiled machine. This is not only applicable to manufacturing organizations but also to service and social organizations.

DEFINITIONS

"Organizational behaviour is a field of study that investigates the impact that individuals, groups and organizational structure have on behaviour within the organization, for the purpose of applying such knowledge towards improving an

organizational effectiveness". The above definition has three main elements; ***first*** organizational behaviour is an investigative study of individuals and groups, ***second,*** the impact of organizational structure on human behaviour and the ***third,*** the application of knowledge to achieve organizational effectiveness. These factors are interactive in nature and the impact of such behaviour is applied to various systems so that the goals are achieved. The nature of study of organizational behaviour is investigative to establish cause and effect relationship.

OB involves integration of studies undertaken relating to behavioural sciences like psychology, sociology, anthropology, economics, social psychology and political science. Therefore, organizational behaviour is a comprehensive field of study in which individual, group and organizational structure is studied in relation to organizational growth and organizational culture, in an environment where impact of modern technology is great. The aim of the study is to ensure that the human behaviour contributes towards growth of the organization and greater efficiency is achieved.

Organizational behaviour can be defined as – **"the study and application of knowledge about human behaviour related to other elements of an organization such as structure, technology and social systems** (LM Prasad). Stephen P Robins defines **"Organizational behaviour as a systematic study of the actions and attitudes that people exhibit within organizations."** It has been observed that we generally form our opinion based on the symptoms of an issue and do not really go to the root cause of the happening. Science of organizational behaviour is applied in nature. Disciplines like psychology, anthropology and political science have contributed in terms of various studies and theories to the field of organizational behaviour. A leader should be able to communicate with his subordinate and keep them in picture as to the happenings in the organization. People promote organizational culture for mutual benefit. Politics is often used to create conflict with the aim of enlarging self-power base to the detrimental of organizational growth. Politics, in Indian context has made inroads based on religion, caste system in the decision making process which has led to formation of informal groups in the organization that often exploit the organization for fulfillment of personal goals at the cost of organizational goals. Conflict and manipulating power bases need to be handled in an appropriate manner to modify human behaviour and stimulate various individuals towards achieving higher productivity. Power dynamics plays a significant role in organization situations in different environment.

CONTRIBUTING FIELDS TO ORGANIZATIONAL BEHAVIOUR

Psychology: Psychology is an applied science, which attempts to explain human behaviour in a particular situation and predicts actions of individuals. Psychologists have been able to modify individual behaviour largely with the help of various studies. It has contributed towards various theories on learning, motivation, personality, training and development, theories on individual decision making, leadership, job satisfaction, performance appraisal, attitude, ego state, job design, work stress and conflict management. Studies of these theories can improve personal skills, bring change in attitude and develop positive approach to organizational systems. Various psychological tests are conducted in the organizations for selection of employees, measuring personality attributes and aptitude. Various other dimensions of human personality are also measured. These instruments are scientific in nature and have been finalized after a great deal of research. Field of psychology continues to explore new areas applicable to the field of organizational behaviour. Contribution of psychology has enriched the organizational behaviour field.

Sociology: Science of Sociology studies the impact of culture on group behaviour and has contributed to a large extent to the field of group-dynamics, roles that individual plays in the organization, communication, norms, status, power, conflict management, formal organization theory, group processes and group decision-making.

Political science: Political science has contributed to the field of Organizational behaviour. Stability of government at national level is one major factor for promotion of international business, financial investments, expansion and employment. Various government rules and regulations play a very decisive role in growth of the organization. All organizations have to abide by the rules of the government of the day.

Social psychology: Working organizations are formal assembly of people who are assigned specific jobs and play a vital role in formulating human behaviour. It is a subject where concept of psychology and sociology are blend to achieve better human behaviour in organization. The field has contributed to manage change, group decision-making, communication and ability of people in the organization, to maintain social norms.

Anthropology: It is a field of study relating to human activities in various cultural and environmental frameworks. It understands difference in behaviour based on value system of different cultures of various countries. The study is more relevant to organizational behaviour today due to globalization, mergers and acquisitions of various industries. The advent of the 21st century has created a situation wherein cross-cultural people will have to work in one particular industry. Managers will have to deal with individuals and groups belonging to different ethnic cultures and exercise adequate control or even channelise behaviour in the desired direction by appropriately manipulating various cultural factors. Organization behaviour has used the studies on comparative attitudes and cross-cultural transactions. Environment studies conducted by the field of anthropology aims to understand organizational human behaviour so that acquisitions and mergers are smooth. Organizations are bound by its culture that is formed by human beings.

BEHAVIOUR MODEL FOR ORGANIZATIONAL EFFICIENCY

Organizational behaviour is a study and application of managerial skills and knowledge to people in the organization to investigate individual and group behaviour. Various concepts and models in the field of organizational behaviour attempt to identify, not only the human behaviour but also modify their attitude and promote skills so that they can act more effectively. This is done scientifically; therefore, organizational behaviour field is a scientific discipline. The knowledge and models are practically applied to workers, groups and organizational structure that provide tools for improved behaviour and dynamics of relationship. The field of organizational behaviour also provides various systems and models for international relationship that are applied to organizations.

Leaders must look for indicators (effects) of individual behaviour and of groups in any organization. Indicators have a root cause beneath. As a leader, it is that symptom, which must be evaluated, and cause of human behaviour established so that if the behaviour is good, the manager can establish the norms of behaviour. If the behaviour is not conducive to achieve the organisastional objective then suitable alternative model can be applied to channelize individual behaviour towards an appropriate organizational value system and thus individual behaviour modified. An organization has three basic elements namely, people, structure, and technology. An organization must have suitable organizational structure, with appropriate number of tier and reporting system properly explained. Principle of unity of command, delegation of authority and responsibility, formulation of objectives and its allotment to various groups is very important so that workers achieve a required level of job satisfaction. They must be trained to handle sophisticated machines and equipment. It is the people, their value system, and faith in the leadership that make an organization. Leader must be able to describe, understand, predict and control individual behaviour in the organization. This is explained in the succeeding paragraphs.

(*a*) **Describe:** Study of organizational behaviour is based on scientific methods, which have been applied on human beings. It is a science, that analyses as to how people behave in different situations in the organization. A manager should be able describe the behaviour of each of the individuals under his command, identify attitude, and be able to pinpoint his behaviour so that the situation in the organization is under control.

(*b*) **Understand:** Leaders must understand human behaviour as to why people behave in particular manner and try to identify reasons so that corrective actions can be taken.

(*c*) **Predict:** By frequent closer interaction, a leader is in a position to identify the nature of workers. Some are more productive while the others are tardy and disruptive. In such situation, a leader should be able to handle each individual differently so that his or her actions can be channalized to higher productivity.

(*d*) **Control:** Managers in the organizations should train their subordinates continuously; aim being development of skills, promotion of productivity and improvement of individual behaviour. It is a continuous process on the part of manager. He must lay down control measures so that the energy of workers is diverted towards organizational objectives. Communication should be used to ensure that the behaviour of individual is controlled. Environment has a great impact on human behaviour. Appropriate internal environment would help organizations to built favourable work environment that will help individuals and groups within organizations to work effectively towards higher productivity.

ORGANIZATIONAL COMPONENTS THAT NEED TO BE MANAGED

People

People are the main component of any organization that has to be managed. Every individual has a personal goal to be achieved. Organizations must identify the ***need spectrum*** of individuals and take suitable steps for its fulfillment to enable them to perform effectively so that they complete their allotted task in time. ***Relationship*** between the workers, with subordinates and superiors should be established based on full understanding and complete faith based on mutual trust so that it is easy to communicate and understand each other's views. ***Work teams*** and ***Groups*** play a vital role in the organization. Individual may have to keep his personal interest aside if it conflicts with team or group goals. It is the team goals, accomplishment of which contribute towards achieving organizational goals. Apart from managing internal workforce, it is also important to manage customers who are the end persons using organization's products or services. Utmost interest of stakeholders, government, employees, social groups and non-governmental organizations (NGOs) must be kept in mind as they play a dominant role in the society. Apart from the above, adequate consideration should also be given to competitors, regulatory agencies, labour force, suppliers and resource persons.

Structure

There are two types of organizations, formal and informal. Informal organizations do not have a specified structure. Formal organizations are build based upon the objective set for it. Organizational structure in such organization is hierarchical in nature, with people at each level having their own objectives, which contributes towards fulfillment of over allorganizational objectives. In such organisastion people at lower levels report to higher level managers. The tier system has the principle of unity of command inbuilt in it. The organization structure may depend upon the size, number of products/services produced, skill and experience of the employees, managerial staff and geographical location of the organization. An organization may have several levels and pyramid like organizational structure or flat structure. The efficiency of the organization will depend upon the free flow of the information, efficient communication system prevailing in the organization, well-defined authority and responsibility supported by detailed policies, rules and regulations. The organization must have well laid out systems, which are understood by workers, supervisors and managers. The leader must keep open mind while dealing with subordinates and exercise full control over various systems, levels and ensure planned productivity and achieve high level of job satisfaction.

Technology

Managing technology is an important job of any management. It is an important element of any unit. Selection of technology, procurement, installation, operation and maintenance is important and no compromise should be made in procuring ***latest or advanced technology.*** Various systems and sub- systems should support technology that exists in an organization. Based on the technology, an organization should formulate job structure and resultant procurement of human resource so that they are complimentary to each other. Adequate attention is also be paid to service industry. For example an appropriate drill, procedures are installed in hospital industry to ensure that the patients' record is maintained properly. On line operations of all systems relating to admission record, past treatment, drugs, availability of beds, schedule of operations maintained so that the level of patients satisfaction is raised. In minimum number of days, maximum numbers of patients should be treated. Various processes required to regulate these functions form the important part of service industry.

Jobs

Job is an assignment assigned to an individual. It encompasses various tasks within it. For example, Personnel manager wants to fill up twelve vacancies in production department within three months. Job will have various tasks inbuilt in it like designing of job specification, selection of media, advertising vacancies, scheduling of selection and recruiting process. Manager, therefore have to manage various tasks to accomplish a particular job. This may form a part of managerial functions. Adequate delegation, supervision, application of various control techniques makes the job simpler for the manager. Introduction of computers have made managerial functions simpler, as required information is available for decision making.

Processes

Management of processes and its inter-dependence is very crucial to high productivity and higher job satisfaction. What is important for a manager is to ensure high morale of the work force. To ensure this, he must identify various managerial dictums. Select appropriate subordinates to carry out a job based on aptitude, personality traits, mental build up and attitude. He should also involve himself and lead subordinates by personal example. In defence services, it is the quality of leadership, that motivates troops to achieve near impossible task where every thing appears to be going wrong. Various role models assist leaders in identifying as to which process, method or approach would be suitable to mould subordinates in suitable frame that may be required by any organization. Nothing motivates workers better if you give them their entitlements in full and train them to take up higher jobs. By doing so, manager must develop and build an organizational culture that will bind employees to a common cultural bond. During day-to-day functions, managers must be transparent and maintain a high degree of value system and display ethical behaviour. There are no short cuts to this and will pay rich dividends in times to come.

External Environment

What we have so far discussed is various components of an organization that should be managed properly. External environment also plays an important role in managing the points discussed above. When we talk about managing people in the organization, what we have to study and manage is the influence of culture and its impact on the individual. A manager should examine as to how he is going to ***cope up*** with the changes. Study of external environment is very wide and encompasses economic, cultural, social, government rules and regulations, legal aspects, political climate, demographics and its impact. If one scans the external environment that is prevailing in Indian context, one will find that individuals are racing to catch up the ***upper class*** as it relates to standards of living, material possession, higher education, attempt to copy western culture, food habits, dressing pattern and the like. Beauty parlors, pubs and cyber cafes around each corner are an ample evidence of the impact of external environment. This trend has an impact on what products or services are on priority in the society and indicates the behaviour of an individual. If the above factors are evaluated appropriately, a manager will be able to examine and predict human behaviour in the organization. It is therefore important to evaluate market situation, competitors, and availability of raw material, technology, availability of skilled, semi skilled and non-skilled personnel. In addition, evaluate prevailing culture and how individuals are likely to respond to the call of the organization. Some factors like government rules, and political stability keep changing, the organizations must cater for such contingencies. Manager must therefore keep in mind the internal and external factors and make the best amalgam and work to achieve organizational effectiveness.

SUMMARY

Study of organizational behaviour is very interesting. It is the art on the part of manager to understand, describe, forecast and modify individual behaviour. Lot of studies have been undertaken in the field of organizational behaviour and vast literature is available, which need to be studied by practictioners in the field of managing human resources. Various models and research instruments are available to investigate human behaviour. Various fields like psychology, social psychology, anthropology, sociology, politics, economics, and medical sciences have contributed to the field of organization behaviour. Various models in the above fields have enriched the study of organization behaviour. It is the field of study that investigates the impact on individuals, groups and organizational structure have on individual behaviour so that the knowledge so achieved can be suitably modified and applied for organizational effectiveness. The study of organizational behaviour relates to the study of attitude, perception, learning, values at individual level. The study is undertaken pertaining to managing stress, conflicts, intergroup behaviour, decision making at group level. Management of change, development of organizational culture, designing and redesigning of jobs, and various organizational development strategies are required to be undertaken by leaders for organizational effectiveness. It is the responsibility of the managers to evolve appropriate strategies to study organizational components. The first component is people. The study of organizational behaviour involves identifying need spectrum of the people, managing interpersonal relationship, understanding of individual objectives and co-relating organizational strategies accordingly. The second component is understanding of organizational structure and its modification based on the need of the hour. Manager should decide upon the nature of structure and ensure unity of command, number of levels that may be required for effective command and control. Communication, delegation of authority, well defined policies, rules, regulation, systems, procedures and processes. Introduction of latest technology is an essential part of organizational development that should be taken care of by the manager responsible for running the organization. Jobs should be allotted to the individual based on the aptitude and the processes must be compatible with the technology being used. One of the most important components is environment. While internal environment relates to various personnel policies and corresponding managerial actions, the external environment relates to cultural, social, legal, and governmental rules and regulations that should be taken care of. Technological changes has made it imperative on the part of managers that they should take care of employees and meet their social expectations so that organizational goals can be achieved.

TEXT QUESTIONS

Q. 1. Define organizational bevaiour. What are various factors that are considered to regulate individual behaviour.

Q. 2. What are various fields that have contributed to the field of organizational behaviour. Explain their contributions.

Q. 3. Explain various components that should be taken care of while studying organizational behaviour.

Q. 4. Explain the field of organizational behaviour. Why the study is challenging.

Case-1

NATIONAL CADET CORPS (NCC) – A BOON FOR SOCIAL DEVELOPMENT

V.G. Kondalkar

National Cadet Corps (NCC) is a national organization having junior wing and senior wing both for girls and boys. Junior wing NCC is meant for secondary school level and senior wing is applicable for college students. The objective of NCC organization is to inculcate discipline for the youth of our nation. An Army Officer of the rank of Lt General called Director General (DG) heads NCC organization at national level. The organization has a vast network at each state level headed by an officer of the rank of Brigadier known as Deputy Director General (DDG) of a particular state. In every state there are number of Group Headquarters located at important cities depending upon school and college density and compositions. Under Group Headquarters there are number of NCC Battalions (Boys/ Girls). Number of battalions in each Group Headquarters varies depending upon the size of the area. In the same fashion, number of groups under a DDG varies.

NCC is applicable to all school/ college going children. It is voluntary organization in nature.

DDGs, group commanders and battalion commanders organize various events round the year. These are as under:

(*a*) Participation in professional training that includes the following:
   - Weapon training, including firing or rifles, sten guns, light machine guns.
   - Drill.
   - First aid training in various contingencies.
   - Basic field craft and guard duties.
   - Basic battle craft at a level of a section (section comprises of ten men)

(*b*) Organization of training camps where teamwork, comradeship, cooperation and events mention in (*a*) above are practiced. The training camps are generally of the duration of two weeks. Such camps are held twice a year.

(*c*) After completion of two and four years of training, B certification and C certificates respectively are awarded to the cadets. The certificates have preference for admission to various professional courses like medicine. It also has a weightage for government jobs. A person having C certificate need not appear in the written examination conducted by UPSC for commissioned officers of the defence services which is a major concession. Such students have to face Service Selection Boards direct, for selection in the defence services as commissioned officers.

(*d*) Individual having C certification (which is achieved after four years of NCC training) gets six months seniority in defence services.

(*e*) NCC is considered as one of the best organizations of our country. The organization has produced better citizens.

During the course of the attachment, the cadets are given full NCC kit. Refreshment is provided during parade days (twice a week). The cadets are provided meals, transportation and medical facility.

The training in the organization is a costly affair to the exchequer of the state government. NCC officers have to interact with civil administration at state level, district level, and with principals/ directors of the colleges. They have to deal with local population, medical authorities, RTO and all agencies related with civil administration. This involves advance planning, good communication and inter-personal relationship. Social, cultural and ethnic activities are promoted in the NCC. Annual training camps are held at state or national level. Cadets, develop friendship with various individuals and learn to live in a community environment during training camps. NCC covers land, air and naval branches and all cadets are put through training in the skill development of respective wings.

Discussion Questions

Q. 1. Why NCC is considered as one of the best organizations.

Q. 2. How does the organization relate to field of organizational behaviour. What are various agencies that the officials have to interact.

Q. 3. What are the benefits of NCC.

Q. 4. How does the management interact with external environmental forces?

Practical Assignment

Visit a NCC unit in your city and find out organizational structure, daily routine of cadets and training schedule.

Case-2

Overcoming Absenteeism at Unique Schweppes Ltd

Unique Schweppes Ltd was multinational Public limited Company with its head office at London. The company's 51 % shares were held by Unique and 49% by Government financial Institutions and individual shareholders. Unique owns three factories and three partly manufacturing units i.e. they had 6 primary manufacturing units located at Jammu, Nagpur, Agra, Pune, Gorakhapur and Hyderabad. The total manpower in these six units was 1900, and was held by Mathew Thomas as managing director. Five directors looking after various financial areas like technical, operations, commercial, HR and marketing, supported him.

Agra unit was situated near Mathura with a manpower capacity of 450 employees, including 41 executives, 12 managers and remaining operators. A representative union was also registered in the name of Association of Chemical Workers in the company. This unit was working in 3 shifts and for all the seven days. The average age of the employees was around 30 years. Agra unit was the only automated plant among the plants of Unique India. It had a unique feature of cross-functional activities at the managerial level with the result a strong networking was observed. Emphasis on financial relations among the employees was given to promote simplified working and better understanding among them. Unique was known for its welfare facilities like – free canteen, free transportation, free uniform, medical re-imbursement up to 5% of the gross salary and all other benefits according to the statutory norms. They also provide with housing loan facilities to employees through HDFC and State Bank of India. Unique re-imbrued the interest amount on house loan exceeding 4%. The loan entitlement is dependent upon the income of workers. Inspite of all the facilities provided to the workers absenteeism was very high thus creating problems in the production.

In July 1995, HR executive, Alok Gupta received a complaint from line supervisor, Prakash Sharma that production was suffering due to absenteeism in his department. Alok Gupta was perplexed. The reason being that with 52 weekly off, 9 casual leaves and 22 earned leaves provided to the workers in line with Factory Act 1948 under Section 52, the absenteeism rate was still 18 %.

In January 1996, a meeting was called by Alok Gupta and in consultation with Prakash Sharma, it was decided that warning should be given to cronic cases and the workers who had started remaining absent should be counseled. Inspite of doing this no change was observed until April 1996. Alok Gupta reported to Priya Kumar, Human resources manager about increasing complaints related to absenteeism. Priya Kumar, Alok Gupta and Prakash Sharma in a brain storming session concluded that punishment was not the solution. An Incentive scheme was felt to be the solution to the existing problem. Thus, the management offered the employees the scheme of doubling the amount of annual interest free loans from Rs 5000 to Rs 10 000 to those who were regular at their work. A plan chalked out for this:

(*a*) Employee who had worked for more than 280 days out of 365 days would get Rs 10,000 interest free loan. Employees who were present for more than 230 working days, amount of free loan would be Rs 5000. For less than 230 there would be no loan facilities.

(*b*) In a period of 4 months, if an employee availed no leave then he would be entitled for additional payment of Rs 500. If a half-day leave, it would be Rs 350 and for one day leave it would be Rs 250. Similarly, some workers who had not shown any improvement in their attendance, it was decided that charge- sheet would be issued. However, when the charge sheet was issued to such cases the union members resisted.

A meeting called by Priya Kumar in which he briefed about the problem of absenteeism and justified the action taken by the management. Ultimately union members were convinced but insisted on counselling and introducing new incentive schemes instead of disciplinary actions alone. During counselling sessions management found some of the reasons which led to absenteeism were high salary, festival celebration, dual employment, very good family background, age factor and defective recruitment policies as fresher were taken from ITI and where less serious about their work and less motivated towards accomplishment of the organizational goals.

It was observed in the beginning of 1999, that the rate of absenteeism had decreased from 18% to 16 %. But it was not satisfactory and hence management decided to put in more efforts in the form of new incentives schemes which were best on social recognition like; tea party, attendance awards, recognition by senior executives at work place and celebrating family day on 17 September i.e., on Vishwakarma Jayanti.

By the end of 1999, they had introduced all monetary as well as social benefits schemes yet three employees among the nine employees who had been issued the charge sheet in September, 1998 had not shown any improvement and remained absent for more than 200 days out of 280 working days. Therefore, the management finally decided to terminate them, and termination letters were issued to them. In the year 2000, a remarkable decline was found in the rate of absenteeism. It had reduced from 16% to 12%.

QUESTIONS

1. In your opinion, which alternative steps would be more effective for reducing absenteeism?
2. What is the role of non-financial incentives over the financial incentives?
3. How do you evaluate the impact of termination on absenteeism?

The case has been adapted from the "Case Method in Management education" edited by Dr Upinder Dhar and Dr. Santosh Dhar. Publish by Excel Books, New Delhi, 2002.

CHAPTER 2

Evolution of Management Thoughts

INTRODUCTION

The origin of management in the organized way can be traced as back as the origin of human beings. They earned their livelihood by hunting that was carried out in groups. Later possession of land mass became important hence there arose conflict between the groups. Local conflicts were resolved by power using primitive weapon system. Management practices were undertaken in a scientific way early 18th century when industrial revolution took place. World War I saw a marked development in evolution of management concepts. In India management practices were in existence in Ramayana and Mahabharata periods. People were administered by the state and their needs fulfilled. The king was considered to be the master. Proper executive, judicial, and state affairs were managed in a very disciplined way. Every individual was morally responsible to the master (king/ruler) for the task assigned to him. Chanakya was a pioneer in evolving principles of economics and warfare in particular and efficient administration of the state in general. Various systems evolved in those days can be seen even today. Water supply system to Aurangabad introduced by King Aurangazeb is even visible today. Management of education, eradication of social evils and various religious systems are evidence of existence of proper management. Management as a field of study was considered early 20th century. Management principles like delegation of authority, empowerment, leadership, scalar chain, unity of command and motivation were clearly demonstrated in Roman Umpire and their ability to organize can be seen from its expansion. Shivaji demonstrated above principles in 17th century.

People have displayed tremendous amount of ability and skill in planning, organising, and directing people as to what is to be done, how it is to be done and anticipating future plans. They also evolved various models of controlling the planned work being executed properly. Various wars have been fought where use of human resources, heavy weapon system, its procurement and use and shifting it to various theatres of war based on threat perceptions are the examples of management. Great war of Mahabharata between Pandavas and Kauravas is an example of managing power, confllict situations, human resource training and development and an art of generalship had been practiced in the most scientific manner. Egyptian piramids, Great Wall of China are the tangible examples where hundreds of thousand of people were involved in construction activity over a protracted period of time. Every individual had a chain of command. He knew as to what is to be done, how it is to be done and the time frame within which it is to be completed. These examples indicate that organizations have been in exixtence for thousands of years and management was being practiced ever since. However, in the past several years, the management has undergone systematic investigation, acquired common body of knowledge, formulated various models to deal with various phenomenon like handling conflict or managing stress and thus became a formal discipline for study. Two landmarks are most important in the management study. ***One***, publication of classical economic doctrines by Adam Smith in 1776 tittled "Wealth of Nations" in which Smith has argued that the economic advantages the organizations and societies would gain from the concepts are: 1) division of labour that promoted 2) skill development. 3) specialised task allotment. 4) time measurement in relation to the quantum of work performed. Smith concluded that, division of work would benefit in higher quality of work and higher productivity. ***Two***. Indudtrisl revolution of eighteenth century, advent of machine power and subsequent development of infrastructural facilities of rail road transportation, communication network, formation of corporations worldwide promoted requirement of people having increased manegerial skills and formalised management practices, which gave birth to the formal theories of management in early 1900s. The concept of management was not clear till about mid of 20th century. There was a contrast between the thinkers. However, Classical approach of management which propogated Scientific Management and General Administrative Theory was a fabulous development. This followed an intensive research work undertaken by Elton Mayo which is known as Howthrone studies. It was followed by more recent concepts of Operatons Research, process management, systems approach, total quality management and last but not the least the contingency approach. In this chapter let us study various theories as the management progressed.

Approaches to Management

As a consequence of industrial revolution in England during 18th and 19th centuries important inventions like lathe machine, power looms and spinning etc. were invented and used

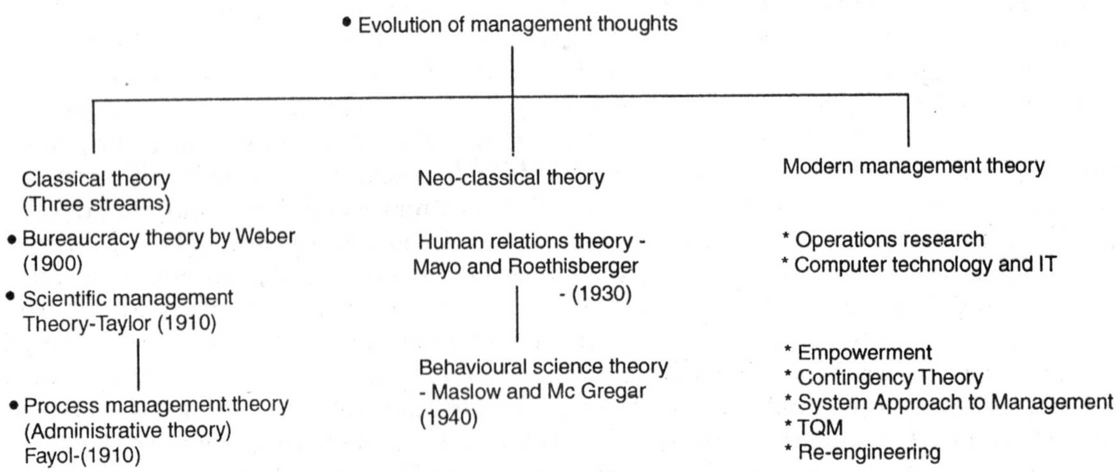

Fig. 2.1. Classification of management thoughts

extensively. Therefore to manage the affairs of large industrial houses, modern management came into existence. This development has led to emergence of various schools of thoughts. Koonz called it as 'management ***theory jungle***. The diagrammatic layout of management thoughts is given in Figure 2.1 above.

CLASSICAL THEORIES OF MANAGEMENT

BUREAUCRACY

Max Weber (1864-1920) a German sociologist introduced the theory of ***Bureaucracy.*** His major contribution to the theory is the concept of authority, structure and its inter-se relationship. Weber in his model of bureaucracy stated that there are three types of authority in any organization. First, ***legal authority*** indicating that a person holds authority based on legal position or a rank within the hierarchy. For example, a production manager in the industry or a battalion commander in the military organization. Secondly, ***Traditional authority***, employees obey a person because he comes from a traditionally recognized power holding family or a person belonging to a royal family. Lastly, ***charismatic authority,*** which indicates special power or an appeal that a leader possesses.

1. Elements of Bureaucracy

Bureaucracy plays a vital role in business, government, education or any other large organization. Though the bureaucratic model was suggested about 80 years ago but it still holds good. For ease of understanding, the structure of bureaucratic model is given in Figure 2.2 below.

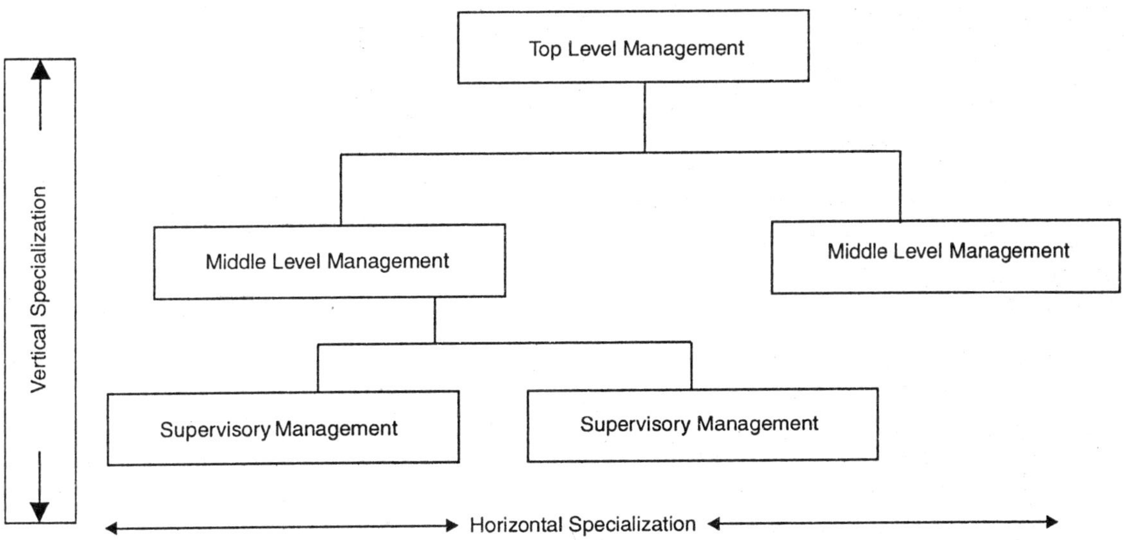

Fig 2.2 Structure of bureaucracy

2. Features of Bureaucracy

Salient points of the Bureaucratic model are as under:

(*a*) Hierarchy of authority exists in the organization, which involves superior-subordinate relationship and chain of command.
(*b*) Division of work based on competence and functional foremanship.
(*c*) System of policy, rules, and regulations is necessary to regulate subordinate behaviour and to ensure rationality, objectivity, discipline and control.
(*d*) In bureaucratic model, rule of law exists that leads to impersonal behaviour of employees. Relations are based on position in the hierarchy.
(*e*) Weber suggests standardization of methods, systems, processes, job contents and tools for smooth operation.
(*f*) Selection and promotion of employees should be based on competence.
(*g*) Bureaucracy recognizes legal power derived from the official position held by an individual.

3. Evaluation of Bureaucratic Theory

The theory is based on rigid rules and regulations having no consideration for interpersonal relationship based on emotions and human qualities. Power has been considered as the dominant factor to administer the organization leading to self-perpetuation. There are glaring drawbacks in the bureaucratic model namely rigidity, impersonal and mechanistic relationship, higher cost of control and umpire building. Lack of co-ordination and interpersonal communication and lastly existence of blind faith in rules and regulations. The system may work in large government organizations or the organization where there is no change anticipated. The theory does not promote fulfillment of human needs and does not exploit full potential of employees.

SCIENTIFIC MANAGEMENT - TAYLOR

Fredrick Winslow Taylor (1856-1915), Frank Gilberth his wife Lillan Gilberth and Henry Gantt have done pioneering work in the field of management They evolved methods and techniques and transformed the field of management in which all works were to be done in the scientific way. ***Taylor's work was so unique that he eventually came to be known as the father of scientific management.*** Taylor joined Midvale steel company as a worker and later he was promoted as supervisor. While working, he completed post graduation in industrial engineering and subsequently joined *Bethlehem Steel Company.* Salient points of scientific management propagated by Taylor are given as under:

(*i*) Effective use of human beings in industrial organizations particularly at the shop floor. He introduced various systems to improve the efficiency of workers.
(*ii*) Taylor stated that managing workforce is an art. He further defined managing as ***'knowing exactly what you want men to do and then see that they do it the best and cheapest way'***
(*iii*) He standardized the work and introduced better methods of doing it.
(*iv*) Time and motion study
(*v*) Introduction of differential piece- rate system of payment offering additional reward for production beyond the standard laid down.
(*vi*) Functional foremanship, creating supervisor having direct authority over the workers

Features of Scientific Management

1. Separation ***of Planning and doing.*** Earlier entire work was done by workers. There were no separate teams for planning and executing the work. Taylor divided the entire work into two parts namely ***planning*** and ***doing***. It was the responsibility of supervisors to plan the work that an individual worker is required to do and ensure that the tools required by them are made available to them.
2. ***Functional foremanship.*** Separation of planning from doing resulted in introduction of ***supervisory*** staff system, which could undertake planning work separately. This has led to introduction of ***functional foremanship*** though it went against the principle of unity of command. The entire work was divided into two parts i.e. planning and doing. Supervisors headed these departments. Each of the departments was further divided into four functional parts. Planning department therefore consisted of route clerk, instrument card clerk, time and cost clerk and disciplinarian. Supervisor "doing" department had under him speed boss, inspector, maintenance foreman and gang boss. The concept of functional foremanship is shown in figure 2.3 below.

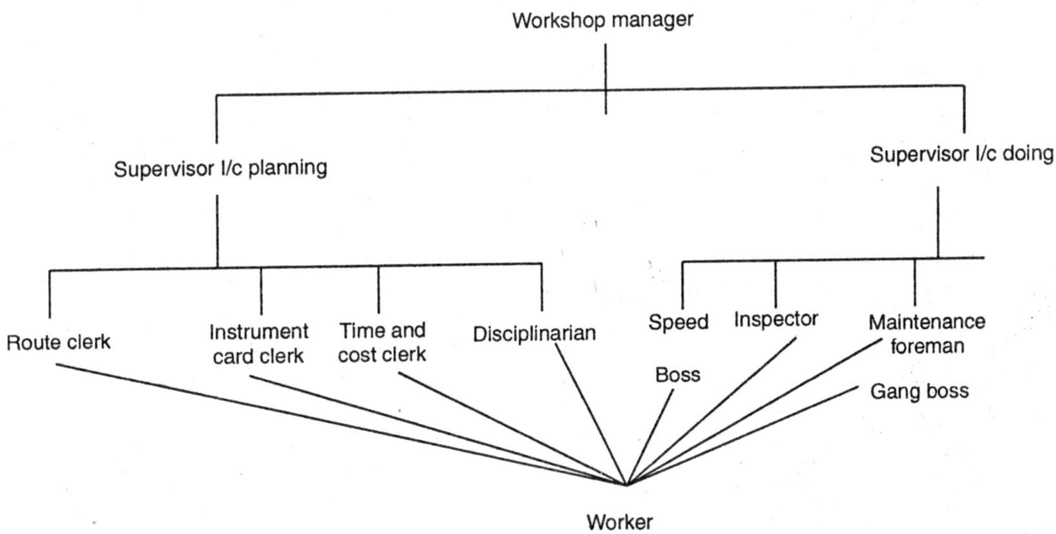

Fig. 2.3. Functional foremanship

3. ***Job Analysis.*** Taylor carried out intensive studies on ***time and motion*** about each job and incorporated such layout in the operations that involved least movement to the workers, minimum operation time and therefore less cost of production. He also carried out studies pertaining to fatigue and incorporated rest periods so that efficiency of the worker is increased.
4. ***Standardisation.*** Taylor carried out job analysis and based on the analysis he standardised tools, instruments, period of work, amount of work each worker has to undertake, working conditions and cost of production. This type of improved work culture and working conditions brought revolution in the production units.

5. ***Scientific selection and training of workers.*** Workers selection should be carried out on scientific basis. Taylor suggested that workers should be given adequate training and work allotted based on their physical and technical aptitude.
6. ***Financial incentives.*** Taylor was a visionary in his approach. He always balanced organizational responsibilities and worker's responsibilities towards the organization. In his approach he tried to introduce scientific way of doing a job and went in details as to how it could be improved at the same time keeping interests of the workers in mind. He introduced various methods to motivate workers by introducing differential piece- rate of payment system. He fixed targets for each work and they were paid based on efficiency. Anybody who worked beyond the laid down target were paid higher rate of wages and any employee who could not meet allotted target was paid below the laid down rate. He also introduced various incentive systems in the organization so that higher productivity was achieved.
7. ***Economies.*** Taylor insisted that internal economy must be ensured by each worker ensuring that there was no wastage in time and material while carrying out the job. Adequate care must be taken at all levels that the work was carried out as per the planning done by the supervisors. Organizations must ensure adequate profitability, which was necessary for survival, he maintained.
8. ***Mental revolution.*** Taylor was a firm believer that there must be sound relations between the management and the workers. All disputes should be resolved by mutual discussion within the organization. Close supervision therefore was a part of supervisors job. Gang boss was responsible for the smooth flow of the work. Workers were provided necessary tools, instructions pertaining to the job, perfect work environment and advise when necessary.

Principles of Scientific Management

1. ***Replacing* Rule of Thumb with Science:** Taylor introduced standardization, differential piece-rate of payment and carried out detailed work-study about each job in industry. He was the first engineer who separated planning and execution of work in the scientific way and allotted specific responsibilities to each of the persons involved in planning and doing.
2. **Harmony in Group Action:** All work groups should work in harmony. They must develop the spirit of give and take.
3. **Co-operation:** Taylor recommended **"co-operation among workers as against chaotic individualism. He insisted peace for war; replace suspicion to mutual confidence, friends for enemy".** From this principles one can find out and imagine that there was a shadow of world war I prevailing at the time he carried out his work. He carried out tremendous work to put the organizations on scientific footing and evolved methods to develop harmonious relations among workers.
4. **Maximum Output and development of workers:** Taylor was of the opinion that development of workers was central to improvement of productivity. He incorporated Gantt graphics in industrial operations. He disliked estimation and insisted precision in measuring the job. Work of Taylor brought near revolution in management and therefore was called the ***"father of Scientific Management"***

ANALYSIS

Scientific management propagated by Taylor made contributions at the production level. It created a near revolution in the field of engineering, production and work performance. It contributed towards efficiency, standardisation, specialisation and simplification of work. Optimum use of men and material was carried out in scientific way. Taylor emphasized five basic concepts to improve theory of management. These are research, standardisation, planning, cooperation and control. He assumed that industrial efficiency could be improved through the application of methods of science. Higher wages were related to higher productivity. He firmly believed that standardisation of working conditions, work methods, time and motion study and lastly the planning of daily tasks as important components of industrial efficiency. Taylor failed to appreciate human potential and treated human beings as yet another source. Indeed, he considered human recourse as component of large productive system. Man was literally equated with machine and his motives and desires had no place in the scientific management. The theory was not people oriented. Man was considered a rational being and not the emotional being. This led to exploitation of the human resources by introducing piece- rate of payment and enhanced payment based on units of production. Scientific management advocated fragmentation of work into small units that led to allocation of small part of a whole job to each individual who was controlled mechanically. It induced in the minds of workers to work more and earn more that reduced them to the level of machines. Very little attention was paid to the welfare, security and health of the employees, if any. A centralized controlled system and excessive rules and regulations were required to be implemented by managers. Taylor's scientific management brought revolution in higher productivity, savings in time, optimum utilisation of machines, expertise, higher rate of payment and materialistic approach in the field of management. The theory was work oriented rather than people oriented.

Taylor described scientific management as under:

"Science not rule of thumb. Harmony not discord. Co-operation, not individualism. Maximum output, in place of restricted out put. The development of each man to his greatest efficiency and prosperity."

PROCESS MANAGEMENT THEORY – FAYOL

The real father of modern management theory is the French industrialist Henry Fayol. His contribution is generally termed as process management and administrative management. Fayol looked at the problems from the top management point of view. He has used the term ***'administration'*** instead of management emphasising that there is unity of science of administration. This administrative science can be applied equally well to public and private affairs. Therefore, management is a universal phenomenon. However he has emphasised that principles of management are flexible and not absolute and are usable regardless of changing and special conditions.

Industrial Activities

Fayol found that activities of an industrial organization could be divided into six groups

1. Technical – relating to production and maintenance
2. Commercial – buying, selling and exchange.

3. Financial – search for capital and its optimum utilization.
4. Security – protection of property and human beings
5. Accounting – accounting of stores and equipment. Statistics is also covered under accounting.
6. Managerial – activities include planning, organizing, commanding, coordinating and control.

Fayol divided his approach of studying management into three parts.

1. Managerial Qualities

Fayol Considered that manager must have following qualities

(a) ***Physical ability:*** relating to health, vigour and ability to effectively addresses the people.
(b) ***Mental ability:*** to understand and learn, judgment, mental vigour and adaptability.
(c) ***Moral ability:*** energy, firmness, initiative, loyalty, tact and dignity
(d) ***Educational ability:*** General acquaintance with matter not belonging exclusively to the function performed
(e) ***Technical ability:*** Particular to function being performed
(f) ***Experience:*** Arising out of work

2. General Principles of Management

In order to develop managerial knowledge, he developed principles of management. These are given below

(i) ***Division of Labour:*** Fayol recommended that work of all types must be sub-divided and allotted to number of persons. Sub-division makes each task simpler and results in greater efficiency.
(ii) ***Parity of authority and responsibility:*** Authority refers to the right of a superior to give orders to subordinates, take decisions on specified matter, use the sources of organization. Responsibility on the other hand includes obligation with respect to the performance and achieving goals in a satisfactory manner. This principle suggests that giving authority without corresponding responsibility leads to arbitrary and unmindful use of authority. Authority relates to the power an individual acquire by virtue of his official position. Personal authority can also be derived from intelligence, moral worth and past experience of an individual.
(iii) ***Discipline:*** In the context of management means obedience, proper conduct in relation to others and complying with the rules and regulations of the organization. Smooth functioning needs discipline. Discipline is also self-imposed in relation to the work environment. If an individual does not display adequate self-discipline and if it has an adverse impact on the work then he should be warned, suspended, demoted or even dismissed depending upon the gravity of the indiscipline.
(iv) ***Unity of command:*** This principle states that subordinate should receive orders and be accountable to one and only one superior. It is necessary for stability, orderly functioning of the organization and accountability
(v) ***Unity of direction:*** According to this principle, the efforts of all the members of the organization should be directed towards common goals. The principle seeks to

ensure unity of action, coordination of strength and focusing of effects. Eg – Production department should have a single plane and all must work to achieve specified goals in terms of quality and quantity.

(vi) ***Subordination of individual to general interest:*** What is in the interest of the organization as a whole must take precedence over the interest of individuals. The efforts should be to bring about convergence of general and individual interest. Organizational interests are common to all employees. These should be above the individual interests. All the employees must set an example and be fair in their dealings. Supervisory staff must be vigilant and carry out supervision of assigned job religiously.

(vii) ***Fair remuneration to employee:*** Remuneration of employee should be fair and reasonable. It should be decided on the basis of work assigned, cost of living, financial and position of business He recommends profit sharing by managers and not by workers. Fayol recommends non-financial incentives for workers.

(viii) ***Centralisation and decentralisation:*** Centralization means the concentration of all powers at the top level of management and decentralization means the authority or the power is shared by middle as well as low level of management. Degree of centralization and decentralization depends upon the size of the organization, experience of the superiors and ability of subordinates.

(ix) ***Scalar chain:*** Fayol defines scalar chain as the chain of superiors ranging from the top management to the lowest rank. The chain also determines the line of authority. The principle suggests that there should be a clear line of authority from top to bottom linking managers at all levels. It is a chain of command as well as communication. An employee (C) could speak to his counterpart (G) by cutting across the formal chain. Same way B could speak to F. This communication was necessary for organizational efficiency.

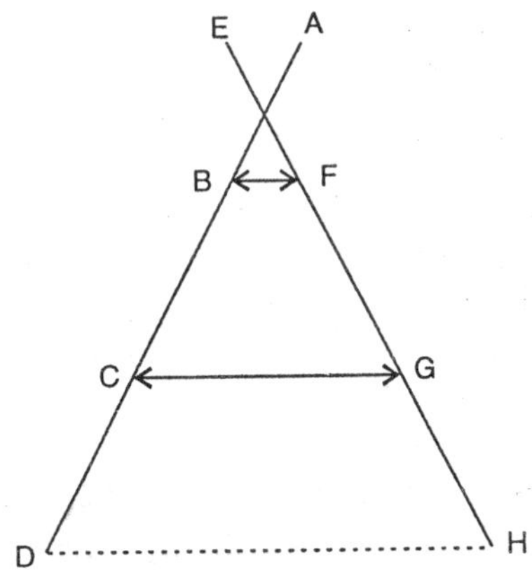

(x) ***Order:*** The principle is concerned with arrangement of things and placement of people. Arrangement of things—material order and and arrangement of people—social order. The people should be assigned specific places of work and that they should be available there and things should be kept at allotted places.

(xi) ***Equity:*** means, similar treatment is assigned to people at similar positions. For example workers performing similar jobs should be paid the same wages. The performance should be judged on the same basis for the same category of employees. Equity is combination of justice and kindness. Equity is treatment to subordinates by their superiors for an exemplary behaviour. It brings loyalty in the organization. It requires good sense, good nature and devotion to duty.

(xii) ***Stability of tenure of personnel:*** Employees should not be moved from their positions frequently. Period of service in a position should be fixed. The individual should not be transferred often as it takes time to settle down in the new appointment. It does not mean that when an employee is due for promotion and a vacancy exists at a new place, should not be transferred. Individual interests must have priority over the other aspects of the organization.

(xiii) ***Initiative:*** Employees at all levels should be allowed to take initiative in work related matters. Initiative means eagerness to initiate action without being asked to do so. However it does not imply freedom to whatever people like to do. Initiative increases zeal and energy.

(xiv) ***Esprit de corps:*** It refers to team-spirit that is harmony in work group and mutual understanding among workers. Managers must take steps to develop a sense of belonging among the members of the work group. If there is team-spirit then everyone comes forward to help each other. It must be remembered that 'union is strength'. Written explanation from erring member complicates matter and all issues should be resolved verbally.

3. Elements of Management

Fayol has regarded the 'Elements of Management' as principles of management. These elements or functions of management are discussed in brief

1. ***Planning:*** It is the most important element or function of management and failure to plan leads to hesitation, false step and untimely changes in directions, which causes weakness in the organization.
2. ***Organising:*** It is the process of bringing together physical, financial and human resources and establishing productive relations among them for the achievement of specific goals.
3. ***Commanding:*** This function is necessary to execute plans. This function includes the influencing the behaviour and work of others in a group to the realization of specified goals in the given situation.
4. **Coordination:** Co-ordination as a function of management refers to the task of integrating the acts of separate units of an organization to accomplish the organizational goals effectively.
5. **Controlling** Controlling refers to the process of ensuring that acts of subordinates and use of resources is in conformity with the pre determined goals.

Contribution of Fayol has made the real beginning of development of management as a separate field of study.

NEO-CLASSICAL THEORIES

Human Relations Era

Human relations era started in 1927 onwards. It was a movement spearheaded by Elton

Mayo. The essence of the movement was the belief that the key to higher productivity was employee satisfaction. Dale Carnegie, Abraham Maslow and Douglas McGregor also made the contribution to above philosophy. In this section we will briefly study the contributions made by these scientists.

Hawthorne Studies

Hawthorne studies were initially sponsored by National research council at the Western electric company's Hawthorne works in Cicero, Illions in the year 1924 but eventually expanded up to middle of 1930s. Engineers of the company carried out initial research, the object of the study was to "examine the effect of various illumination levels on productivity." The study envisaged formation of ***control group*** and ***experimental group***. Control group members worked under constant illumination intensity while the experiment group was subjected to varying intensity levels. It was expected that the individual output be directly related to intensity of light.

Conduct and Findings of the Study

As the illumination was increased in the experiment group, output increased in both the groups. As the light level was dropped in the experimental group, productivity continued to increase in both the groups. Productivity decrease was observed in the experimental group only when the light intensity had been reduced to that of moonlight. These findings baffled the engineers of the Western electric company, who concluded that illumination levels were not responsible for higher productivity. No reason could be ascribed for this phenomenon.

Further studies were conducted in Western electric company. Elton Mayo who at that time was working at Harvard University as professor, joined the study group along with his team. Following studies were undertaken by him, which started in the year 1927 and lasted up to 1932.

1. Redesign of jobs.
2. Changes in the length of workdays and workweeks.
3. Introduction of rest period.
4. Individual versus group wage plan.
5. Evaluation of effect of group piece incentive pay system

Elton Mayo and his colleagues carried out the studies where number of variables were tested. These were place of work, place and length of rest pause, length of working days, length of work, method of payment, free mid morning lunch etc, in relation to productivity.

Relay Room Experiment 1 and 2

Mayo started relay room experiment in 1927, which may be treated as actual beginning of Hawthorne studies. Two female assemblers were selected for the experiment. They were permitted to choose four other members to join them in test room, which was segregated from rest of the plant. Complete freedom was accorded to the members of the test group. Each test period yielded higher productivity than what was in the previous period. The relay room experiment did not yield the expected result as in normal environment, also the productivity increment was noticed.

Second Relay Room Experiment was related to the impact of wage incentives on output was under investigation. The norms suggested that output should not vary with the wages – There should be "no rate busters,' 'no chisellers, and 'no squealers'. The groups imposed controls through peer pressure, and sometimes through physical means". The study was undertaken where Experiment group and Mica splitting Test Room study group were under investigation. Experiment group was placed on a separate small - group piece rate incentive system while Mica splitting group members worked under their normal individual piece – rate plan. Continuous increase in output in Relay Assembly Test Room may be attributed to the wage incentive factor. The wage incentive factor was so dependent that it was virtually impossible to consider it as an independent factor. Researchers did not succeed in proving the above hypothesis.

Mass Interview & Bank Wiring Experiment

Mayo did not succeed in Relay Room experiment to identify the impact of changes in workdays and workweek and individual versus group wage plan. In the third experiment it was viewed to determine the factors that may be incorporated to improve supervisory training programme, no worthwhile results were achieved. Bank wiring study made an observational analysis of the informal work group objective. Data was collected with the help of the observer and an interviewer. It was concluded that there was no improvement in productivity. It was further observed that all (*i*) men stopped work before Quitting time, (*ii*) Workers were able to turn out more work and (*iii*) Tests of dexterity and intelligence indicated no relationship between capacity to perform and actual performance, fear of raising of slower workers acts have really affected production in Bank wiring experiment.

Mayo Concluded that

1. Individual behaviour and sentiments are closely related.
2. Group influences significantly affected individual behaviour.
3. Group standards established individual output.
4. Money was less a factor in determining output.
5. Group standards, group sentiments and security provided by the group were Responsible for higher productivity.

Elton Mayo made a new beginning on human factor in functioning of the organization and attainment of organizational goals. Hawthorne studies have proved that experiment and behavioral research can play a vital role in management and decision making. Mayo's contribution will ever be remembered for its contribution to the behavioral approach to management.

Sekaran[1] concluded that while the classical theorist subscribed to the notion that appropriate changes made in the work setting with regard to the job will automatically result in increased performance if the workers are trained and rewarded, the human relations theorist had other ideas. Evolving from the Hawthorne studies, the human relations school recognized that workers respond to appropriate changes made in the work setting with their feelings and sentiments and by what they perceive to be the social norms in the work setting. Thus, the study of management shifted from a stimulus – response notion to understanding the stimulus – the worker's feelings and reactions. Thus, the concept the "Rational Man" to "Social Man".

Dale Carnegie

Dale Carnegie published his work on "How to Win Friends and Win People. The theme of his work was to achieve success through winning the co-operation of others. He proposed four principles.

1. Make others important through a sincere appreciation.
2. Strive to make good first impression.
3. Win people to their way of thinking and by "Never telling a man that he is wrong".
4. Change people by praising their good traits and giving the offender the opportunity to Save face.

Need Hierarchy Theory-Abraham Maslow

Abraham Maslow's original work of needs theories was undertaken with the rehabilitation of people in mind. Today, the need hierarchy theory of Maslow is often quoted and used in management to motivate workers. Maslow's theory generally state five needs of human beings Viz, Physiological, safety, belonging, (Social) esteem and self-actualization. One thing that must be remembered is that the original hierarchy needs theory has six needs Maslow called them "Meta" needs, comprising a range of different needs such as 'cognitive' and 'aesthetic' which exists between esteem and self – actualization needs. Original theory of Maslow did recognized that peoples needs varied at different times, and in hierarchical order. Before a person enters to fulfill higher order needs he must achieve minimum two basic needs (Physiological and Safety). He further stated that needs do not disappear but its potency is reduced and the next higher order need takes precedence, once that is fulfilled the next needs becomes dominating and so on. Needs which are commonly used in the theory and it's meaning is given below.

Physiological Needs – Decoration, Vibration, Temperature, Space, Noise, Gas, and Canteen facilities.

Security Needs – Job description, regularity, role clarity, structure, communication, safety report meetings, agreements, and contracts.

Social Needs – Joint Tasks, appreciation, sharing offices, recognition and team membership.

Self – esteem – Being consulted, rank, success, achievement, encouragement, recognition, pre-requisites.

Self – actualization – Personal or professional growth, autonomy, worthwhile job.

Maslow's hierarchy of needs theory can be applied to the individual's life span. In the early years of life a person is concerned about fulfillment of basic needs. But when a person takes up a job and experiences independence, which is marked by crave for autonomy, he feels that he should be consulted and works to achieve recognition. Employees first want physical and job security later a suitable working environment, appreciation, job stability, recognition, growth and autonomy. Thus making a full cycle of need beginning with physiological needs to self-actualization needs.

Theory X and Theory Y - McGregor

Theory X and Theory Y were introduced by Douglas McGregor based on two diagonally opposite views of human behaviour.

Theory X

McGregor assumed that average human being dislikes work and will try to avoid it if possible. Employees are lazy, they must be controlled, coerced and even punished to achieve organizational goals. Average employee do not accept responsibility and seek direction from their superiors. They lack ambition. McGregor therefore recommends organizations so structured that enable close supervision, tight control and mangers must exert energy to achieve organizational objective.

After Theory X, there were certain changes in external environment. Entrepreneurs took business seriously and on the scientific manner. There was industrial revolution; management practices were being applied in the business. Because of these changes McGregor proprogated Theory Y.

Theory Y

Theory Y suggests that average human being likes work and takes it as natural as play. Employees can exercise self-direction and self-control and given the proper working conditions, average person seeks responsibilities. McGregor felt that wisdom is widely spread among the employees and they are innovative and can take quality decisions. It therefore assumes that management must appreciate the potential among employees and adopt such management practices like delegation, job enlargement and management by objective. Management must appreciate the individual and organizational goals and create such environment, which is conducive for its attainment. Reward System, recognition and facilities for creativity should be provided.

McGregor in his theory displayed a total recognition of humanistic approach. He laid stress on delegation of authority, setting organizational objectives and leaving it to the employees to attain the same. He carried forward the behaviour approach proposed by Mayo, Maslow in mid 20th century. McGregor's theory Y is as valid to day as it was 50 years ago.

MODERN MANAGEMENT THEORIES

Re-engineering

Michael Hammer has coined the concept of re-engineering. Re-engineering is the fundamental rethinking and radical redesign of business processes to achieve dramatic improvements in critical, contemporary measures of performance, such as cost, quality, service and speed[2]. Re-engineering involves total redesign of the job. The process of re-engineering begins with a clean slate and a job is planned from beginning till end, the objective of re-engineering is to improve efficiency, performance and overall productivity.

Steps in Re-engineering Process

Under the re-engineering process, employees are an important element; they must understand the new way of carrying out the task.

1. **Mission**: The first step of re-engineering is managements rethinking of identifying the basic mission of the organization and deciding what business they are in and what they want to do. This facilitates the desired approach to carry out various processes to attain mission.

2. **Process:** Top management plays an active role in leading the process, thus ensuring the overall co-operation from the personnel.
3. **Creation of Sense of Urgency:** An atmosphere of urgency among the personnel regarding the need for re-engineering is necessary. This will ensure commitment of efforts to the case of re-engineering.
4. **Identification of Customer needs:** Identification of customer needs for re-engineering efforts to be successful is essential. To know the customer needs and wants and then creating an organizational structure and team work providing it.
5. **Organizational Support:** When needs have been identify an organizational support of various departments is essential so that the processes and systems are modified for higher efficiency and increased productivity. Sight of the mission and fulfillment of customer needs is the focus.

There are number of examples of re-engineering efforts i.e. conduct of on line interviews, examinations and declaration of results of various technical institutes, introduction of E-business and transfer of money etc.

Benchmarking

Benchmarking is the process of comparing work and service methods against the best practices and outcomes for the purpose of identifying changes that will result in higher quality output. Benchmarking incorporates the use of human resources techniques such as goal setting to set targets that are identified, pursued, and then used as a basis for future actions. The benchmarking process involves both inside and outside the organization for ways of improving the operation (Fred Luthans)[3]. Benchmarking offers following benefits to the organization.

1. This technique helps organization to compare themselves against the best practices available in the field.
2. Identification of improvement strategies.
3. Assist in learning from others.
4. It helps organsiation create a need for change in work procedure and assignments.

Benchmarking procedures are practically used by most organization to identify cost of production, expenses on research and development activities. Identifying cost of training per individual. At international levels caparison of business is carried out.

Empowerment

Empowerment is defined as **"a process that enhances intrinsic work motivation by positively influencing impact, competence, meaningfulness and choice."** (Thomas K.W. & Velthouse B.A.)[4]. Empowered people believe that they are competent, and valued, that their jobs have meaning and impact and those they have opportunities to use their talents. Brown and Brown define the process of empowerment as **"the orientation of all forces, values, and beliefs which determine human behavior in organizations so that the support and liberate the individual rather than reduce their range of thought and action."** (Randolph W.A.)[5]. He believes that empowerment is not just "giving people the power to make decisions". He holds that they already have the power to make intelligent decisions to help the company operate more effectively. He defines

"empowerment as recognizing and releasing into the organization the power, which the people already have in their wealth of useful knowledge and internal motivation."

Empowerment is very closely tied to the study of organizational behaviour. "Empowerment is the authority to make decisions within one's area of operations without having to get approval from anyone else. (Luthans) there are two major characteristics of empowerment.

1. Personnel are encouraged to use their initiative.
2. Employees are given not just the authority but resources as well, so that they are able to make a decision and see that it is implemented.

In the highly competitive and rapidly changing environment caused due to globalisation and liberalization of market economy there has been growing concern for empowerment. Those organizations, which liberate themselves by empowering their people, can survive in the present environment. It must be noted that empowerment is most effective tool of managerial effectiveness to obtain the full potential of employees. In bureaucratic form of organizational structure, there is an established hierarchy of command and the higher authority controls the subordinates down the line. But in organizations where empowerment is practiced, performance of individual is achieved. Empowerment envisages participation, innovation, access to information and accountability. Maximum productivity is achieved from the front line operators supported by management in creating value. Empowering organization can be designed through the following:

1. Management by trust, Quality of work life and by implementing other organizational development strategies.
2. Organising flexible production systems rather them mass production.
3. By introducing customized product with variations for customer needs.
4. By reducing waste and achieving global competitiveness in price.
5. By enhanced efforts in research and development activities.

Systems Approach to Management

Kast and Rosenzweig[6], **"defines system as an organized, unitary whole composed of two or more interdependent parts, components, or sub – systems and delineated by identifiable boundaries from its environmental suprasystem."** From the above definition following aspects stand out.

(*i*) A system has several parts. These are dynamic in nature and therefore interact with each other.

(*ii*) The parts or systems are interdependent and interrelated.

(*iii*) The interdependence is required due to specialized nature of job, division of labour, sharing of limited resources and scheduling of activities.

(*iv*) Creating various departments that carries out the work in the organization, sub-departments and sections.

(*v*) Work is carried out by teams and groups who performed specialized task to accomplish overall organizational objective.

(*vi*) Change in one department affect the other departmental work.

A system is therefore composed of several sub system and sub-sub system. Every system or sub-system has its own objective and various processes. Personnel employed to manage the system have to play their roles and work under systems that are open. Katz and Kahn include importation of energy, throughput, output, phenomenon. Organization import resources, energy and information from environment, transform them into product and services and export it to the environment where society uses the same. Organizations do not export all that they produce but retain certain portion for its survival and growth. Organizations carry out modification and improvement based on performance feed back. Organization must also develop the ability to absorb the shocks and influences from the environment by developing inbuilt flexibility and responses.

In order to obtain clarity of this concept, take an example of soft drink bottling plant. The plant is a system. Filling plant, Marketing of bottles, advertisement may be considered as a sub-systems of bottling plant. Collection of empty bottles from the consumers, washing the bottles and making them ready for refilling may be considered as sub-sub system. All the systems, sub-systems and sub-sub systems are interdependent and intertwined. Without the support of each of the sub-system and sub-sub system, soft drink bottling plant cannot function effectively. If empty bottle collection sub-sub system fails, the bottle plant will come to a virtual halt. The plant draws raw material, technical know how, machinery, human resources, land and plant from the environment, transform it into soft drink bottles and export product and services back to the environment, retaining a part of it for survival and growth. A strong bottling plant has to receive shocks from other bottling plants in the form of price war, shortage of raw material and yet ensure survival and growth by using various business strategies. There can be several ways of classifying systems and one may follow any basis. Broadly speaking, Carzo and Yanouzas gave three kinds of sub-systems in an organization as a system – technical, social and power. The technical sub-system represents the formal part of organization and the remaining two, the non-formal one. These are discussed in the following paragraphs:

1. Technical Sub-System

When an organization is formed, there is a technical sub-system, which is nothing but an entire formal organization. Organization is structured based on technology, product and market that one is required to serve. Policies, rules and regulations are framed, span of management is created and authority and responsibilities are delegated based on need. Appropriate engineering, information technology and other considerations are laid down. The organization imports necessary resources from the environment, transform them and export the finished product/services to the environment. In the process, decision making, communication and control measures are implemented. Administrative system ensures balance in the organization, so that no department becomes powerful while carrying out the job. Due care is taken about the status, norms, attitudes and behavioural pattern of employees. The whole arrangements are synchronized, all details are tied up and everybody knows as to what he has to do to achieve the organizational goal. Therefore, this sub-system is called technical sub-system, which exists in all the organizations irrespective of product/ services they produce.

2. Social Sub-System

Social Sub-System provides social security and social satisfaction to its members. Enrolment of human resources is carried out to match the requirement of job. Individuals have varying degree of interests, capabilities attitudes, beliefs, likes, dislikes. Based on these they join groups of like-minded employees to meet their social aspiration even by cutting across hierarchical barriers. It has often been noticed that employees join various social organizations, groups, sports club to enhance their image in the work environment. The employees thus seek a power base to meet the social needs. The process thus leads to emergence of social groups who have their own objectives, structure and role to play. These groups develop a pattern of social norms, image in the society and subsequently exercise immense power in the society. Members of Rotary or a golf club are some of the examples.

3. Power Sub-System

Every job is important in the organization. People have to be, not only dependent on others, but also inter-dependent so that the individual, group and ultimately the organizational objectives are met in given time. Specialization has become an important aspect in organization. Individuals display power behaviour based on the ability, skill, importance of their job, the critical appointment they hold and lastly the proximity to decision making authority. Some people have more influence areas than others while those who do not care for organizational norms engage themselves in politicking and play an opportunistic games. Power sub – system take its firm root based on personality traits, dominant nature, relationship with superiors, ability to influence others, the success story and the like. Therefore the power – holders enjoy extra privileges, status and turn the situation in their own interest.

Technical, social and power sub – systems do not function independently, there is an overlap. Infact they are intertwined to a great extent. Individual behaviour is displayed and guided by these sub–systems. On occasions individual may behave in such a way that it is difficult to make distinction between various sub – systems. These sub – systems are a part of larger system say organization as system. Organization itself can be a sub-system of larger system like society and society a sub–system of environmental system. Since the entire sub – systems /systems are interdependent and must function with great precision and coordination. Each of the systems must contribute positively as they are influenced and get influenced by other sub- systems / systems. What in effect emerges as an outcome of this interaction is called **emergent system**.

The emergent systems remain valid and operative as long as there are no changes in the environment. Once there are changes in environmental factors like technology, marketing variables, social changes etc., the emergent system take a new form. It is a continuous process and therefore we say change is a constant phenomenon.

4. Contingency Theory of Management

Contingency theory of management is an extension of system approach to management. There cannot be a suitable management solutions for all situations. External and internal factors keep changing. Since systems approach cannot appropriately suggest relationship between organization and environment, the gap so created has been fulfilled by contingency approach. The theory suggests:

1. What a manger should do in a particular situation based on the examination of the facts relating to each situation?

2. Contingency theory suggests active inter-relationship between various variables in a situation and managerial action devised. It not only suggests solution to the given situation but also examines various influences of the situation on behaviour pattern of the individual and groups in the organization.

The contingency view of organization may be explained in the words of Kast and Rosenzweig as follows : "The contingency view seeks to understand the inter-relationship within and among sub-systems as well as between the organization and its environment and to define patterns of relationship and configuration of variables. It emphasizes the multivariate nature of organizations and attempts to understand how organizations operate under varying conditions and in specific circumstances. Contingency views are ultimately directed towards suggesting organizational designs and managerial actions most appropriate for specific situations (Ref. Kast, F.E. and J.E. Rosenzweig)[6].

Tosi and Hammer states that when a sub -system in an organization behaves in response to another system or sub – system, we say response is contingent on environment. Hence a contingency approach is an approach where the behaviour of one sub- unit is dependent on its environment relationship to other units or sub-units that have control over the consequences desired by that sub-unit.

Features of the Contingency Theory

1. Management action is contingent on certain actions outside the system or the sub system.
2. Organizational action should be based on the behaviour of action outside the system so that organization can be integrated with the environment.
3. Because of the specific organization – environment relationship, no action can be universal. It various from situation to situation.
4. Internal functions of the organization are generally consistent with the technology, demand placed on the organization by the society, external environment and needs of the members of the organization.
5. Contingency approach suggests suitable alternatives for those managerial actions, which are influenced by external and internal environment like organizational design, strategy formulation, decision systems, leadership styles and organization improvement.
6. Organizational systems are not absolute. They have to adjust or modify considering social, political, technical and economic situations.

Implications

Contingency approach to management is an important addition to the management theory. It is a very sophisticated approach because it takes into consideration increasing complexity of organization. The approach emphasizes multivariate nature of organization and suggests organizational designs and managerial actions to specific situations. The theory is contingent on environmental factors like politics, technology and economic situation prevailing from time to time. Sharma (1997)[7], explains that contingency views tend to be more concrete and to emphasize more specific characteristics and pattern of inter-relationship among sub-systems. The view recognizes that the environment and internal sub-systems of each organization are somewhat unique and provide a basis for designing and managing specific organizations. Contingency view recognizes the complexity involved in running modern organizations and uses pattern of relationship and /or configurations of sub-systems in order to search a way out. However there are certain drawbacks in this approach. It is not considered as unified theory of management because there is inadequate literature. It does not suggest any action in a contingency. Management actions depends upon situation is not adequate. The theory is difficult for empirical testing. It is complex because there are large number of variables and large number of managerial actions involved. The theory is not proactive, it is reactive.

TOTAL QUALITY IN HUMAN RESOURCES MANAGEMENT

The concept of Total Quality Management (TQM) essentially revolves around the effective use of the available human resources. Hence emphasis on training and continuous personal improvement is essential. TQM means that an organization's culture is defined by and supports the constant quest for customer satisfaction. This involves continuous improvement of organizational processes, resulting in high quality products and services (Kreithner and Kinicki, 1995)[8].

Deming's Pioneering Work

Pioneering work in TQM was done in Japan through the efforts of Edward Deming. He stressed the need for all the individuals involved to work in a cohesive team, keeping in mind the fulfillment of the given objectives in time. Training in statistical process control techniques is necessary for all, so that quality control of the product being manufactured is maintained in accordance with the standards laid down and corrective measures are taken while the product is being manufactured. In other words TQM is not just a technique that can be turned on when quality improvement is required. TQM is rather a philosophy that requires active participation on the part of both owner and employees. TQM is an on-going process that is to be approached from the standpoint of continuous improvement by incremental stages. The ability to ensure the quality of a product or a service is, therefore, dependent on the quality of the working relationship between the human beings at the work place. It involves the dynamics of the behavioural processes. For the six best companies of Europe, TQM means continuously improving processes and performance by involving people so as to delight customers (Binney, 1992)[9].

Deming's framework of Total Quality Management is aimed at improvement in the quality of the product, reduction in the cost of production, gaining an increased market share, thus ensuring the prosperity of the business. Deming was fully aware of the potential of human beings and knew that TQM could be achieved only by changing the nature of the organization, stressing the importance of leadership and the need to reduce variations in the organizational processes. Deming proposed 14 principles of TQM:

1. Create consistency of objectives and plans
2. Adopt a new philosophy of quality
3. Cease dependence on mass inspections
4. End the practice of choosing supplies based solely on price
5. Improve the system constantly and continuously
6. Institute training on-the-job
7. Strengthen leadership
8. Drive out fear

9. Breakdown barriers between departments and units
10. Stop requesting improved productivity
11. Eliminate work standards that prescribe numerical quotas and quality standards
12. Remove barriers to pride in workmanship
13. Institute vigourous education and self-improvement programmes
14. Put everyday in the company to work to accomplish the transition to total quality

(Shani and Lau, 1996.) TQM is an approach that fosters quality leadership, quality production and full utilization of organizational resources. It can transform an organization's culture.

Based on the above 14 principles, Deming coined the following four practical policies of TQM:

1. Do it right the first time so as to eliminate costly rework
2. Listen to and learn from customers and employees
3. Make continuous improvement an every day matter
4. Build teamwork, trust and mutual respect

Though Deming's Total Quality Management revolved around ensuring quality products and services, he nevertheless paid full attention to developing individuals and the organizational culture. This is evident from the fact that of the 14 factors he enumerated, ten pertain to the human beings in the organization that is involved in providing quality products and services. He laid stress on training and development of subordinates, which he believed, was the key to Total Quality Management, as it relates to the improvement of the human resources. Removing barriers to pride in workmanship and improvement of various systems in the organization were other suggestions given by him.

Juran's Framework of TQM

Joseph Juran, an electrical engineer was Deming's collaborator in Japan. He suggested ten principals of TQM.

1. Build awareness of the need to improve
2. Set goals for improvement
3. Organize so as to reach the goals
4. Provide training
5. Conduct projects to solve problems
6. Report progress
7. Give recognition
8. Communicate results
9. Keep score of progress achieved
10. Maintain the momentum by making annual improvement part of the regular system and processes of the company.

Juran too laid down stress on the human resources of an organization. He firmly believed that human resource development by various techniques could help bring about Total Quality Management in a company. Selection and maintenance of personnel is not the important pre-requisite for any organization. What is important is that all personnel should keep the company's objectives as the focus of all their activities and identify ways to accomplish them. Further, the objectives or goals for each department or unit and all resources including the personnel should be deployed for their attainment. Efforts to improve human performance should be taken up as an ongoing process.

Training and development, therefore, merit the serious attention of the management. Training must be progressive in nature, realistic and preferably done on the job to be of real value. Freedom of action should be encouraged among the trainees and the bogey of Zero Defects should not be flauted during training. The trainer should encourage discussion and full participation in a free environment, so that contributions from all the participants enrich the contents of training. Once the stage of tutorial discussion is over, the inputs should be tried out by subjecting the trainees to various exercises and later to practical cases. Their reactions should be observed and corrected by the facilitator. No compromise should be allowed. Those found fit should be allowed to go up. Psychological testing, especially of managers, during the recruitment stage is recommended. It should be the endeavour of each head of unit to ensure that all employees are trained in such a way that they are capable of undertaking jobs one step above the existing one, without losing time and without any additional efforts. This will ensure higher performance and job satisfaction for each individual.

Steps must also be taken to relate performance to recognition. Recognition fosters job satisfaction and promotes a sense of belonging in the organization one is serving.

Juran's teachings emphasize the idea of managing for quality and getting it "**right the first time**", rather than inspecting things into finished products (Thiagrarjan and Zairi, 1977).[10]

Philip B Crosby's Approach

If Deming and Juran are credited with jump-starting the quality movement in Japan, Crosby can be credited with the quality awakening in the United States through his 1979 bestseller **Quality is Free: The Art of Making Quality Certain:** Croby's approach to quality is based on management commitment to quality goals, prevention of defects and respect for employees and their efforts. Crosby advocates zero defects as the quality performance standard for every one in the organization. This calls for a change in the culture of the organization.

Crosby lists four new essentials of quality management, which he calls "**the absolutes**".

1. Quality is defined as conformance to requirements
2. Quality is achieved by prevention not by appraisal
3. The quality performance standard is zero defects
4. The cost of lack of quality is measured by the price of non-conformance

The key points which are derived from the absolutes are: The need to understand customer requirements; a management commitment to satisfying the customer; communicating customer requirements to the workforce; training the workforce to produce to customer requirements; prevention of errors by a proper understanding of the process involved in producing products and services; doing things right the first time as a management performance standard; creating an enabling environment to achieve such standards; and measuring and publicizing the cost of rejects, reworks and waste. Crosby talks about the three stages in the evolution of a total quality culture: first, the conviction that quality is an asset; next a commitment to implement quality as a way of life; and finally, the conversion of the entire organization to this way of life.

Leadership

The top management is the main driver of TQM (Zairi, 1992)[11]. Therefore, the most important factor in TQM is leadership. What is expected of a leader is first to know his subordinates, their social background, their financial status, the number of dependents, and the level of their dependency on the employee. This will enable a leader to judge what job to assign to each individual and how much to expect from him. Secondly the leader must be professionally competent, so that subordinates can look up to him as a person who has solutions to the problems they face. He should display an ability to adjust to changing situations and to different people. A leader should be able to work effectively in adverse circumstances and not show signs of creaking up. He should display professional honesty and be known for integrity. This is essential to obtain the willing obedience of subordinates and to accomplish his mission. Hence a leader should adopt a code of conduct for him and for the organization.

People have been concerned about the nature of leadership, so as to identify the difference between leaders and non-leaders, and between successful and unsuccessful leaders. Research suggests the six most important characteristics that a leader should possesses are:

(*i*) A high level of personal drive
(*ii*) A desire to lead
(*iii*) Personal integrity
(*iv*) Self confidence
(*v*) Analytical ability
(*vi*) Knowledge of the job and of the organization

Apart from these factors, charisma, creativity and flexibility are highly desirable qualities in a leader. Finally successful leadership depends more on appropriate behaviour skills and action and less on personal traits. The traits only provide the latent potential and the behaviour is the successful release and expression of this potential. Leadership of this kind is indispensable to build up an organizational culture suitable for Total Quality Management.

Appraisal and Recognition

Performance appraisal has assumed great significance. It is the measure of the effectiveness of an individual, a barometer for furtherance of one's career. An individual's performance must measure up to the objectives assigned to him. He must accomplish his job at least in the given time, since time management is a key factor in any job. The attainment of quality standards is a necessary element in effective performance appraisal. Besides a person displaying innovative ideas should be recognized and facilities should be accorded to him to show his worth. Outstanding performance must be recognized in public. This has a strong motivational effect on all the employees. Remuneration must also be compatible with the job and merit should be the sole consideration for promotion. An award system should be introduced and fairly implemented. All these actions on the part of the leadership are bound to bring about an organizational culture conducive to Total Quality Management.

TQM in human resource management should be looked upon as a central company policy. It should originate at the highest level and percolate down to last person doing his job. It should be treated as a movement. However, this is possible only when autonomy is accorded to leaders at various levels in the performance of their jobs. Mutual trust and respect for each other's ideas is most helpful. If Total Quality Management is undertaken in an organization, then, re-engineering and quality control at various stages becomes outdated as all these factors are at the very core of the TQM concept.

SUMMARY

Management has been in existence since the birth of human race. Only the form and the intensity differred. However management has been recognised as an independent field during 18th century and it made its mark during World War I. At the beginning of 20th century classical theories gave a solid foundation to the field of management. Three streams emerged during that period namely 1) Bureaucracy Theory by Max Weber-1900; 2) Scientific Management Theory by Taylor-1910; and 3) Process Management Theory which is also called Functional management and Administrative Theory by Henry Fayol-1910. Major contribution of this period has been tremendous. Max Weber has been pioneer in putting the business on a correct footing by introducing strict rules and regulation, hierarchy of command and control system, standardisation, rule of law leading to impersonal behaviour, selection and promotion based on skills and competence and concept of power, which is derived from the official position held by the individual. Taylor transformed the industrial floor processes. His major contribution to the field of management is 1) Concept of functional foremanship. 2) Time and motion study. 3) Differential piece-rate system of payment. 4) Concept of supervision. However, Taylor failed to recognise the real potential of human beings and treated them yet another source. Taylor described scientific management as under:

"Science not rule of thumb. Harmony not discord. Co-operation, not individualism. Maximum output, in place of restricted out put. The development of each man to his greatest efficiency and prosperity." He is called Father of Scientific Management.

Henri Fayol has developed Administrative managemet theory, thereby propagating suprimacy of administration over management. He identified 14 principles of management. He proposed that authority and responsibility go hand in hand. Paid special attention to division of work, unity of command, scalar chain, spirit–de corps, justice, and evolved policies that promoted human resource in terms of reward and growth. He was known real father of management by virtue of his extensive work. The principles are still valid even today.

Classical theories failed to appreciate the significance of human element in management. Too much standardisation, rules and regulation and bogie of improving productivity had stalled to recognize the importance of human beings. The study carried out by Elton Mayo envisaged the consideration of human element and adopted a humanistic approach. Following studies were undertaken by Mayo between 1927 to 1936.

(*a*) Effect of illumination on productivity
(*b*) Relay room experiments 1 and 2.
(*c*) Mass interview and bank wiring experiment

The studies established:

1. Individual behaviour and sentiments are closely related.
2. Group influences significantly affected individual behaviour.
3. Group standards established individual output.
4. Money was less a factor in determining output.
5. Group standards, group sentiments and security provided by the group were responsible for higher productivity.

The studies established the need for changes for job design as under:

(*a*) redesign of jobs.
(*b*) Changes in the length of workdays and workweeks.
(*c*) Introduction of rest period.
(*d*) Individual versus group wage plan.
(*e*) Evaluation of effect of group piece incentive pay system

With this the concept of worker shifted from that of the **"rational man to social man".**

In middle of the 20th century Dale Carnegie published his work on how to win friends. Abraham Maslow introduced Need Hierarchy Theory. In his theory he stated that there are five needs of any human being. The needs are in a particular order. Once the lower level need is satisfied, its intensity reduces and the new need emerges which has higher intensity and therefore individual attempts to satisfy the same. Needs do not disappear but its intensity is reduced. The five needs mentioned by Maslow are 1) Physiological need. 2) Security need. 3) Social need. 4) Esteem need. 5) Self-actualisation need.

Mc Gregor during the same period introduced Theory X and Theory Y. Theory X relates to the assumption Mc Gregor made about human beings. He stated that human beings are basically lazy, donot like work, are irresponsible, lazy and lack ambition. He therefore, recommended that the organization structure should be so designed that should lend itself to close supervision, tight control over the employees. Theory Y, on the contrary suggests employees as ambitious, hard working, responsible, innovative and self directed. He therefore, recommended manegerial practices like delegation of authority, job enlargement, management by objective and creation of such enviornment that is condusive to higher productivity. The Human Relations Era though still continues, but due to technological advancement, and introduction of computer and information technology a need has emerged to fasten the space of production and maintenance of quality. Hence a modern management era began. Processes of re-engineering, bench marking, management by objective and empowerment were introduced. Total quality management concepts of Deming and Juran have created a revolution in Japan and US. These concepts were introduced so that customer satisfaction is achieved, competiveness is maintained and satisfaction of stake-holder is achieved. Zero error syndrome was in vougue. Systems approach tried to be practiced by all organizations, which envisaged latest technology, process upgradation and adoption of systems that cut down operation time and were economical to the organization. This did not cater for any contingency and managers had to evolve fresh strategies every time. Hence contingency theory was intoduced. The theory caters for managerial actions in various contingencies. Contingency theory suggests organization designs and manegerial actions should be specifc for a particular situation. Information technology, electronic media and introduction of computers had made a near revolution in the society. Communication efficiency increased tremendousely. Managers are in position to acquire information of value that enables them to take fast and quality decisions. This phenomenon has improved the effeciency of organizations.

TEXT QUESTIONS

Q. 1. Trace out the evolution of management theories. Identify major landmarks in the process.

Q. 2. Explain in detail the Bureaucracy theory of Max Weber. What were the strong points of this theory? Are they still valid? Discuss the concept in detail with suitable examples.

Q. 3. Explain Scientific management theory of Taylor. What is his contribution to science of management?

Q. 4. "Process management theory was one step ahead of scientific management". Do you agree with this statement. Explain various factors considered by Fayol. Discuss principles of management propagated by him. Are they still valid in the present enviornment?

Q. 5. What are various experiments carried out by Elton Mayo? Explain in detail the illumination experiment carried out at Howthrone. What are its findings?

Q. 6. Explain Systems Theory to manage an organization. What are its drawbacks?

Q. 7. Explain Contingency approach to management.

Q. 8. Explain Need hierarchy theory of Abraham Maslow. Carryout analysis of the theory.

Q. 9. Explain the following concepts

(*a*) TQM

(*b*) Re-engineering

(*c*) Empowerment

(*d*) Bench marking

REFERENCES

1. Sekaran Uma. ***"Organizational Behaviour"*** Text and Cases, Tata McGrow Hill, New Delhi
2. Michael Hammer and James Champ, ***"Re-engineering the Corporation".*** A thorniest for Business Revolution, Harper Collins, New York, 1993, P. 32).
3. Fred Luthans, ***"Organizational Behaviour"***, McGraw Hills, International Edition, 7th Edition, 1995.
4. Thomas K.W. & Velthouse B.A. ***"Cognitive Elements of Empowerment – An interpretative model of intrinsic task motivation"***, Academy of Management Review 1990. 668 – 81).
5. Randolph W.A. ***"Navigating the Journey to empowerment"***, Organizational Dynamics, spring, 1995 – 19 – 32)
6. Kast, F.E. and J.E. Rosenzweig, ***"Organization and Management"***, McGraw–Hill New York, 1979).
7. Sharma, R.A. ***"Organizational Theory and Behaviour"***, Tata McGraw Hill. Publishing Co. Ltd., New Delhi.

8. Kreitner Robert and Angelo Kinicki (1995). ***"Organizational Behaviour"***. Third Edition, Chicago; Irwin.

9. Binney George (1992) ***"Making Quality Work"*** Lessons from Europe's Leading Companies.London: The Economist Intelligence Unit.

10. Thiagarajan, T.and Zairi, M.(1997) ***"Understanding the Fundamentals of TQM in Productivity"***. 3 (1), 87 – 102.

11. Zairi M. (1992). ***"Managing User – Supplier Interactions"*** Management of R & D Activity in Management Decision, 30 (8).

PART TWO

Individual Dimensions of Organizational Behaviour

CHAPTER 3

Individual Dimensions of Organizational Behaviour

INTRODUCTION

Study of human behaviour is very complex. It is affected by various environmental factors. It is based on various cultural factors in which an individual is brought up and various social systems in which he is working. Every individual behaves in a different manner, his behaviour is individualistic in nature, and therefore cannot be changed easily without any strong stimuli. There exists a cause and effect relationship in individual behaviour. For example if an organization pays good dividends to its employees, the productivity can be improved. This means that the increased productivity is an effect of receipt of handsome dividends by the workers. These are monetary in nature which is extrinsic value addition. People are more prone to change in behaviour due to intrinsic value addition like recognition or change in status. It is therefore necessary for the managers to identify "need" of individual employee and evolve such strategies that would give an employee an intrinsic value satisfaction so that the productivity is increased and individuals are satisfied with the job they have been assigned to. An individual may be satisfied with subsidized lunch the organization provides, while the other may be dissatisfied with the menu, preparation or the method or even timings of the lunch. Human activities are innumerable. It may be maintenance of machines, delegation of authority, or writing a report on appraisal system. In general it could be both mental and physical process. All the activities of human beings cannot be measured, what goes psychologically or inside the thought process of an individual cannot be observed. Individual behaviour cannot be easily predicted due to interplay of various variables, that are very complex to examine and implement. The job of a manager therefore is to *predict* the behaviour based on knowledge of individual his experience with him in an identical situation and behaviour pattern prevailing, based on the organizational culture. A manager at best can generalize a situation and should implement his managerial skills so that workers satisfaction level is increased. No two individuals are alike and they behave different in similar situations. In relation to work, individuals differ in the following respects.

1. **Intrinsic/Extrinsic rewards:** Intrinsic rewards are related to recognition that a worker gets in an organization. It is related to inner satisfaction of a person and

not related to material wants. Extrinsic rewards are related to maintenance or hygiene factors which are related to increased monetary compensation. Intrinsic reward is related to change in right direction of human behaviour, which is permanent or long lasting. Monetary rewards prevent motivational level to come down however it does not help to increase. Workers differ in this respect and hence there is a difference of behaviour of workers in a particular situation, though the situation may be the same.

2. **Compensation:** Compensation is another factor, where most of the individuals have their own way of expression, while some workers would appreciate the mega-work the management is doing in running the organization and be satisfied with the reward or the compensation they are getting while the others may be unhappy and resort to various grievance.

Foundation of Individual Behaviour

Individual behaviour is influenced by various factors. We will study those personal factors, which has influence on productivity, job satisfaction, absenteeism and turnover. These are given in Figure 3.1 below:

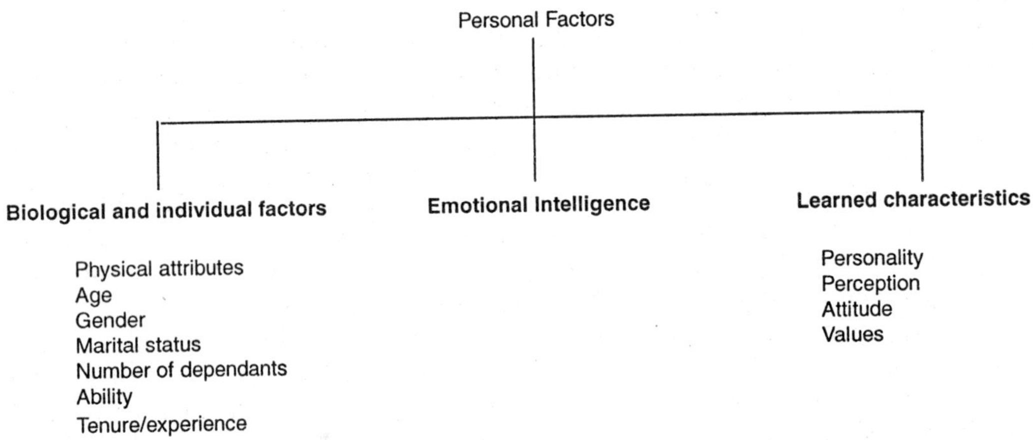

Fig. 3.1. Personal factors having influence on productivity job satisfaction, turnover and absenteeism

BIOGRAPHICAL CHARACTERISTICS

Biological and Individual Factors

There are certain factors which are inherited by an individual. A person inherits physical appearance, way of talking, analyzing, and taking initiative in a group. Physical attributes of a person are important in work enviornment. If a manager is able to identify these factors he will be able to deal with each of individual employees effectively. These factors are as under:

(*a*) **Age:** Age is one of the important factors to generate productivity. The relationship between job and performance is an issue of increasing concern. Younger employees are expected to be more energetic, adventurous, ambitions and risk takers. On the other hand old people are considered to be more conservative, having slow speed of work and are less adaptable. Job performance and turnover declines with increasing age and therefore less job opportunities, hence there are less of resignation. Older people generally get higher wages, longer paid vacation and they stick on to the job because of pensionary benefits. However productivity is related to attitude and behaviour of employees irrespective of age factor. Speed, agility, strength and coordination reduces by age. Experience, the older employees enjoy is of a great significance, disadvantages caused due to declining age is off set by experience.

(*b*) **Gender:** Traditionally some jobs were reserved for females like nursing jobs. Over a passage of time, there is no gender differenciation between male and female. We observe successful female entrepreneurs working around the world. In the Indian defence services, the women fighter pilots had done a wonderful job during Kargil operations. They can undergo physical and mental stress and display exemplary capabilities. There is no gender difference for skills that are required for problem solving, analytical skills, competitive drive, motivation, sociability and learning ability. It has been established that women are more willing to conform to authority. Men are more aggressive and have a greater expectations from the organization. There is no difference in productivity and job satisfaction. Women absents more as compared to the men, this is because of the social responsibility and domestic problems. Women have to stay longer at home for child care, illness of dependants and the like. As far as turnover is concerned, there is no difference between men and women.

(*c*) **Religion:** Religion and culture play an important role in determining various aspects of individual behaviour. There is a great impact on individuals who have been brought up in ideal religious culture concerning moral, ethics and a code of conduct. Religion and culture determine individual attitude towards work and compensation. Employees having high religious value are generally found to be hard working, honest, dependable, sociable, who can fit in the organization well. They are productive, innovative and think well of the organization.

(*d*) **Marital Status:** Marriage imposes increased responsibilities on an individual, therefore an individual desires to have a steady job. Married employees have fewer absences, lesser turnover and higher job satisfaction. Number of dependants is also a factor to be considered. There is no clear cut information about the impact of marital status on productivity, absenteeism, turnover and job satisfaction. Since marriage increases the family commitment, an individual does not change organizations.

Tenure

Tenure is referred to as experience. The impact of experience on performance is an issue which is subject to a lot of misconception and speculation. Work experience is considered to be a good indicator of employee productivity. There is a positive relationship between seniority and job performance and negative relationship between seniority and absenteeism. Employee turnover is negatively related to seniority. Research indicates that experience and satisfaction are positively related. Seniority and experience is a better indicator of job satisfaction than the age of a person.

Ability

Ability is individuals' capacity to perform various tasks in a job. Ability is made up of two sets of skills:

(A) Intellectual skills or ability and

(B) Physical skills or ability. We are not created equals. It does not mean we are inherently inferiors to others. Everyone has strengths and weaknesses in ability. What is important is to identify level of ability or skills and put it to optimum utilization to improve performance.

(A) Intellectual ability: It is an ability of a person that is required to do mental activities. Higher IQ is not necessary to perform the job successfully. For any high job a general level of intelligence is adequate. Intellectual ability can be further divided into the following skills:

(*a*) **Number Aptitude:** A person having number aptitude displays speed, accuracy and arithmetic inclination in the work. Such individuals can be best employed in accounts and sales tax departments.

(*b*) **Verbal Comprehension:** It refers to ability to understand what is heard or read. It is relationship of words to each other. People having verbal comprehension can be best employed as plant managers. They would be ideal to draft corporate polices.

(*c*) **Perceptual Speed:** It is an ability to identify visual similarities and differences. Such individuals can be gainfully employed for investigative jobs.

(*d*) **Inductive Reasoning:** The ability is related to individual's skill to identify logical sequence in a problem and later solve the same. Such individuals can be assigned the job in research and development departments / organizations.

(*e*) **Deductive Reasoning:** The ability refers to use of logic and assess the implications of an argument. People with this skill can ideally foot the bill as supervisors.

(*f*) **Spatial Visualisation:** It is an ability to imagine how an object would look if its position in the space were changed. Interior decorators have this skill.

(*g*) **Memory:** It is an ability to recall past experience. Sales persons depend upon this ability in performance of their job.

(B) Physical Ability: Physical ability refers to strength factors which includes dynamic strength (muscles force), trunk strength (abdominal muscles), static strength (exertion of force against external object) and explosive strength. Other factors relate to body coordination, balance and stamina. It is the responsibility of the manager to identify physical skills in the individual and assign them suitable jobs commensurate with their ability. High importance of physical skills are given in police, railways, defence, revenue and agriculture fields where various skills are important. In industrial setting, it must be ensured that ability is co-related to the job requirements so that an optimum output is achieved.

Emotions

For many years wisdom of a person and his ability to perform was measured by Intelligence

Quotient (IQ). IQ was a measure for admission to schools, measurement of performance in studies, for seeking jobs and performance evaluation while on the job. However studies indicate that Emotional Intelligence (EI) is now considered as greater predictor of success than IQ.

Wechsler and Robert Thornadike carried out work on non-cognitive aspects of intelligence like social intelligence. In 1990, Salovey and Mayer coined the term 'Emotional intelligence'. They described emotional intelligence as **"a form of social intelligence that involves the ability to moniter one's own and others' feelings and emotions, to discriminate among them, and to use this information to guide one's thinking and action"**. Cognitive abilities are related to IQ of an individual and non-cognitive with emotions. It has been found that emotional and social skills actually help to improve cognitive functioning also.

Emotional Intelligence at Work

Optimism

Martin Seligman developed a construct that he calls "learned optimism". It refers to the causal attributions people make when confronted with failure or setbacks. Optimists tend to make specific, temporary, external causal attributions while pessimist make global, permanent, internal attributions. In research at Met Life, Seligman and his colleagues found that new salesman who were optimists sold 37 percent more insurance in their first two years than did pessimist. When the company hired a special group of individuals who scored high on optimism but failed the normal screening, they outsold the pessimist by 21 percent in their first year and 57 percent in the second. They even outsold the average agent by 27 percent. Optimism was a better predictor of students' actual grades during the freshman year than high school grades. The ability to manage feelings and handle stress is another aspect of emotional intelligence that has been found to be important for success. A study of store managers in a retail chain found that the ability to handle stress predicted net profits, sales per squire foot, sales per employee and per dollar of inventory investment. A study carried out at Yale University by Sigdal and Barsade indicated that emotional intelligence has as much to do with knowing when and how to express emotions. Good feelings led to improved co-operation, fairness, and overall group performance. It has been established that most effective leaders in the US Navy were warmer, more outgoing, emotionally expressive, dramatic and sociable. Empathy is a particularly important aspect of emotional intelligence, and researchers have known for years that it contributes to occupational success. People who are best at identifying others' emotions are move successful in their work as well as in their social life. (Reference: Cherniss Cary, Emotional Intelligence: What it is and Why it Matters, Graduate School of Applied and Professional Psychology Rutgers University Piscataway, NJ 08854).

Emotional intelligence is important for success in work and in life. Goleman and Mayer, Salovey & Caruso have argued that by itself emotional intelligence probably is not a strong predictor of job performance. Rather it provides the bedrock for competencies that are. Goleman has tried to represent this idea by making a distinction between emotional intelligence and emotional competence. **"Emotional competence refers to the personal and social skills that lead to superior performance in the world of work. The emotional competencies are linked to and based on emotional intelligence. A**

certain level of emotional intelligence is necessary to learn the emotional competencies", for instance, the ability to recognize accurately what another person is feeling, enables one to develop a specific competency such as 'influence'. Similarly, people who are better able to regulate their emotions will find it easier to develop a competency such as initiative or achievement drive. Ultimately it is these social and emotional competencies that we need to identify and measure, if we want to be able to predict performance.

FRAMEWORK OF EMOTIONAL COMPETENCE

A model of Emotional competencies is given below in Figure 3.1 below.

	Self Personal Competence	**Other** Social Competence
	Self awareness	**Social Awareness**
Recognition	Emotional self-awareness Accurate self-assessment Self confidence	Empathy Service orientation Organizational awareness
Regulation	**Self management** Self control Trustworthyness Influence Connsciousness Adaptability Achievement drive Initiative	**Relationship management** Developing others Communication Conflict management Leadership Change catalist Building bonds Teamwork and collaboration

Fig. 3.1. Framework of emotional competencies

The above model reflects recent statistical analysis by Richard Boyatzis that supported four domain as seen in the diagram above. These are Self-Awareness, Self-Management, Social-Awareness, and Relationship Management (Boyatzis, Goleman, and Rhee, 2000). They administered the emotional competence inventory, a questionnaire designed to assess the twenty EI competencies to nearly six hundred corporate managers and professionals and engineering, management, and social work graduate students. Respondents were then asked to indicate the degree to which statements about EI-related behaviours- for instance, the ability to remain calm under pressure–were characteristic of themselves. Their ratings were then compared to ratings of those who worked with them. Three key clusters into which the twenty EI competencies were grouped emerged: Self Awareness, Self-management and Social awareness (which subsumes Empathy), along with relationship management, which, in the statistical analysis, subsumed the Social awareness cluster. While the analysis verifies that the competencies rest within each EI domain, it also suggests that the distinction between the Social awareness cluster and the Relationship management cluster may be more theoretical than empirical.

Learned Characteristics

1. **Personality:** Personality is sum total of ways in which an individual reacts and interacts with others. It is a dynamic organization within an individual of those psychological systems that determine his unique adjustments with his environment. It is the charm, positive attitude, smiling face, growth and the development of a person that adds to personality. Personality is greatly influence by the environment that a person has been brought up and the factors of heredity.

(*a*) **Environment:** It refers to culture in which a person is raised. Culture establishes norms, values and attitude that are passed on to generations. Early conditions, norms in the family, friend and social groups and other influences that are formative of personality.

(*b*) **Heredity:** Heredity is transmitted through genes that determine hormone balance and leads to physique formation which shapes personality. Heredity refers to those factors like physical stature, facial attractiveness, sex, temperament, muscle composition, reflects and energy level. Heredity is made up of biological factors. Traits like shyness, fear and distress are passed on to generations. Traits are characteristics of an individual when exhibited in large number of situations. More consistence and more frequent occurrences in diverse situations, the more predominant the trait in an individual are. Common traits found in a person are shyness, aggressive, submissive, laziness, ambitious, loyal and timid. Perception is the process by which information is interpreted in order to give meaning to the world around us. Different people perceive the same thing differently. It should be noted that we should evaluate each situation / individual carefullv before forming an opinion. Perceptual errors should be avoided. Perception will be studied in greater details in chapter 8.

(*c*) **Attitude:** Attitude is a tendency to act/think in certain ways either favourably or unfavourably concerning objects, people or situation. For example, If I say I am satisfied with my job, what actually I am doing is expressing my attitude towards the job. An attitude is the way a person feels about a person, a place, a thing, a situation or an idea. Attitude could be positive or negative. Attitude can be measured either by observing the action of the individual or simply asking him the questions about how he would behave in a particular situation.

(*d*) **Values:** Values are beliefs that guide actions and judgments across a variety of situations. Values represent basic convictions that a specific mode of conduct is personally or socially preferable to an opposite mode of conduct. Values are of two types, **terminal value** that are ultimate values like freedom, salvation, truth and non-violance. **Instrumental values** relate to means for achieving ends. It is a tool for acquiring terminal values. For example obedient, capable etc.

Individual values are formed in the initial stages. They are influenced by the parents, teachers, friends and other social groups. Values vary from person to person. Values help in understanding the attitudes, and motivational level of the individuals. It helps to change the individual behavior. Values are of a great help to determine as to what is good and what is desirable. Values are so strong an instrument that it at times ulter rational decisions. An organization having right value system have greater chances of growth.

DEVELOPING AN ORGANIZATIONAL BEHAVIOUR MODEL (OB MODEL)

Objective of model development is to **understand** human behaviour, **predict** and **control** the same. The behavioural approach is used for controlling human behaviour as individuals and as a group, to measure organizational effectiveness.

Development of OB model involves studying individual, group, organizational structure and systems that should be finely interwoven. The basics of OB model is an individual in an organization. Two or more individuals make a team or a group (work group). There are various systems and sub-systems in any organization like recruitment system or communication system under which an individual or group has to function. Study of OB relates to studying individual behaviour, group behaviour and various organizational systems. It has been observed that Individual behaves differently in different situations. For example an individual will be very enthusiastic on the sports ground, very sober while worshiping in the temple and gay during the dinner party. Though the individual is the same but changes his behaviour based on norms that has been associated with different situations. Two people often act differently in any one situation. For example, worker would display different type of behaviour under different patterns of leadership. His behaviour would be affected, to a large extent on the style of leadership. Individual level behaviour forms a base for group behaviour. It is a study which involves step by step approach, first studying individual behaviour, later group behaviour and in the end studying various organizational structures, which have impact on organization as a whole.

Individual, groups and organization structure have a direct impact on the productivity of an organization. High productivity is directly related to high job satisfaction of the employees. While employee turnover and absenteeism is inversely proportionate to productivity and job satisfaction. More satisfied employee would be more productive. He would be absent on less occasions unless forced by the situation and would render dedicated service and display high degree of loyalty unless forced by domestic constraints. The health of the organization can fairly be judged by the absenteeism and employee turnover. Greater the absenteeism and turnover poorer is the productivity and dissatisfied employees. It is therefore fair to assume productivity, job satisfaction, employee turnover and absenteeism as dependent variables in the study of organizational behaviour. Some management scientists also include job stress, individual dissent and innovation as additional variables. It is stated that an individual or group of people who undergo high level of job stress would either absent themselves frequently or leave the organization. Therefore the study of stress and dissent is integral to absenteeism and employee turnover and need not be studied separately. Innovation is a personal characteristic of an individual who is innovative by nature and likes a challenging job, which ultimately would lead to higher job satisfaction and a better quality of life and higher productivity. It is therefore the field that the study of innovation as dependent variable need not be undertaken separately as this would be covered under the personality traits of the individual that have an impact on organizational effectiveness. Most of the management experts have accepted only four independent variables i.e. productivity, job satisfaction, employee turnover and absenteeism. Let us briefly study these factors.

Dependent Variables

Productivity: When we decide to study productivity, actually what we want to know is the factors that would influence high productivity. The study reveals that it is effectiveness and efficiency of individual, groups and organizational structure that have a positive impact on productivity. It should therefore be an endeavour of any organization to introduce such management practices, which will enhance job satisfaction level of an individual group and organization as a whole. Productivity can be measured in terms of number of items produced by an organization or percentage of profit earned at the end of the production cycle or financial year. It can also be measured by output of production per hour. In case of service industry like hotels or hospitals, occupancy of suites in a hotel on daily basis and turnover of patients per day can express the productivity of the service organization.

Job satisfaction: Job satisfaction can be explained as a general attitude towards one's job. Job satisfaction is the difference between the amount of rewards workers receive and the amount they believe they should receive. It is a difference between material/ money gains in terms of wages, salary and expectations. Job satisfaction sphere can be enlarged to promotion, organizational policies and its implementation, wage structure as compared to the industry norms. Job satisfaction is important because it displays demonstrated relationship to performance and value preferences. Job satisfaction is an attitude rather than a behaviour. It is negatively related to absenteeism and employee turnover. Challenging jobs should be provided to the employees and total quality management of workers is undertaken. Higher management must take quality decisions, which has an equal bearing on quality production. Organizations should evolve such policies that would increase the satisfaction level of employees and must count on intrinsic value that employees believe in.

Absenteeism: Absenteeism refers to individual absenting himself from the job or work place without any notice. While leave is also absenteeism but it is a forewarned phenomenon. In the work-setting, a supervisor is expected to be aware of individuals proceeding on leave in advance so that adequate measures are taken to hire individual in place of the person proceeding on leave. When an individual is not happy with his work, he generally absents himself. Apart from causing personal loss in terms of wages, it also causes great amount of inconvenience to the organization and hampers work schedule and productivity. If an organization works on a process manufacturing like bottling plant, the link of process is disturbed due to the individual being absent and a substitute is required to be hired at the last moment, who may not be skilled to do the job. If a large number of individuals are absent at any one time, the quality of product is reduced because of poor quality of individuals hired. Even a situation may arise to shut down a plant when absenteeism is at an optimum degree.

It may be noted that absenteeism reduces work stress and fatigue of the workers. When they join on the duty, they are fresh and it has been noticed that the production level increases. It has also been observed that managers joining on duty after a long leave of absence, give quality decisions. It is therefore necessary that the individual working in any organization should be adequately motivated, their leave appropriately planned and suitable relief arranged when they proceed on leave of absence. An organization having zero percent of absenteeism is generally considered to be a high productive unit with a good morale of workers and high esprit de corps.

Turnover: Turnover of employees could be voluntary or involuntary. Voluntary turnover takes place when an individual leaves an organization to join another, where he believes that there may be better prospects or opportunities for growth. Apart from the above, an individual may leave the organization purely on administrative grounds like new organization being close to the residence, availability of schools in the new area etc. Involuntary turnover refers to permanent withdrawal of an employee from the organization at the organization's will. This turnover may be planned or unplanned. Persons leaving organization on retirement is a planned turnover because the management knows well in advance as to the date of retirement.

The study of employee turnover is important because it relates to manpower planning of the organization. It is the prime function of a HR manager to identify where and when the employee is leaving the organization and ensure the vacancies so caused are kept filled. Turnover has an adverse impact on productivity. High rate of turnover leads to increased cost on recruitment, selection and training the employees. It also causes disruption in production due to various posts remaining vacant over a long period of time. It should be borne in mind that employee turnover should be kept zero if possible apart from planned turnover. This would ensure smooth functioning of the organization, sticking to the production schedules that will ultimately have a possitive impact on sales revenue. Greater turnover leads to extra expenses in terms of time and efforts that could be avoided. Social scientists and management experts feel that employee turnover to some extent is good for the health of the organization. They feel that due to employee turnover, new opportunities are created to the individuals, certain amount of undesirable individuals can be replaced, new blood with higher skills, fresh ideas and motivated people can be inducted, who may have a vision and give a new look to the organization.

Independent Variables

Independent variables influencing the organizational behaviour are as under:

(*a*) **Individual Variables:** Individual has value system which is exhibited by him through his personality. Apart from this he has preferences, attitude, ego and learning. All the variables influences the work environment. Managers do not have control over the individual behaviour. The knowledge of these factors is important as it has direct bearing on the organizational effectiveness and growth. These factors have a direct impact on productivity, job satisfaction, turnover and absenteeism.

(*b*) **Group Variables:** Group variables are important factors influencing organizational behaviour. A group has a deciding impact on various events in the organization. The contribution of people in group is more than the sum total of individual contribution made to the organization. Study of group behaviour is carried out under several concepts like group dynamics, group decision making, power politics, leadership, inter-group and intra-group behaviour, conflict management. All these variables are studied so that the energies and skills are diverted towards goal achievent in the organization.

(*c*) **Structural Variables:** Structural variables are related to command and control, reporting channels, specilisation, training and development, organization development and other variable pertaining to organizational make up, job design procurement and utilization of organizational resources. If organizational structure is flat, the people would be accountable and more responsible. Formal and informal organizations have its merits for contribution to the organization.

TYPES OF MODELS OF ORGANIZATIONAL BEHAVIOUR

The models of organizational behaviour are developed considering input, process and output. Input contains various independent variables. Processes involve interaction with other individuals, groups formally or informally and take into consideration organisatioin resources, managerial roles, leadership styles, motivational factors, level of conflicts, stress factors, channels of command and control, organisatioal development measures undertaken by the organization, prevailing organizational culture and hosts of other factors. These factors then culminate into output in the form of dependent variables discussed earlier. The models of organizational behaviour have been developed through the historical development of management thoughts discussed in chapter two of the book. In India, organizational behaviour models differ from organization to organization. Every organization adopts one or more models of behaviour. The different types or organizational behaviour models are discussed in succeeding paragraphs.

Fuedal Model: Feudal Model treats employees inferior. The concept is based upon Theory X where actions, polices and procedures are considered superior to human beings. In fuedal model employees are treated sternly and hire and fire principle is applicable in the organization. A fear psychosis is created among the employees. These models have been practiced world over by various organizations where people have been laid off for cost cutting. Employee desires, value, emotions are not considered pragmatically by the organizers. People are treated as another resource for all purposes.

Autocratic Model: Autocratic model is based on the concept that managers are superior. They have power to hire and fire any employee. Managers' words are considered final. Autocratic model believes in power and authority of the manager. Employee have to obey the orders of the boss. Autocratic model proposes that minimum employee needs are met. It believes that higher salaries given to employees is sheer waste of resources as they spend money for unproductive needs. Individuals are controlled by the managers based on official authority and power attached to it. Employees are driven to work as this model assumes that nobody wants to work unless he is forced to do so. Managers are considered neutral born leaders who are obeyed and respected in all areas. The autocratic model is very commonly used in Indian organizations like, railways, defence organization, police organization, banks etc. Autocratic model has however proved to be partly in-effective because of introduction of human rights commission. This has reduced the scope to abiding by rules regulations and written instructions of an organization.

Custodial Model: Custodial model imply that owners are custodian of resources in the organization and they are bound to look after the welfare of employees. It considers that assets of organization belong to industrialist, managers and employees in equal measures and that nobody has monopoly rights. Employees are given opportunities to bring their problems to the notice of the employer and it is the duty of the latter to solve the same. Redressal of grievance procedure exists in the organization. Employees depend on the organization for security and their welfare. The organizations provide wages and salary while employees are in service. They also provide pensionary benefits to the employees so that they can sustain their post retirement life comfortably. While in service employees get fair wages rather than subsistence wages. They depend on the organization rather than the boss. Employees devote themselves for the organizational development because they feel that the organization look after the employee welfare not only during service but also post service periods. Employees are interested in economic rewards and benefits. The model proposes passive involvement of employees and money as the only motivating factor. Direct cooperation of employees is not sought. Employee value, preferences, attitude, emotions and psychological motivational factors are not considered for organizational effectiveness. The model however is useful for organizational growth.

Supportive Model: Employees are considered active workers who have their value, attitude, desire, and preferences. Leaders use attitude and value system of employees to motivate them. Supportive model believes that employees are active and with ideal environment and support, they can use their energies and skill for higher productivity of the organization. If employees are given oppourtunities they can increase their capacity to do a particular work. Owner has to provide and support various activities for individual, group and organizations. The employees should develop sense of belonging and feeling of participation in over all organizational growth. The model does not support the custodial model concept where money is considered as motivating factor. Employees get oppourtunities for recognition. They develop positive outlook towards work culture. Managers and workers participate together in the development of organization while achieving development of their own skills. Many organizations have developed as a result of adopting the supportive model. The model helps in the development of individuals, groups and organizations. It is more effective in developed countries. It has not been proved very effective in developing nations because of restrictive social and cultural environment. Supportive model is used in many organizations with modifications.

Collegial Model: Collegial model refers to body of persons having common objective. The basis of the model is the partnership of the employees with owners. The emphasis is on team management between workers and owners. Employees are given responsible and trustworthy jobs. They are self-disciplined and self-motivated. Managers and workers have similar activities, work environment and understanding. Managerial cadre is not considered superior to the employees. They contribute jointly rather than bosses or leaders. They have to develop as a team with employees and impress upon quality and performance. Combined efforts contribute to the growth and performance of the organization.

Human Value Model: The natural process of behaviour is **Stimulus, Organism, Behaviour** and **Consequence**. It is generally known as SOBC. Every organization should provide enough incentives in the form of intrinsic and extrinsic stimuli. Intrinsic stimulus is achieved by encouraging individuals by recognition, empowerment, delegation of authority, better inter-personal relations and cognitive behaviour in general. Extrinsic stimuli refers to economic incentives in the form of reward for the job done. It is monetary in nature and are exercised for influencing organism of employees. The aim of these incentives are to stimuli the employees in the desired direction so that productivity and growth is achieved. Organizations should identify best social, cultural, physical and tecnological stimuli so that positive consequences in the form of behaviour is achieved. It must be understood that people work in the organization for achieving psychological satisfaction. They want to belong to a social group so that they are mentally at peace and that would lead to desired behaviour in the organization. Enviornment of the organization therefore must be condusive to work and quality of work life should be very rich.

Contingency Model: Contingency model of organizational behaviour refers to complex variables that influence individual, group and organizational structures. Contingency model is designed to meet the contingent situations like management of conflict, handling of stress, achieving growth and managining the complexities caused due to changes in organization structures. In the contingency model relations between manager and employees are based on co-operation, trust and desire of well-being. Promotion to employees are assured. No distinction is made between specialist and non-specialist. It is also known as the hybrid model where long term employment is assured to the employees.

Environmental Factors

Environment has impact on individual's behaviour. When a child is born, he is raised in a particular culture that establishes values, norms and attitude. These are passed on to subsequent generations. Early conditions have permanent impact on the child. Family norms and social group influences an individual to a great extent. First born child and later born child may display different attitude and approach to life. Environmental factors that have impact on individual behaviour are 1) General economic situation of the organization one is serving. An individual serving in government/ public sector undertaking has a job security. Those serving in private organization may be worried about retrenchment. 2) Wages is another issue. It will determine the social norms an individual is able to practice. 3) An individual who has employability is able to secure job in organization of own choosing. In the recent past software professionals shifted their jobs very frequently. Technical qualification is therefore an important factor that has impact on human behaviour. Monetary and psychological aspects play a decisive role in human behviour. 4) Political, social, legal and tecnological enviornment should be sound and condusive to work culture. Owners should analyse the situation and be vigilent about employee attitude, behaviour and pre-empt any dangerous behavioural situation.

SUMMARY

Individual behaviour is very complicated. An individual behaves differendly in various situations. It is necessary for a manager to identify "needs" of the individual and evolve such strategies that satisfy them. Based upon knowledge, skill and experience, a manager should be able to predict individual behaviour. Motivation of individual differes when intrinsic and extrinsic rewards are given to him. He reacts in a different way as it relates to compensation. Individual behaviour is founded on 1) biological and individual factors that include Physical attributes, age, gender, marital status, number of dependants and experience/tenure. 2) emotional intelligence of the individual and 3) learned characteristics that include personality, attitude, perception and value system of the person.

Emotional intelligence is now considered as a measure of one's feelings and application of social skill. Learned optimism is an ability of an individual to perform. There are two types of persons. They are either optimist or pessimist. An optimist makes specific, temporary natured exernal causal attributions while pessimist makes global, permanent external attributions. Goleman states that emotional intelligence is bedrock of individual competencies. He further clarifies that "emotional competency refers to personal and social skills that are based on emotional intelligence. These are futher clasified into self awareness, social awareness, self management and relationship management competencies". Learned chareceristics include personality, culture, heridity, attitude and values. These have tremendous effect on job performance growth and job satisfaction. These characeristics and emotional intelligence factors that have a direct impact on productivity, Job satisfaction, absenteeism and turnover. The later are therefore called dependant variables. Various organizational models are fuedal model, autocratic model, supportive model, collegial model, human value model and lastly the contingency model.

TEXT QUESTIONS

Q. 1. Explain individual behaviour. What is its relationship with intrinsic and extrinsic rewards?

Q. 2. What are various biological and individual factors that have impact on productivity, job satisfaction, absenteeism and turnover?

Q. 3. Explain concept of emotional intelligence.

Q. 4. What do you understand by learned optimism?

Q. 5. Draw out a framework of emotional competence and explain individual behaviour?

Q. 6. What are various learned characteristics of an individual. How these affect behaviour?

Q. 7. What are various dependant variables. Explain each of them in detail?

Q. 8. What are various OB models. Discuss?

Q. 9. What enviornmental factors have influence on individual behaviour. Discuss?

Case

THE UNATTENDED ACCIDENT

Mrs. S. Madhuri

Vinod Khanna left Bombay for Surat on official work on 3rd November, by 10.45 p.m. train. On the following day in Surat, Vinod received a phone call from a colleague in Bombay saying that his mother and his children had met with a car accident. He phoned back his sister in Bombay and got the details about the accident. As he felt concerned about the nature of injuries to his mother, he felt it advisable to return. He therefore, took the evening plane back to Bombay. Vinod Khanna stays in the housing colony of the company with his parents and his children. The company and its housing colony are situated at a place not easily accessible to the mainland city of Bombay. On the previous evening, when he was leaving for Surat, he had requisitioned the office car at 7.45 p.m. for commuting to the station. On the way to the station, he had picked up his mother and children from his sister's house in the mainland city.

After seeing him off at the railway station. His family members were returning to their company quarters by the same car. Half the way up, the car was hit by a truck. The driver received minor injuries. Vinod's daughter got some bruises. His son's jaw was badly hurt endangering one of his teeth. His mother was hurt on the face, her denture was thrown off and her ears started bleeding. The car was badly damaged. An RTO officer who was around directed the driver and Vinod's relations to the nearest police station. From the police station the driver called the company's Administrative Officer and informed him about the accident. Vinod's son contacted his aunt who came and took care of the children and the mother. They were taken to a hospital where the children were treated and allowed to go, and the mother was hospitalized.

The next morning, that is on 4th November, Vinod's sister called the company's Administrative Officer and was informed as to where Vinod could be contacted. She also called a colleague of Vinod and told him about the accident. On reaching his office on 5th November, Vinod complained to the Chief Executive about the neglect and lack of concern shown by the administration regarding the accident. The Administrative Officer had not taken any immediate action consequent to the driver's phone call. Vinod also complained that while commuting to the office that morning by the company's bus. The Administrative Officer confirmed that he received the driver's phone call at 11.30 p.m. He maintained that the driver had said that he had been slightly injured. Where after he had talked to the police sub-inspector on duty, who also informed him that the driver and Vinod's son had received minor injuries; and that he would release the driver and the car immediately. The Administrative Officer further contended that the driver did not ask to be picked up also that he did not know that Vinod's mother was also in the car and that she had been badly hurt. The driver submitted his report the next evening.

The driver contended that after phoning the Administrative Officer from the police station, he went back to the car at the site of the accident and spent the night with his injuries untreated. He said since the police officer talked to the Administrative Officer in English, he did not know what conversation took place between them. In the morning, he phoned the transport incharge, whence he was picked up and the car towed to the company premises. The transport incharge, Mr. Kashyap maintained that the car and the driver were assigned for duty only upto the railway station and back. He said he also did not know that Vinod's mother had been in the car until the driver filed his report. Nor, he said, did he notice Vinod on the bus on the morning of 5th November.

On 6th November, the Chief Executive received a memorandum from the Employees Association of the company complaining about the inaction of the Administrative Officer concerning the accident.

QUESTIONS

Read the above case carefully and answer the following questions.

Q. 1. Identify the human relations problems in the case.

Q. 2. Is it possible to deal with the problem through formal procedures? What are the likely consequences of dealing with it formally?

Q. 3. What may be other methods of resolving the problem?

Q. 4. What kind of behavioural change is required on the par of different functionaries involved?

CHAPTER 4

Personality

PERSONALITY

Personality is a very complex and multidimensional construct of a human being. No common definition of personality has so far been arrived at. Every individual defines personality in different way which includes trait factors and physical appearance.*" Personality is a dynamic organization within an individual of those psychological systems that determines his unique adjustment with the environment. It is a sum total of ways in which an individual reacts and interacts with others."* As far as physical aspect is concerned it relates to individual charm, attitude while dealing with others and smiling face can also be included into personality. Uma Sekaran states that one can examine personality in terms of a set of relatively stable characteristics and tendencies that determine our thoughts, feelings and behaviour and which have some continuity or consistency over time. Maddi (1980) defines personality thus: *Personality is a stable set of characteristics and tendencies that determine those commonalities and differences in the psychological behaviour (thoughts, feelings, and actions) of people that have continuity in time and that may not be easily understood as the sole result of the social and biological pressures of the moment.* The above definitions indicate the commonality of characteristics and human tendencies amongst people who display consistency in their behaviour over time. Maddis definition suggests that people do change due to biological and social pressures. Thus by understanding certain dimensions of personality one can predict human behaviour to a great extent.

Determinants of Personality

Personality is determined by heredity, environment (culture) and situation under which an individual works. This is shown in diagrammatic form in Figure 4.1. Let us study these concepts.

Heredity

Heredity is transmitted through genes, which determine hormone balance, which later determine physique and subsequently the personality. Heredity refers to acquiring from parents certain biological, physical and psychological commonalities, which are further reflected in physical stature, facial attractiveness, sex, temperament, muscle composition and even reflect. They often decide energy level. These factors have a deciding influence

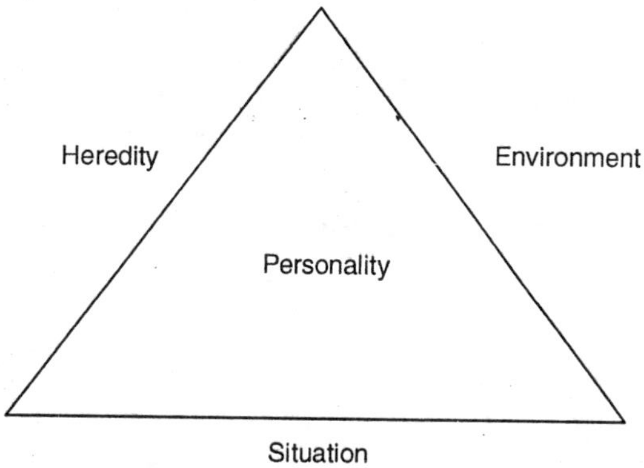

Fig. 4.1. Determinants of personality

on how a person in an organization would display his reactions in a particular situation. Nature of health and psychological make up that an individual enjoys can be traced from the traits his parents possessed. Parents prominently pass on shyness, fear and distress to the next generation. In good organizations and particularly in defence services a detailed screening is carried out of the candidates based on the background of the parents as it relates to physique, psychological make up, disability and transferable disease as it has far reaching impact on the general health of the organization.

Environment

Every individual is born and brought up in a particular environment. Environment leaves an imprint on the personality of an individual. It is commonly seen that a doctors son preferring his father's profession and a child of a soldier entering into Defence Services. More advanced the socio-economic conditions of the society more would the children be forward thinking. Environment should be viewed from the point of view of norms, ethics and value that are observed and the attitude displayed by the social group. These factors actually formulate the culture of the society from which the organizations draw their human resource requirements. The cultural background is important to evaluate personality. In childhood, parents, uncles, aunts and even neighbour's behaviour is copied by a child. It is therefore necessary to display an ideal behaviour on the part of all the adults who come in direct contact with the children. Family moulds character of children through role models re-enforcements, rewards and punishments. Other influences like first born and later born child will have different personality traits. First-born child would generally be commanding. Female child would be more responsive and pass on sobering effect on younger brothers/sisters. It is therefore important to study early conditions under which the child has been brought up, norms followed in the family and the existence of cultural value system in the society. All these factors have a marked influence on the personality of an individual.

Situation

Individual has to interact with number of problems in a given situation, which does not remain constant. It is subject to change and hence fluid in nature. There is therefore a need to recognise the *person-situation* interaction. It can be social learning activity of personality. Thus personality is situational, the uniqueness of each situation and any measure of personality must be examined. Personalities therefore mean how people affect others, how they understand and view themselves, pattern of personality traits and person-situation interaction. For example individual modifies his behaviour based on situation. When an individual goes to temple he would be sober, generally put on plain clothes and bow. When the same individual goes for interview he would be armed with knowledge of the organization while in the club he would be merry making having a drink in his hand and meet friends and generally be in gay mood.

Personality Traits

Personality traits are the characteristics of an individual when exhibited in large number of situations. More predominant the traits in an individual are, more consistence the individual is and more frequent occurrences in diverse situations. There are thousands of traits that have been identified. Cattell[1] isolated 171 traits but concluded that they were superficial and lacking in descriptive power. What he sought was a reduced set of traits that would identify underlying pattern. The result was the identification of 16 personality factors, which he called the source, or primary traits. These and their opposites are given below :-

1	Reserved	vs	Outgoing
2	Less intelligent	vs	More intelligent
3	Affected by feelings	vs.	Emotionally stable
4	Submissive	vs.	Dominant
5	Serious	vs.	Happy go lucky
6	Timid	vs.	Venturesome
7	Expedient	vs.	Conscientious
8	Tough minded	vs.	Sensitive
9	Trusting	vs.	Suspicious
10	Practical	vs.	Imaginative
11	Forthright	vs.	Shrewd
12	Self assured	vs.	Apprehensive
13	Conservative	vs.	Experimenting
14	Group dependent	vs.	Self-sufficient
15	Uncontrolled	vs.	Controlled
16	Relaxed	vs.	Tense

THE MYERS-BRIGGS TYPE INDICATOR (MBTI)

This is one of the most commonly used Personality test consisting of 100 questions. On the basis of the answers the individuals are classified into following categories

(*a*) **Visionary:** A person who has been classified visionary based the MBTI results has an organised mind, has a great drive for new ideas and purpose. An individual is skeptical, critical and stubborn. He displays traits like working independently and has a high determination to achieve the desired goals, which are often challenging.

(*b*) **Organizer:** A person having great organizational ability would be practical, realistic and believes in what he sees. Organizers are generally successful businesspersons,

persons involved in basic engineering jobs, and persons who are involved in assembling resources to run the organizations.

(*c*) **Conceptulisers:** Persons who take quick decisions, they are ingenious and good at many things. They are resourceful, problem solver and have a tendency to neglect work, which is of a routine nature.

Locus of Control

Major personality attributes which affects organizational behaviour is *locus of control*, that is the degree to which people believe that they are masters of their own fate. It is the concept, which determines whether an individuals control events or the events control the individuals and that they become only the pawns of situation. People have both internal locus of control and external locus of control, only the degree varies.

(*a*) **Internal Locus of Control.** Persons having internal locus of control believe that they can manipulate events to their advantage and therefore they are capable of deciding their fate For example, a manager having dominant internal locus of control would be able to effectively control resources, decide events, which benefits him. He manipulates communications, resources, events, programmes in such away that enhances his position and he creates an aura around him that he is an indispensable person. Individual feels that he is decider of his own future and that no external events (power) can interfere with it.

(*b*) **External Locus of Control.** Person having dominant external locus of control believe that what happen to them is controlled by outside forces such as luck or chance. These types of people lack initiative, decision-making and do not even take calculated risk. They wait and see events take place and things happen.

PERSONALITY ORIENTATION

1. Achievement Orientation

Achievement orientation of an individual also indicates the personality of an individual. Every person possesses need to achieve (nAch) phenomenon in his personality. It could be high degree nAch or low degree. A person who possesses high nAch displays very dominant personality. He is generally very ambitious, hard working and fixes his goal at a very high level and strives to achieve the same. He is achievement oriented and undertakes a task which is neither easy, because easy task is generally attained by a common person nor a very challenging or tough task because there would be chances of failure of achieving the same. He therefore prefers to undertake task of intermediate nature so that its achievement would satisfy him to a large extent and he would feel that he is above than the normal individual. People having high nAch are found to be good organizers, efficient managers. Sports persons are generally high achievers as they strive to achieve that extra point or mark than his competitors. High nAch generally do well as sale persons as it calls for hard work and achieving higher targets of sales every time.

2. Authoritarianism

Close to the personality trait that a person possesses who is achievement oriented is a person who believes in having a reasonably high authority in the organization Theory of authoritarianism is related with status and power. The theory states that there should be status and power difference between various people in the organization. While there would be some people who will have more power and authority hence more authoritative yet there would be people with low power and authority hence minimum degree of being authoritative. One would therefore find in an organization, people with low authority and high authority. Person who possesses high authoritarian is intellectually rigid, they display varied behaviour patterns. They are submissive with those who are superior (senior) to them and behave in an exploitative manner to those who are subordinates or below them. They resist change and display insensitivity while dealing with people. They are task oriented.

3. Theory of Machivellianism

Niccolo Machivelli introduced theory of Machivellianism. The theory refers to degree to which an individual is pragmatic and maintains emotional distance with co-workers while accomplishing any task. A person who practices this theory believes in "end justifies means." In any organization people can be classified as having high Machivellianism or low Machivellianism tendencies. A person having High Machivellianism (H Mach) generally displays variety of personality traits like manipulation, win more, persuade others to do a work while they do not get persuaded by others. They generally flourish in face-to-face situation where there are minimum rules and have enough space for maneuver. They have high bargaining skills and believe in giving substantial rewards to their subordinates on accomplishment of tasks. They are highly productive. Machivelli believed in one doctrine, that a work must be finished whatever be the means.

4. Self-Esteem

Self-esteem refers to individuals' degree of liking or disliking himself. People's self-esteem has to do with their self-perceived competence and self-image. Most recent studies indicate that self-esteem plays an important moderating role in areas such as emotional and behavioural responses and stress of organizational members. As was recently noted, "Both research and every day experience confirm that employees with high self-esteem feel unique, competent, secure, empowered and connected to the people around them (Luthans)[2]. People having high degree of self-esteem take more risk in job selection and take up unconventional assignments while those possessing low self-esteem display dependency, seek approval from others for the decision they make, respect others and seek confirmation in beliefs. Managers with low self-esteem do not take unpopular stand, which may lead to displeasing others.

5. Self-Monitoring

Self-monitoring is related to self-efficacy. It is situation specific. A person must always examine efficiency and attribute it to his behaviour with subordinates and improve upon it. This quality displays high degree of adaptability and high sensitivity of an individual. A person possessing self monitoring trait is likely to behave differently in different situation.

6. Risk Taking

Risk taking trait is commonly seen in various entrepreneurs. They display rapid decision-making ability.

Types of Personality

Type A: People having Type A personality are always moving, walking and eating rapidly. They feel impatient with the speed the events take place. They always strive to do two or three thing at any one time and cannot cope with leisure. They are generally obsessed with work involved with numbers.

Type B: People possessing Type B personality never suffer from sense of urgency and take thing as it comes coolly. They do not discuss achievement and leave it to the superiors to identify it. People having B type of personality play for fun and relaxation rather than to show off. These people have the tendency to relax without guilt.

Studies indicating personality traits of Indian Managers

Individual's behaviour is influenced by various factors studied earlier. Behaviour has an impact on how an individual acts and interacts with superiors and subordinates in the work environment. Various studies have been conducts in this field.

Dwivedi Study

R.S. Dwivedi has carried out study of 52 managers in public and private sector organizations. Findings indicate that managers give high importance to the following traits:

- Cooperation.
- Intelligence.
- Energy.
- Sociability.

Low importance was assigned to the following personality traits:

- Aggressive.
- Confronting.
- Independent.

Flexibility, preserving and self-monitoring has been accorded moderate importance. The co-relation co-efficient between managers of public sector and private sector accounted for as high as 90. Saiyadain and Monappa carried out studies to identify personality traits of middle level managers from public sector and private sector organization (N = 172). The respondents represented major functional areas of respective organizations. Results, first an Authoritarian and Machiavellianism traits indicated an equal distribution. Secondly, above two third of the managers scored higher than average on competence need for achievement (NAch) traits.

SUMMARY

It is difficult to identify ones personality because individual behaviour is complex and construct multidimensional. Personality of a human being can be determined by identifying stable characteristics of an individual. Personality can be influenced by environmental factors and situation under which an individual is working. Heredity has an influence on individual's physical appearance, facial attractiveness, sex, temperament and reflects. These factors have deciding influence on individual behaviour in the organization. Individual behaviour is shaped as per the environment he is brought up. Cultural background, socio-economic conditions, parents profession are some of the factors responsible for individual personality. Every individual possesses various personality traits. Locus of control could be internal or external. People who feel, they can decide their own fate are internal and those who believe that luck, opportunity and other external factors are responsible for their future are externals. Every individual behaviour display personality traits, Locus of control, authoritarianism, self-esteem and self-monitoring aptitude. Individuals can possess A Type or B Type personality. Indian managers believe more on competence and achievement orientation traits as most important.

TEXT QUESTIONS

Q. 1 Define personality?
Q. 2 What are major personality determinants?
Q. 3 What are various personality traits that are generally found in each individual?
Q. 4 Discuss Locus of control
Q. 5 What are various factors that shape individuals personality?
Q. 6 How is an employee likely to behave who has external Locus of control, Low Mach, Low Self-esteem score?
Q. 7 Write short notes on the following
- (*a*) Type A and B personality.
- (*b*) Authoritarianism.
- (*c*) MBTI model.

REFERENCES

1. Cattell R.B. ***"Personality Pinned Down"***, Psychology Today, July 1973.
2. Luthans Fred, ***"Organizational Behaviour"***, International Edition 1995, Mc Graw Hills.

Case

HAZARDS OF HILLS

INTRODUCTION

This case is based on an actual incident which took place in an Army Unit deployed in field area. A part of a Battery (about ¼ of an Artillery Regiment) was deployed in a snow bound high altitude area of Kashmir. This was the first time, an artillery unit was deployed in an area with roads and tracks still under development. Preparation of this area for such a deployment needed a lot of digging for guns, pits for ammunition storage, living place of the personnel, slit trenches and weapon pits for local defence against any possible enemy/ terrorists' attack on the position, place for storage of rations, cook-house and communication trenches, etc.

The total strength of the party deployed there was

(*a*) Officer – 1 (second Lieutenant with about one year service)
(*b*) Junior Commissioned Officer (JCO) - 1
(*c*) Jawans - 40

The Battery Commander (BC) remained with the Regiment Headquarters at Srinagar (with the remaining part of the Battery) as per the orders of the commanding Officer. There was a vehicle with the part of the Battery which was deployed at high altitude to assist in the daily administration of the troops like collection of ration, stores for preparation of defences, water, ferrying of personnel from one place to another. The vehicle could go only upto a limited number of places due to bad road conditions and steep gradients. Only one driver was kept for this vehicle to reduce administrative problems due to more number of personnel. The vehicle completed about 35 to 40 kms. of running daily in its routine commitments.

The party had just been inducted about two weeks back. The defences were being prepared which involved lot of effort in digging of hardened ground due to the cold winter months of November. The defence stores were to be collected, once the digging was complete, from another Engineering Unit located about 5 kms. to the rear. The roads were treacherous; with a number of stones and slides falling down occasionally during a drizzle due to precipitation in atmosphere, there were steep gradients, narrow roads with sheer falls on one side due to the road having been cut into the side of hills. The digging was complete by end November. In the month of December, snow fall at that location was expected any time, as it had already started snowing in the higher reaches and tops of mountains. The digging had been completed in a record time of two weeks. The party under the stewardship of the young officer had done a commendable job.

In the first week of December, the only driver of the vehicle reported pain in the chest and problem in breathing. He was evacuated by helicopter the next day with instructions to inform the unit to sent another driver for the vehicle. It took about three days for any one to reach this area, with staying of two nights enroute in order to acclimatize by stages. The detachment was to be without any driver for about three days. Another driver was detailed to proceed to this area, after having been medically examined and found fit. A day after the dispatch of the driver, the young officer with this party arrived in the unit and reported that the vehicle had fallen from a hill-side road and was completely damaged. The officer was in a complete state of disarray and shock. What actually had happened, goes something like this.

After the first driver of the vehicle was evacuated, the weather started turning bad and it seemed that it was going to snow that day. The officer realized that in case of snow fall all the efforts put in by the troops would go waste, if the dug-ins were not covered. Realizing this, he borrowed a driver of an ambulance from a local medical unit to direct his vehicle for collection of defence stores. After the stores had been collected and dumped at the site of defences, the vehicle was being driven back to the party's location. Before it could reach this location, it had to negotiate a dusty and steep track. At a steep climb the vehicle stalled and got switched off. All the men got down, prevented the vehicle from reversing by putting stones behind the wheels and started checking what had gone wrong.

After the check on the engine had been carried out, the bonnet cover slipped off the hands of the driver while closing it and fell to closing position with a bang. Because of the jerk thus created, the stones placed behind the vehicle slipped off. It was later discovered that there was glassy smooth layer of ice under the thin layer of dirt which could not hold the stones firmly and they slipped off, with the result, that the vehicle moved backwards and toppled thrice and stopped upside down because of the obstruction created by a big boulder. As there was no one in the vehicle, there were no injuries to personnel. On close inspection by the officer, it was found that the vehicle body, cabin, bonnet, steering wheel and two of the four wheels were badly damaged. The officer, being quite young and inexperienced, could not ascertain the real condition of the engine and chassis. He thought those too were damaged, whereas, because of some providential chance, the chassis and engine remained intact.

The BC was given the responsibility of getting the vehicle back to the unit. He was given a vehicle fitter and recovery vehicle with a driver. The BC took two more Non-Commissioned Officers (NCOs) and proceeded to the location to retrieve the vehicle. It took two days to reach with a few hours of the last leg of the journey in complete darkness in that snow bound area with treacherous slippery roads. On reaching the location, the Commanding Officer of the local unit, who happened to be the Station Commander of that sector, expressed his happiness on their taking such a great risk. With the assistance of all ranks of that unit, who came in willingly, it took two days to get the vehicle out of the boulder strewn area on to a track. It was a minor military operation in 'itself' in that hostile terrain, and inclement weather of high altitude. The troops and officer had a very good rapport with chose of the local unit and there was not much of a problem in getting the men of that unit to assist.

While coming back, the hazards of night journey were very obvious. There was a thick layer of snow on the road with slope towards the khuds as layers after layers kept on accumulating, freezing before the water could roll down the compete slope. There were steep falls on one side. Both these phenomena, peculiar to hilly terrain, were not very discernible because of the darkness. The headlights of the vehicles exposed very little. There were frozen nalas where the vehicle would skid, aligning itself in the direction of the frozen nala, which tended to prove quite dangerous at times. At such places, the few troops and officer available would get down, push the vehicle to keep it aligned to the road and in turn slip down themselves on the frozen snow, most of the times face-down, in an attempt to push the vehicle. Though the situation was quite grave, it sometimes bordered on being humorous with everyone laughing spontaneously. At one place, the BC, pushing the vehicle to keep its tail and aligned to the direction of road, fell down, slipped a few feet down in the frozen nala and landed up head down in a frozen khud about five feet deep. But for the direction of landing, the slip and fall could have proved quite dangerous. There was complete silence. The vehicle was gently stopped on the snow itself, secured with pegs along the wheels and rescue operation commenced for the ditch. There were several humorous remarks by the BC and the tension was relieved at once, with troops working on the vehicle with renewed vigour and strength once again.

At another place, the recovery vehicle with the damaged vehicle behind it at suspension toe slipped, but because of the dexterity of the driver, it was saved from going down a nala by putting it on the left. The BC himself was in the recovery vehicle to give encouragement and moral support to the diver, sharing all the risks which his troops were facing. He did all that the troops did, while directing, controlling and executing. The party with vehicle, reached the unit location on the evening of the second day starting from the high altitude area. The problem of recovery of the vehicle being resolved. The question of enquiry into the cause of accident arose. An enquiry into such an accident would have caused embarrassment to all those in authority in the unit and also the officers and jawans of the sub-unit/battery. Meanwhile, the inspection of the vehicle was carried out to assess the extent of damage. It was found that the engine and chassis were intact and the rest of the items of the body or fitment were damaged, either lightly or severely. To avoid embarrassment to the unit and loss to the exchequer, as well as in view of the administrative difficulties, the BC decided to have the vehicle put on road with the units' efforts and at the earliest. Meanwhile, the cabin-hood of the vehicle had been purchased for about Rs. 650 and was paid for by the BC, from his own pocket, thus setting an example to others. The JCO and jawans were also keen to pay for other damages. The offer was appreciated but declined.

The Officer-in-charge of the local Army Workshop happened to be an officer with commendable helping attitude, positive bent of mind and with an understanding of peculiarities and problems of the area where such accidents were quite frequent and possible. When approached to assist, he listened to the whole incident very sympathetically and promised to assist in whatever way he could. This officer was a contemporary of the unit in a previous station and had excellent relations and interaction with the unit. Some items were offered by the workshop officer and replaced accordingly. The vehicle was made road-worthy again within a fortnight and put on road for duty. All the enquiries were dispensed with and there was no loss of face by face by anyone at any level. It is pertinent to mention that it had snowed in that location as soon as the recovery party came out of the hills.

QUESTION

1. What are the qualities of a good leader? In this case, how were they applied?
2. Which factors contributed to motivate the troops to go ahead for such a difficult task as recovering a damaged vehicle from such a difficult and treacherous terrain and getting it repaired in such a short time?
3. Which incidents indicate the importance of good interpersonal relationship with juniors, peers and superiors and what is the importance of good interpersonal relationships?

This case has been adopted from "Case Method in Management Education – Text and Illustrations edited by Upinder Dhar & Santosh Dhar, Excel Books, A–45 Naraina, Phase–I, New Delhi, 2002.

EXERCISE TO DETERMINE PERSONALITY

Type A - Type B Self – Test

To determine your Type A or Type B profile, circle the number on the continuums (the verbal descriptions represent end points) that best represents your behaviour for each dimension.

Am causal about appointments	1 2 3 4 5 6 7 8	Am never late
Am not competitive	1 2 3 4 5 6 7 8	Am very competitive
Never feel rushed, even under	1 2 3 4 5 6 7 8	Always feel rushed pressure
Take things one at a time	1 2 3 4 5 6 7 8	Try to do many things At once; think about what I am going to do next
Do things slowly	1 2 3 4 5 6 7 8	Do things fast (eating, walking, etc.)
Express feelings	1 2 3 4 5 6 7 8	"Sit" on feelings.
Express many interests	1 2 3 4 5 6 7 8	Have few interests outside work.

Total your score: ________________ Multiply it by 3: ______. The interpretation of your score is as follows:

Number of points	Type of personality
Less than 90	
90 to 99	B
100 to 105	B+
106 to 119	A-
120 or more	A+

Source: Adapted from R.W. Bortner, "A Short Rating Scale as a Potential Measure of Pattern A Behaviour", Journal of Chronic Diseases, Vol. 22, 1966, pp. 87-91.

LOCUS OF CONTROL – QUESTIONNAIRE

Want to test your locus of control? Just answer the 16 questions given below as frankly as possible using the following response scale.

1 = Disagree very much	4 = Agree slightly
2 = Disagree moderately	5 = Agree moderately
3 = Disagree slightly	6 = Agree very much

1	____________	A job is what you make of it.
2	____________	On most jobs, people can pretty much accomplish whatever they set out to accomplish.
3	____________	If you know what you want out of a job, you can find a job that gives it to you satisfaction.
4	____________	If employees are unhappy with a decision made by their boss, they should do something about it.

5	________	Getting the job you want is mostly a matter of luck.
6	________	Making money is primarily a matter of good fortune.
7	________	In order to get a capable of doing their jobs well if they make the effort.
8	________	In order to get a really good job you need to have family members or friends in high places.
9	________	Promotions are usually a matter of good fortune.
10	________	When it comes a landing a really good job, who you know is more important than what you know.
11	________	Promotions are given to employees who perform well on the job.
12	________	To make a lot of money you have to know the right people.
13	________	It takes a lot of luck to be an outstanding employee on most jobs.
14	________	People who perform their jobs well generally get rewarded for it.
15	________	Most employees have more influence on their supervisors than they think they do.
16	________	The main difference between people who make a lot of money and people who make a little money is luck.

SCORING AND INTERPRETATION

You have just completed the Work Locus of Control Scale developed by Spector (1988). To find your score, subtract your responses to questions 1, 2, 3, 4, 7, 11, 14 and 15 from seven. For example, if you gave a response of 3 to question 1, give yourself a 4 (7 minus 3). Then add up your resulting scores to all 16 items. Your total should be somewhere between 16 and 96. The lower your score the more internal you are – you see what happens to you to be a result of your own actions and initiative. The higher your score, the more external you are – you see what happens to you to be a result of luck, chance, or connections. The average score of 1165 people in a variety of occupations was 38. Thus, these people tended to see themselves as somewhat more internal than external.

CHAPTER 5

Learning

INTRODUCTION

Learning brings relatively permanent change in human behaviour that occurs as a result of experience. All complex behaviour is a learned behaviour. If we want to predict and explain behaviour, we must understand how people learn. Learning involves change in behaviour. It is continuous process, which occurs all the time. We cannot see learning but we can see changed behaviour as a consequence of learning. Learning changes attitude of individuals to a large extent. An individual reacts to any situation or responds to instructions in particular fashion, that fashion or style is caused due to learning. Theoretical approach to learning incorporates ***behaviourist, cognitive*** and newly emerging ***social learning*** theories. Understanding of these theories is important to the study of organizational behaviour.

THEORIES OF LEARNING

Classical Conditioning – behaviourist theory

> ***"Classical conditioning can be defined as a process in which a formerly neutral stimulus when paired with an unconditional stimulus, becomes a conditioned stimulus that illicit a conditioned response.*** (Luthans 1995)[1]

Ivan Pavlov a psychologist who won Nobel prize introduced classical conditioning theory. The experiment envisaged dog as a subject. Pavlov carried out this experiment in three sequential stages. In ***stage one***, he presented meat (unconditional stimulus) to the dog. He noticed a great deal of salivation (unconditional response). In ***stage two*** he only rang up the bell (neutral stimulus), the dog had no salivation. In ***stage three***, Pavlov was to accompany the offering of meat to the dog along with ringing up of bell. After doing this several times, Pavlov rang up only bell (without offering of meat to the dog). This time the dog salivated to the ringing up of bell alone. Pavlov concluded that the dog has become classically conditioned to salivate (response) to the sound of the bell (stimulus). It will be seen that the learning can take place amongst animals based on stimulus – response (S-R) connections. The study was undoubtedly single most famous study ever conducted in behavioural sciences. It was a major break through and had a lasting impact on understanding of learning.

This stimulus – response connection (S-R) can be applied in management. Historically when a CEO visits an organization, production charts are updated, individuals put on a good dress, window panes are cleaned and floors are washed. What all one has to do is to just say that the Top Boss is visiting. You will find that all above work is undertaken (response) without any instructions. Because the people in the organization have learned the behaviour (conditioned). It has caused a permanent change in the organization (S-R connections). Robbins[2] states that classical condition is passive. Something happens and we react in a specific way. It is elicited in a response to specific, identifiable events. As such, it can explain simple reflective behaviours. But most behaviour – particularly the complex behaviour of individual organizations is emitted rather than elicited. It is voluntary rather than reflective.

Operant Conditioning

Operant conditioning deals with Response—Stimulus (R-S) connection. The concept was originated by B.F. Skinner. He felt that more complex behaviour couldn't be explained by Classical Conditioning concept. He states that most human behaviour operates based on the environment. ***Operant Conditioning*** is concerned primarily with learning as a consequence of behaviour (R-S). In Operant Conditioning particular response occurs as a consequence of many stimulus situations. Stimulus typically serves as a cue for a particular response. In his concept a "response" is first evaluated out of many stimulus, which is environmental in nature. Behaviour is a function of consequences. It is voluntary in nature. Re-inforcement increases the probability of occurrence. Behaviour is learned and is not a matter of reflects. If we create learning consequences, the probability of specific forms of behaviour increases. For example an individual will take a long trek (Response) to library because he knows he would be able to get a desired book (Stimulus), (R-S connections). Individual would work hard(R) because he knows that he would be able to get praise, or even promotion (S). Operant Conditioning has greater impact on learning as compared to Classical Conditioning.

Cognitive Theory – Cognitive Approach

Edward Tolman was recognized as pioneer of Cognitive Theory. The theory consists of relationship between environmental (cognitive) cues and expectations. He used white rat in his psychological experiment of Cognitive theory. He found that the rat could run through critical path with particular intention of getting food (goal/objective). In the experiment, Tolman established certain ***choice points*** where expectations were established. The rat learned cognitive ***cues*** at various choice points, which would raise its expectation to move forward to the objective (food). Thus the rat turned to acquire food, based on relationship of ***Cues and Reward*** or expectations. This theory was later applied on human resources where incentives were related to higher performance.

Social Learning – behavioural approach

Social learning approach is a behavioural approach. The approach basically deals with learning process based on direct ***observation*** and the ***experience.*** It is achieved while interacting with individuals. In social learning people **observe, alter** and even **construct** a particular environment to fit in the social behavioural pattern. Individuals learn a great deal from watching attractive models and they copy their behaviour and display the same.

Children copy the behaviour of their parents, adults, and copy cinema actors/actresses in various styles. Social learning is practiced in organizations by observing various cultural, and social practices. This phenomenon is distinctly visible in defence services where cadets opt for a particular regiment based on the performance of their instructors (role model). In industrial organizations leader must display a role model so that subordinates copy the style of functioning. An appropriate behaviour can be predicted that would contribute towards achieving higher individual satisfaction level and organizational goals. The influence of model is central to the theory of Social Learning. The following processes determine the extent of influence that a model may have.

Attention Process

It is human tendency to get attracted to impressive models especially those, which suits the individual's temperament and match expectations. This causes social learning.

Retention Process

Learning is basically adapting to a change on permanent basis. Models retention will depend upon the attractiveness of the model. Advertising agencies therefore project attractive models in promotion to their product or services. The advertisement retention aspect is at the core of the concept of the theory that the buyer must be able to retain maximum of what has been projected in the advertisement. Evaluation of such retention (learning) is measured by pre- test and post-test (advertising experiments). This will measure the effectiveness of learning through observation of a particular model.

Motor Reproduction Process

Motor reproduction deals with evaluating the impact of the model on individual. Does individual display the same behaviour as is displayed by the model? If the learning were effective then the learner would be able to display a desired (reproduction) pattern of behaviour.

Re-inforcement Process

Individuals will be able to display positive behaviour or even attitude if a particular activity is rewarded by way of positive incentives. An accountant would be able to maintain accounts correctly and produce a balance sheet when needed if he is encouraged, his work is appreciated or he is given monetary or non-monetary incentives. Re-inforcement is being practiced by various organizations to achieve a patterned behaviour free of conflict situations.

APPLICATION OF REINFORCEMENT TO SHAPE BEHAVIOUR

Management of human resource plays a dominant role in the growth of an organization. Various material inputs in the organization can be put to its optimum utilization if the employees display positive attitude towards organizational systems, processes, activities and have an appropriate interpersonal behaviour. This is possible if a manager is able to identify human requirements (needs) try and satisfy them in an unambiguous manner. This can be achieved by applying re-inforcement to individuals in the course of their performance. If a cleaner keeps the workshop floor neat and clean at all the times, he should be awarded so that he continues to display the same behaviour.

A soldier was publicly congratulated for smart salute by his commander showed an over all higher standard of salutation in the entire defence unit. It has happened (at no cost) because of the re-inforcement received and soldiers showed an overall higher standard in the performance of their duty. Application of re-inforcement model developed by Skinner could be applied with positive results in the organization.

Continuous Schedule

Continuous re-inforcement re-inforces the desired behaviour of an individual in the organization. When a worker is required to do a particular assignment and if he does it on time he should be rewarded for the same. Because he would continue to display the same behaviour every time with the hope of reward. It has been seen that when the re-inforcement (reward) is withdrawn the individual is unlikely to do the job on time. It is not possible for the manager to keep a tag of each and every individual and the activities they perform in the organization. It is therefore important to lay down the policy in this respect so that employees achieve higher productivity by displaying desired (standard) behaviour.

Partial Re-inforcement Schedule

In partial re-enforcement every positive act of individual is not re-enforced (rewarded). In this schedule individual's behaviour is re-enforced after a long gap and his accumulated behaviour is rewarded. It has been observed that partial re-enforcement has a fair chance of individual behaving in a positive and desired manner because he feels that sooner or later his work would be recognised. Partial re-inforcement has a wide application in the organizations. Partial re-inforcement can be classified into four categories as shown in Figure 5.1 below.

Schedule of re-inforcement		
	Interval	Ratio
Fixed	Fixed interval	Fixed ratio schedule
Variable	Variable interval	Variable ratio schedule

Fig. 5.1. Schedule of re-inforcement

Fixed Interval Schedule

The re-inforcement is related to the hygiene factors or administrative factors of the organization like salary, organizational policy, interpersonal relationship, status and the like. In the interval schedule the critical factor is time. As a manager, one has to apply re-inforcement schedule on a fix interval of time. Daily wagers will look forward to get their salary at the end of the day and those on piece rate of payment would work hard to earn maximum. Fixed interval re-inforcement is not very effective. The re-inforcement is of temporary nature and does not motivate individuals on a long-term basis.

Variable Interval Re-enforcement

In this method re-enforcement is not based on the fix period of time. It varies from job to job. Individual's behaviour can be modified based on incentives on a variable time period basis. Promotion, upgradation, or incentives in salary structure coming on different timings that are not on a pre-fixed basis motivate individuals and increment in productivity is achieved. Variable interval re-enforcement schedule generates higher rate of responses and is more consistent.

Fixed Ratio Schedule

Fixed ratio schedule is related to administration of reward system after the individual accomplishes a particular volume of work. A worker is paid or a re-inforcement is administered after manufacturing of particular pieces of product under piece rate of payment. The individual works hard and displays a sense of devotion to his work because of the proposed reward for which a particular quantity has to be manufactured. The response level under fixed ratio schedule is higher than under an Interval ratio schedule.

Variable Ratio Schedule

Variable ratio is similar to fix ratio schedule except that in variable ratio, quantity is not fixed. Re-inforcement is awarded to an individual based on the situation to situation. For example a sales person may be awarded a higher commission on the sales he made irrespective of volume of sales. The incentive may also be given based on number of successful sales calls made by the sales person. Variable ratio schedule has been most effective to modify individual behaviour or ensure sustenance of a particular behaviour. The method draws a very rapid and positive response at a desirable level This type of re-inforcement is considered to be very effective tool to obtain willing obedience of subordinates in a particular situation. The impact largely would depend upon the timings and volume of work performed by the individuals in the organization and the skill of the moderator.

RE-ENFORCEMENT

There are four types of re-enforcement namely ***Positive, Negative, Punishment* and *Extinction***. Positive and negative re-enforcement seeks to achieve a desirable behaviour by two different approaches while punishment and extinction prevents undesirable behaviour. These are discussed in the succeeding paragraphs.

Positive Re-enforcement

Positive re-enforcement is institution of reward for a particular desired behaviour. The intensity of reward must stimulate a desired behaviour. "Shram Shri" award is a re-enforcement or a reward for innovation in production. This is instituted so that individual works to achieve a high standard. The awards instituted in film industry is to stimulate artistic display by artists, which will have a lasting impact on the public. An array of awards in defence services is to stimulate bravery during peace and war environment amongst soldiers and improve over all efficiency. Arjun awards in the area of sports are to achieve excellence in sports with a view to achieve skill and efficiency. Positive re-enforcement to be effective should have following pre-requisites

- The reward should match the expected behaviour graph and need spectrum of awards. Monetary rewards activate some people while others would be happy with just a praise or recognition.

- The re-enforcement or rewards should be contingent to the degree of performance. Higher the performance required, higher must be the recognition (Reward system).
- Rewards must be given on time. Delay in awards may not have desired effect and the impact of reward would be lost. Field Marshal Slim used this tool very effectively during World War II when he used to give gallantry awards to the soldiers for their acts of bravery on the spot in the battle field (front line) thereby intending to achieve high morale and success in fierce battle actions.
- Re-enforcement must be applicable universally without any structural variations. Disparity in rewards is counter-productive.

Negative Re-enforcement

In organizations acts are committed or omitted. For commission of desired acts a reward is given while rewards can also be given for displaying behaviour by terminating undesired consequences. Both, positive and negative re-enforcement techniques are for strengthening desired behaviours. In former employees put in their best and work hard to get financial and other rewards but in the later case of re-enforcement employees work in such a way that they do not invite negative comments or reprimand from superiors. In work places, parking of vehicle at right places, following instructions on training, abiding by safety regulations, assisting employees in performance of their duty are the forms of negative re-enforcement. Because employees would follow instructions to avoid negative consequence of undesired behaviour.

Punishment

Punishment is awarded to an individual for undesired consequences of behaviour. It is a method of decreasing frequency of occurrence of unpleasant behaviour and a tool generally used by organizations for corrective or modification of individual behaviour. It is generally treated as an unpleasant consequence contingent upon undesired behaviour. It is corrective in nature and intended to reduce probability of its recurrence. Punishment acts as deterrence to other individuals and prevent them from doing an undesired act. Punishment should not be given collectively to a group. Punishment should be awarded to an individual who is habitual of undesired behaviour. Punishment can be reduction of salary, non-granting of increment, fine and even removal from service. The gravity or the scale of punishment will depend upon the nature of behaviour displayed by an individual. Punishment should be used sparingly and not as a matter of routine. It should be corrective in nature and not punitive. It should focus on an act deserving punishment and not the subject person. Punishment must be awarded with due care and made public so that it acts as deterrence. While applying punishment as behaviour modification for skill development, due care must be taken by organizations to avoid legal and social fall out. Following points should be kept in mind while applying punishment

Authority

Authority who is entitled to award punishment must be specified and notified to all concerned.

Process

All employees should know the process of punishment. If required this should be included in training programme so that awareness is brought about.

Show Cause

Individual must be given opportunity to justify his actions. No arbitrary decision should be taken.

Board for Inquiry

An impartial body of persons should be formed to investigate each event to decide whether the punishment is required to be awarded. The gravity of the offence, the probable scale of punishment and the individuals involved in the commission of an act.

Time Bound

All actions must be time bound and individual awarded punishment in time

Gravity

Punishment must be commensurate with the gravity of the offence.

EXTINCTION

Extinction refers to withdrawing of re-enforcement or reward so that the happening becomes less frequent and ultimately dies off. The method involves withdrawing positive re-enforcement earlier granted. Eliminating any re-enforcement is called extinction. For example students are given extra coaching for higher performance. Over a period of time this positive re-enforcement leads to students increased dependency on coaching by a teacher. So if this facility (re-enforcement) is withdrawn, it is with the aim of modifying behaviour by extinction, so that the students form the habit of self-study and therefore the learning takes place that leads to behaviour modification in a group. Ignoring an individual in organization for his unsuitable behaviour or ignoring a lazy person in a group is some of the forms of extinction. Because it is expected that extinction would lead to behaviour modification.

APPLICATION OF LEARNING AND ORGANIZATIONAL BEHAVIOUR MODIFICATION

Some of the behaviour modification techniques are given below which may be used in the organization

1. Use of Lotteries to reduce Absenteeism

Attractive prizes can be included in lottery that can be used gainfully to achieve reduction in absenteeism. It has been found that there was no absentee in an organization with the above scheme because management decided that only those individuals could participate in the lottery that has no absenteeism. This has led to individuals attending work regularly and brought about behaviour modification. Absenteeism reduced to a large extent and workers displayed a sense of responsibility that led to increased productivity and higher job satisfaction.

2. Work pay Vr sick pay

Organizations have leave policy. Apart from other leave, there is a provision for few days of sick leave in a year. It has been noticed that most of the employees avail sick leave with impunity whether they are sick or otherwise and therefore organization cannot avail of their services. But if sick leave can be converted in to payment of bonus up to a certain extent, the employees would choose to avail of financial benefits and would not absent themselves under the pretext of being sick. This will improve satisfaction level of employees and would not hamper productivity.

3. Training and Development

Training and development programmes must be run systematically and in a preplanned manner. The author had asked employees in an organization as to what are the expectations of workers from owners of any organization? I was glad to hear that the employees expected two things. ***First,*** they should be so trained in their profession that they are able to take up next/ higher job position and the ***second,*** employees expect that all their entitlements be paid on time. This is biggest contribution an organization can make to the employees. The training and development programmes must be very effective. Social learning theory must be applied and a role model displayed during training. Apart from imparting job related training, it must also enrich value system, adapt a way of life, new life concept and develop a total ethics based approach to life. If this were achieved, all organizations would have conflict free behaviour. Employees would develop a sense of belonging to the organization. Japanese precisely developed this and followed social learning concept. The efficiency of training and development will depend upon the skill of the trainer, the organization culture that management would like to practice and the level of commitment.

4. Mentoring Programmers

2nd lieutenant of an Army regiment was asked as to why he chose to join that regiment. The officer replied that his mentor was from that regiment which interested him the most during his training period. Most of the newly commissioned officers chose their regiment because of the smartness of their mentors, dress they wear and skills they display during tactical exercises, briefings and on firing ranges. Mentors therefore must display model behaviour so that subordinates emulate them. Mentors should ensure to develop sense of responsibility amongst the subordinates who should be able to take higher jobs and work for the organization. They are expected to develop positive attitude towards subordinates, job in hand and achieve a sound personality based on culture and social values. This can be achieved by full dedication on the part of both mentor and the trainee.

5. Discipline

Behavior modification can be achieved by laying down minimum standard of discipline in the organization. Defense organizations are most disciplined organizations because they do not compromise on the standards, be it related to training, work, supervision, accounting or disbursement of salary and wages etc. The leader should set an example for his subordinates. In organization be it production intensive or service sector, managers should insist that all his subordinates strictly follow the timing of work, dress code, display courteous behaviour when interacting with others and accomplish their assigned task on time. Defaulters should be dwelt with strictly. Any lethargy in programme implementation will not bring behaviour modification. Manager must work in the same environment as the workers, eat the same food and wear the same dress and should display alertness and physical toughness. They should be able to work effectively under stress and strain and should not show any signs of tiredness to their subordinates. It is combination of leadership qualities and role played by the managers that will establish high standards of discipline amongst all employees of the organization.

5. *Self-Management*

Learning concepts are meant for modifying the behaviour of others. These theories are also applicable for self-management. Individuals should lay down personal standards, objectives relating to personal growth, identify various courses of action to adopt and modify self-attitude and behaviour. Individuals should be able to compromise on self-interests for overall good of the organization. Regulating various activities and achievement of personal as well as organizational goals would be easier in an environment of self-managed organizations.

SUMMARY

Learning refers to permanent change in behaviour of the individual. It is a continuous process. Ivan Pavlov has suggested classical conditioning theory of learning where stimulus – response (S-R) concept has been applied. Pavlov suggests that S – R phenomenon can be applied in the management and employees should be so trained that they act in a desired manner. Skinner on the other hand recommends Response – Stimulus (R-S) concept. The researcher believes that an individual behaves because of higher probability of response. Edward Tolman has propagated Cognitive Theory of learning. He explains the relationship of environment and expectations. In the recent times social learning has been quite popular because of its simplicity. It is related to modification of behaviour based on observation. The change in behaviour is based on the attention process, retention process, motor reproduction process and lastly the reinforcement process. For behavioural change reinforcement plays a vital role. Managers must apply positive reinforcement based on various schedules. Negative reinforcement deals with the restrictions like preventing promotion etc. Punishment is also considered as a factor for behaviour modification. Punishment must be timely, awarded only by the competent authority. This has a salutary effect on employee behaviour. Learning process must be planned properly and executed sincerely in the organization. Use of incentives, training and development schedules, mentoring programmes, self-management and laying down minimum disciplinary standards are some of the learning strategies that may be adopted by organizations.

TEXT QUESTIONS

Q. 1. Explain the concept of learning. How learning leads to behaviour modification.

Q. 2. How do you relate Pavlov's experiment to human behaviour?

Q. 3. What are various theories of learning? Explain in detail with suitable examples.

Q. 4. Explain in detail the four basic reinforcement strategies to achieve desired behaviour

Q. 5. Explain punishment as a strategy for behaviour modification. What special care must be taken?

Q. 6. Explain schedule of reinforcement. In your opinion, which one of these schedules is most desirable for behavioural change?

REFERENCES

1. Luthans Fred, ***"Organizational Behaviour"***, Mc Graw Hills, International Edition, 1995.
2. Robbins. Stephen P. ***"Organization Behaviour"***, Prentice Hall India 2001, 9th Edition.

Case

MR. VICE CHANCELLOR NEEDS LEARNING THROUGH DOINGS

Often changes surface the organizations with the new Heads of the Organizations. So is true in case of an infant Central University in the North-Eastern Region of India. As the Vice Chancellors in the University system are migratory birds for a certain period of 3 or 5 years to stay in the University, the previous Vice Chancellor left and the New Vice Chancellor joined the University with his own type of mission and vision for the University. He, from his first day in the University, started thinking and working to achieve his mission and vision. In order to monitor the things/ happening in the University in right direction, he formed an informal advisory committee consisting of some 20 Professors of the University. He also evolved a *modus operandi* for this advisory committee.

Fortnightly, he started holding meetings with the group of advisory committee in order to keep them informed and teach them the specifics of any new change in the Government and the University Grants Commission policies and procedures that might affect their work. He also used to discuss priorities and assignments for them. This meeting was also a time and place when the members can share some of the problems and concerns of their respective departments. The meeting is scheduled to begin at 3 P.M. sharp every second and fourth Saturday of the month. Initially, when it was non-teaching duration, the members came on time. Lately, when classes in the Semester System gained momentum, the members have been filtering in every five minutes or until almost 4 P.M. This made the Vice Chancellor delay the start of the meeting until all the members arrive. During the last few weeks when classes are running in full swing, the meetings have not started until 4 P.M. In fact, at 3 P.M., nobody has shown up. The Vice Chancellor could not understand what has happened. The facts unknown to him were mainly missing a single class in the semester system costs as lot, most of the Professors-Members were two-in-one i.e, the Deans of the Schools and the Heads of the Departments, and non-availability of transport after 5 PM from the University Campus to the city with a distance of 20 kms. Though the Vice Chancellor was seeing the crowd of the students, teachers and non-teaching employees standing by the road-side waiting for highly irregular public transport, everyday while passing through the bus stop in his black glass official vehicle, but was oblivious to think over how they will come back to the city which is 20 kms away from the Campus.

The Vice Chancellor was only concerned how to conduct the Advisory Committee meetings on time. For a moment, he thought to start meeting at 3 P.M. so that meeting is over by 5 P.M. before all, the advisory committee is informal and, thereby, the members are volunteers by nature, and, therefore, he cannot push them or make them get to the meetings on time. On the other hand, the Professor- members, who are in no way less qualified than the Vice Chancellor, didn't care for this advisory committee meetings which are not under the purview of their official duties or jobs.

QUESTIONS

1. If you were a consultant to the Vice-Chancellor, what advice would you give to the Vice Chancellor?
2. In terms of re-inforcement theory, explain what is happening here and what the Vice Chancellor needs to do to get the meeting started on time.

Adopted from "Organizational Behaviour", S.S. Khanka, Edition 2004, S. Chand & Company Ltd., New Delhi – 110 055.

CHAPTER 6

Value, Attitude and Job Satisfaction

INTRODUCTION

Value, attitude and behaviour are interlinked with each other. All these factors decide the personality of an individual. Value represents individual's standards, faith, ideals or even events and activity. When we say that the individual should be loyal to the organization one serves, is an expression on individual's standard, faith or an ideal he carries with him as a part of his personality. Attitude can be defined as "individual's feelings about or inclinations towards other persons, objects, events or activities." Attitude encompasses such affective feelings as likes and dislikes and satisfaction and dissatisfaction. Our needs, past experience, self-concept and personality shape the beliefs, and opinions we hold towards the perceived world[1].

Value shapes our attitude and behaviour. For example all employees must be truthful (value) and I find Mr. X is not speaking the truth in a particular situation and if he persists in lying, I therefore do not like Mr. X [my perception] and do not take him at the face value [attitude]. When an opportunity arises, I try to get rid of him [Behaviour]. It is therefore necessary that our attitude is not formed on the basis of wrong inputs and the behaviour is controlled. Attitude is either favorable or unfavorable, concerning object or people. When I say, "I like my job", what I am doing is expressing my attitude towards the job I do. Parents, teachers and peers shape an individual's attitude. We try and behave as our parents, teacher or peers do. We try to imitate them throughout our lives. Value is very important constituent of an individual's life. It is the broad frame of behaviour. Values are imbibed by an individual based on inheritance and environment. Value is more permanent while the attitude is less stable and can be changed. Advertising agencies do precisely the same and attempt to alter your attitude towards a particular product or services. In an organization, attitude is more important because it affects the job behaviour.

VALUES

Is racial discrimination right? Is quota in education institutes and government jobs right? The answers to these questions are value laden. Somebody will say positive while the large number of people may be against it. Values are beliefs and are defined as beliefs about what is desirable and "good" (freedom of press) and what is undesirable or bad (dishonesty). Value represents basic conviction that ***"a specific mode of conduct or end state of existence is personally or socially preferable to an opposite or converse mode of conduct or end state of existence".*** A manager who believes strongly in the work ethics will tend to voice attitudes towards workers or work practices as a means of reflecting this value and say "you got to work harder, that has been the custom and tradition of the organization and reason for being in the present position". Value has contents and conviction element. Every person has value inbuilt in him; it is faith that he deposes in certain ethical aspects. The list of such values is endless, nonetheless a person has hierarchy of value system. It is nothing but various values that he nurtures and its relative importance, which can be called as content and intensity. Value system is identified by the relative importance we assign to various values such as truth, non-violence, equality and so on.

Values are stable. They are genetically inherited to a large extent of the total value possessed by an individual. Balance is environmental. They are stable in nature and do not change. If you like non-violence, or equality, you would always tend to live in peace, preach peace and give equal opportunities to your subordinates.

Value is important in the study of science of human behaviour. Value will dictate attitude and human behaviour in the organization. Organization culture plays a dominant role in the productivity of the organization[2]. Culture is formed by value system practiced by all employees. If promotion is related to the performance, the workers would put in the hard work. On the contrary if promotion is based on seniority the efficiency of the individual will be drastically reduced. Value and culture therefore plays a decisive role in motivation and employee productivity.

Types of Values

1. Allport and associates described six types of values. These are discussed briefly as follows:

(*a*) **Theoretical value:** Theoretical value is related to importance and discovery of truth through rational approach. If all the employees practice truth in true sense, the organization would operate itself and there won't be any need for supervision. Truth is such a powerful value that the British Empire had to leave Indian soil.

(*b*) **Economic value:** It emphasises usefulness and practicability of resources, efforts put in by individuals and the consequent value derived there from. If the project is economically viable (in a very large sense) then it can be undertaken. Economic value is appreciated from a very broad sense and it spells apart from economics of the issue. It also adds human value to it when it is considered. It is the human aspect, which makes economic value enlarged.

(*c*) **Aesthetic value:** It is form of Harmony. We believe that all work must be done in a smooth manner and that there is mutual understanding and sense of participation among all human elements. Aesthetic value is displayed by cordial relations between various levels of organization, effective communication, conflict free atmosphere and very congenial work environment. The work in organizations, which has aesthetic value system among workers, is done in harmony, peace and participation of one and all.

(*d*) **Social value:** Is related to love of people, sense of belonging and an attitude of 'we' feeling. Such value is very important in the organization that brings together the employees which are bound by a sense of participation that leads to high level of motivation and high productivity.

(*e*) **Political value:** It refers to power and influence in the organization. Right people must be placed at the right positions so that they are able to influence the people

(*f*) **Religious value:** As name suggest it is related to display of value which would bring unity and understanding amongst the people in the organization based on common religious platform. This value is no more is being preached in organization as cross section of people are now working in organization world over. However, the positive impact on work environment in the organizations cannot be under-estimated based on religious value.

Rukeach Value Survey

Milton Rokech is a pioneer in studying human values. His research is known as the Rokeach value survey (RVS). The RVS consists of two sets of values. Each of the sets contain 18 value items. The first sets of ***Terminal value*** refers to desirable end state of existence. These are the goals that a person would like to achieve in lifetime. The second set is called ***instrumental values***, it refers to preferable modes of behaviour. These are means of achieving Terminal values. The details of both the value sets is given below in Figure 6.1.

Values

	Terminal values		Instrumental values
1	World of peace	1	Honesty
2	Happiness	2	Hardworking
3	Prosperous life	3	Broad minded
4	Equality	4	Capable
5	Peace	5	Cheerful
6	National security	6	Forgiving
7	Freedom	7	Helpful
8	Salvation	8	Imaginative
9	Social recognition	9	Independant
10	Wisdom	10	Intellectual
11	Mature love	11	Logical
12	Self-respect	12	Loving
13	Friendship	13	Obedient
14	Inner Harmony	14	Polite
15	Sense of accomplishment	15	Responsible
16	Self respect	16	Self controlled
17	World of Beauty	17	Ambitious
18	Family security	18	Clean

Fig. 6.1. Details of terminal and Instrumental Values

Value, Loyalty and Ethical Behaviour

Indians have a rich value system and culture. Children are brought up in an appropriate atmosphere especially in the rural setting. However during the past two decades, electronic media has brought western culture right at the doorsteps of Indians. Indian culture and value system is deep rooted. Workers are generally loyal to the superiors. Obedience as a value is strictly adhered to by Indian workers and managerial cadres. Organizational culture must emanate at the top ladder of the organization. They have to practice right value system so that subordinates down the line also practice the same. Ethical behaviour at the top level is very important. Recent example and scams in UTI, co-operative bank and various other organizations display breakdown of ethical behaviour. The very fact that politics is playing a decisive role in Gujarat riot, the executive wing of the Government has proved to be ineffective. This is indicative of breakdown in ethical standards in the organization. In this situation the police force must act at all cost and display total value system and behave ethically beyond the party politics and act by conscious decisions and quell the riots. Because of break down of value system, the government machinery of law and order has come to a standstill. The society therefore is suffering. It is a matter of great understanding that value and loyalty has an impact on ethical behaviour. Every individual must possess a high degree of value system, he must be loyal to his work, the superior and behave ethically in lager interest of the society. Wherever there is a conflict because of the external pressures, the manager/leader must behave by dictates of conscious. As of now the industrial scene is worth examining. The young executives are seen to be loyal to their job. They change jobs frequently based on high pay and perks. Middle-aged managers are loyal to their jobs because it gives them lively-hood. The old ones display greater loyalty to the organization due to expected pensionary benefits. In each of the categories the motive is predominant in performance. Whatever be the case, loyal workers with right value system will display ethical behaviour.

ATTITUDE

According to G.W. Allport, ***"Attitude is a mental and neutral state of readiness organized through experience, exerting a directive or dynamic influence upon individual's response to all objects and situations with which it is related."***

Krech and Crutchfield defined ***"attitude as an enduring organization of motivational, emotional, perceptual and cognitive processes with respect to some aspect of the individual's world"***

According to Katz and Scotland, ***"Attitude is a tendency or predisposition to evaluate an object or symbol of that object in a certain way".*** In effect attitude is used in a generic sense, as to what people perceive, feel and express their views about a situation, object or other people. Attitude cannot be seen, but the behaviour can be seen as an expression of attitude.

Components of Attitude

(*a*) **Cognitive component:** Cognitive component of attitude is related to value statement. It consists of belief, ideas, values and other information that an individual may possess or has faith in. Quality of working hard is a value statement or faith that a manager may have.

(*b*) **Affective component:** Affective component of attitude is related to person's feelings about another person, which may be positive, negative or neutral. I do not like

Maya because she is not hard working, or I like Mina because she is hard working. It is an expression of feelings about a person, object or a situation.

(*c*) **Behavioral component:** Behavioral component of attitude is related to impact of various situations or objects that lead to individual's behaviour based on cognitive and affective components. I do not like Maya because she is not hard working is an affective component, I therefore would like to disassociate myself with her, is a behavioural component and therefore I would avoid Maya. Development of favourable attitude, and good relationship with Mina is but natural. Individual's favourable behaviour is an outcome of the fact that Mina is hardworking. Cognitive and affective components are bases for such behaviour. Former two components cannot be seen, only the behaviour component can be seen. Former is important because it is a base for formation of attitude. These components are explained in Figure 6.2 below.

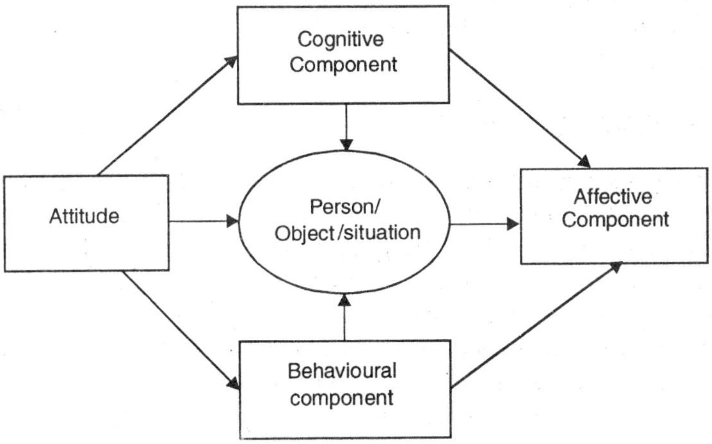

Fig. 6.2. Components of Attitude

Types of Attitude

Job satisfaction: Job satisfaction is related to general attitude towards the job. A person having a high level of satisfaction will generally hold a positive attitude while dissatisfied people will generally display negative attitude towards life. When we talk about attitude, we generally speak about job satisfaction because they are inter-related in organizational behaviour.

Job involvement: Job involvement refers to the degree to which a person identifies himself (psychologically) with his job, actively participates and considers his perceived performance level important to self-worth. (Robbins) . High level of involvement indicates that the individual cares for his job, that has an impact on high productivity. Higher the job satisfaction, lower will be absenteeism and employee turnover.

Organizational commitment: Organizational commitment refers to degree to which an employee identifies himself with the organizational goals and wishes to maintain membership in the organization. He wants to "belong" to the organization and take an active part in the its functioning. Absenting or resigning from the job versus job satisfaction is a predictor of organizational commitment. The concept has been very popular in the recent times. Organizational commitment depends upon job enrichment factor and degree to which the workers enjoy autonomy and freedom of action while performing.

Attitude and Consistency

As stated earlier that the attitude of an individual is not visible but is reflected through his behaviour as a mirror of his attitude. It is seen that people seek consistency among their attitudes or between attitude and behaviour. They seek to reconcile their attitudes and align their attitudes with behaviour so that it is rational and consistent. If there is inconsistency between attitude and behaviour, outside forces act upon an individual, which leads to attaining of equilibrium state, thus consistency is achieved. For example an individual may buy an old car while praising the new model. Reconciliation like, 'why invest more for a new model', or 'the old model is as efficient as the new one, because the same had been sparingly used'. Such feelings are expressed to soothe the attitude (praising new car) and behaviour (Buying the old model) to achieve consistency between them. (Attitude and behaviour)

COGNITIVE DISSONACE THEORY

Leon Festinger proposed cognitive dissonance theory in 1950s. The theory seeks to explain linkage between attitudes and behaviour. We have often observed workers saying that working conditions in an organization are poor. Does it mean that if the working conditions were improved the workers will achieve higher productivity? It is a difficult question to answer, because there is in-consistency between working conditions and its impact on changing of attitude of workers in relation to productivity. Festinger explains that dissonance is inconsistency, and cognitive dissonance refers to any inconsistency or incompatibility that an individual might perceive between two or more attitudes, and attitude and behaviour. He further argues that

(*a*) Any form of inconsistency is uncomfortable and individual attempts to reduce dissonance or discomfort.
(*b*) Individual tries to reduce dissonance to achieve stable state of behaviour. For example Non-payment of tax (behaviour) while recommending payment and displaying honesty towards social obligation (attitude)

Reduction of dissonance

Reduction of dissonance depends upon following three factors.

(*a*) **Importance of the issue, element or situation.** If elements creating dissonance are unimportant, the pressure to correct behaviour will be low. For example to prevent pollution (non-use of polythine bags) is not so important for an individual. Therefore, though prevention of pollution is important but individual rarely show the concern and keep using polythine bags in day-to-day Life. On the other hand train driver, though does not want to run the train at odd hours of night but he has to make the living and hence he runs the train (behaviour) in spite of the high degree of dissonance because it is related to high degree of rewards.

(*b*) **Degree of influence individual believes he has on issue, element or situation.** If one perceives that the dissonance is uncontrollable then one is less likely to change the attitude. Attitude change is a matter of conviction. It is voluntary in nature. In such situation (because it is from within) the pressure to change the attitude is more to reduce the state of discomfort. For example voluntary disclosure of Income Tax scheme (VDIS) introduced by the government. If an individual wants to reduce dissonance (tension of being caught if not paid) and if the degree of influence is high, then the pressure to reduce dissonance will be high and therefore individual will disclose his income (behaviour).

(*c*) **Reward that may be associated to the dissonance.** Rewards influence the degree to which individuals are motivated to reduce dissonance. If high rewards are associated with dissonance (discomforts) then individual will reduce tension, which is inherent in dissonance. A reward acts as positive attitude change agent and further achieves consistency in human behaviour. VDIS is a scheme where government had asked people to disclose their income and that it would not ask the individuals about its source. The scheme therefore attempted to reduce dissonance that led to heavy deposits in the banks.

Organizational implications

(*a*) The theory can help predict individual attitude and behavioural change.

(*b*) Greater the dissonance (incompatibility or discomfort) the greater would be the pressures to reduce the same (after they have been moderated by choice, importance and rewards). Attitude –behaviour relationship can be improved by considering moderating variables of attitude and behaviour relationship. These are personal involvement, social constraints like group pressure and the experience the individual has.

JOB SATISFACTION

The study of Job satisfaction is one of the most important factors in the study of human behaviour in the organization. Job satisfaction focuses on employee attitude towards his job. It has three important dimensions:

(*a*) Job satisfaction can be measured by the emotional response to a job situation, hence it cannot be seen, and it can only be inferred.

(*b*) Job satisfaction is related to what you actually get as reward and what you expect to get. If the difference between the actual reward and expectation is minimum or negligible them a person will display a positive attitude and if there is wide difference between the two, a person will display a negative attitude towards his job and therefore the satisfaction level will be low.

(*c*) Job satisfaction is related to job dimensions. These can be expressed in terms of job content, remuneration, attitude of co-workers, and opportunity of growth that job is able to provide in terms of promotion and last but not the least the expert loyal and experienced leadership is available in terms of supervision.

Factors determining job Satisfaction

There are number of dimensions which effect job satisfaction. Value system possessed by an individual and the culture supporting the value system in the organization can be called as an important and basic for job satisfaction. However some of the important factors that determine job satisfaction of the employees in the organization is as under: -

1. **Work Content:** Content of the work itself is a major source of satisfaction. The work must be challenging. It should lend itself opportunities to use employee skills, ability and experience. The content of the work should be encouraging and interesting and have variety inbuilt in it so that it is not boring. Positive feedback from the job and autonomy has been considered to be important for motivation of employees. Too tough or job having two little challenge brings frustration and feeling of failure hence the job should be moderately tough so that the individual has to stretch his ability, imagination and skills. Once such job is completed successfully, the workers get a great sense of satisfaction.
2. **Pay and promotion policy:** Salary and wages play decisive part in the study of job satisfaction. Equitable rewards is multi-dimensional in nature. The benefits are of varied nature namely pay, perks and rewards are associated with motivation of employees. Pay system and promotion policy of the organization must be just, unambiguous and in line with the prevalent industry norms and employee expectations. Employee wages and salary must ensure him the social status and should be able to fulfill the expectations. Individual must perceive salary administration and promotion policy as being fair. Organization should ensure that their polices are growth oriented and incremental in nature so that employees take on an additional responsibility voluntarily. Apart from financial benefits, organization must provide adequate perks and non-financial benefits so that they are motivated and display high level of satisfaction.
3. **Supportive working condition:** Working conditions have a modest but lasting effect on job satisfaction. Due to fast development of technology, it is necessary that the organizations are operating on upgraded technology, latest systems and procedures. The layout of work place must be ideally suited from operational point of view and the employees should display great degree of satisfaction. The place should be neat and clean with necessary facilities as per Factories Act. Light, ventilation, cleanliness, enough space for work, immediate availability of supervision, adequate latest tools and generally good surrounding will definitely add to job satisfaction. If the work place were closer to home, it would add to employee retention.
4. **Work group:** The concept of work group and work teams is more prevalent to day. Work group of multi skilled persons with one goal will be able to function effectively if they are friendly and co-operative. The work group serves as a source of support, comfort, advice and assistance to individual worker. A good work group makes the job more enjoyable. The factor of work group support is essential for job satisfaction. If the reverse conditions prevail, the people may not be able to get along with each other and the level of job satisfaction will be reduced.
5. **Supervision:** Supervision is one of the moderate factors, which affect job satisfaction. Qualified supervisors should be available for advice, guidance and problem solving. Supervisors should be placed close to the place of work and should be available. They should take personal interest in the affairs of employees both on

personal and official level. Supervision is related to leadership. In Defence Services the leadership is so proactive that the leader carry on him details of each soldier under his command. The details include dependants of soldier's family, their economic position, details of children, the class they study, home address and other demographic details, soldier take his boss as guide and philosopher who is always available to him for advice. Such supervision improves the morale and job satisfaction of employees. The concept of supervision has changed. What is in vogue and in practice to day is self-serviced teams and work group. The group prefer more freedom of work in relation to work hours, time management, frequent breaks between work hours and autonomy as long as job is completed in time. Flater organizational structure therefore has come into practice. Steps in command structure has reduced. There is a participative management and work has to meet the established standards in terms of quality and quantity. The levels might have been reduced but not the value of supervision as a factor of job satisfaction.

6. **Personality job fit:** Individuals should be assigned the job, that suit their interest. Recently it has been seen that MBA graduates are satisfied with their job if they get the job related to the "specialisation" they have chosen during the MBA degree. Persons having analytical approach should be assigned job in R&D department so that their level of job satisfaction increases.

EFFECT OF JOB SATISFACTION ON PERFORMANCE

1. Satisfaction and productivity

Based on research carried out in Hawthorne studies, further research to prove that "happy workers are productive" was carried out, which has been proved negative. Based on the conclusion of Hawthorne studies, managers began their efforts to make their employees happier by improving work conditions, providing participative type of leadership, expanding various facilities to the workers, but it has been found that there is no direct relationship between happiness and productivity. Robins concluded that productive workers are likely to be happy workers. Further research on the subject suggests that organization having happy workers might have increased productivity. On individual level it may not be true due to complexity of environment, work processes, various systems and sub systems having impact on the individual employee. But it can be said from organizational point of view that organization that are able to evolve such policies that make employees happy bound to have improved productivity. V.H. Vroom[3]. Productivity is considered as reward for hard work which is due to high level of satisfaction. However globalisation, speed of machines and knowledge explosion, impact of media on workers, social awareness and high expectations of employees to meet social obligations are important factors to ensure high satisfaction level of employees. While evolving industrial practices, above factors should be considered favourably and employee growth achieved so that organizations grow automatically.

2. Satisfaction and absenteeism

There is an inverse relationship between satisfaction and absenteeism. When workers are more satisfied the absenteeism is low. When satisfaction level is low absenteeism tends to be high. There are certain moderating variables like sick leave and degree to which people feel that their jobs are important. Where there is a provision for sick leave, employees would take the benefit and absent themselves. As far as the importance of work is concerned, it has been observed that people attend to their work when it is important to accomplish. Employees having high satisfaction would not necessarily result in to low absenteeism but those having low satisfaction level would definately have high absenteeism.

3. Satisfaction and turnover

It has been found that employees who are not satisfied with their jobs will have high turnover. Employees who are satisfied will not have high turnover. Satisfaction is also negatively related to turnover but the co-relation is stronger than what we found in absenteeism. Employee performance is a moderating factor of the satisfaction—Turnover relationship. In recent times a phenomenon amongst the software engineers whose performance is high, their turnover has been noticed as high because of competition for personal growth. Organization lures the competent person for their organizational growth. Organization cares for such high performers and their retention. Poor performers do not leave the organization for fear of lack of job opportunity outside.

Dissatisfied workers may express their satisfaction as given in Figure 6.3 below. The responses are based on two dimensions i.e. constructive/destructive and activity/passivity.

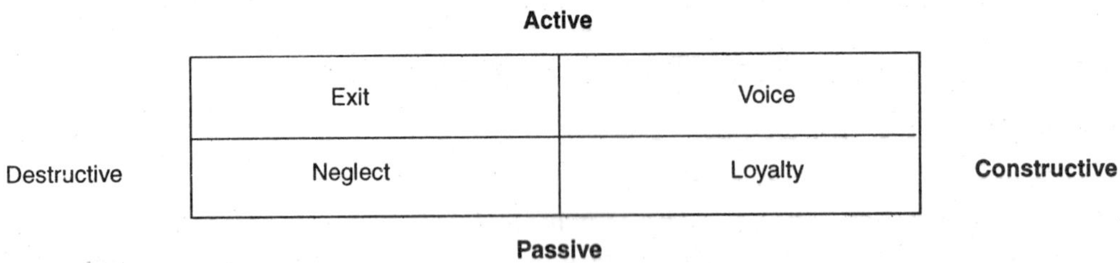

Fig. 6.3. Expression of dis-satisfaction

Exit – individual starts searching a new job and resign from the current job.

Voice – employees tries to improve working conditions. In the process suggestion to management are submitted, increased union activates and communication is important.

Loyalty– workers behave passively in situation like external criticism. They wait for things to improve on their own.

Neglect – deliberately and consciously allow conditions to worsen by long absenteeism, lack of interest for quality control, targets, quota, etc. They put in reduced efforts and display lack of interest.

Organizational Commitment

Organizational commitment is defined as (*a*) a strong desire to remain member of a particular organization (*b*) willingness to exert high level of efforts on behalf of the organization, and (*c*) a definite belief in and acceptance of value and goals of the organization. (R.T. Mowday, L.W. porter, and R.M. Steers)[4]. In other words, employees display an attitude of belonging to the organization, a sense of "MY" organization. They continue to do so even after they leave the organization. Of late a concept of *organizational citizenship is* used. It indicates a sense of belonging to a particular organization as if you were citizen of that organization, but it depends as to the contribution made by organization to have developed such feelings.

SUMMARY

Value attitude and behaviour of an individual indicates his personality. Value represents individual's faith, standards, ideals and belief. Attitude indicates feelings about another person or events. It encompasses satisfaction level about an individual. Individual behaviour is based on value system and attitude he possesses. Value is the strongest element of human personality and therefore it shapes human behaviour. Value is a permanent phenomenon while attitude is comparatively less stable and can be changed. Value are belief—what is desirable and good. Values are end state of existence. It is a faith in certain ethical aspects. It has content and conviction element inbuilt in it. In social environment, there exist a value system. Values are permanent in nature. They form organizational culture that has impact on higher productivity and growth of the organization. Allport and associates have described six types of values. These are theoretical, economic, aesthetic, social, political and religious value. Milton Rokeash has suggested two types of value in the survey carried out by him called Rokeach Value Survey (RVS). These are Terminal values and Instrumental values. Terminal values are end state of existance like freedom or justice and instrumental values are preferable mode of conduct or means of achieving terminal values like hard working, and dependable person. Attitude has three components ie cognitive component, affective component and behavioural component. Individual's attitude can be judged based on level of job satisfaction he enjoys, job involvement and organizational commitment he displays. It has been observed that individual tries to maintain an equilibrium between attitude and attitude, between attitudes and attitude and behaviour so that he conducts and interacts rationally. Leon Festinger has proposed "Cognitive Dissonance Theory" in 1950s that explains linkage between attitude and behaviour. He explains that individual tries to reduce incompatibility or inconsistency between attitude and behaviour so that a stable state of behaviour is achieved. Reduction of dissonance depends upon (*a*) importance of the issue, element or situation; (*b*) degree of influence that individual enjoys and any (*c*) reward that may be associated with it. Job satisfaction is an emotional response. Job satisfaction is difference between what one actually gets and what one wishes to get . If the difference is minimum the job satisfaction will be higher. Job satisfaction is related to job dimensions. Work contents, pay and promotion policy, supportive working conditions, work group phenomenon, supervision and personality-job fit determine the job satisfaction. If workers are satisfied productivity will improve, reduce absenteeism and turnover. Dis-satisfied workers express their dis-satisfaction by leaving the organization. Some of the dis-satisfied workers will passively observe deterioration of the organization while the others may come forward with solid suggestion for the improvement. Organizational commitment is an important part of job satisfaction. It is related to the desire of an individual to maintain the organizational membership and putting in best possible efforts to realise selfworth. Organizational citizenship is also a part of organizational commitment where an individual considers himself a part of the organization one is serving.

TEXT QUESTIONS

Q. 1. Value, attitude and behaviour are inter-linked? Explain.
Q. 2. Define value. Explain the model of Allport and Associates.

Q. 3. Explain Rukesh Value Survey (RVS). Explain how instrumental values assist in achieving end state of existence.

Q. 4. Value and loyalty has an impact on ethical behaviour? Explain.

Q. 5. Define attitude. What are various components of attitude. Give examples.

Q. 6. Discuss various types of values.

Q. 7 How dissonance can be reduced and a state of equilibrium can be achieved. Discuss with the help of Cognitive Dissonance Theory of Leon Festinger.

Q. 8. Explain in detail the concept of Job Satisfaction? What are various factors that promote job satisfaction?

Q. 9. What is the effect of Job Satisfaction on employee performance?

Q. 10. How dis-satisfied workers display their behaviour. Explain with the help of a model.

Q. 11. Explain the following concepts.

(*a*) Attitude and consistency

(*b*) Organizational commitment

(*c*) Dissonance

REFERENCES

1. Uma sekaran, ***"Organizational Behaviour, Text and Cases, 1989"***. Tata McGraw hills Ltd. Ninth reprint 2000.
2. M.Rokeach ***"The Nature of Human Value"*** New York" Free Press, 1973, p.5.
3. V. H. Vroom ***"Work and Motivation"*** New York: Wiley 1964; and M.T. Iaffaldano and P. M. Muchinsky ***"Job Satisfaction and Job Performance."*** A Meta-analysis' psychological bulletin, March 1985).
4. L.W. porter, and R.M. steers, ***"Employee-Organization Linkage"***, academic press, New York, 1982.

Case - 1

WHAT RIDES OVER-PROFIT OR ETHICS?

Nagesh Iron and Steel Company Ltd. was established by Nagesh Samuel in the year 1980 with its head office at Delhi. The company was established in 400 acre of land at Bilaspur in MP in which four plants were situated viz. Sponge Iron, Powerhouse, Furnace and Rolling Mill. The project cost was around Rs.650 crore and annual turnover was around 1000 crore and the company was recognized as a profit making unit. The workforce was 3000 in number, out of which, 1200 workers were on the company's pay roll while remaining were affiliated to INTUC. The unit was headed by the chairman and managing director, Nagesh Samuel. He used to operate from Delhi and was supported by the president and other three VPs in the field of finance, marketing and technical fields respectively. There were also general managers appointed for respective plants and divisions at Bilaspur. Nagesh Iron and Steel Company Ltd. had constructed huge township for the staff and managerial personnel and almost seventy families including few workmen resided in the township. Most of the workers hailed from Orissa, Bihar and Madhya Pradesh. The literacy rate was very low amongst the workers and the local anti-social element often influenced the activities of the union.

The CMD was 42 yrs of age and a religious, dynamic person who believed in quick decision making with an autocratic style of leadership. He was a qualified engineer from USA and occasionally visited the factory. He used to control the plant from the Delhi head office. The recruitment at senior level was not based on proper procedure and nepotism was encouraged by giving chance to the relatives of CMD. The market for Nagesh Iron and Steel Company Ltd. was exclusively on the domestic front however, it had to face competition from Jindal, Nova and Special Steels. The relationship between management and the union was bitter since the beginning. The CMD was directly involved in day to day activities and the president reported directly to the CMD. The working capital involved per day was Rs. 30 lakhs as a result of which CMD wanted to continue with production at any cost.

An undue advantage was taken by union members towards this approach of CMD and as and when the union got the opportunity, it threatened to go on strike and became dominating while interacting with the management. With the result the tactics of pressuring was made for even minor demands. A fresh charter of demand was served to the VP (Comm. & Admn.). Pratap Verma and Manager (P & A) held several meetings with the union members and wanted to build a harmonious relationship with the members of the union.

On Dec. 2, 1996, the President of the unit was shocked upon receiving a fax from CMD stating that the listed 12 employees including the GM, Quality control and other officers were to be sacked with immediate effect. On being inquired by the President about the termination, the CMD from Delhi, on telephone replied that he had information that their were close links of these people with the union leaders.

A meeting was called immediately by the president which was attended by VP (Comm. & Admn.) VP (Technical) Manager (R & A) HR Manager. After long discussion, every member was of the opinion of terminating the officers and managers, gradually in phases, because immediate termination would have resulted in bad consequences on the company and the process of agreement with the union might have taken a ugly shape.

The opinion was conveyed to the CMD at his head office. However, the CMD did not agree with the opinion and strongly told the President to sack the listed twelve employees immediately. The President called GM Quality, Arnab Ray and asked for the resignation on the ground of lack of confidence and similar reasons were given to all other employees. Some of them had tendered the resignation immediately while others had asked some time to think. Arnab Ray and others met the union leaders the same evening to discuss the issue.

As the news of termination spread within the premises, simmering discontent started and the atmosphere become tense. As a result, next morning i.e., on December 3, 1996, at 6.30 A.M., all workers at the behest of the union went on strike. Workers from all the four plants came out of the factory to the main gate and even workers form night shifts were not allowed to start their machines. With the result half of the plat was running without attendant and the remaining plant was closed at 8.30 A.M. The staff members also formed the union and got associated with labour union and revised charter of demand were served before the management, clearly indicating the reinstatement of sacked employees. Management refused to accept the new charter of demands and as a result, situation became violent to the extent in that even telephone connection and electricity supply was disconnected. Police was called in for maintaining law and order situation and for the protection of executives. Only six managers stood by the management and they were gheraoed and locked for twenty four hours inside the plant without food and water. A meeting was conducted by the local management, police and union leaders, so that the officers who were inside the plant got food from their houses. The strike continued for next eight days and though there were number of rounds of negotiations, no results were obtained.

An application was submitted to the labour court by the local management through their consultants and advocates and a strike was declared illegal by the labour court and the same was published in the newspaper. Since CMD started direct dialogue with the union, the local management became powerless and the union stopped listening and interacting with them. Strike had started in the first week of the month and salary could not be distributed therefore, restlessness could be observed among the workers and management reached to a conclusion that strike might be called off within a day or two and this was communicated to the CMD also but the CMD didn't succumb to the advise given by the management as he was facing financial loss costing Rs. 300 – 400 crores and on December 9, 1996 he himself reinstated all the sacked employees and bowed down before the union and accepted the charter of demand.

In the next six months the president called back to the Delhi office, HR Manager and VP (Technical) resigned and VP (Commercial & Administration) was transferred to another unit at Jabalpur.

QUESTIONS FOR DISCUSSION

Q. 1. Was the decision of CMD to terminate 12 employees right ?
Q. 2. Had you been in the place of CMD, what would have been your decision ?
Q. 3. What was wrong in the organizational cultural of the unit ?
Q. 4. What can be the implications of the decision taken by CMD ?

This case has been developed by S. Rangnekar (IIITM, Gwalior), Y. K. Singh (MGCVV, Chitrakoot), Manoj Patwardhan and Hemant Soni (Prestige Institute of Management, Gwalior).

Case - 2

FUNCTIONING UNDER FEMALE CHIEF EXECUTIVE

Dr. (Mrs.) Anjali Ghanekar

"Ajit, I'm finding it little bit difficult to cope-up with the situations in my organization. You see, how much ever hard and sincere efforts you may put in, your superior work performance does not count. What matters more is how much and to what extent you can 'subordinate' yourself and carry out the wishes of your boss!" exclaimed Rajesh.

Ajit replied, "Yes, I know, that is the most common experience with male bosses. On the contrary' look at my organization. We all feel very happy and comfortable with our leading lady Mrs. Leena Modi. She is very considerate and sympathetic. She always puts very reasonable demands and for team there is neither any embarrassment nor any discomfort".

Rajesh found it difficult to believe and said, "Well, frankly speaking instead of 'Mrs. Modi' if you were having some 'Mrs. Joshi' as your CEO, I'm sure, things would have been a lot different. Also, I feel it is humiliating for men like us to accept orders from women bosses on both the fronts that is at home as well at work place!"

Rajesh had typical stereotyped negative attitudes towards women manager and his entire thinking pattern was highly prejudiced. In case of Mrs. Modi, Rajesh had reinforced his negative viewpoint since he had once experienced her open confession in an informal get-together that she had experienced certain reluctance and resentment from her male subordinates in carrying out her orders. She was wondering whether to attribute it to her being a 'woman', or, to her being 'young and inexperienced'. Anyway, much to his astonishment, she seemed to be quite sure that once they accept her as competent and efficient manager, they will offer wholehearted cooperation in implementing the order and decisions.

Ajit had observed that in general people's perception about Mrs. Modi as CEO was rather ambivalent – it was mostly a wonderful intermixture of admiration, resentment, competitiveness, anxiety, pride and animosity. He understood that people like Rajesh were also having a feeling that Mrs. Modi has a specific need to 'over-achieve' in order to prove herself that is why she insists on consistently high levels of work performance. Moreover, they were having their own doubts about the team-building efficiency of Mrs. Modi.

Becoming aware of this fact, Ajit narrated his own experience of functioning under Mrs. Modi : "You see, Rajesh, over these four years I'm fully convinced that Mrs. Modi is paying particular attention to the quality and substance of what she is doing. She is a highly independent woman with a strong positive self-image. She is able to recognize and accept the strengths of those who work with for her. Her involvement, commitment and contribution has gone a long way in making our organization effective and efficient.

Moreover, she has the right perspective as well as clear and sharp insight to build an effective team. I tell you, I still remember the first meeting she had with our team. At that time I discovered that she was extraordinarily good at not only listening but showing that she was listening. Nevertheless, she summarized what the other fellow had said and actually expressed his view better than the way it had been originally delivered.

Till that meeting, for every problem that came up, few of my colleagues and myself seemed to have a ready answer and yet the problems kept coming up. You know, during the meeting, Mrs. Modi used two flipcharts. One she marked 'Problems', the other she divided into two columns : 'Causes apparent' and 'Causes deeper!. Emerging out of that meeting, I learnt two things – one was about looking deeper into problems and the other was about how to make the best use of the intelligence of seven people working together".

After this long narration, Rajesh uttered his heartfelt words : "Is it really so ? Now I realize how biased my views were regarding women executives!"

QUESTIONS

Q. 1. Do you agree with this if you were in place of Rajesh ?

Q. 2. What difference would it make to employees if they work under a female Chief Executive ?

Adopted from The book titled "The Process of Management" by Dr. M.L. Bhasin, Published by Global Business Press, Abhinav Publishing Industrial Pvt. Ltd., Delhi – 110 095.

CHAPTER 7

Motivation

INTRODUCTION

It is essential to increase overall efficiency of human beings to improve performance of an organization. While machines, processes, technology of high order can be made available to the individuals, but high productivity can only be achieved if workers are highly skilled and adequately motivated. Motivation perhaps is a single most important factor of the study of organizational behaviour that concerns each and every executive today.

Definition: Motivation is defined as **"inner burning passion caused by need, wants and desire which propels an individual to exert his physical and mental energy to achieve desired objectives"**. Efficiency of a person depends upon performance. Performance can be expressed as under

$$\text{Performance} = \text{Ability} \times \text{Motivation}$$

Terms liked motive, motivation and motivating are commonly used in Organizational Behaviour. It is important to fully understand the meanings of these terms so that they can be appropriately used to derive maximum benefits.

Motive: As per Burleson and Steiner, (1964) 'motive' is defined as **"an inner state that energises, activates (or moves) and directs** (or chanalises) **the behaviour towards certain goals."**

Difference between motive and needs. Motive is a strong need which has a certain degree of strength that propels a person to act for its fulfillment. If the need or motive is not fulfilled a person remains restless and when fulfilled a person enjoys a certain degree of satisfaction. Certain amount of tension is harbored by a person when need exists. If incentives for accomplishing are given, the person is more enthusiastic for its implementation. Greater the motive, greater is the tension and higher the desire to fulfill. A high degree of satisfaction is experienced by an individual once the desire is fulfilled. For example a clerk who knows manual typing on typewriting machine. He is aware that if he learns computers he would be more skilled and he would be able to achieve higher performance in his job and would probably get higher rewards for the work. Therefore, there exists a motive to learn computer, due to its higher benefits, the need gets transformed into motive because of its greater strength. Till the time individual does not learn computer the tension won't be released. Once this is done (due to higher motivation) the individual and organizational objective (growth) is achieved. This is explained in Figure 7.1 below:

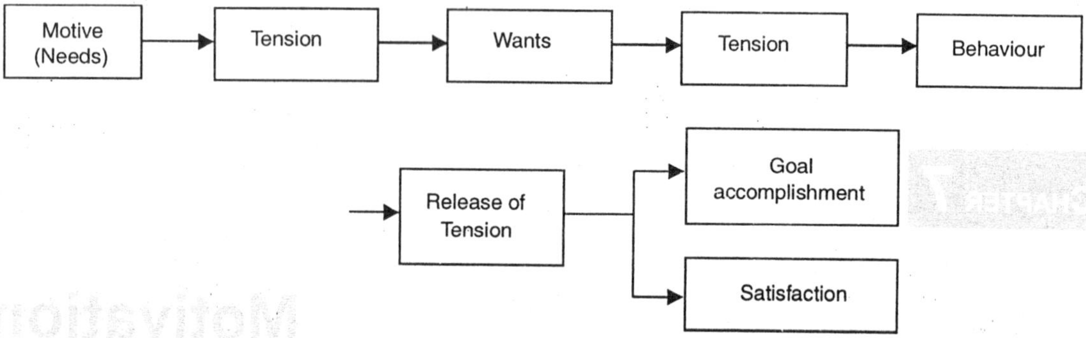

Fig. 7.1. Process of motivation

Motivating: Managers must create situations wherein a person/employee is stimulated to undertake activities, that may motivate him to achieve higher goals. Creating a situation by alleviating restlessness of a worker. To achieve higher goals a person should work so that the restlessness is reduced and later removed. This is possible when worker feels to achieve something and divert all his energies towards achievement. This process could be called motivating subordinates. For example, a sepoy can be selected as commissioned officer in the defence services provided he acquires competency as a specialist in any field may be accounts, equipment management, weaponry and the like. If a leader has been able to ignite a spark and create certain amount of restlessness among deserving sepoys (combatants) to work towards one of the above specialisation so that in course of time he is commissioned as an officer in a particular branch. The entire process could be called motivating. Leader can continuously identify such situations in the work environment and motivate his subordinates for self-development and organizational growth.

Motivation: Scot defined motivation as **"a process of stimulating people to action to accomplish desired goals"**. Mc Farland has defined **"motivation as the way in which urges, drives, desires, aspirations, strivings needs direct, control or explain the behaviour of human beings"**.

The Encyclopedia of Management: Motivation refers to degree of readiness or an organism to pursue some designated goals and implies the determination of the nature and locus of the forces, including the degree of readiness.

Memoria: "A willingness to expand energy to achieve a goal or reward. It is a force that activates dormant energies and sets in motion the action of the people. It is the function that kindles a burning passion for action among the human beings of an organization".

The author defines **"motivation as inner burning passion caused by needs, wants and desires that propels an individual to exert physical and mental energy to achieve desired objective"**.

Characteristics of Motivation

(*a*) Motivation is a psychological phenomenon. It is the inner desire of an individual to accomplish something more. The very deficiency forces him to undertake certain amount of work. More is the individual motivated better the performance and organization relations.

(*b*) Motivation is a continuous process. Since need is a continuous phenomenon if one need is satisfied the other need emerges and so does individual propels to work and thus the continuous chain is created.

(*c*) Motivation is caused due to anticipated perceived value from an action. Perceived value is the probability or the expectancy. Therefore

$$\text{motivation} = \text{valance (value)} \times \text{expectancy.}$$

(*d*) There are unsatisfied needs. A person remains disturbed till they are satisfied. This disturbance or tension causes disequilibria in human behaviour. More the motivation level, the higher will be efforts to get over the tension and in the process job accomplishment would take place.

(*e*) Individual is motivated by positive motivation. It refers to incentives offered by the organization to achieve efficiency. Incentive can be monetary like increase in pay, allowances, and payment of bonus. Payment for additional or overtime work. It can be non-monetary like issuing of certificates for excellence, awards, recognition, status, job enrichment, competitions, and the like. Monetary rewards prevent individuals from getting demotivated or they do not motivate so to say. However non-monetary awards motivates individual as it is related to the inner/psychological aspects.

Importance of Motivation

(*a*) ***High level of performance***: It is the duty of every manager to ensure that the employees have a high degree of motivation. He should offer monetary and non-monetary incentives. Highly motivated workers would be regular for work, and have a sense of belonging for the organization. Quality of product will be improved, wastage will be minimum and there will be increase in productivity, and performance level will be high.

(*b*) ***Low employee turn over and absenteeism.*** Employee turnover and absenteeism is caused due to low level of motivation on the part of managers. When dissatisfaction is increased employees do not enjoy the work assigned to them. Therefore there is a tendency of absenteeism. The workers hunt for an alternative job and leave the organization whenever they get an opportunity. High level of absenteeism causes low level of production, wastages, poor quality and disruption in production schedules. Increased turnover is disastrous for any organization as it puts strain on financial position of the organization due to additional recruitment, selection, training and development. Motivation is therefore a very important management tool to achieve organizational excellence.

(*c*) ***Acceptance of organization change.*** Management must continuously scan the external and the internal environment. There has been a great impact of. Social change and technology evolution on the motivation level of employees. Social change increases aspirations of workers and put an additional demand on the organization, which must be considered positively so that conducive working environment is created. Technical innovation, better working conditions, better R & D facilities, encouragement to employees and existence of better personal policies should be part of any organization. This will facilitate retention of employees. Management must ensure that the changes are introduced in the organization and its benefits explained to the employees so that there is no resistance to change and organizational growth is achieved. Re-engineering, empowerment, job enrichment, job rotation, introduction of new technology and processes will go a long way to boost employee morale and achieve high degree of motivation.

(*d*) ***Organizational image:*** Employees are the mirrors of any organization. Managers must lay down high performance standards coupled with high monetary and non-monetary rewards. Training & development programmes should be regularly organized and employee skill improved. It will have a positive impact on the employees and the image of the organization will be improved. It will also reduce employee turnover and better employee will look forward to join the organization. High organizational image will contribute towards brand image of the product and services the organization is marketing.

MOTIVATION THEORIES

- Maslow's Theory of Need Hierarchy
- Motivation and Hygiene (Two Factor Theory)
- Theory X and Theory Y
- ERG Theory
- Vroom's Theory of Motivation. (Performance Satisfaction).
- Porter — Lawler Theory.

MASLOW'S NEED HIERARCHY THEORY

Abraham Maslow was a clinical psychologist in USA. His motivation theory is widely accepted and studied. Maslow suggested that every individual has complex set of needs at any particular moment and his behaviour is determined by the existence of strongest need. He stated that human beings have five types of needs and physiological need is the strongest hence the individual behaves in a particular manner to satisfy that need. Needs are hierarchal in nature and only one need dominates at any one point of time. Once the strongest need is satisfied then the second need emerges as being the strongest need and human behaviour is regulated in process of achieving satisfaction in series of need requirements. Maslow further started that there is only one need satisfying process is underway at any one time. They do not disappear once they are satisfied but their intensity is reduced (relegated) below the subsequent need. He has arranged the needs as per **Figure** 7.2 given below.

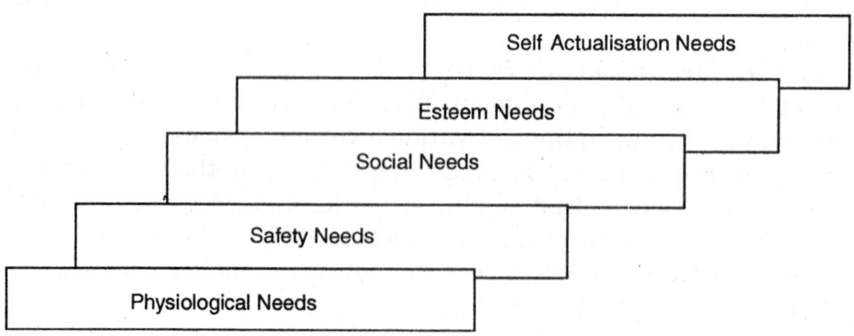

Fig. 7.2. Hierarchy of needs

Let us discuss the hierarchy of needs theory:

1. ***Physiological Needs*** - As per Maslow physiological need is strongest in every human being and hence it has highest strength as compared to the other needs. Individual behaves in a particular manner to satisfy basic bodily needs like hunger; thirst, shelter and clothing. These needs keep dominating unless they are reasonably satisfied. Human being is therefore motivated to work in that direction.
2. ***Safety Needs or Security Needs*** - Once the physiological need of an individual is satisfied, the safety need /security need arises and is dominant at that point of time. This need is related to the following:–
   - (*a*) Every worker is concerned about his personal safety and wants to be free of physical danger.
   - (*b*) There are various dangerous processes in the work setting. Individual desires to be free and work toward self-preservation.
   - (*c*) Safety need is also related to employee/employer relationship, which should be cordial and free from any threat to job security.
   - (*d*) There should be certainty in the job and non existence of arbitrary action on the part of management/employer.
   - (*e*) Administration policy of any organization must cover various points that are related to safety of an individual like pay, pension, insurance, and gratuity. Individual should be given opportunities for choice of job so that he derives satisfaction. He must also be given adequate security against being fired, laid off or demotion.
3. ***Social Needs*** - Once the safety need is satisfied, third need i.e. social need arises. People want to belong to some social group where their emotional need of love, affection, warmth and friendship are satisfied by being member of sports club, social organizations or being the company of friends and relatives. In the work setting individuals want to be member of work group and contribute towards it so that the social need of the individual is fulfilled.
4. ***Esteem Need or Ego Need*** - Fourth need in the hierarchy of needs as suggested by Maslow is Esteem need or Ego need. Individual wants self-recognition, appreciation for the work done. It is related to self-respect, self-confidence, praise, power and control. It these needs are satisfied it gives an individual a sense of self-worth and ego satisfaction.
5. ***Self-actualization Need*** - Self-actualization is the last need in the need hierarchy. Once esteem need is satisfied, there appears the self-actualization need of human being. It is related to an intense carving for something supreme one wants to achieve in life. It is transcended and related to achieving the very best that may be possible of human endeavour. People set high goals, achieve them and set a higher goals again and to achieve the same by utilising fullest potential. It is related to development of intrinsic capabilities. An individual seeking to satisfy self-actualization need seek situations or jobs that are challenging in nature - achievement of highest value out of the work. Mahatma Gandhi wanted to achieve freedom for India by unique weapons of peace and non-violence. He strived hard, faced various challenges but ultimately achieved his goal. With his innovative

ideas he bound the whole nation in one thread of to-getherness for the cause of freedom.

In essence Maslow's Motivational Theory covers the following.

(*a*) There are five levels of human needs.

(*b*) These needs are hierarchical in nature.

(*c*) A satisfied need is no longer a need. Once that need is satisfied, the next level need becomes stronger.

(*d*) Needs do not diminish. It is the gravity that changes. Individual strives to satisfy the need that has a strong appeal at any point of time.

ANALYSIS

Maslow has taken a deprivation gratification approach to need satisfaction (Uma- Sekaran, 2000). That is, he extended that an unfulfilled or deprived need would activate a person to engage in behaviour that would satisfy or gratify that need. Once one level of need is gratified, the next level of needs will emerge as the deprived needs seeking to be gratified. Relationship of various needs is given in Figure 7.3 below.

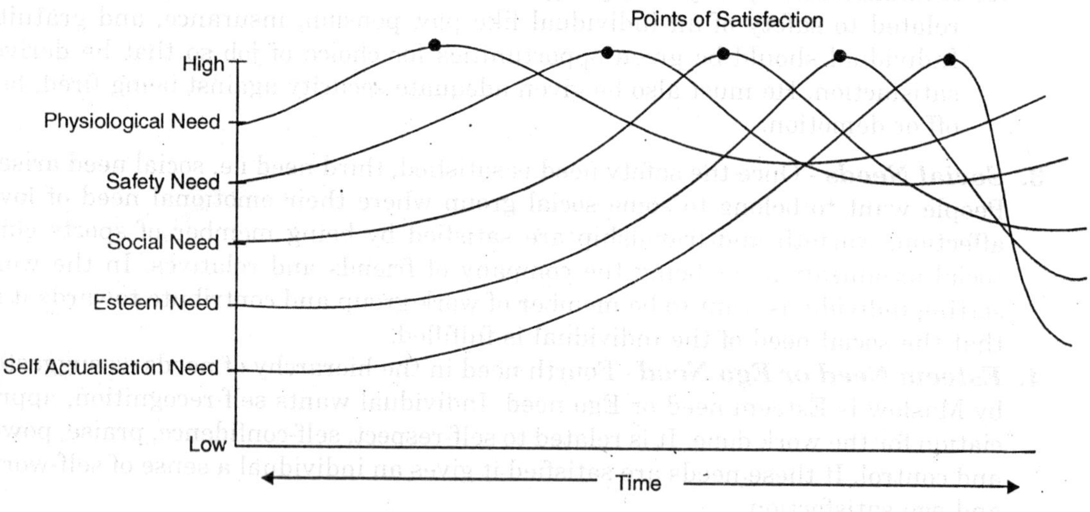

Fig. 7.3. Relationship of various Needs

From the above figure, the following points emerge

- Desire levels of various needs are overlapping to each other.
- All needs are inter-dependent.
- Each higher level need emerges before lower level need is satisfied.
- Need does not disappear when it is satisfied. Its gravity is reduced when another need emerges.
- When peak of a particular need is passed that need ceases to be primary and next need starts dominating.

Critics of Maslow's Hierarchy of Needs Theory and Its Application

Maslow's theory of motivation and its nature of hierarchy of needs lays down a systematic approach a manager can apply to motivate his subordinates. It will be seen that needs are generally in the order. Maslow has suggested that when a worker is employed he is concerned about his basic need of food, water, shelter and clothes and wants a minimum level of rewards so that the above need is fulfilled (physiological need). Once the first need is satisfied, a manager must strive to fulfill second need (security need) of his subordinates by providing them physical security, job security and laying down various policies, which are required for smooth running of an organization. Management must enjoy cordial relationship with employees and ensure free flow of communication so that employees devote maximum attention towards organizational work. Workers can "belong" to a particular organization (social need). By creating work groups and extending facilities for social interaction so that esteem need and self-actualisation needs, which are of intrinsic nature can be accomplished by workers.

Maslow has laid down that individual has a particular pattern and hierarchy of needs which may not be true. There are craftsmen, poets, sculptures, painters who have devoted their entire life towards fulfillment of self- actualization need without having satisfied physical, safety or even social needs. Renowned poet Galib was a poor person and always had the problem for two squire meals a day. Though he was deprived of lower order needs but tried all his life to accomplish self-actualisation need. To some people esteem need may be more important than social need. Therefore, they may seek self-assertion. There is a lack of direct cause and effect relationship between need and behaviour as propagated by Maslow. A person feeling thirsty may not always drink water but he may switch over to cold drinks soda or even a glass of beer to squint thirst. Level of need satisfaction generally differs from person to person hence the theory cannot be universally applied.

Maslow has been criticised for laying down needs in particular order. But in reality it may not be so. For Example a person may like to 'belong' to a particular organization or a social group and his social need may be dominant as compared to the physical need or the safety needs. On the other hand a worker who is a sole income earner for the whole family may feel job security as his most dominant need. It is therefore fair to state that we may not find the needs in the given order and that the strength of particular need is situation-based. It is therefore necessary that the contingency approach should be adopted by various managers while applying the model to real life situations in the organization.

HERZBERG'S MOTIVATION— HYGIENE THEORY (Two factor theory)

Fredrick Herzberg and his associates developed Motivation Theory based on two main factors in late 1950's. This theory is also known as Two Factor Theory. Herzberg carried out research in nine different organizations where 200 respondents comprising accountants and engineers were subjects. A structured interview was carried out. The purpose of the study was to identify various factors for goal achievement and also the factors that could be included so that motivation levels do not fall.

Findings of the study: Herzberg concluded, " There are two types of needs, independent of each other".

(*a*) **Motivational Factors:** There is a set of job conditions, which operates primarily to build strong motivation and job satisfaction. These factors are called motivational factors.

They are intrinsic in nature and help increase one's output. These factors have positive effect on morale, productivity, and job satisfaction and over all efficiency of the organization. These factors are as under:

Achievement
Advancement
Possibility of Growth
Recognition.
Work Itself
Responsibility

(*b*) **Maintenance Factors:** There are some job conditions which operate primarily to dissatisfy employees when these conditions are absent. These factors are also called **hygiene factors**. When these factors are present they do not motivate in a strong way, when absent they dis-satisfy, That is why these factors are called **dissatisfiers**. These factors are.

- Company Policy and administration.
- Technical supervision.
- Interpersonal relationship with superiors.
- Interpersonal relationship with peers.
- Interpersonal relationship with subordinates.
- Salary.
- Job security.
- Personal Life.
- Working condition.
- Status.

Above factors are not an intrinsic part of a job. They prevent losses due to work restrictions. These factors are necessary to maintain a reasonable degree of satisfaction of employees. As stated earlier they are demotivators if they are not present. For example minimum level of working conditions must be maintained by the organization to ensure that minimum level of satisfaction exists. If working conditions are poor, the employees will be dissatisfied and it would have adverse effect on goal achievement. Potency of various factors does not increase the motivational level. It is influenced by personality and characteristics of individual employee. Herzberg has identified that employees are either maintenance seekers or motivation seekers.

ANALYSIS

Herzberg's Theory indicates the following:

(*a*) It has been found that most of the people are capable of satisfying their lower level needs considerably as they are not motivated by maintenance factors/hygiene factors.

(*b*) Any improvement in Hygiene factors do not motivate workers but their reduction below a certain level will dissatisfy them. For example increase in status or salary need not motivate an employee because he feels it, as a matter of happening but if he was not to get an increase in salary or if his status is not increased he would be dissatisfied. Hence the hygiene factors are called dissatisfiers. Therefore they do not contribute towards motivation.

(*c*) The model suggested by Herzberg is not applicable in all conditions. There is a mixing up of both factors in a job, which cannot be separated, as intrinsic and extrinsic. Because the level of personal need and relative strength of each of the needs is different from person to person.

(*d*) Job satisfaction and job dissatisfaction are two opposite points on a single continuum. It has been seen that individuals are affected more by job environment or job contents when we want to achieve this, what we are actually doing is keeping hygiene factors constant and increasing the motivational factors in a job like improving the work itself or having growth orientation or we delegate the job to an individual and vest in him the full authority and responsibility.

(*e*) Herzberg's theory of motivation is not conclusive as the scope was narrow. Only 200 respondents were interviewed and that to persons belonging to white collar jobs [engineers & accountants] hence affect of various hygiene factors may be positive on workers.

(*f*) The study is "Method bound". It has not shown any positive results in actual work environment.

(*g*) Herzberg's study of motivation is important, as it has identified two main factors as Motivational factors and Maintenance or Hygiene factors. They should not be divided in strict water tight compartments. Certain overlap is bound to happen. Since these are applied in relation to various human beings.

Comparison of Maslow's need hierarchy theory and two-factor theory of Herzberg

On comparing both the studies, certain similarity has been noticed. Maintenance factors propagated by Herzberg are identical to lower level needs of Maslow. Higher level needs in the hierarchy of needs are identical to motivation factors suggested by Herzberg.

Division of esteem need in two parts has become necessary. Advancement and Recognition are considered to be motivational factors while, achievement, work itself, possibility of growth and responsibility could be clubbed along with Maslow's lower needs.

Maslow has achieved "Universality" in his strides. Any unsatisfied need, as per Maslow is a motivator, irrespective of whether higher or lower order. Herzberg could not achieve the same; there is still a deference of opinion regarding hygiene factors, which fails to motivate.

It has been observed that people get motivated when they achieve a feeling of being worth, accomplishment and recognition for the good work done. Over a period of time the needs, demands and expectation of employees have increased. They achieve greater satisfaction if there is a sense of freedom in work place, which relates to authority. Young managers serve those organizations which accord them two things one, opportunity for personal growth and two, development and opportunity to achieve fast promotions. Prestige of the organization outside in the society is also a factor, which is referred to by employees. They feel satisfied by virtue of being a part of an organization, which is widely recognized world over for example "Microsoft" or "TATA" organizations. Pay, allowances job security especially for old managers and perks that is being offered by the organizations promote motivational level of employees. They therefore dedicate themselves to achieving organizational objectives. These factors are applicable for high motivational level of various employees in organization. However for managerial class, it has been seen that autonomy, higher responsibility, promotion and growth opportunities are important and favored for motivation. Manager must therefore create favorable conditions and environment in the organization to enable employees to fulfill their aspirations and expectations so that the individual objectives are achieved and would lead to achievement of higher organizational goals.

McGREGOR'S THEORY X AND THEORY Y

Douglas McGregor introduced Theory X and theory Y which are diagonally opposite to each other. McGregor is aware that human beings are rational in their thought process and they are social by nature. They display very high degree of behaviour relating to achieving self-actualization. There is interaction of variety of need fulfillment phenomenon and complex nature displayed by an individual in different situations.

Theory X

Theory X is a traditional theory of human being McGregor assumed that with respect to ***Managerial action.*** Management is responsible for organizing various element of an enterprise like money, material equipment and people. *With respect to people*, it is a process of directing people, their efforts, motivating them, controlling their actions, modifying their behaviours so that they fit in the organizations. In Theory X McGregor assumed that people would be passive therefore management must persuade, reward and punish the worker to achieve the desired behaviour of workers.

Human nature –McGregor further stated that Human being have indolent nature, he works minimum. McGregor summaries workers as lacks ambition, dislike responsibility, prefers to be led. An individual is self centered and indifferent to organizational needs, by nature he resist change. Lastly he gullible and not very bright.

In theory X, McGregor states that those who subscribe to the views expressed above, the manager will have to structure, control and closely supervise employees.

External control has to be exercised towards immature and irresponsible behaviour of the employees, so that there energies can be regulated towards productive work. Theory X is applicable to traditional organizational and characterized by centralized decision making hierarchical pyramid and external control.

After Theory X was proposed, McGregor observed that some changes in human nature have taken place. It was not due to the changes in human behaviour and reactions to various situations but due to change in industrial organizations, management policies and practices that have tremendous effect on human nature. At this point he proposed. Theory Y as under:

Theory Y

(*a*) Expenditure of physical and mental efforts on the pant of employees is as natural as play or rest. The average human being does not inherently dislike work.

(*b*) Workers seek direction and exercises self control. He dislikes punishment.

(*c*) Commitment to organizational objective is associated with rewards like pay promotion etc, ego satisfaction and satisfaction of self-actualization needs.

(*d*) Average human being learns under proper conditions. He accepts seeks responsibilities. At times, it will be seen that certain individuals display phenomenon like avoidance of responsibility, lack of ambition and lay undue stress on security. McGregor suggested that these are due to inherent human characteristics.

(*e*) Capacity to exercise high degree of imagination, ingenuity and creativity is widely distributed among workers that must be identified and fully utilized.

(*f*) Intellectual potential of workers is partially utilized. In the above situation McGregor recommends that the organization should reorient based on the human behavioural change. More co-operation, maximum output with minimum control and self-direction is predominant among workers. It is also seen that there is no conflict between individual and organizational goals. The emphasis is on very smooth running of organization with greater participation of individuals.

Assumption about human nature that underlines Theory X and theory Y propagated by McGregor

Theory X	*Theory Y*
(*a*) Work is inherently distasteful to most people.	(*a*) Work is as natural as play.
(*b*) Most people are not ambitious, have little desire for responsibility and prefer to be directed.	(*b*) People display extreme degree of self-control, which is necessary for achieving goals.
(*c*) Most people have little capacity for creativity in solving organizational problems.	(*c*) The capacity of creativity in solving organizational problems is widely distributed in the population.
(*d*) Motivation occurs only at the physiological and security need levels.	(*d*) Motivation occurs at social, esteem and self-actualization need levels.
(*e*) Most people must be closely controlled and often coerced to achieve organizational objectives.	(*e*) People can be self-directed and creative at work.

Analysis Paul HERSEY has analysed Theory X and Theory Y. He states that managers who accept theory X assumptions about human nature usually direct, control, and closely supervise people, whereas theory Y managers are supportive and facilitating. We want to caution against drawing such consolation because it could level to the trap of thinking that Theory X is "bad" and Theory Y is "good".

It is unusual to find exclusively Theory X people or Theory Y people in any organization. There would always be a mix of both type of employees in varying proportions. Managers therefore will have to tailor their motivational application in appropriate manner suiting behavioural patterns.

ERG THEORY OF MOTIVATION

Clayton Alderfer of Yale University carried out further studies on Maslow's theory of need hierarchy. He identified three basic needs of human being against five needs of maslow.

These are as under:

(*a*) **E-Existence need** - These are related to provision of basic material requirement of human being and are related to Maslow's Physiological and safety needs.

(*b*) **R-Relatedness** - This need is related to desire of an individual to maintain sound interpersonal relationship. It is related to Maslow's, Social need and External component of Esteem need i.e., status, recognition and attention.

(*c*) **G-Growth** - Growth is an intrinsic desire for personal development. It is related to intrinsic component of Esteem Need like advancement, self respect, autonomy, achievement and self-actualization need.

Evaluation

(*a*) Alderfer advocated three need patterns of an individual as against five steps proposed by Maslow.

(*b*) Alderfer recommends that all the needs, need not be in rigid stepwise progression. Any need may be stronger and individual is forced to fulfill that need.

(*c*) More than one need may be operative at any one time. It gratification of higher need is stifled, the desire to satisfy lower level need may increase. ERG Theory contains a frustration — regression dimensions (when there is a frustration in higher level need, lower level needs may get more activated.)

Alderfer recommends satisfaction - progression patten of need. i.e. when one level need is satisfied then higher level need arises (satisfaction-progression).

EXPECTANCY THEORY-VROOM

Vroom has propagated Expectancy Theory based on employee expectancy. He believes that employee is motivated to exert high level of efforts when he believes that efforts will lead to good performance and therefore organizational rewards that will satisfy achievement of personal goals. The focus of the theory has three elements.

(*a*) **Efforts - Performance relationship.** It is related to the probability perceived by individual that exerting a given amount of efforts will lead to performance (Expectancy).

(*b*) **Performance - Reward Relationship.** The degree to which the individual believes that performing a particular level will lead to attainment of desired outcome (Instrumentality).

(*c*) **Reward-personal goal relationship.** The degree to which an organizational reword will satisfy individual needs and its attractiveness for the individual (Valence).

The concept is explained in Figure 7.4 below:

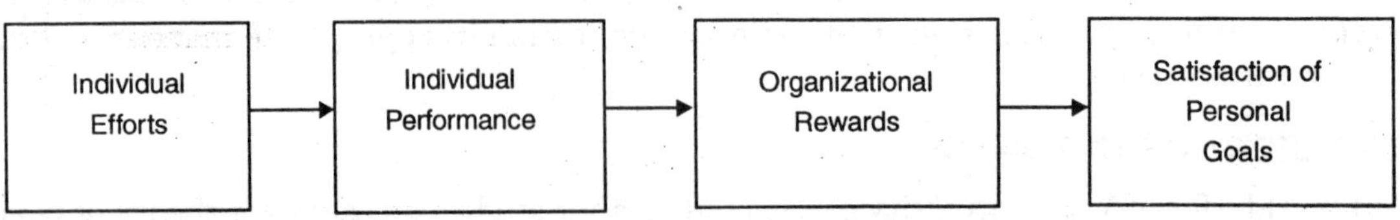

Fig. 7.4. Expectancy Theory-Vroom

Individual invariably asks questions to himself like probability of good performance, assessment based on the skill and non-performance criteria and personal likes and dislikes. In second stage he evaluates performance-reward relationship in terms of award of seniority or the amount of co-operation he is liked to get in the organization and lastly the rewards attractive enough to fulfill his personal goal of promotion. Management must therefore identify individual goal pattern and lay down performance criteria and reward system. The key is to understanding of an individual's goal linkage between efforts and performance, between performance and rewards, and between rewards and individual goal satisfaction.

Analysis – Maslow's theory is basically need satisfying concept. Vroom has gone one step ahead to identify individual expectations from the organization, and its impact on work behaviour of an individual. If a system of performance appraisal and its resultant benefits are attractive, then the individual will put up his best to achieve organizational objective. The behaviour of an individual has been taken as rational. The theory helps managers to work beyond Maslow and Herzberg and create work environment and set organizational goals in such a way that individual is stretched to achieve higher performance. However the theory is difficult to implement because of the organizations inability to provided required resources and time.

PORTER AND LAWLER MODEL OF MOTIVATION

Lyman Porter and Edward Lawler came up with a comprehensive model of motivation. They combined adding two more components to Vroom's theory of motivation. The model is more comprehensive as it includes various aspects that we have studied so far. This is a multivariate model which explain the relationship that exists between job attitudes and job performance. This model is based on four assumptions of human behaviour as under:

(*a*) Individual behaviour is determined by a combination of factors that exist in the individual and are present in the environment.

(*b*) Individuals are considered to be rationale people who make conscious and logical decisions about their behaviour when they interact with other people in the organization.

(*c*) Every individual have different needs, desires, and their goals are of varied nature.

(*d*) On the basis of their expectations, individuals decide between alternate behaviours. The outcome of the efforts is related to the pattern of behaviours an individual display.

Porter and lawler model of motivation is explained in Figure 7.5.

1. Value of rewards. People try to find out the rewards that are likely to be received from undertaking a particular job will be attractive enough. This phenomenon is equal to that of valence in Vroom's theory of motivation. If rewards are attractive, an individual will put in an extra efforts, Otherwise he will lower the very desire of doing a job.

2. Efforts. Efforts refer to the amount of energy which an individual is prepared to exert on a job assigned to him.

3. Perceived Efforts - Reward Probability. People try to assess the probability of a certain level of efforts leading to a desired level of performance and the possibility of that performance leading to rewards. Bases on the valence-reward and the efforts-rewards probability, people decide the amount of efforts they would like to put in.

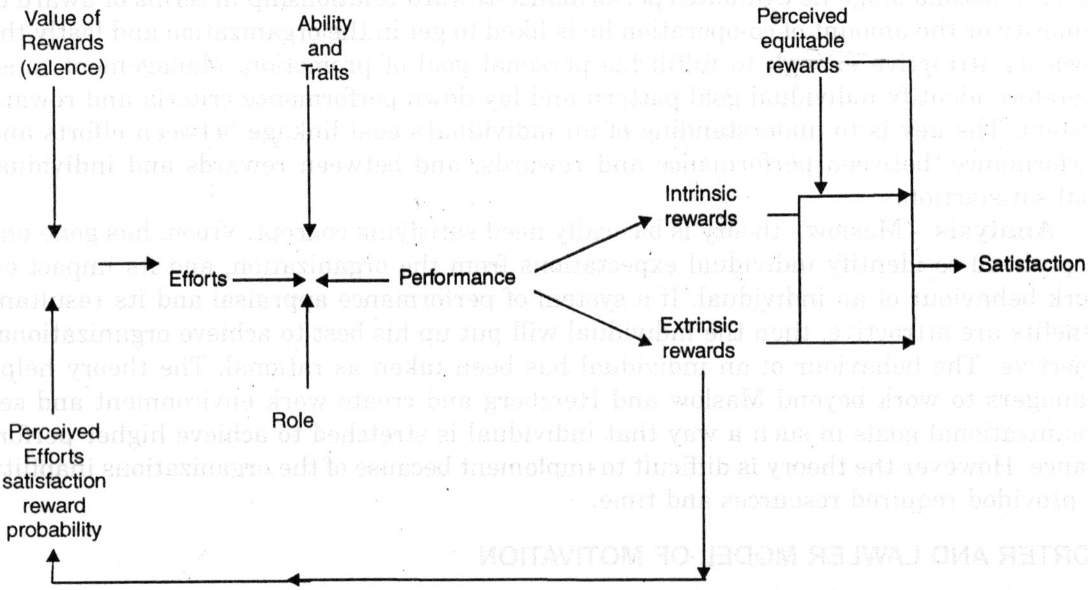

Fig. 7.5. Porter and Lawler's model

4. Performance. Efforts leads to performance. The level of performance will generally depend upon role perception as defined in the standing orders/ policy instructions, the level of efforts, skills, ability, knowledge, and intellectual capacity of the individual. Traits also play a role in performance equation. Thus, ability and personality traits will moderate effort-performance relationship. Performance of the individual is directly related to reward he is likely to get. Reward is of two type i.e., intrinsic and extrinsic. Individual is generally motivated by intrinsic rewards. It is therefore necessary that the organization pay an adequate attention to the reward system in the organization. Extrinsic Rewards are in the form of money or other material elements that have been included in hygiene factors of Hertzberg's motivation theory.

5. Satisfaction. Satisfaction results from intrinsic rewards. Individual will therefore compare his actual rewards with the perceived rewards. If actual rewards are equal or greater than perceived rewards the individual would feel satisfied. On the contrary if they are less than perceived rewards, an individual will put in reduced efforts, and obviously he will be less satisfied.

Significance of the Model

Porter and Lawler Model is a complete model and is a departure from the traditional performance—satisfaction relationship. The model is of a great significance to managers as it sensitizes them to focus their attention to achieve employee motivation. Following points need more attention.

1. Matching of individual traits and ability with the job.

2. Managers must explain to the employees the role they play in the organization and its relationship with reward system.
3. Managers should carry out job analysis carefully, lay down actual performance levels, which should be attainable by the individuals.
4. Job expectations, performance levels, and reward associated with the job should be clearly laid down and implemented.
5. Motivation of employees is important. Make sure that the rewards dispensed are in line with employee expectations. Carry out the review of reward system periodically.

SUMMARY

Motivation is inner burning or passion caused by need want and desire. Stronger the need higher would be efforts on the part of an individual and therefore the performance would also bee higher. Performance therefore can be put as under:

$$\text{Performance} = \text{ability} \times \text{Motivation}$$

Motive can be defined as "an inner state that energises, activates and directs the behaviour of the individuals to achieve goals". Motive is a strong need. When one need gets fulfilled another need arises and again individual attempts to satisfy the same. This is a continuous process. It is the responsibility of a manager to create such environment that individual is motivated to achieve higher goals. Motivation is therefore is a way in which individual strives to fulfill desires, urges and aspirations that explains the individual behaviour. Motivation is inner passion that propels an individual. It is a psychological phenomenon. Motivation should be continuous process. It is caused due to anticipated value. Motivation is intrinsic in nature and therefore caused by non-monetary incentives. Monetary incentives keeps the minimum level of motivation amongst the employees. Motivation probably is the single most important factor that a manager is required to do in the organization. It may be noted that high motivation leads to greater performance, higher cohesiveness and leads to higher job satisfaction. Employees accept change that leads to increased organizational image, low turnover and absenteeism.

Abraham Maslow, the pioneer in the studies of motivation has suggested that every individual has a complex set of needs and his behaviour is determined by the strongest need existing at a particular moment. He propagated need hierarchy theory of motivation and classified human needs into five categories namely physiological needs, safety needs, social needs, esteem needs and self-actualisation needs. He states that needs are hierarchal in nature. Only one need is strongest at any one time and that an individual attempts to fulfill the same. Once that need is fulfilled the second need arises as strongest need and individual keeps on fulfilling each need as it arises. Maslow has taken deprivation – gratification approach to need satisfaction. Once one level of needs is gratified, the next level of need will emerge as the deprived need seeking to be gratified.

Fredrick Herzberg and his associates developed motivation theory based on two main factors. The theory is therefore called two factor theory. The first factor is **"motivation factor"** which includes a set of job conditions which primarily operates to build strong motivation and job satisfaction. The other factor is called **"maintenance factor or hygiene factor."** This include job conditions that dissatisfy when these are absent and do not in any way increase satisfaction when they are present. They however maintain a certain level of job satisfaction. These factors are not intrinsic part of a job. The theory has been widely criticized as being method bound and inconclusive.

Douglas McGregar introduced Theory X and Theory Y. Theory X states that managerial actions are contingent to human behaviour. As regards to human nature McGregar states that human nature is indolent, does not like to work, he is lazy, resist change, does not take responsibility, lacks ambition, prefers to be led and gullible and not very bright. As far Theory Y is concerned, human being takes work as natural as play, display self-control, they can be self-directed and creative.

Clayton Aldefer carried out further studies on motivation theory of Maslow. He identified basic three needs of human being. These are: existence need, relatedness need and growth needs. Aldefer recommends satisfaction-progression pattern of need.

Vroom has put forth Expectancy theory of motivation. The theory is based on efforts, performance and reward relationship. He believes that employee is motivated to exert high level of efforts when he believes that effort will lead to good performance appraisal and therefore organizational rewards that will satisfy personal goals.

Porter and Lawler have presented a motivational model which is a step ahead of Vroom's theory of motivation. They have related satisfaction of employees with traits, skills, efforts, performance and its relationship with the reward system. Managers can effectively implement this model in their organizations.

TEXT QUESTIONS

Q. 1 Explain Motive, Motivation and Motivating.

Q. 2 Explain in detail the motivation theory of need hierarchy propagated by Maslow. Carry out analysis.

Q. 3 Explain two factor theory of Herzberg? What are hygiene factors and why they are called demotivators?

Q. 4 Explain ERG Theory of motivation of Aldefer. What do you understand by satisfaction-progression pattern of need satisfaction.

Q. 5 Explain Expectancy Theory of Vroom.

Q. 6 Explain Porters and Lawlers motivational theory. Do you feel that the theory is any significant and that it has made a change in the motivation pattern in the organization.

Q. 7 Theory X Theory Y are concerned with the nature of the people. What are its implications.

Q. 8 Explain in detail the ERG theory of motivation. How does it significantly differ from Maslow's model of motivation.

Q. 9 Explain Mc Gregar's Theory X and Theory Y. How is theory Y an improvement over the traditional view that you can motivate employees by paying them the money.

Q. 10 What do you understand motivation. How does it affect behaviour. What happens when a person is not able to satisfy his needs.

Q. 11 Can motivation be increased. Discuss various factors that influences motivation.

REFERENCES

1. Burleson, B, and Steiner, ***"Human Behaviours"***, New York, Harcourt Brace and Jovanovich, 1964.
2. Uma- Sekaran, 2000.

Case

MR. ALOK BANARJEE

Mr. Alok Banarjee is the Chief Executive of a medium- sized pharmaceutical firm in Calcutta. He holds a Ph D in Pharmacy. However, he has not been involved in research and development of new products for two decades. Though turnover is not a problem for the company, Mr. Banarjee and his senior colleagues noticed that the workers on hourly basis are not working upto their full potential. It is well known fact that they filled their days with unnecessary and unproductive activities and worked only for the sake of a pay cheque. In the recent past the situation has become quite alarming as the organization began to crumble under the weight of uneconomical effort. The situation demanded immediate managerial attention and prompt remedial measures. Mr. Banarjee knew very well that the only way to progress and prosper is to motivate workers to peak performance through various incentive plans.

One fine morning, Mr. Banarjee contacted the Personnel Manager and enquired: "What is the problem with the workers on hourly basis? The wage bill shows that we pay them the highest in the industry. Our working conditions are fine. Our fringe benefits are excellent. Still these workers are not motivated. What do they require really?" The Personnel Manager gave the following reply: "I have already informed you a number of times, that money, working conditions and benefits are not enough. Other things are equally important. One of workers in that group recently gave me a clue as to why more and more workers are joining the bandwagon of 'non-performers'. He felt bad that hard work and efficiency go un-noticed and un-rewarded in our organization. Our promotion and benefit plans are tied to length of service. Even the lazy workers, accordingly, enjoy all the benefits in the organization, which, infact according to workers, should go only to those who work hard."

Mr. Banarjee then wanted the Personnel Manager to look into the problem more closely and find out a solution to the problem of workers on hourly basis.

Answer the following questions

Q. 1 Explain the motivational problem in this case by relating to Herzberg's theory.

Q. 2 What would be your response to Banarjee's statement, if you were the Personnel Manager of the Company?

Q. 3 If you were the manager, how would you motivate the employees so that they work better.

CHAPTER 8

Perception and Individual Decision Making

INTRODUCTION

Perception is like beauty that lies in the eyes of beholder. Individual differs in the way he sees, interprets and understands a particular event. A manager may perceive non-attendance of duty by the subordinate in a different way. Individuals may also differ in their opinion though the event or situation may be the same. For example, in an organization where lunch is served in a subsidised manner may be interpreted by the employees in a different way. An employee may perceive it as "right" to get a subsidized lunch, the other may feel that it is being given out of surplus of profits achieved by the organization while the third individual may state that it is mandatory for the management to provide lunch free of cost and that the management is not doing any favour to them by providing the lunch.

Definition

Perception is defined as ***"a process by which individuals organise and interpret their sensory impressions in order to give meaning to their environment (Robbins)[1]"*.**

(*a*) What one perceives may be different from objective reality. A person coming late on duty may be perceived as casual and tardy while there may be social problems faced by him.

(*b*) There is often disagreement among the individuals in the organization in relation to pay and allowances, administrative back up, policies and procedures and the place of work itself. An individual who displays a positive attitude may perceive above factors as good and conducive to work environment while the others may consider them inadequate. Employees also compare themselves on job assignment. If a job is assigned to one individual who may consider the assignment in excess to his job entitlement on the contrary if he is not given the job, he may consider it as neglecting him in allocation of responsibilities.

(*c*) It would often be observed that the manager is rated differently by his subordinates because of the different perception of the individual about the manager. The study of perception is very important in the organization because it is necessary for the manager to perceive individuals correctly irrespective of their status and perceive each of the situation as close to the real fact or as it exists by interpreting the sensory reflects in correct way. Sensation and perception are complex phenomenon. Perception is outcome of sensation and is much broader in its nature. Perception involves observing data, selecting, and organizing the data based on sensory reflects and interpreting the same as per personality attributes of the perceiver. That is why no two individuals can perceive an employee in the same manner, for one he may be efficient while for the other he may be perceived as useless.

Factors Influencing Perception: Following three factors influence the perception

Perceiver	**Situation**	**Object/Target**
Attitude	Time	Shape
Motives	Work setting	Size
Interests	Social setting	Shade
Experience		Sound
Expectations		Silhouette
		Movement
		Background

Perceiver: When an individual looks at the object and attempts to interpret the same, what he or she sees it is largely influenced by the personal characteristics. Perception is a matter of **attitude** that can be positive or negative. Some workers would feel and perceive that the prevailing working conditions in the organizations are congenial for work and it contributes positively while for others, it would be inadequate and demand improvement.This is indicative of positive and negative attitude patterns. **Motive** is another factor that plays an important role in perception. Motive is nothing but unsatisfied needs. This exerts considerable influence on perception. Boss who is insecure perceives subordinate who does well as threat to his position. Personal insecurity is a threat to personal survival in a job especially if one is frequently transferred. **Interest** is persons liking for a particular thing in an individual. May be some people get attracted to eyes of a girl because he has interest in the eyes while other person may be interested in hair style, therefore different person (perceiver) will perceive a girl based on perceivers' interest. It has also been observed in the work places that workers would display interest as per their liking. Students in the class when preoccupied are not attentive in the class. **Past experience** also plays an important role in perception. Just as interest narrows down one's perception so does past experience. In contrast past experience nullifies an object interest. For example second or subsequent visit to a historic place. Object or events that have not been experienced before are more noticeable and creates an interest. For example a female manager. **Expectations** can distort one's perception in what one sees and what one expects to see. For example power hungry police officer to be strict regardless of his actual traits.

The Target: Objects, events that are similar to each other tend to group together and have a tendency of perceiving them as common group for example. Blacks, Whites or Indians etc irrespective of their different characteristics. Physical and time proximity also leads us to perceiving a situation in a different form than actual reality. Increase in the sales volume may be attributed to newly posted sales manager. In actuality the increase in sales may have been the outcome of hard work done in the past by sales representatives and public contact. Soldiers in identical uniform and their uprightness is perceived as being strict, ruthless and tough, on the contrary they are sober, soft and very delicate at heart. It is therefore important to analyse the event, situation, or an object in its correct perspective and be led by similarity, physical and time proximity. An object can be identified by its size, shade, shape, sound it makes and background. It can be distinguished based on its movement. In darkness it may be identified by its silhouette, for example caravan moving on skyline at the dawn.

The Situation: Change in situation leads to incorrect perception about a person. Time is one factor, which influences the perception. Time is related to work setting and social setting. A person decked up for party may not be noticeable but the same dress in office would be noticed distinctly, though the person has not changed. You would have very frequently heard people say that their manager is different during working hours and 180^0 opposite while in social setting. Infact person is the same but the perceiver perceives the manager as per business like setup while on work, while the person is observed on a private or a personal platform when meeting him in the club or at home. What is important to remember is the perception should be done in a correct manner not to be led due to work setting or social setting and that the situation is not allowed to perceive wrongly.

Attribution Theory of Perception: In day-to-day life, we come across people with whom we interact. Motives, intentions, belief and attitude of people have an impact as to how they behave. It has been seen that our perception about the people is greatly influenced by the assumption we make about a person and not by reality. There are two factors, which has an impact on human behaviour. First is internally caused behaviour – refers to internal factors on which individual has a full control, secondly the externally caused behaviour- refers to the behaviour which has been caused due to external factors and that the individual has no control over it. Attribution theory suggest that when we evaluate human behaviour, it is either internally caused or it is caused due to external factors as explained above. The determination however depends on the following three factors. See Figure 8.1 below:

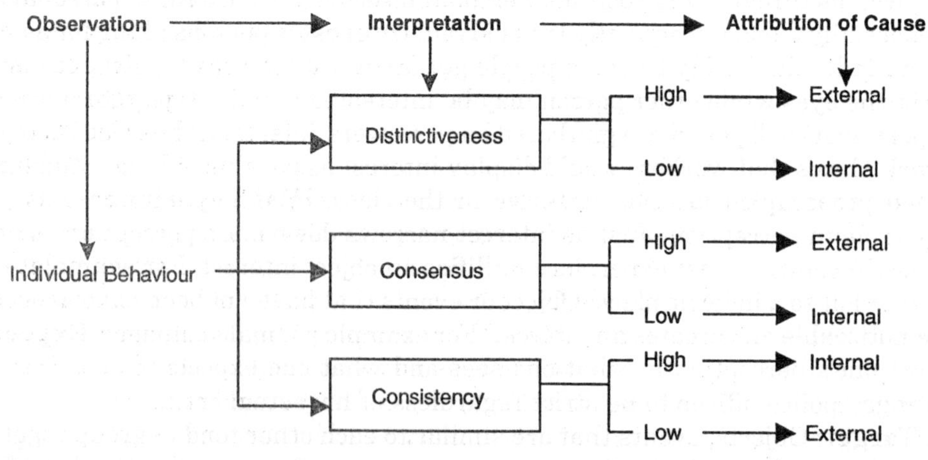

Fig. 8.1. Attribution Theory of Perception

(*a*) **Distinctiveness:** Let us for evaluation purposes take an example of X worker coming late for duty. When we carry out interpretation there are two factors, one whether arriving late is usual or unusual behaviour. If it is usual, it is attributed to internal factor on which X has full control. When the behaviour is unusual then it can be attributed to external factors. In the former situation individual could be counselled appropriately in the later situation, the external factors cannot be corrected. If the external factors are high, then late coming should not be attributed to the individual behaviour.

(*b*) **Consensus:** This factor refers to group behaviour. If the entire group taking the same route came late on duty, the causation is attributed to external factors. But by some chance if X only was late then the causation would be internal.

(*c*) **Consistency:** If the behaviour of Mr. X is consistence, that is if he is consistently coming late then attribution should be to internal factors. In such cases there is a high internal causation. If X came late once in a while the causation would be low and attributed to external factors. More consistence the behaviour, the more the observer is inclined to attribute it to internal causes. It has been seen that we have the tendency to under estimate the influence of external factors and over estimate the influence of internal factors or personal factors while carrying out perception. This phenomenon is called the ***fundamental attribution error.*** Fall in sales of a commodity is generally attributed to inefficiency of sales force rather than market trend, recession or innovative product launched by the competitor. There is also a ***self-serving bias*** error caused by the individuals who tend to attribute their own success to internal causation like ability, hard work and self-worth and the failure, to external factors like Luck. This phenomenon is called a self-serving bias displayed by the individuals. There are bias, which distorts attribution universally across culture. During World War II it was considered by Allies that Japanese are invincible, but the attribution proved to be false at later date when tide took the turn and Japanese had to suffer total annihilation. Self-serving bias does not apply to all organizations, where cultural identity has been established like Defense Services of India. Where the leader takes the responsibility for the failure of group task and attribute success to collective efforts. This is the main reason that soldiers have great faith in their leader and his ability and that is how the soldiers are led in war and they follow the leader blindly because they have a correct perception of their leader.

Aspect of personality that influence perceptions: Costello, Zalkind (1962) and Hamacheck (1971)[2] indicate the following relationship between personality factors and perception

(*a*) Secure person perceives others as warm individuals.

(*b*) Thoughtful individuals do not perceive situation in terms of Black and White but understand that there can be different shades of gray. Hence they do not make judgments based on single piece of evidence.

(*c*) Self-accepting people perceive others liking and accepting them. Those who are not self-accepting tend to distrust others.

(*d*) Self-accepting person also accepts others easily which is not true of those who are not self-accepting.

(*e*) People tend to perceive others more accurately when they are more like the ones they perceive than if they are different from those who are being perceived.

Common Errors While Judging Others

1. **Selective Perception:** People selectively interpret what they see based on their attitude, interest, background and experience. An individual might have been appointed on a key position on the day of the visit of CEO and the appointment may be incidental but we may perceive appointments as a consequence of CEO's visit. In an organization so many things keep happening but different people will perceive one fact differently based on individuals selectivity in perceiving which is generally based on his past experience and attitude towards work. It is important that when we read others, we make a mistake reading with speed and putting seal of what has been selectively seen by a perceiver. For correct perception an individual must be observed, studied, tried and later perceived without an individual bias.
2. **Halo Effect:** Halo effect refers to judging an individual based on single characteristics, such as intellectual ability, sociability and appearance. Sales Manager's visit to sales territory and consequent increase in sales volume may be attributed to the visit of the sales manager to a particular sales territory. Perceiver in this situation did not notice the cause of increased sales to probably higher demand, change in market forces, subordinate sales employees past efforts to woo customers to buy the product and host of other factors that go with increase in the sales volume. This type of perception is quite common in any organization, which is called halo effect in perceiving an individual or situation. A rater may rate a subordinate based on dominance of a single trait of the subordinate. The halo effect has been very frequently noticed in performance appraisal.
3. **Projection:** You assume a person based on your own traits and not what he actually possesses. If you were hard working and dependable you would expect others to be so. If a person projects the above characteristics in his dealings he is rated high or perceived in a different way than what he actually is. It is commonly found that subordinates do or exhibit the same behaviour as desired by the boss. This phenomenon is called the 'projection', an error that is common in any organization.
4. **Contrast Effect:** We do not evaluate a person in isolation. Our reaction to one person is relative to the other. During selection process, interviewer selects a particular person for a particular job not because he fulfils all requirements but he is generally selected in relation to the other candidates. Individual selected may be academically, skill wise, experience wise better than those not selected. So it is a comparative or contrast phenomenon of perception. We generally hear, people say that Mr. X presentation was good thereby meaning it was better in relation to other people who would have made presentations in a particular session.
5. **Stereotyping:** In order to simplify matters, we often tend to classify people and events into already known categories. For example we generally perceive man as executive and woman as secretary even if the situation may be different. For police person, it is generally believed that they are generally tough and law abiding which may not be true. In our mind we have established certain categories with certain attributes. For example, category of teenagers would generally be independent, indisciplined and so on. In reality this may not be true. Similarly we

attach positive attribute to judges, professors and doctors and negative attributes to school dropouts, addicts although they may not be really so.

INDIVIDUAL DECISION MAKING

Managers have to take decisions and communicate the same to subordinates for implementation. Decisions can be of routine nature or may have strategic consequence. It is the judgment of the individual to arrive at a particular solution. The process that takes place in mind is fast and based on ability, nature, skill and experience of the individual. Hilter took a decision to attack Europe in the West while he had captured half of Russia. Opening war on two fronts led him to defeat. Otherwise the map of the world would be different. Such are the consequences of faulty decisions. Due to information technology revolution, a manager has to his disposal pleanty of information on product, market trends, customer choice, availability of various resources that go in to run an organization. He has also to use statistical tools before arriving at a decision. This at times cause an information overload for a manager to take decision. Decision must be rational and based on the available facts and future expectations of the user. Decision is studying various alternatives and selecting the best alternative to the problem. When a decision is taken, a mental appreciation is carried out. It leads to following three questions :

Q. 1. What is my aim/objective/goal ?
Q. 2. What does it involve ?
Q. 3. How far can I plan now ?

Once this exercise is carried out, an individual is generally in a position to take an appropriate decision. Decision must be taken in time and implemented. Studies have been conducted by Taylor et al[3] to see if there is a co-relation between certain characteristics of a decision maker such as age, level of intelligence, experience, aptitude for creativity and level of motivation and such variables as decision accuracy, confidence in the decisions and time spent in studying the problem and reaching the decision.

These studies have shown that biggest unknown and the most mysterious factor is still the decision maker himself. How and why an individual acts is still a mystery.

Factors Affecting Decisions

1. **Information :** Adequate information must be available to the decision maker. Due to computers lot of information may now be available but it is of little consequence. What is important is the amount, quality and the format in which the information is made available to the decision maker. Inadequate information is as dangerous as too much of information.
2. **Bias :** Every individuals' decision is highly affected by value attitudes and beliefs. Individual has preconceived ideas about an issue and accepts what he wants to, and throws away information which is not acceptable by him. Prejudice and bias that may lead to faulty decisions. It is therefore necessary to have an open mind and take decision without any prejudice. Organizational culture plays a decisive role in decision making. If an organization is known for its promptness, honest dealings etc, a manager in such organization would definitely take just and appropriate decisions.

3. **Personal habits :** Some people are rigid and stick to their own decision even if it is wrong. Others blame their subordinates for failure and take credit for successful job. There are individuals who have an external locus of control and blame outside agencies/ situations for their failure for decisions to be effective.
4. **Time constraints :** A problem is identified and a solution is sought within a specified time. As the complexity of impact of external variables, the enhanced time may be required. In the fast moving era it is necessary to carry out time and space appreciation of the problem involved. A rigid time schedule may be necessary that can be followed. There are mangers who can take effective decisions under the pressure of time. However most people under time pressure rely on "Heuristics" approach which means limiting the search for facts and data using the limited information for decision making. Under the above circumstances the quality of decisions are "Workable" rather than "Optimal".
5. **Risk Taking :** Risk is related to various factors. A manager's risk taking attitude is dependant on personal characteristics, organizational culture where risk is rewarded and not penalized for failed decisions, intelligence level and the expectations of the decision maker. High intelligent managers are found to be generally conservative and do not take bold step. People with high expectations are generally highly optimistic and take decisions even with minimum required level of information. Social and cultural influences also play a dominant role on the quality of decisions.

SUMMARY

Perception depends on the attitude of the individual. Individuals differ in the way they see a particular event or observe an object or a situation. Perception is a processes of interpretation of sensory impresions of the enviornment. What one perceives may be different from the objective reality. There are three factors that affects the perception of the individual. These are, 1. ***the perceiver.*** Perception differs from individual to individual based on attitude, motives, interests, experience and the expectations. 2. ***the object.*** Individual has a tendency to group together the items, situations, and people to physical and time proximity. This leads to perceiving the situation in a different form. Objects can be perceived differently based on shape, size, shade, sound, movement and its background. 3. ***the situation.*** Individual behaves differently in different situations. Therefore he should be perceived in the correct fashion. Work setting and social setting play decisive role in perception.Human behaviour is caused due to internal or external factors. These factors are related to ***distinctiveness, consensus and consistency.*** It has been observed that we have a tendency to under estimate the influence of external factors and over estimate the influence of internal factors. This is said to be a fundamental attribution error. Costello, Zalkind and Hamchek have indicaed very close relationship between personality and perception. Common errors while judging others are ***selective perception, halo effect, projection, contrast effect, and steriotyping.*** Individual decision making relates to 'identification of problems, what does it involve to solve the problem and how far one can plan now.' Decision must be taken in time and implemented. Studies have been conducted by Taylor et al to see if there is co-relation between certain characteristics of a decision maker such as age, level of intelligence, experience, aptitude for creativity and level of motivation and such variables as decision accuracy, confidence in the decisions and time spent in studying the problem and reaching the decision. There are various factors that affect decision making. These are availability of informatiom of correct type, personal bias, habits, time available and risk taking ability of a decision maker.

TEXT QUESTIONS

Q. 1 Define perception. What are various factors that affect perception?
Q. 2 Explan Attribution Theory of perception.
Q. 3 Explain fundamental attribution error with suitable example.
Q. 4 How does personality affect individual perception?
Q. 5 What are common errrors that an individual does while judging others?
Q. 6 What are various factors that affect decision making?
Q. 7 What is the relationship between personality factors and perception as proposed by Costello et al.

REFERENCES

1. Robbins Stephen, ***"Organizational Behaviour"***, Ninth Edition, Prentice Hall, New Delhi, 2001.
2. Costello and Zalkind (1962) and Hamacheck (1971).
3. Taylor R.N. and M.D. Dunnette, ***"Relative Contribution of Decision makers attributes to Decision Processes"***, Organizational Behaviour and Human Performance, Vol. 2, 1974 pp 286 – 298)

Case

WHO IS RIGHT

Prof. V. G. Kondalkar*
Dr. Upinder Dhar**

ABOUT THE ORGANIZATION

A high powered Indian delegation had paid a visit to China in the beginning of the sixties and started a green revolution in India based of Chinese experience. Initially, it was related to agriculture later it was extended to forestry and wasteland development also. To ensure the natural balance of flora and fauna, an organization called Ecological Survey of India (ESI) was established in 1964 at the national level and had one centre in each of the states. The locations of the state centers were Udhampur, Chandrapur, Silchar, Pathankot, Hyderabad, Tezpur, Palampur, Cochin, Imphal, Bikaner, Ootcamund, Nainital, Rewa, Gopalpur, Dehradun, Jamnagar, Shillong, Chhindwada and Guwahati.

ESI had its headquarters at Shimla in Himachal Pradesh and controlled all the state centers in the country directly. The major functions of ESI were related to field work. The staff had to identify wasteland, plan for its development, plant tress, and shrubs, and sand

* Professor, VNS Institute of Management, Bhopal.
** Director, Prestige Institute of Management and Research, Indore.

stabilization plants in the desert of Rajasthan and pine, fur, deodars in the higher ridges of J & K, himachal Pradesh and in the Eastern States. Since it was a speacility work, the staff had to be selected, trained and posted to various state centers centrally by ESI. ESI had 1000 officers of various grades. 10,000 supervisors in various categories and approximately 50000 field staff. The field staff was divided into various categories like agriculture assistants, surveyors, draftsmen, planters, field guards, clerks, drivers and other administrative staff like cooks, barbers, washmen etc. the requirement for enrolment of staff was projected by state centers to ESI on a yearly basis and ESI took action by advertising the requirement in national dailies.

Training Institutes

ESI during its development had established institutes to train various categories of staff. The Agriculture Engineering Institute which was located at Shillong was training employees who were sent by ESI after selection and recruitment. The Driving and Maintenance Institute which was located at Trivandrum trained drivers in driving various types of vehicles and mechanical plants and were also supposed to carry our basic maintenance of such vehicles and plants on the spot as moving of these vehicles and plants from remote areas was neither economical nor practical. The Clerks and Computer software Institute was located at Nagpur and trained a raw individual into a full fledged clerk. The training period for them was of 14 months. During the period an individual selected as a clerk was to have a typewriting skill of 40 words per minute, and had to be physically tough to be able to sustain in the mountainous terrain that prevaild in Ladakh region of Jammu & Kashmir in the North and Arunachal Pradesh in the East.

CLERKS AND COMPUTER SOFTWARE INSTITUTE

The Institute had a capacity to train 2000 individuals at any one time. It also conducted head clerks, office supervisors and PA's modular courses ranging from three month to six months duration. These courses had proved to be an asset to the organization. The training institute was headed by the director from within the ESI cadre of officers and had teaching staff of ESI which reverted back to field work after completion of the tenure.

FUNCTIONS

Each of the state centers had self- sufficient sub-centers spread over in the state where ecological work had to be undertaken. Each centre generally had 7 to 8 projects going on at any given time. Each project took about five years after it was launched. The staff once posted to any of the sub-centers was dedicated and was not transferred except on extreme compassionate grounds. All the staff had to be physically fit, mentally robust and psychologically sound to sustain the hostile climatic conditions that prevailed in the areas of work. Officers, supervisors and class IV staff had to stay in a temporarily erected camp or close to the site of project, generally away from habitation. Project camps in central Indian states were close to a city/ town and therefore, the families could stay with them on a permanent basis, subject to transfer.

Review

A systematic procedure existed at ESI to review the work of each of the sub-centers and training institutes on a yearly as well as five yearly basis as net outcome was only possible once the project was complete. However, for training institutes, the yearly review was in vogue. In the review of the training institutes conducted in the year 1988, the Review committee of ESI recommended that the Clerks and Software Institute, Nagpur should be closed down as it was proving to be a "White elephant". The recommendations were based on Pran Kishore, director general's personal views, who was of the opinion that "Teeth to Tail" ratio be reduced and that the training of clerks and computer software programmers, etc. could be conveniently undertaken by state centers under direct control of state centre directors who would train within their own recourses before being posted to sub-centers/ project locations. To facilitate initial training he agreed to pool some training staff of the institute to various state centers against the field vacancy. He further appreciated that the saving so accrued could be fruitfully utilized in the main project work. The views of the Director General prevailed and closure of the institute was ordered in the year 1990. On the above analogy, the Driving and Maintenance Institute, Trivandrum was ordered to be closed the following year.

Process of Closure

The process of closure took about six months. All typewriter machines, training material, furniture, vehicles, and administrative staff had to be sub-allotted to various state centers on the approval of the director general, ESI. The work of closure was smooth but painful because an institute which had proved its excellence in training and the staff that had graduated from the institute stood the test of time in varied areas with different climatic conditions. Pran Kishore retired and Chaman Lal took over as Director General, ESI in 1990. He stalled the decisions of closure of the driving and maintenance institute, Trivandrum as he felt that vehicle and plant drivers if recruited from the mainstream of the country would not be able to undertake work for a prolonged period of time in hostile terrain and climatic conditions.

Aftermath

The closure of the Clerks and Computer Software Institute at Nagpur by the previous Director General, ESI was a topic of discussion during the dinner hosted by the state unit of ESI. Most of the officers of ESI felt that off late they had noted with concern the decline in quality of staff work in various state centers. Office procedures had declined and compilation of current work had accumulated making it difficult to retrieve the old data. There had been a lack of administrative staff support. Reports and returns were not being forwarded to ESI HQ regularly. Some of the officers felt that the situation was likely to worsen further.

QUESTION FOR DISCUSSION

Q. 1 Discuss the decision making process adopted by the two senior executives in this case.

Q. 2 Who is right? Support your answer with relevant arguments.

Q. 3 What should be the next decision of chaman lal? Should the Clerks and Software Institute Nagpur be reopened?

Part Three

Group Dynamics

CHAPTER 9

Interpersonal Behaviour (Transactional Analysis)

INTRODUCTION TO TRANSACTION ANALYSIS (TA)

Study of human behaviour is very complex. Human behaviour is affected by behaviour of others. It is based on basic psychological facts like perception, learning, motivation and personality of the individuals interacting with each other. Interpersonal behaviour could be **mutually cooperative** where complementary transactions take place, such behaviour is possible where there is mutual trust, respect for each other's view point and ideas, concern for each other's needs and when both have a complementary ego state. Such behaviours are mutually gratifying to each other. On the other hand, interpersonal behaviours can be **conflicting.** Reasons for such behaviour can be attributed to personality differences, different value system, and conflict of interest and last but not the least role ambiguity between the two individuals.

Transactional analysis is the study of individual in the organization when he is interacting with other individual on social front or professional front. Eric Berne is credited to the movement for psychotherapy, which he started in 1950s. He observed that there are several persons within one person and therefore an individual transacts in different ways with different persons in different situations. People spend considerable time interacting with each other. They transact in a way that may provide connecting tissues between two individuals, which may hold them to-gether. This type of pair relationship is called **Dyadic relationship**. Transactional analysis offers a mode of expression of personality and dynamics of self and its relationship with others. It is a method of analyzing and understanding inter personal behaviour. Transactional analysis involves the analysis of the following factors:-

(*a*) Study of awareness
(*b*) Ego State
(*c*) Analysis of transactions
(*d*) Life Script
(*e*) Psychological games
(*f*) Study of life positions

(*g*) Stroking
(*h*) Games analysis

Definitions

"Transactional analysis is a technique used to help people better understand their own and other's behaviour, especially in interpersonal relationship."

Johari Window

Joseph Luft and Harrington Ingham have developed a model to look at one's personality that can be known and unknown to self and known and unknown to others. The concept known as Johari Window is shown in Figure 9.1 below. It is a technique to analyze and improve interpersonal - Transaction.

	Information known to self	Information not known to self
Information known to others	1 Open Self (Public Area)	2 Blind Self (Blind Area)
Information not known to others	3 Hidden Self (Private Area)	4 Unknown Self (Dark Area)

Fig. 9.1. Johari Window

The above figure indicates that there are four parts (**self**) in all of us that has been indicated by four quadrants. These are explained below:

(*a*) **Open Self:** Open Self is known as **Public area**. This quadrant indicates information about self is known to oneself and also to others. The information relates to feelings, motivation and behaviour of an individual, which he is willing to share with those whom he comes in contact. The individual behaves in a straight forward manner and is sharing. In an organizational setting, because of the openness of the individual the chances of conflict are reduced to minimum.

(*b*) **Blind Self:** This quadrant is related to information is not known to self but known to others, who interact with you, know more about you. This is known as blind area. It is important that an individual should reduce blind area to the minimum by interacting with people more intimately and by asking questions about self. For example, an individual may not be aware of the fact that he is extremely task oriented and employees do not like it. In other words, others know and perceive the individual as a hard taskmaster and dislike him because of this. This is blind area that a person is blind to the fact that he interacts with others in the professional manner. This situation is likely to create an unpleasant atmosphere in the organization. Individual therefore should reduce blind area and increase public area. This will reduce conflict situations to a great extent in interpersonal behaviour.

(*c*) **Hidden Self:** Certain aspect of personality has formed this quadrant. Self knows information but others do not know it. There are certain aspects, which are private. Individual therefore does not want to share it with subordinates and wants to keep hidden. The area is also called **Private Area.**

(*d*) **Unknown Self:** This area is characterized by facts unknown to the self and to others. This is dark area, which is not pregnable. There is nothing much that can be done about it. It should be an endeavor to improve upon one self by obtaining feed back from others about self. Individual should carry out improvement and perceive one self correctly so that one perceives each person in the right manner. There are certain factors to improve Interpersonal relations. (Public Area).

Development of Inter-personal Relationship

(*a*) **Develop positive attitude:** We have already studied attitude, perception and values and its relationship towards accomplishment of given task. It should be an endeavour of every manager to look at the individuals, situations from positive point of view and remove distortion if any in a particular situation. Personal bias is dangerous and acts as bloc in improving relationship. If a manager is unbiased, have positive feeling towards his subordinates, advices them when in trouble and supports them in day-to-day functioning will develop a positive feeling about the workers, which will reduce blind area and convert it in to public area. This will bring an excellent work environment in the organization.

(*b*) **Be Empathetic:** Manager must look at from the employees' point of view. He should be able to identify subordinates need pattern and try and fulfill them. He should display high degree of sensitivity towards the subordinates and rise above the personal interest for the well being of employees.

(*c*) **Improve Self Concept**: Every individual must improve his self-image. This is possible when work is assigned to an individual based on his skills, aptitude, experience, knowledge and qualification. In case there is distortion between the individual's expectations and job requirement, a person is bound to develop frustration that would lead to the feeling of inadequacy (for a highly skilled person). In this situation a job rotation or even change of organization is recommenced. This will bring to him new challenges, and have a greater degree of freedom of action and job satisfaction that will lead to increased degree of self-concept. In nutshell, self-concept is achieved by achieving an ideal fit between individual competency and job requirement.

(*d*) **Communication**: Communication is an important factor in developing an ideal interpersonal relationship. All barriers of communication should be removed. Managers should conduct themselves in such a manner that the subordinates feel that the former is approachable. One must also be a good listener. Mis-perception should not be allowed to set in for want of communication. Subordinates should be kept posted about the latest happing in an organization so that they are prevented from imagining the situation that may distort perception. In the organization vertical, horizontal, diagonal communication be permitted. Formation of social clubs should be encouraged.

(*e*) **Perception errors:** Common perceptual errors like stereotyping, halo effect, selective perception, attribution errors and distortion should be avoided. Managers must be able to lend credence to what they preach by practicing. This will enhance their image in an organization.

(*f*) **Culture:** Development of organization culture emanates from top level. Work ethics, value based practices must be rewarded. Development of culture is a continuous process, which is unending. For short-term gains compromise on ethical practices will doom the best of the organizations.

PRINCIPLES OF CHANGES IN AWARENESS

Awareness in self is not static and subject to change. Quadrant to which Psychological state (information known to self and information known to others) is assigned also changes. Joneward has assigned eleven principles of such change.

1. Change in one quadrant will affect change in other quadrant and hence the changes in interpersonal behaviour can be noticed.
2. It takes energy to hide, deny or be blind to behaviour.
3. Threat tends to decrease awareness while mutual trust increases awareness.
4. Forced awareness (exposure) is undesirable and usually ineffective.
5. Interpersonal learning means a change has taken place. Therefore when one quadrant enlarges the other becomes smaller.
6. A large enough area of free activity, more resources and skill facilitates working with others.
7. If No 1 quadrant is smaller it is indicative of the poor communication.
8. There is universal curiosity about the unknown area due to customs, social training and diverse fears.
9. Sensitivity means appreciating the covert aspect of behaviours in quadrant numbers 2, 3 and 4, and desire of others to keep them so.
10. Learning about group processes help to increase awareness. It will increase quadrant number 1 for both group and individuals.
11. Value system of a group and its members may be observed in the way the group deals with unknown in the life of group itself.

EGO STATE

Study of ego state is an important part of transactional analysis, it explains psychological behaviour pattern of an individual. Study of ego state is related to the way an individual thinks, his feelings and subsequent behaviour. People interact with each other in terms of psychological positions of behaviour known as ego state. **Sigmund Freud** was the first to advocate that in every individual there are three ego states residing within him i.e. parent ego, adult ego and child ego. They stimulate, monitor and control individual behaviour. The ego state is not related to the age of an individual. He further states that a person can change ego state depending upon situation and modify his behaviour. **Berne** states, "Although we cannot directly observe these ego states, we can observe behaviour of an individual and can infer which of the three ego states an individual is transacting at a particular moment". Let us study these ego states.

Parent Ego

Parent Ego refers to the personality attributes like value, attitude and behaviour of parent like people, inherited by a person when he was child. This behavioural pattern becomes basics for behaviour as individual copy parent figures like teacher, father, mother, brother or any other person who is elderly and displays an advisory behaviour, which is copied by a child and subsequently displayed in his lifetime when such situations arise. Parent ego can be of two types.

(a) Nurturing parents

Nurturing parent ego is characterized by over protectiveness, helpful, distant, dogmatic, indispensable and upright parent behaviour. When such behaviour is displayed to a child, he inherits the same pattern of behaviour.

(b) Critical parents

Critical parents ego state is characterized with the behaviour, which is hurtful, waging finger at the other and conveys displeasures. The behaviour is strict which usually quotes rules, laws and has great reliance on successful people.

Adult Ego

Adult Ego is based on reasoning, seeking from subordinates and providing information. A person having adult ego views people equal, worthy of undertaking any job and responsible. They behave rationally and think logically. Physical signs can identify their behaviour, which displays controlling type. People with adult ego, verify their behaviour and update their parent and child ego continuously. They block parent and child ego state based on experience. The person updates data to determine what is valid thus he controls emotional expression. Adult ego is considered to be valid ego state comparatively.

Child Ego

Child ego state is inner feelings, experience and adaptation. Person having child ego generally displays creativity in his action. He conforms to the situation and people who interact with him and displays anxiety, depression, dependence, fear and hate. Child ego can be perceived by observing an individual who displays physical signs like silent compliance, attention seeker in certain situations he displays temper, tantrums, giggling and coyness. The individual thinks non-logical and wants immediate action on various issues. Such behaviour is formed unto 5 years of age by accepting inputs of behaviour of various individuals around in childhood days. Child gets a social birth and inherits various patterns within the child ego state. These are:-

(a) Natural Child

Natural child generally displays following behavioural pattern

- Affectionate
- Does what come in the way
- Fearful
- Self-indulgent
- Self-centered

- Aggressive

(b) Adaptive child

Adaptive child is psychologically trained in obeying instructions from parents though not to his liking and does whatever because parents insist to do so. It has the tendency to get involved in NOT OK transaction. Rebellion, frustration becomes part of his personality.

(c) The little professor

The little professor is intuitive, creative and manipulative. He believes in magic and uses this ego state with adult ego state and achieves good interpersonal relationship. He responds to non-verbal communication and play hunches. He is imaginative.

ANALYSIS OF TRANSACTIONS

One of the barriers of communication is crossed transaction. TA is a technique for examining the nature of interpersonal communication between the two individuals and to analyse its effectiveness. Every piece of conversation is treated as a transaction. For example when A talks to X it is one transaction and when X replies to A it is another. Each transaction of an individual emanates from parents ego, adult ego or child ego state. As stated earlier, parent ego state (P) is authoritarian, the adult ego state (A) is rational and logical in approach and lastly the child ego state (C) is impulsive. Every person transacts from all the three ego states but each one of us has one ego state as dominant. Transaction is effective when stimulus and response is from the same ego state and the complementary in nature. Crossed transactions create conflict and problems for interpersonal behaviour. Let us study patterns of complementary transaction.

(a) Complementary Transaction

Complementary transactions are those communications where stimulus and response (S—R) is from identical ego state. Message from one person gets almost predicted response and the transaction is parallel. There are nine such complementary transactions:-

(i) Adult – Adult Transaction

Both individuals are transacting from adult ego state. The stimulus and response are based on logical thinking and rationale. This type of communication is considered most ideal in any organization. There is least chance of conflict among the workers. See figures below:

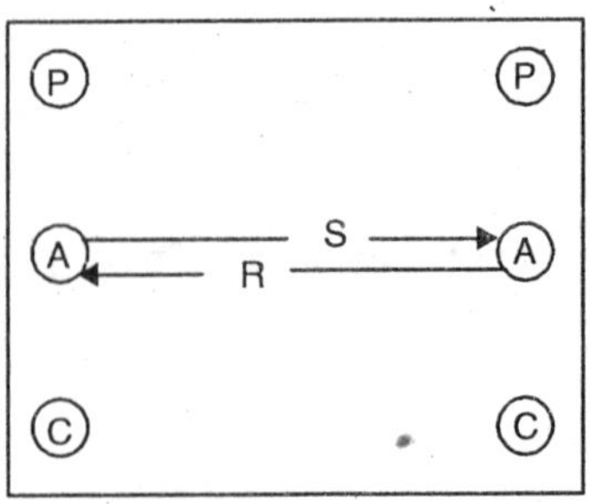

Adult – Adult Transaction

(ii) Adult – Parent Transaction

In adult – parent ego state, manager speaks from adult ego state which is rational and backed by rules and regulations while the employees speak from the parent ego state which is authorization, is not likely to smooth in the long run. Parent ego state (workers) will try to control and dominate the manager. The employees may develop hostile attitude towards the boss. See figure below:

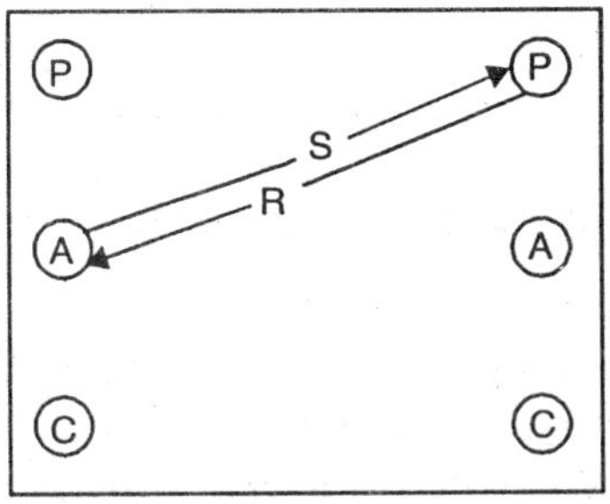

Adult – parent Transactions

(iii) Adult – Child Transactions: Adult-child ego transactions are shown below:

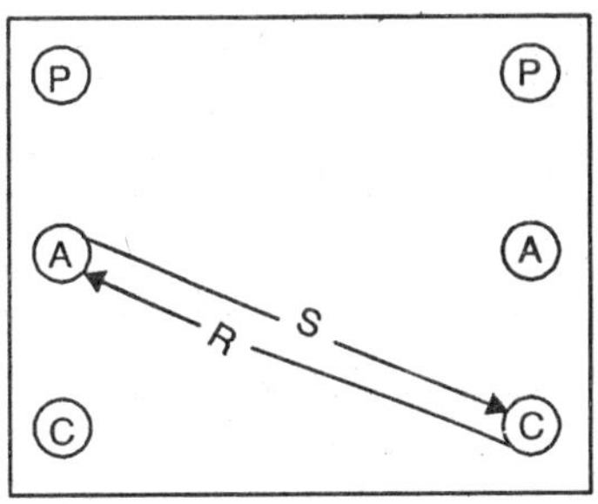

Adult – Child ego state Transactions

This type of transaction is effective if child ego is of little professor category where employees can work with certain amount of creativity. Manager in this type of situation has to keep guiding and tolerating childlike behaviour of employees which is characterized by loose control, and lot of fun and enjoyment, which is not productive for the organization.

(iv) Parent – Parents transactions

Parent ego state is characterized by admonitions, rewards, and work by rule, praise and punishment. If both i.e., the manager and employees have the above characteristics of ego state, the stimuli and response will be dominating from either side. While manager would put forward his ideas, the employees would reject it and put up a fresh idea and would want to be accepted by the manager. Manager will have to take up a nurturing parent attitude for transaction to be fruitful and thus have a productive communication. See figure below:

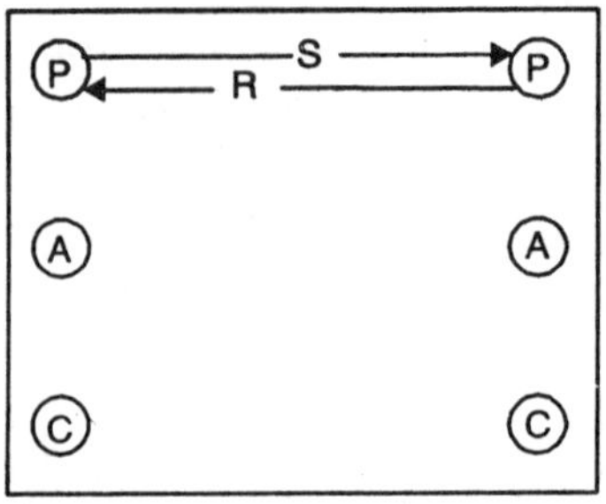

Parents – parent ego state Transaction

(v) Parent – Adult ego state

The boss is transacting from parent ego while he subordinate is responding from adult ego state. Such type of relationship may not last long. Employees rational and logical thinking will be marred by parent ego state, which may diminish good working relationship of the two parties. One will have to switch over to the corresponding ego state. See figure below:

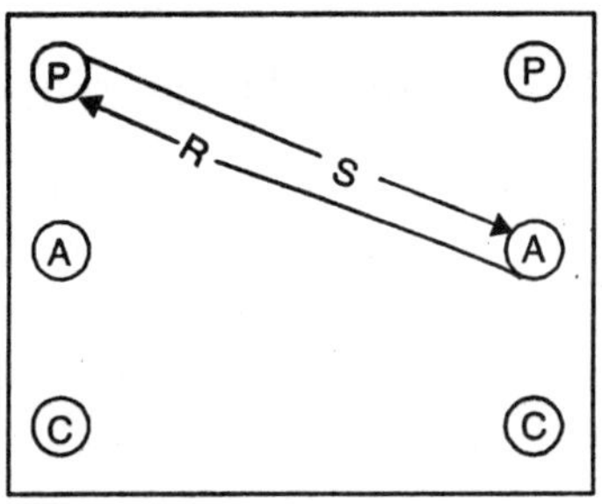

Parent – Adult ego state

(vi) Parent – Child ego state

This transaction is workable in the organization where the manager will get the work done from subordinates by advising, guiding, and by assigning rewards for good work and punishment for non-performance. The subordinates (Child ego) will listen to manager and look forward for advice, guidance, and assistance at each stage of production cycle. Manager may get frustration because he may develop the feeling that he is controlling an inefficient work force. See figure below:

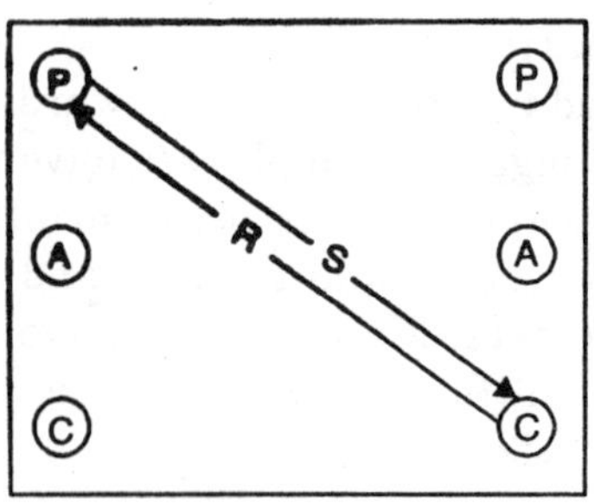

Parent – Child ego Transaction

(vii) Child – Parent ego state

This is not a very effective style of communication whose manager has a child ego state and employee's parent ego state. In such situation employees would control the manager. The latter would always perceive employees as threat and look forward for their advice from time to time. It will be lassie-faire type of command. Instances of manager being ridiculed and talked about loosely by subordinates will be a common phenomenon. See figure below:

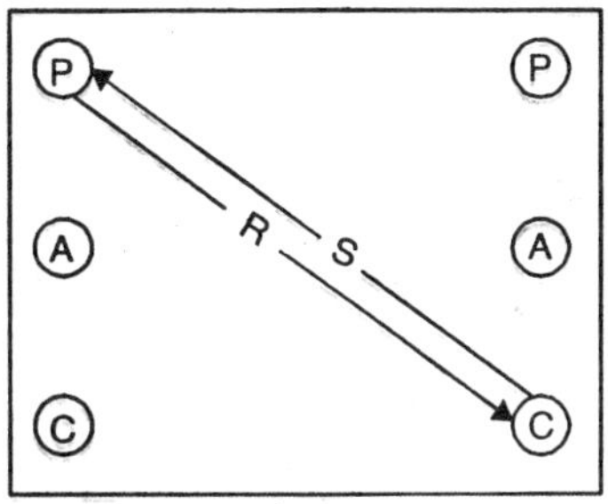

Child – parent ego state

(viii) Child – Adult ego state Transactions

When manager acts from child ego, there will be poor decisions based on whims and fancies and emotions. This will pose a problem for employees who want to work rationally. Unless the ego state of the manager is changed, this is going to be problem in the organization. No growth can be expected with child ego manager at the helms of affairs. See figure below:

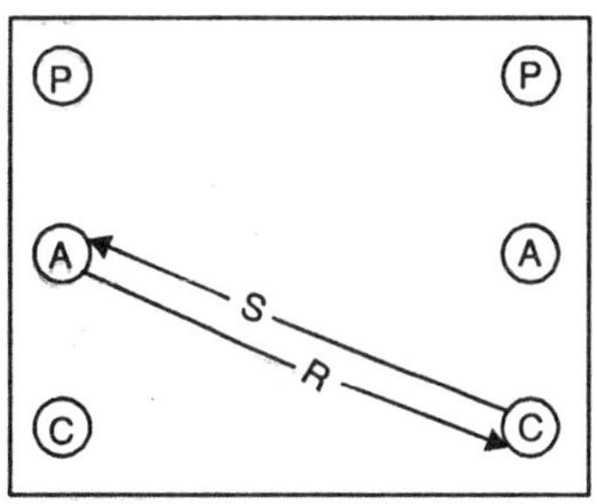

Child – Adult ego state Transactions

(ix) Child – Child ego state

Such transaction is not good for the organization. This organization even can be called as leaderless. Manager with child ego dominant is more of a liability to the organization. Performance of the organization will be poor, no growth, no new ideas, and lithargy will prevail in the system. In such situation, the manager should be replaced. See figure below:

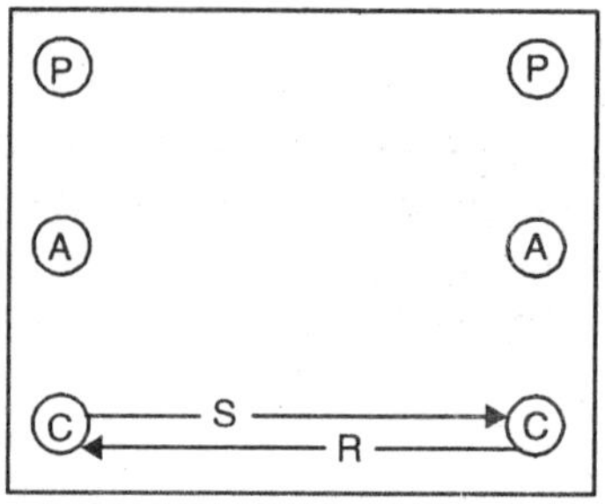

Child – Child ego state transaction.

Non-Complimentary Transactions

Non-Complimentary transactions are those transactions which a sender sends the message on the basis of his ego state, but the response is from an uncompatible ego state on the part of receiver. Such behaviour occur when stimulus and response is not parallel. Following figure depicts non-complimentary transaction.

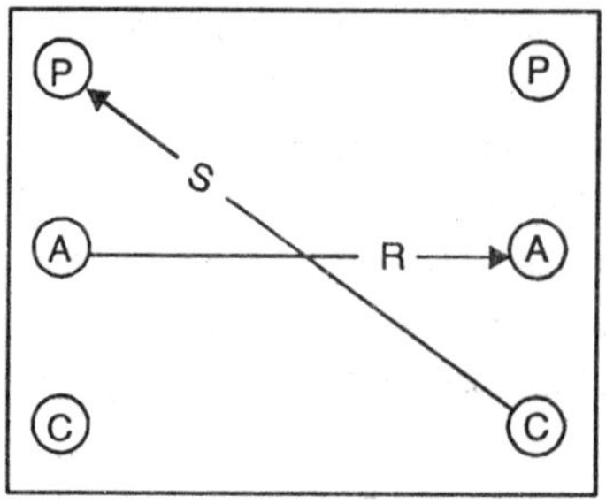

Non-Complementary Transaction

(c) Ulterior Transactions

Ulterior transactions are most complex transactions because if involves more than two egos states working at the same time with double meaning in the stimulus. This type of transaction is very common i.e. diplomatic circles when you say something but mean the other. For example read the following newspaper reports. "Newly appointed Pakistani Ambassador to UN, Mr. Munir Akram said "India would have license to kill' (Pakistani) if Pakistani relied only on its non-nuclear firepower. If India reserves the right to use conventional weapons (because of no first use of nuclear weapons) how can Pakistan – a weaker power – be expected to rule out all means of deterrence"? In the above message, Pak Ambassador is speaking to India from child – parent ego state when he says Pak is a weaker power but at the same time conveys (from Adult to Adult ego state) that she reserves the right of using nuclear weapon (all means of deterrence) this type of communication where ulterior meaning is different are dangerous and should be avoided as they are not desirable for better relationship and understanding.

LIFE SCRIPT

Script is a text of play motion picture, TV serial or a radio programme. Life of a person is compared with the play or motion picture or a Radio programme. Because human being's life script emerges out of the role he plays all his life and life is quasi- programmed. In transactional analysis the script is compared with life span. Every person writes his or her own script right from childhood under the personal influence and form attitude, behaviour pattern that does not change with age. Whatever has been learnt in the childhood is enacted by all of us all our life as if we are enacting a play on the stage of life. If you have been told not to speak lie by your parents, you would not like a person to speak lie and in turn you will teach your children "Not to lie". If you have been told in childhood that one must not butt in when two people are speaking, you would also practice and preach the same in life what one is doing is what one has learnt. One is repeating (enacting) the script of what has been learnt. Berne states that life script is a complete plan of living. He further states that the script is full of offering based on structures of injections, prescriptions for various situations as to how one should behave and permissions. In the process, the person is either successful called **winner** or unsuccessful called **loser**. Winner programming (of script) is more adaptive because the person with above life script enjoys more autonomy in his dealings, while the loser has strong injunctions and inner demon who disturbs the whole life plan and therefore a person does not succeed in life. Joneward has gone further and stated that every person plays a drama on public stage and private stage in life. She further states that life script resembles as a script of drama whose characters, dialogues, actions, scenes and themes is learned in life and enacted as drama/play culminating towards a climax and ends in final curtain. Life script is nothing but a formation of personality in early stage and its display in life span that has a great impact on how a person transact with other person. If he is winner, the organization where he is employed will achieve growth and display positive outlook in all his dealings. If one has a looser script, he will behave negatively, be critical and may bring negative growth to the organization. It is therefore necessary to know about a person, his childhood, environment, society he comes from, schooling, habits, likes and dislikes so that one knows, though partly about the life script of a person on being employed. Mc Clelland states that stories read or heard by children and movies seen have an impact. When a child reads or hears stories based on successful leaders, the reader turns out to be achiever in life. If the stories of risks are read or told to children they turn out to be power-oriented leaders.

LIFE POSITIONS

Child develops life philosophy by experience. As child grows he tries to develop philosophy for itself based on self-identity, sense of worth and an ability to perceive people in the right sense. Harris identified life positions where individual knows about himself and the perception of people about him. Transactional analysis constructs the following four life positions.

(*a*) I am Okay you are Okay.
(*b*) I am Okay you are not Okay.
(*c*) I am not Okay you are Okay.
(*d*) I am not Okay you are not Okay

For above analysis see figure 10.2.
Let us discuss the above four life positions.

1. I am Okay your Okay (C)

This is an ideal life position because this position is rationally chosen one. In this position individual behaves rationally and accept significance of others. People feel happy and life is worth living. Individual with this life position expresses confidence in his subordinates, work with high level of delegatation of authority, and believes in give and take. Manages enjoys good communication network, work with confidence and there is work sharing and positive attitude towards work. People remain happy and have high level of job satisfaction. People work with adult ego state. There is no conflict situation and there is total understanding among subordinates and peer group. An Ideal life position.

	I am NOT OK	I am OK
You are NOT OK	A Avoidant/Averse	B Bossing
You are OK	D Difficult	C Competent/Confident/ Creative

Fig. 9.2. Life positions

2. I am Okay, you are not okay (B)

This is distrustful psychological life position taken by individual who feel that others are wrong. They blame others for their failure. People who have been neglected by parents in their childhood take this position. They generally operate from rebellion child ego state that feel victimized and blame others for their miseries. Mangers lack trust, confidence in the intellectual level, skills and talent in their subordinates and do not believe in delegation of authority. They perceive delegation as threat to their personal existence. Managers are critical, oppressive and point out flaws in the working of subordinates. They operate from critical parent ego state and rarely give positive remarks. They feel their workers lazy, irresponsible and find them as stated in theory X of Mc Gregor. Expresses bossing attitude.

3. I am not okay, you are okay (D)

This life position is common to persons who feel powerless in comparison to others. Persons in this life position always grumble and feel at the mercy of others. They have tendency to withdraw and at times experience depression that may lead to suicide in extreme cases. People with this life position operate from child ego state. Managers tend to give and receive bad feelings. They are unpredictable and display erratic behaviours. It is not a good life position. People are diffident in this life position.

4. I am not okay, you are not okay (A)

This is the worst life position in which individual feel defeated and sees whole world as miserable. It is a desperate life position where people loose interest in living. In extreme cases people commit suicide or homicide. This position is caused due to children having brought up by servants and very scant or no attention having been paid by the parents. At managerial level, no decision is taken in time and managers make mistakes. They at times provoke others in the negative direction and display a lack of personal potency. Manager with this position look to others for final decision and often delegate in-appropriately.

On analysis, it is seen that everybody has elements of various life position. But one of the four-life positions is dominant. **"I am okay your are okay"** is the best life position All- individual must try and modify life position in various situations. **Adult – adult transaction from the above life position and positive life script will make an outstanding manager.**

STROKING

Stroking is an important aspect of transactional analysis. Stroking is an act of implying recognition to other person. Stroking is recognition that a person gives to his subordinates for good work done or even bad work done. Lack of stroking has an adverse psychological and physiological effect on individual.

Stroking is a basic unit of motivation that can be seen from the following

(*a*) The quantity and the quality of strokes serve as either positive or negative motivation for employees.

(*b*) Good share of psychological satisfaction we get from work is from strokes available from other persons.

(*c*) We get strokes from the work itself.

There are positive and negative strokes. Positive strokes are recognition, pat on the back and affection shown by superiors, who make subordinate feel okay. It is the recognition of the work that employees get boost to do even better. Negative strokes on the other hand are the feeling "you are not okay" conveyed by superiors by way of criticism, hating and by scolding for the job not done well. It serves as negative encouragement and a feeling of failure is created among the workers. Negative strokes received by individual also serves as positive strokes because an individual who has done a mistake expects a negative stroke from his boss, so that mental tension is relieved and a social equilibrium is achieved in the relationship. When the work is challenging, the worker gets an ultimate satisfaction from the work itself that serves as a motivator. It is therefore necessary that managers/supervisors assign to their subordinates the work, which, in itself is rich and has a motivational value. Positive strokes must be used as frequently as possible.

PSYCHOLOGICAL GAMES

Psychological games are set of transaction, which has following characteristics:-

(*a*) Transactions are repetitive

(*b*) Transactions tend to make sense on superficial or social level.

(*c*) One or more transaction has ulterior value.

The set of transactions, which has negative pay offs, prevent people/organizations becoming winners. Psychological games are played by individuals to fill up time, provoke attention and re-enforce early opinion about self and others to fulfill a sense of destiny. Psychological games are not good as they prevent open, warm and intimate relationship. These must be discouraged. Joneward has suggested the following steps:

(*a*) Avoidance of complementary hand.
(*b*) Avoidance of victim role
(*c*) Avoid putting other people down.
(*d*) Avoidance of putting one-self down.
(*e*) Practice giving positive strokes in all transactions and avoidance of negative strokes.
(*f*) Investing more of life's time in activities of intimacy.
(*g*) Leveling of thinking with others.

BENEFITS OF TRANSACTIONAL ANALYSIS

1. In this chapter we have studied awareness improvement, ego state, and analysis of transactions, script analysis, life positions, Psychological games and stroking. These are all psychological factors that must be applied intelligently in working environment so that performance of each element is positive and contribute to better understanding. Some of the benefits of TA are given below

(a) Development of positive thinking

Transaction analysis brings positive feelings in the individual, which has remarkable impact on attitude change

Present states	**Transformation**
Confusion	Clear thinking
Defect	Victory
Fear	Courage, achievement
Frustration	Gratification
Loneliness	Feeling of togetherness
Pessimism	Optimism
Suppression	Friendship

(b) Interpersonal effectiveness

Transactional analysis improves:

- Interpersonal relationship
- Understanding of ego state
- Better Communication
- Problem solving

(c) Motivation

Transactional analysis is basically applied to improve motivation of employees. When applied, it satisfies the human needs. Enrichment of job is achieved by helping fellow workers thereby achieving intrinsic value. It helps to change management style from theory X to Theory Y whose transformation takes place from parent – Child relationship to transaction involving adult – adult relationship, from "I am Okay, you are not okay to I am Okay – You are okay life positions.

(d) Organisational development

Organization development refers to development of humanistic value system in the organization. Joneward has recommended that TA plays an effective role in the following area:-

(*i*) Maintaining adult – adult transactions.
(*ii*) To give an okay to natural child.
(*iii*) To identify and avoid crossed transactions.
(*iv*) To minimize destructive game playing.
(*v*) To maximize and development of various support systems and policy and improvement of work environment.
(*vi*) In transaction analysis, leadership theory propagated by Blake and Mouton can be fruitfully practiced. Manager who works from 9:1 position actually behaves from parent to child ego state, 1:9 acts from child to parent ego state and, 9:9 position is nothing but managers working from adult ego state. These ego states can be modified based on the situation and ability of subordinates.

SUMMARY

Transaction analysis is a study of human behaviour. It is based on basic psychological factors. Interpersonal behaviour could be mutually gratifying or conflicting. This will depend upon the awareness about each others needs, ego state, life script the individual possesses and formation of personality in the childhood. Transaction analysis is therefore a technique to help people better understand others' behaviour. Joseph Luft and Harry Ingham have developed a model of interpersonal relationship, which is commonly known as **Johari Window**. The model is based on two factors i.e. information known to self and not known to self, and information known to others and not known to others, about each other (transacting parties). Based on the above parameters four quadrants are formed. Quadrant one is open self that is also known as public area where information is known to each other and therefore a gratifying transactions take place. Quadrant two is known as Blind self, Quadrant three Hidden self and Quadrant four as Unknown self, where the transactions may not be gratifying and conflict may take place. It is therefore necessary to enlarge Open-self-quadrant. Larger the area of quadrant one, better the inter-personal communication. One should develop positive attitude, be empathetic, improve self-concept and improve communication skills to be able to improve transaction.

Ego state is an important part of transactional analysis. It explains psychological behaviour pattern of individual. Sigmund Freud, in his study on ego state has stated that every individual has three ego states within him. These are parent ego state, adult ego state and child ego state. Within the parent ego state, there could be nurturing parents and critical parents. In child ego state there could be natural child, adaptive child and little professor. Every person transacts from dominant ego state. Transaction may vary from situation to situation. Basically, transactions are of three types, one, the complimentary transaction, two, crossed transaction and three, ulterior transactions. One must try and always involve into complimentary transaction that is smooth, likeable and free of any conflict. While crossed and ulterior transaction is not recommended as it is conflicting and does not improve organizational functioning.

Life Script is inheritance of what one has seen, heard and experienced in childhood. Formation of personality is complete in five years of age. Mc Clelland states that human life is like a script one writes in early days. Human being only enacts it repeatedly in the lifetime. If one has heard the stories of bravery; a child turns out to be brave. If one has heard the stories of successful leaders, a person in all probability will be an achiever. A person writes his life script right from the childhood under the influence of parents and form attitude and behavioural pattern, which does not change with age.

Harris in his studies identified four life positions where individual knows about himself and the perception of others about him. These are, **one** I am okay you are okay, **two** I am okay you are not okay, **three** I am not okay you are okay and **four** I am not okay you are not okay. Everybody has elements of all the four life positions, but one of the four life positions is dominant. I am okay you are okay is the best life position. All individuals must modify life position in various situations. Adult –adult transaction from above life position with a positive life script will make an outstanding personality.

Stroking is an act of recognition given to a person for good work done. It is an encouragement given by superior to his subordinates. Stroking can be positive or negative. Individual even gets stroke from work itself when work is challenging and he is able to complete the same.

Psychological games are a set of negative transactions that have negative payoffs. Psychological games are not good as they prevent open, warm and intimate relationship.

Transactional analysis has following benefits:

(*a*) It helps in development of positive attitude.

(*b*) It assists transformation of individual status.

(*c*) Transactional analysis improves interpersonal relationship, understanding of others ego state and helps in problem solving. It motivates individuals.

(*d*) Transactional analysis is a tool for organizational development.

TEXT QUESTIONS

Q. 1 "Transaction analysis offers a mode of expression of personality and dynamics of self and its relationship with others". Explain the above statement.

Q. 2 Explain Johari Window. How can the awareness be improved? Explain with suitable diagram.

Q. 3 What are various methods to improve interpersonal transactions?

Q. 4 What are various ego states? Explain complimentary transactions.

Q. 5 Explain crossed (non complimentary) transactions with the help of diagram.

Q. 6 What is ulterior transactions? Please quote an incidence of such transaction you have known in the recent past.

Q. 7 What do you understand by life script? How would you ensure that children form a winner personality?

Q. 8 Explain various life positions, explain the model of Harris - I am okay, you are okay.

Q. 9 Write short notes on the following:

(*a*) Stroking

(*b*) Psychological games

(*c*) Benefits of transactional analysis

(*d*) Ulterior transactions

(*e*) Little professor

CHAPTER 10

Foundation of Group Behaviour

INTRODUCTION

When we study management, we carryout planning for the organization. One of the most important elements of planning is to set objectives depending upon the resources available. The organizational objectives are later categorized into departmental objectives and group objectives. What we have done in the process is division of work. To accomplish the organizational objective, each group has to accomplish its group objective so that a "whole" can be achieved by co-ordinating various activities of groups. It is therefore division of work and coordination, that provides synergy to the organization. Let us take an example of automobile industry for which the yearly target is producing 10,000 cars. The engine department has to produce 10,000 engines, body manufacturing department has to make 10,000 car bodies. chassis manufacting department have to make equal number of chassis. This work is also divided into monthly, weekly and daily basis and further broken down to group levels. It is therefore important that at lower level, the accomplishment of group objective will contribute towards achievement of organizational objectives. If there is lack of coordination of various group activities, an end product can not be attained and the organizational goals can not be effectively achieved. Thus as Uma Sekaran[1] has stated that "the synergy is a function of both division of labour and coordination of activities in organizations since group provide synergy through specialization and coordination, they are integral to the organizations functioning. There are socio psychological factors which come into play when a particular work is undertaken by the group. Personal objectives or interest have to be kept aside for the over all group objectives."

Understanding Group

A work group is collection of two or more individuals, working for a common goal and are interdependent.They interact significantly to achieve a group objective. For a manager it is difficult to manage group because of varied nature, personality traits, attitude of individuals and personal interest in the group job the group members display. It is therefore important for managers to understand group member behaviour and deal effectively with the group because of the synergy they provide. Manager should be able to achieve not only group objective but should be able to fulfill individual objectives within the overall organizational frame work.

Group members should be able to achieve greater (volume and quality) than the sum total of individual contribution. This is achieved by joint idea generation, finding out various courses open, and selecting and implementing the best course of action. Because of the joint efforts of the group, it possible to use skill, knowledge and experience of group members to achieve quality decisions and achieve group goals. Fred Luthans states that if a group exists in an organization, its members :-

- Are motivated to join
- perceive a group as unified unit of interacting people
- contribute to various amounts to the group processes
- reach agreement and disagreements through various forms of interaction.

Types of Groups

A typical group layout is given at Figure 10.1 below:

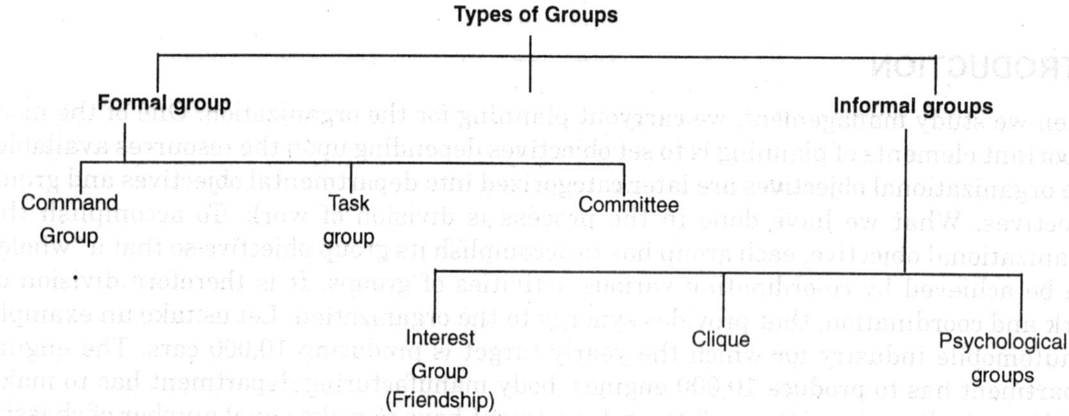

Fig. 10.1. Types of groups

1. Formal Group

Formal group is designated work group defined by the organizational structure. It is collection of employees who work together to contribute towards achievement of organizational objective. For example aircrew. Formal groups are formed based on the work and human resources required by skill, knowledge and experience to achieve organizational task. In a manufacturing unit, the organizational task is sub divided into groups and teams. Each group is composed of various members based on the human resource requirement. The members of the group report to a designated leader. They interact with each other on official level.

2. Command Group

It is formed to carry out a specific task. There is a leader in a group who is also designated by the organization. He receives orders from his superior and reports to him about group activities and performance. A task group is made up of individuals from across the functional areas. They work together to complete a job/task. Task group boundaries are not limited to its hierarchical superior. Once the task is complete the group members fall back to their respective parent groups/units.

3. Committee

The other form of formal group is committee. It can be of permanent or temporary nature. Planning committee, finance committees are of permanent nature, they keep working all along and have a designated authority to control the work. There are temporary committees, which are formed to accomplish a one-time works like committees formed at district levels to issue identity cards to citizens. They are formed for specific work and disbanded once they have completed their work.

Informal Groups

Informal groups are groups that are not formally organized in the work system to get the job done but develop on their own randomly at workplaces because of common interest and mutual liking of the group members. For example members of production department, body manufacturing department, HR department members and few individual from finance dept may form a friendship group. This development takes place because of the interaction they have with each other during the official work. Members from within one group or members from different departments or even an organization can form an informal group. The features of such groups are as under:

(*a*) Informal groups are formed by various members themselves, it has no official sanctity.
(*b*) These groups are formed based on commonality of culture, religious function, liking for each other and common interests.
(*c*) Their contribution for success of formal group is immense if properly handled by official authority.
(*d*) These groups evolve their own structure, elect their own leaders and have followers. They work based on group norms, social norms and code of conduct.
(*e*) They represent the human side of an organization.
(*f*) The group exists without any rigid rules. Their common interest is bond for existence.

Psychological Groups

We had earlier discussed 'emergent' behaviour that is related to behaviour of group members in informal group and involving themselves in various activities, interactions and sentiments based on common interests, value system and social bondage they develop. When such informal group members develop highest level of sentiments or affinity among themselves and become aware of each-others needs and potential contribution to further group objectives. these groups are called psychological groups. The distinct feature of such informal group is that the members become close knit, develops strong feeling of togetherness and get identified by the group. A feeling that 'we' belong to a particular group sets in deep into the behaviour pattern of all group members. At times the strength of informal group identity becomes so strong that the members are more loyal to their friendship group as compared to their normal group. The managers restructuring the task activities and using appropriate group processes should channel the emergent behaviours in such a way that will help organizations to achieve its goal. This phenomenon can be used effectively for the betterment of organizations. See Figure 10.2 below:

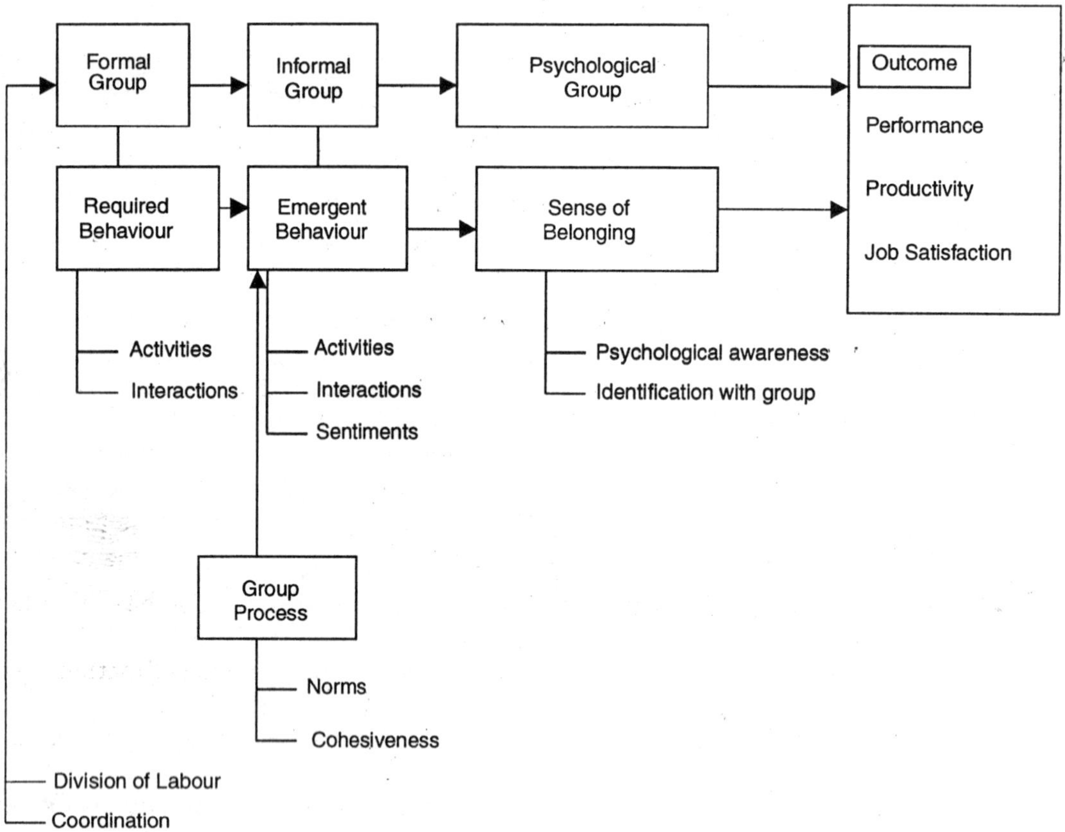

Fig. 10.2. Psychological groups

THEORIES OF GROUP BEHAVIOUR

Propinquity Theory of Group Behaviour (George Homes 1950-60)

Propinquity means affiliation which may be due to spatial or due to geographical proximity. Group Behaviour refers to activities, interactions and sentimements. In any organization, the behaviour of a group is analysed based on 'required' behaviour that refers to those actions the organization expects employees to perform effectively. It relates to the job that each group has to perform. The instructions for job performance are communicated to the group by way of job description, meetings, instructions by supervisors to the workers and other formal instructions that may be used from time to time. The managers expect that the employees follow these instructions in letter and spirit. While on the contrary, members of the group display an emergent behaviour. It refers to the activities the members get involved in the workplace which are of private nature and applicable to common interest of the members of the group. Whatever be the type of behaviour, each member is involved in various activities, carryout interaction with group members and develops sentiments. Let us see as to how does this phenomenon occur? Activities are those behaviours when a group member is involved with other member or group to perform his duties as is laid down in the work schedule. More complex the job and critical nature of work, more will be the activities involved. These are certain activities like chatting or taking coffee together is called emergent activities that the group often gets involved. Activities that are required to be carried out officially with the other members of the group involves interaction. Group member also interact with other members on social platform, which may be called emergent behaviour that relates to feelings, beliefs and values held by group members. All these activities require interaction and exchange of knowledge, knowhow and ideas to perform. More of such interactions develop a bond of friendship (or even hate) among the group members. Apart from official side there are certain impersonal side of organizational systems and process that must be promoted for better group member relationship for higher productivity and conflict free organizational work environment.

Balance Theory

Balance theory was proposed by Theodore Newcomb that states **"persons are attracted to one another on the basis of similar attitudes and common interest relevant to some object or a group goal"**. See Figure 10.3 Below:

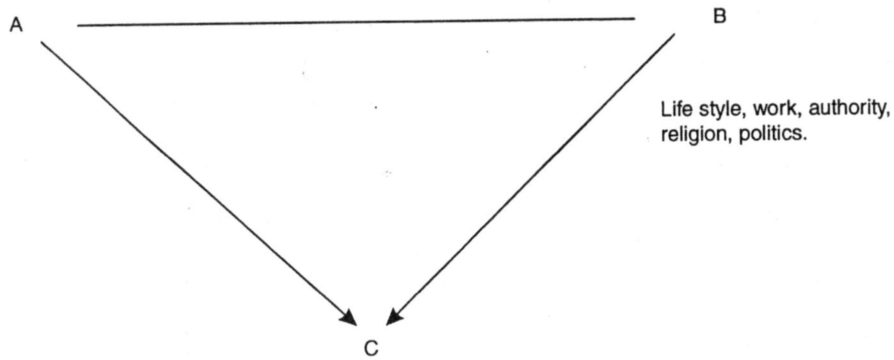

Fig. 10.3. Common attitude and value system

As long as there is a balance, the relationship lasts. If due to some reason an imbalance is created efforts are made by both to restore the balance by compromising. If that does not work the relationship breaks. Reasons for maintaining relationship is based on common interest in politics, religion, similar life style, authority etc. In the Organization interest, it is the responsibility of the manager to ensure effective functioning of the group.

Exchange Theory

Exchange theory is based on cost-reward relationship. Every individual before joining the group evaluates its outcome. If he feels that the outcome (reward) is greater than the cost he joins the group, he will form the part of the group. It should be noted that an individual joins group if a minimum positive level of outcome exists in order to establish attraction and affiliation to take place. The cost of relationship or affiliation is measured in terms of outcome that relates to fulfillment of various levels of needs of an individual.

Group Dynamics

Group dynamics is concerned with interaction and forces between group members in a social situation. Concept of group dynamics was first evolved by Kurt Lewin in 1930s who viewed the concept from the perspective of internal nature of group, why they form, how they form, the structure of group, how they function and its effect on other group members, other groups and the organization. Following concepts are relevant for the study of group dynamic.

Norms

"Group Norms are set of beliefs, feelings, and attitude commonly shared by group members. These are also referred to as rules of standards of behaviour that apply to group members". These are prescriptions of behabiour accepted and determined by the group. As per the Handbook of Industrial and Organizational Psychology, the Norm is defined as "acceptable standards of behaviour that are shared by the group members." All groups have established norms, that is - norms tell members what they 'ought' and 'ought not' to do a thing under certain circumstances. From an individual stand point, they tell what is expected of them in certain situations. When agreed to and accepted by the group, norms act as a means of influencing the behaviour of group members with a minimum of external control. Norms differ among groups, communities and societies, but they all have them.

A study conduct by P.C.De La Porte showed that the group norms that are favourable to the organization were — organizational pride, team work, honesty, security, planning and customer relations. The norms about profitability and supervision were unfavorable to the organization (De La Porte, PC)[2]. Behaviour of an individual as a group member must be acceptable to all the members, this will give an individual "Good standing" and recognition in the group. If norms are violated by an individual, corrective measures such as strokes are applied. In case the individual persist in his behaviour contrary to the group norms he will be totally neglected by other members and can even loose the membership of the group by way of total ignorance by other members of the group and thereby loosing status in the group.

Types of Norms

Norms may differ from organization to organization, nature of work and the location. Following norms are generally found and practiced by all the organizations.

(a) **Performance Norms:** Performance standard is set by the individual worker and approved by the superiors. These are general norms, industry standards prevailing in a particular type of industry and restricted to geographical limits. All the individuals are expected to fulfill their task within the stipulated time. If some worker is slow and can not cope up with the work load, is assisted by other group members. On the contrary if some worker produces more than what is required to do is reprimanded by the group members and discouraged to produce more than upper limits set by the organization so that management does not raise their expectations.

(b) **Appearance Norms:** Appearance norms is related to dress code and code of conduct in the organization. In good organization dress while on work, dress for sports function or for dinner are laid down. In defence services such norms are inbuilt in the organizational culture. As regards to code of conduct, an individual is expected to be loyal and display total dedication to the organization he serves. Workers are not expected to report about fellow workers to the superiors. In the same way members are not expected to divulge company secrets to any other organization, no matter how much tension prevails between workers and management. Group norms is a very powerful tool for high productivity and maintenance of peaceful relationship among the fellow workers.

(c) **Behaviour Norms:** Guidelines for general behaviour are issued by the management so that all the employees display behaviour in an identical manner. These guidelines may cover various aspects relating to the work. This may include time management,. punctuality, salutation, showing respect to the views of other members behaviour while on shop floor and level of professionalism that an individual should possess. These norms eventually take the form of organization culture and are very useful for bringing down the conflict or stress level among the group members

Development of Norms

Norms are developed over a long period of time. They ought to have sufficient time for it to be formalized and called as norms that can not be violated by group members. Explicit statement made by group members like "when going gets tough the tough gets going". This may ultimately be a norm and members of a group would work overtime and utilize their full potential to resolve a critical situation and complete a job, which was tough. Critical events in the groups history may be called as norm. For example donation of blood by group member when required by another group member injured while on the work. Primacy refers to the first (initial) behaviour by one of the group members like 'wishing smooth working on a turbine' which has now become a norm and every member before going to the work wishes his fellow workers accordingly. Past experience is also important in forming a group norm, where a member brings with him good ideas from other organization like having lunch together.

Status

Status refers to the official position enjoyed by an individual in an organization. It is 'importance' and 'deference' that people give to others. People at higher level who have devoted themselves and brought credit to the organization enjoy higher status. They therefore exercise more control over their subordinates. Those who are more competent have more say in group decision making as compared to low status individual. All the members in a group do not enjoy equal status. Standing of a person in a group depends on various factors as mentioned below:

- Personal attributes
- Charismatic disposition
- Demographic characteristics
- Educational level, experience, length of service in the organization
- Expertise
- Proven track record in accomplishing group task.

In certain cultures female children are accorded low status. It has also been observed that in Indian culture, low status is accorded to the individuals coming from low caste system that is socially and legally incorrect. Influence of social, cultural and family background play a dominant role in according status to individual. Employee whose father is on the board of directors enjoys a special (high) status irrespective of his personal achievements.

Cohesion

Cohesiveness defines the degree of closeness that the members feel with the group. It identifies the strength of the members desires to remain in the group and degree of commitment to the group. Cohesiveness of the group is reflected to the extent of unity displayed by the group members and adherence to the group norms. It is "WE" feeling displayed by the members of the group. Cohesion can be achieved when there is a feeling of attraction and adherence to group norms. Cohesiveness of a group can produce miracles in the organization if group objectives and organizational objectives are complementary to each-other. If they differ then the group cohesiveness can be disastrous for the organization. For example if organization wants to improve sales by 10%, this can be achieved provided group is assured of devidants out of additional revenue accrued by additional sales. If no incentives are provided then the cohesiveness of sales group will become counter productive and dysfunctional for the organization. If the organization and the group can subscribe to the common goals, then the high cohesive group will be valuable. In such situation required and emergent behaviour of the group become identical. But if group does not subscribe to the organizational goats then the cohesive group will be detrimental to the organization's goal. In this situation required and emergent behaviour are incongruent and cohesive group become dysfunction to the organization. It is therefore important for a manager to use group cohesiveness to the best advantage of the organization by identifying group member goals and aligning the same with organizational goals.

Conformity

Members in the organization want to belong to a group for various reasons. **First** they want to belong to a group to fulfill the need of social security. The **second** reason is the conformity to group decisions in conflicting and confusing situation as a best bet. When individual belong to a group he abides by group norms and the group decision against ones own judgment. Individuals need for affiliation is satisfied when an individual is fully accepted in the group by group members. In conflicting situation an individual goes by the decisions made by the group. Conformity with group norms and group decision provide an individual enough emotional strength to cope up with organization stress.

There are some individuals who have dominant ego factor, may not accept group decisions and therefore refuse to accept conformity. These individuals are called **deviants.** Such non-conformist have strong individual views and independent opinion on a particular issue. They can survive as group members for being non-conformist. They are subsequently isolated from the other members of the group.

Groupthink

Groupthink is a phenomenon in which the norms for consensus overrides the realistic appraisal of alternative course of action(Robbins OB 2000). Groupthink is a situation when all the members of a group are aligned to each other in the group and blindly abide by the group decisions. No external pressure is applied. In the process it has been seen that poor decision are made by the group as no one resist the decision, groupthink phenomenon is bad for group decision making because group members don't take decision based on rationality, non use of available data, and over estimation about ability. Too much of group cohesion is dangerous for equality decisions.

GROUP COHESIVENESS: Following factors contribute to group Cohesiveness. Refer Figure 10.4 below:

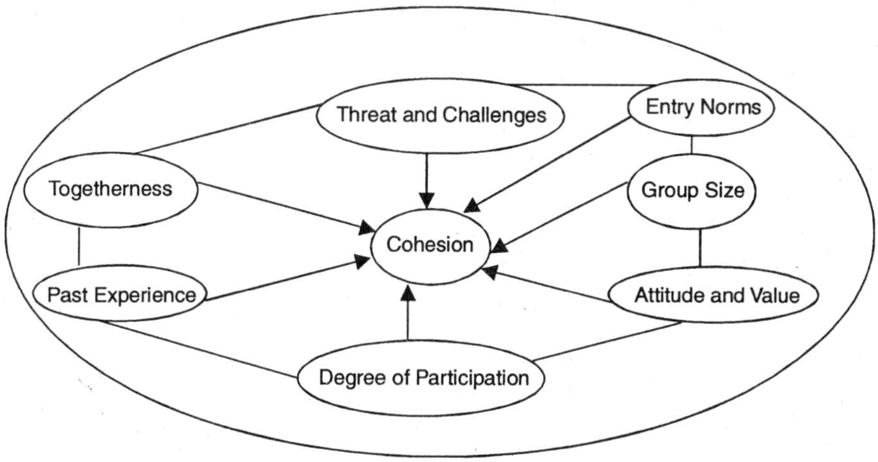

Fig. 10.4. Factors contributing to group cohesiveness

Togetherness

It is a natural tendency that people want to remain together. When they interact they know each other better and are attracted by their nature and behaviour pattern. People share their happiness and hardships and a bond of togetherness is formed. In organizational setting, people on the same floor, department, residing in the same colony, bus stop friendship are attracted to each-other because of their close proximity. It will invariably be found that the people who are closely associated by virtue of even seating arrangement in the work-place share their views and display more cohesiveness than those who are located away.

Group Size

Cohesiveness of a group depends upon the close interaction of the group members with each other. In a large group it not possible for the individual to communicate with each-other hence there is likelihood of large group being less cohesive than the small group. In work environment small group is more effective. If a group is large, there is also a possibility of formation of small sub groups within a large group. This will lead to delusions of group norms and power politics within the sub group, which is not desirable. Another interesting factor about group cohesion is the sex, whether the group composes of all male members of female members. Studies showed that if all member were of the same sex then small group had better cohesion than large ones (Robbins stephon)[3]. In a mix group situation, even larger group has a better cohesion because people like to be a part of mix group and are more interactive with opposite sex that increases group Cohesion. What should be the optimum size for a effective group cohesion can not be decided, as other factors like attitude of group members and demographic factors play a decisive role. However 8 to 10 members could be an ideal group size for optimum group cohesion to be achieved. Beyond the above limit the cohesiveness of the group decreases gradually. Large groups are least cohesive.

Entry Norms

There are organizations whose membership is difficult to obtain. There are also clubs which are reserved for exclusive members of a particular background like Defence Services Officers club. Joining of such group elevates the status, position and members feel a sense of pride and accomplishment. Because the membership of such clubs is exclusive. At times, there is also a long waiting list to join such groups. More exclusive the group more cohesive it will be. More difficult to get entry, more cohesive the group would be.

Threat and Challenges

Every group has its objectives. It has been experimented that whenever there is a threat to disturb the group norm or group objective, group members get more united to protect the group objective from the party threatening the same. It will be noticed that external threat brings higher degree of cohesion to the group. In the fast moving world to day, the importance of group has increased many fold. Employees have sacrificed their perks and privileges to ensure higher productivity by adhering to group norms. For example employees in a well organized industry work beyond specified time to achieve group goals. Meeting higher challenges brings personal satisfaction to group members and higher level cohesiveness to the group they are part of.

Degree of participation in group Activities

Participation in group activities is important as it leads to more frequent interaction between group members. Success in group activities also bring cohesiveness as each of the participants feels that he has been the contributor for achievement of group goals. For example participation in sports team and achieving the victory.

Attitude and Value

"Birds of the same feather flock together". Group members having identically attitude and high level of value system will behave themselves identically and promote group norms and achieve Cohesiveness. In such situation decision making and implementation of group task is comparatively easy . Conflict situations are avoided and a smooth sailing is achieved. Interest of the group is well protected due to cohesiveness of the group.

Relationship between Cohesiveness Performance Norms and Productivity

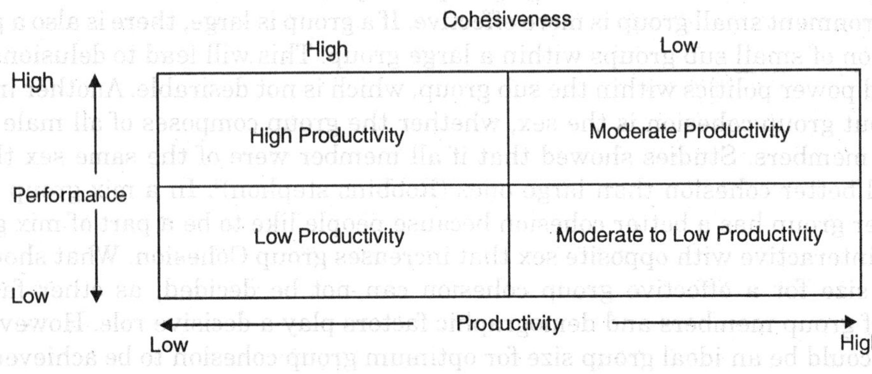

Fig. 10.5. Relationship between cohesiveness, performance norms on productivity

Study of cohesiveness is important because it has an impact on productivity of the organization. Relationship of group Cohesiveness, performance norms and productivity is given in Figure 10.5 above.

Performance norms are those work and behaviour related activities that have been accepted as norm like Cooperation, Quality of output, interpersonal behaviour etc. A cohesive group will be more productive than a less cohesive group. If cohesiveness is high and performance norms are low, productivity will be low thereby establishing the superiority of performance norms. If cohesiveness is low and performance norms are high, productivity will increase. When performance norms and Cohesiveness is low, productivity will fall.

To achieve group cohesiveness following suggestion are made (J L Gbson and J M Lvancevich)[4]

(*a*) Small group have better Cohesiveness.
(*b*) Encourage unilateral acceptance of group goals.
(*c*) Time spent by members for group activities should be increased.
(*d*) Increase status of group and group members.
(*e*) Create an environment of perceived difficulty in attaining group membership.
(*f*) Competition with other groups.
(*g*) Introduce reward systems.
(*h*) Physical Isolation of group increases cohesiveness.

Consequences of Cohesiveness: See Figure 10.6 below:

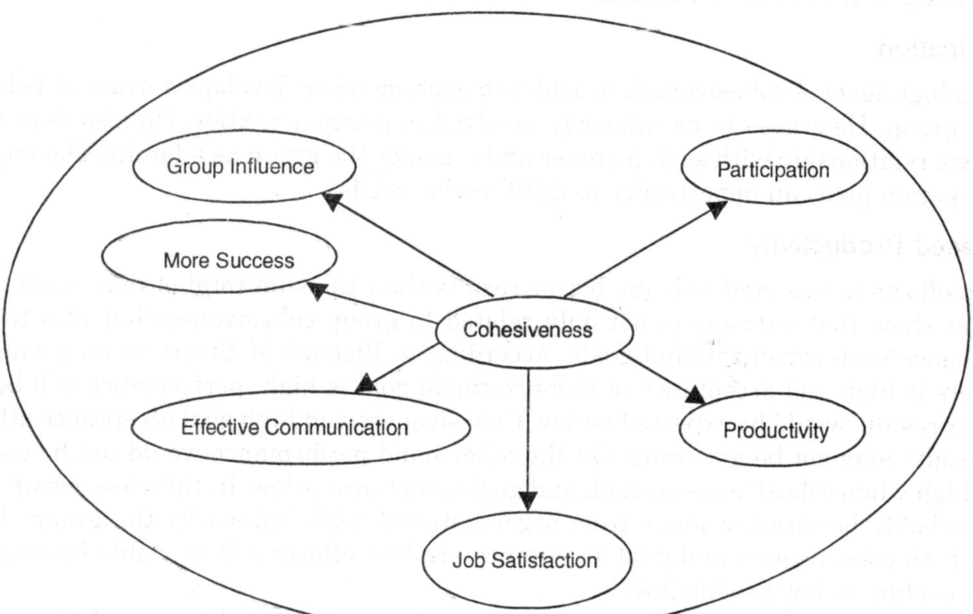

Fig. 10.6. Consequences of group cohesiveness

More Influence

Every group has a leader. If it is a formal group then the leader will be appointed by virtue of organizational structure. If a group is informal and a leader is not nominated, then the leader will automatically arise due to various situations and requirements. Leader who apart from being appointed, exercises considerable influence over the group members is accepted as leader by the group members. Leader who is autocratic exercises even move power to handle the external situation. Leader must be sincere and care for the expectations of the group members. Leader's decisions will be accepted when he displays considerable amount of concern and well of the majority of members. For example, Leader's agreement with union on a particular issue would be accepted by members of the group if leader wields internal power over the group members.

Success

Group is formed to achieve a particular group objective. When achieving group objective, the personal objective takes a back seat. Group Cohesiveness and success are interdependant. When group is highly cohesive the success is almost assured. On the contrary if the group is not cohesive the members will display separate interests and fulfillment of group objective will merely remain as an objective and its accomplishment will be difficult. For example, take a crew of the passenger aircraft flying from Bombay to Paris. The objective is clear, there is a common objective, every member of the crew (group) is contributing to safe passage. Flight engineer, Navigator, pilot, attendants all are committed to achieve group goal and personal interest (goal) if any is kept aside. It is therefore necessary to achieve a high degree of cohesiveness by adopting to group norms and conforming to it to achieve success.

Participation

Once a high level of cohesiveness is achieved each member develops a sense of belonging to the group. He craves to be intensely involved in group activities. He also develops an intimate relationship with each member and consider the group as a family. The members participation gives an opportunity to fulfill social needs.

Increased Productivity

Group efforts is expected to bring better results than the sum total of individual efforts. Studies show that outcome is not only related to group cohesiveness but also to group compliance with organizational goals. According to Richard M Steers when group cohesiveness is high and acceptance of organizational goal is high, performance will be high. Similar results would be expected for low Cohesiveness and high goal acceptance although the results may not be as strong. On the other hand performance would not be expected to be high when cohesiveness is high and goal acceptance is low. In this case, group efforts will probably be directed away from organizational goals valued by the group. Finally when both cohesiveness and goal acceptance are low, efforts will probably become dissipated leading to low productivity[5].

Satisfaction. In a group environment, satisfaction is guided by cumulative effect of external factors like respect for each other, support from group members, expert guidance, achievement and sense of safety in group environment. These factors bind members to each other and achieve cohesiveness. If members are not satisfied they would seize to be part of the group.

Better Communication. Members form a group, remain member of the group because of the value system they share with each other. By virtue of this an effective communication is evolved that reduces conflict to a large extent. Members of the group enjoy the freedom of action by virtue of respect for each other and the social relationship.

SUMMARY

Concept of group came in existence along with division of work. The group is collection of two or more indivisuals working for a common goal and are inter dependent. To achieve organizational objective the group has to accomplish its (group) objective so that the 'whole' is achieved. The same can be achieved by co-ordinationg group activities. It is difficult for a manager to understand each individual because of different behavioural patterns of the members. Concept of Group dynamics was first introduced by Kurt Lewin in 1930s. There are two types of groups. These are formal group of which command group, task group and committee form the part. The second type of group is informal group. This contains interest group, clique and psychological group. There are various theories of group behaviour. Homes proposed Propinquity theory of group behaviour. The theory deals with activities, interactions and sentiments of individuals that leads to affiliation caused due to spatial or geographical proximity. It has been observed that individuals display required or emergent behaviour in work enviornment. Second theory of group behaviour was introduced by Theodore Newcomb called 'balance theory'. The theory explains as to how people are attracted to each other based on common attitude and value system. This may include life style, work, authority, religion and politics. Exchange theory deals with affiliation that takes place based on cost-reward relationship that is measured by psychological aspects like feelings anxiety and so on.

Following concepts are relevant for the study of group dynamics. These are as under:

Norms are set of beliefs, feelings, attitudes commonly shared by group members. Norms are of various types. These are performance norms, appearance norm and behaviour norms. Development of norms is a continuous process and are based on behaviour displayed by various members of the group on various occasions. These include explicit statement made by group members, critical events in the life of the group, primacy of behaviour and the past experience. **Status and cohesiveness.** Cohesiveness identifies the strength of the members' desire to remain in the group and degree of commitment displayed by them. Cohesiveness of a group can be developed by conforming to the group norms by according secondary position to individual interests as against the group interests.

Groupthink is a phenomenon in which norms overrides any alternative course of action if a group is required to be strong. Togetherness, group size, entry norms and ability of group members to face threats and challenges posed by various situations. Degree of participation in group activities, attitude and value displayed by the group members are also important for group cohesiveness.

There is a close relationship between cohesiveness, performance norms and productivity. For high productivity a group must ensure high cohesiveness and high performance norms.

Low performance norms will lead to low or moderate productivity. A highly cohesive group displays, greater participation in group activities, higher productivity, more influence among group members, effective communication, more success in the organizational mission and above all a higher job satisfaction.

TEXT QUESTIONS

Q. 1 Explain the concept of group.
Q. 2 What are various types of group?
Q. 3 Explain various theories of group behaviour.
Q. 4 Study of norms and status is essential for the study of group dynamics. Explain.
Q. 5 "Cohesiveness is the degree of closeness that the members feel with the group". In the light of the above statement explain cohesiveness and factors contributing to it.
Q. 6 With the help of a diagram explain relationship between group cohesiveness, performance norms and productivity.
Q. 7 What are the various consequences of group cohesiveness.
Q. 8 Why people join group. Explain.

REFERENCES

1. Uma Sekaran, ***"Organization Behaviour"***, Tata McGraw Hills, 9th edition 2000.
2. De La Porte, PC, ***"Group Norms Key to Building a Winning Team personnel"***, Sept./Oct. 1974, pp. 60-67.
3. Robbins stephon, ***"Essential ‹f Organizational Behaviour"***, Prentice Hall of India, 2000.
4. J.L. Gbson and J.M., Lvancevich, ***"Organizations"***, 8th edition Irwin, 1994.
5. Steers Richard. M, ***"Introduction to Organizational Behaviour"***, Scott, Foresman and Company, 1988.

Case

Balchandra belongs to an economically backward family. He is the only educated member of his family. With much difficulty he could complete his matriculation, earning the credit of first matriculate in the family. His approach and behaviour can be seen as subjected to his economic handicap. Though he has a little inferiority complex and is a little introvert, he is hardworking. At the age of 22 he has joined a public sector organization as a junior clerk. While in service, he has completed intermediate, B.A. and M.A. He has then been promoted to the post of a senior clerk. Being ambitious, he has expected to get a better promotion. Hence he worked hard. He took a management diploma also.

All the four unions in the organization have asked him to join their unions, which he did not take heed. Hence all the union leaders are unhappy with him, while his colleagues have a jealousy. He has been sincere and hard working. Though he has not joined any of the unions, he has tried to keep moderate relations with all of his colleagues. However, the union activists and some of his coworkers have kept some sort of grudge and whispered against Mr. Balchandra.

Considering the hardworking nature and additional qualifications, Balchandra has been promoted to a junior executive position. But as soon as he took charge the union leaders have protested against the promotion. They have interpreted it as an incentive for not joining the union. As a result of their strong protest, the promotion order is cancelled within a week. It was a great blow to Balchandra. Earlier he was working with the Research & Development Dept., which was according to his liking. But after being reverted, he has been placed as a senior clerk in the Accounts department, where his supervisor has been one of his strongest critics. Moreover, he did not like accounting work; and he could not get job satisfaction in the new position.

His adversaries have rejoiced, while he lost interest. He started showing disinterest in the work, and has become irregular in attendance. Gradually, he become disgruntled and moody, and started absenting frequently. Accounts section supervisor has not waited to call for explanations of Balchandra a number of times, which adversely affected his morale. He lost hopes and applied for causal leave for three days, he left the office without waiting for the sanction of the casual leave. He did not care to report back for duty even after three days. The Accounts section supervisor and other union leaders have promptly approached the personnel manger on the 15th day of his absence with a detailed note of the case and a recommendation from the Accounts Departmental head to serve a show cause notice on Balchandra, to conduct a departmental enquiry and to finally remove him from service.

The union leaders have persuaded the Personnel Manager to promptly act on the recommendation of the Accounts Dept. Head. Some of Balchandra's friends have informally reported the matter to his family, which is perturbed too much because Balchandra is the sole bread-winner of the family. A detailed analysis of the line of events throws light on group behaviour, interaction of individual and group behaviour, morale and job satisfaction of Balchandra in the context of the line of events, group dynamics, conflict between individual goal and group goal, lack of cohesion and its reasons, etc. We shall also consider the questions like : Is there anything wrong with Balchandra ? Which are the various groups with which Balchandra is associated ? Can we remark that the behaviour and approach of the various groups have been correct? What would be the appropriate action on the part of the personnel manager in the particular situation ? Is it possible to motivate Balchandra and to improve morale, cohesiveness, and job satisfaction in the existing situation?

CHAPTER 11

Conflict Management

INTRODUCTION

To study the dynamics of organizational behaviour, study of conflict management deserves attention. In present corporate environment conflict has become very common phenomenon. Conflict is bad as it has adverse effects on the individual performance. If conflict is beyond control it takes a destructive dimension. When employees do not cope up with the conflict situation, there is an increased absenteeism and exit of employees. It can be so disastrous that can lead to demise of an organization. American Firm Shea and Gould perished due to high degree of conflict. On the other hand it has been opinioned that conflict is good for the organization as it produces new ideas, increases competitive sprit, cohesiveness in the team and instills an atmosphere of brotherhood in the organization. This is only possible if ideas are properly chanalised and there is proper delegation of authority, empowerment and autonomy in functioning.

Definitions

Conflict can be defined (Thomas K.A.)[1] as the **"process that begins when one party perceives that another party has negatively affected something that the first party cares about."** Conflict must be perceived by either of the parties. Stiff opposition due to incompatibility of organizational goals characterizes it. Conflict can also be caused due to difference about interpretation of facts or issues involved. Conflict takes an ugly turn and take a form of violence due to disagreement based on behavioral expectations. It could be covert or overt and can be seen when one observes violent acts of individual in organizations. Austin et al[2] defines conflict **"as a disagreement between two or more individuals or groups, with each individual or group trying to gain acceptance of its views or objective over others."**

Nature and scope of conflict

Every organization has its objective. It is further broken down as departmental objectives, group goals and lastly individual goals. When individual interacts with another individual there is perceptual and communication problems that causes misunderstanding and leads to individual conflict situation. It is also true of groups. Group conflicts indicate the way of inter-group behaviour in an organization. This is more relevant in the Indian context, where inter-union rivalry is most cognigible. Inter-group conflict occurs due to group competition and group cohesiveness. This leads to a feeling of **'we'** and **'they'**. "We are always right and they are always wrong". Hence a beginning of conflict. Aims and objectives of various organizations differ drastically that give rise to greater competition hence a high level of conflict. Conflict can arise between employer and employees, management and workers, one department and another, stakeholders, shareholders, producer and customers and between various trade unions that are often politically motivated. Schein[3] has pointed out that, this problem exits because as groups become more committed to their goals and norms, they are likely to become competitive with one another and seek to undermine their rivals' activities, thereby becoming a liability to the organization as a whole. The overall problem, then, is how to establish high productive, collaborative inter-group relations. Michael[4] states that conflict can lead to breakdown in standard mechanism of decision making so that an individual or group experiences difficulty in selecting an action alternative. The breakdown may be because of competing demands on an individual or group rivalry and competition. There can be vertical and horizontal conflicts; or individual conflict, group conflict and organizational conflict.

Conflict can be considered as expression of hostility, negative attitude, aggression and gross misunderstanding. It is caused due to varying interest of individual or groups. Pondy[5] has described that the term 'conflict' is used in four ways to indicate

1. Antecedent conditions of conflictual behaviour, such as scarcity of resources.
2. Affective states of individuals involved such as stress, tension, hostility, anxiety etc.
3. Cognitive state of individuals, that is their perception or awareness or conflictual situations.
4. Conflictual behaviour, ranging from passive resistance to overt aggression.

Functional and Dysfunctional Conflict

Conflict that supports the individual and group goals, which leads to higher performance is called **functional conflict** while the conflicts that hinders individual or group performance is called **dysfunctional conflict**. The latter generally takes destructive form. There is thin margin between the two types of conflicts mentioned above. While evaluating the impact of conflict on goal achievement, individual perception and effect of group performance should be evaluated. If the conflict contributes towards higher performance then the conflict should be called *functional* or otherwise dysfunctional. Conflict can be broadly classified in three types i.e. ***task oriented conflict, behavioural conflict* and *structural conflict* or *process conflict.*** Task conflict relates to the group goals or objectives to be achieved by the group while behavioral conflict relates to individual's value system, approach, attitude, ego state, skill and norms being followed by him. Studies reveal that most of the dysfunctional conflict fall under this category. Process conflict is related to how a task is being accomplished in the organization. It is related with various processes, procedures, drills and instructions that are being followed on a particular job. When individual differs in this regard, conflict arises. This type of conflict can be eliminated to a large extent by following strict discipline in the work procedure and adhering to the rules and regulations. Positive points of functional conflict are as under:

Functional Conflict

1. Conflict develops cohesiveness within the group members. A group goal therefore becomes a priority. Individual goals are then relegated to secondary position.
2. Conflict leads to innovation and creativity, as there is competing sprit among various groups.
3. Conflict provides challenging work environment and enhances opportunities for self-development of group that leads to formation of group norms.
4. Enhance work culture leads to upgradation of various systems within the organization and therefore growth is achieved.

Dysfunctional Conflict

Conflict may turn out to be detrimental and disastrous and having deleterious effects. Dysfunctional nature of conflict can be identified in the following circumstances:

1. When conflict does not lead to solution.
2. When basic goals of the organization are neglected.
3. People should be treated with due respect. If it is violated and a climate of distrust and suspicion is created people feel defeated and demeaned which develops antagonism and leads to conflict.
4. Conflict may lead to absenteeism and subsequently to increased turn over if not controlled in time.
5. Dual management style may create hatred and lead to dysfunctional conflict.
6. Disagreement with management may be considered as disloyalty, if this environment prevails, an opportunity for creativity would be lost and employees would loose interest in their job. This would lead to increased conflicting situations.

TRANSITION OF CONFLICT

1. Traditional view

During 1930-40s, conflict was considered to be bad and viewed negatively. It was considered harmful, unnecessary and considered synonymous to violence, destruction and irrational. The view held that the conflict arose due to poor communication, lack of openness, lack of trust and failure of managers to be responsive to the needs and aspirations of their employees. The view further held that the conflict must be avoided at all costs. During the same period, the scientific management and administrative school of management that were in the state of evolution, developed such organizational structure where responsibilities had been properly laid down, rules, regulations and policies had been inbuilt in the system. Thus a proper mechanism was introduced in the management systems and an adequate attention was paid by the managerial staff to ensure that there was no misunderstanding among the employees and that the conflict was avoided.

2. Human Relations View

Human relations view, which prevailed between 1940-70 states that conflict is a natural occurrence of individual behaviour and that the conflict cannot be avoided. The theory propagated that we must accept conflict since we can not eliminate the same. It further states that organizations must lay down proper policy and procedure, set achievable goals. Have proper communication and thereby avoid stress and strain. Resources should be properly allocated and steps taken to avoid occurrence of conflict. An environment of trust, cooperation, friendship and sharing is built amongst the employees so that increased productivity for the organization is achieved. Avoidance of conflict and trust building is the key for the prosperity of the organization.

3. Behavioural View

Behavioural scientists encourage conflict on various grounds. They feel that a group having inter group harmonious relations, peace and cooperation among group members is likely to be non-vibrant, static in nature and can display apathetic attitude towards group members. In this situation the groups are non responsive. What is required today is innovation, creativity and an ability of the group to meet the social obligations. Hence there is a need for maintaining minimal level of conflict within the group. This would lead to group being viable. Group members should be self-critical and develop creativity. Minimum level of conflict between the groups would increase competitiveness that will lend itself to higher productivity and increased job satisfaction. It must be borne in mind that only minimum level of conflict is necessary for it to be beneficial. Behavioral view proposes that because people differ in their attitudes, values and goals, conflict is but a natural outcome in any group of people and that it can be helpful and constructive. (Chandan Jit S)[6]. The neo-classicists emphasized the understanding of individual psychology, development of informal groups, informal leadership, and a democratic-participative leadership style so as to avoid conflicts and establish harmony in the organization.

4. Modern View

The *modern view* holds that conflict may be necessary for organizational effectiveness. It is believed that harmonious, peaceful and cooperative groups can become static and uninnovative. Minimum level of conflict that keeps the group alive, self critical and creative is desirable. Modernists believe that conflict is structural in nature, is inevitable and endemic to the organizational milieu. It is a product of systems and determined by structural factors and integral to the nature of change. When groups interact there is bound to be difference of opinion and disagreements, which is a cause for conflict. It exists even when there is single individual who is faced with organizational problems like decision making. Conflict should be welcomed and managed effectively. Some of the positive points of minimum level of conflict are as under:

(*a*) Conflict should be expressed. By doing so, communication between two groups is restored that promotes growth.

(*b*) Minimum level of conflict serves as pre-requisite for organizational development. Conflict brings changes.

(*c*) Conflict helps achieve cohesion within the group that develops group identity and members of the group follow group norms setting aside personal problems. This tendency leads higher level of productivity, sense of identity with the organization and increases group ability to compete with groups and departments.

(*d*) Poor decisions are detrimental to organizational growth. Minimum level of conflict promotes stimulus for analytical thinking, which may challenge views, policies and systems prevailing in the organization. It will lead to reviews hence new policies may be introduced in the organization.

(*e*) Conflict can serve as power equalizer between two parties. This is clearly observed during management union meetings. While management is powerful at the beginning of the discussion it however tends to equalize itself as the discussion proceeds.

Causes of Conflict

Communicational Aspect: Communication is an important process in the organization. Poor communication, passing of an incomplete information to a department may cause conflict because this may have far reaching consequences in attainment of organizational goals. Importance of full and complete communication cannot be over emphasized in the fast moving organizations in the present era of information technology. Some of the reasons for poor communication are as under:

(*a*) *Inadequate communication:* where too much or too little information is passed from one department to the other.
(*b*) *Filtration effect:* where end receiver receives very scant information having little or no value.
(*c*) *When information is not received on time*: it must be noted that delayed information has no value as the decision might have already been taken without the information.
(*d*) *Barriers of culture, language.*
(*e*) *Inadequate training of sender and receiver.*
(*f*) *Noise problems.*

Behavioural View

Types of Conflict

As discussed earlier, organizations exist based on various groups and departments where scares resources have to be put in to use through various processes. Systems and sub-systems exist in the organizations that are managed by individuals and work teams or work groups. While interacting with each other on individual, team or group levels, there may be occasions when conflict occurs due to perceptual differences. The conflict may be intra-personal, inter-personal, intra-group, inter-group or intra-organizational in nature. These are discussed below.

Intra-personal Conflict: Intra personal conflict is also called the conflict within the individual. This type of conflict can be of two types

(*a*) ***Value conflict:*** Every individual has to play certain roles, which conforms to his value system. However, there are certain situations when an individual may have to compromise on value system and beliefs. For example, finance manager of an organization, while submitting tax returns to the government may conceal some facts, which may go against his belief and value system. This situation may cause tension and conflict within the individual.
(*b*) ***Decision-making:*** Problem solving is one of the important jobs every individual has to undertake in work environment. Every problem has various courses open. At times it is difficult for a person to select an appropriate course of action. This

situation causes conflict within the individual. He therefore will have to take decisions based on the past experience and the knowledge. It may be noted that decision-making has become simpler these days due to *firstly*; information technology where required data is available and *secondly*, group decision is the norm in most of the organizations.

Inter-personal Conflict

Inter-personal conflict relates to conflict between two or more individuals and is probably the most common and recognized form of conflict. Interpersonal conflict is caused due to disagreement over goals and objectives of the organization. These are heightened due to difference of opinion of individuals and when issues are not based on facts. Every organization is full of unresolved issues, problems and differing situations that leads to conflict. Conflict can also take place between one person of a group with another person of the same group or another group on issues relating to decision-making. Individuals may have a difference of opinion on selection of a particular course of action that will lead to disagreement and often result in the conflict. It is the merit of the issue, and willingness of members of the organization to accept the others point of view that will avoid the conflict situation.

Intra-Group Conflict

Intra-group conflict relates to values, status and roles played by an individual in the group and the group norms. Individual may want to remain in the group for social needs but may disagree with the methods and procedures followed by the group. The conflict may arise when social changes are incorporated in the group. When group faces new problems and when values are changed due to change in social environment. Intra-group conflict is like Inter-personal conflict except that the people involved in the conflict episode belong to a common group.

Inter-Group Conflict

Conflicts between different groups, sections and departments are called inter-group conflict. For example, conflict between production and sales departments over the quality being produced and the customer requirements. Inter-group conflict causes due to factors inherent to the organizational structure like independence, inconsistency in various policy matter, variance on promotion criteria, reward system and different standards being adopted for different sub-units and departments. Organizational objectives can only be achieved when all departments work towards attainment of organizational goals. This is possible when interactions between departments are smooth and cordial. Conflict can be avoided by better communication between departments, joint decision making, removing disparity in group goals and paying due respect and displaying concern for other group's views.

Inter-Organizational Conflict

Inter-organizational conflict takes place between two dependent organizations. Conflict can take place between government organization, unions and the operating industry. Government organizations function to ensure that minimum standards are followed by the organizations. Managers must try and reduce inter-organizational conflicts by adopting positive approach and by following strictly, the rules and regulations laid down by the government agencies. Conflict can also take place between seller and buyer organizations.

Intra-Organizational Conflicts

Intra organizational conflict encompasses *horizontal, vertical, line–staff and role based conflicts.* Let us briefly study these situations.

Horizontal Conflict

Horizontal Conflict is caused due to incompatibility of goals, sharing limited resources and difference in time orientation. It leads to tension, misunderstanding and frustration on the part of both the parties. Horizontal conflict relates to employees or group at the same level. Organizational goal at implementation level vary from department to department. Finance department may not be able to spare additional amount as may be required by research and development department for new product development, that may cause tension, misunderstanding between two individuals or departments. Individuals may not be able to meet the targets of production in given time due to variety of reason that may cause conflict with sales department as the latter would like to flood the market with their product to make the presence felt. It has been seen that due to increased interdependence of individuals or groups to carry out various functions, situations do arise where there is difference of opinion on issues that cause conflict between individuals or groups.

Vertical Conflict

Vertical conflict refers to conflicts that might take place between different levels of hierarchy. Conflicts between subordinates and superior occur due to incompatibility. It is generally caused because of differences in perception, value system, goals that may be assigned, cognition and difference in individual behaviour. Conflict is also caused due to inappropriate communication between individuals at two different levels.

Line and Staff Conflict

Line and staff conflict has been traditional. Line authority creates product and services and contributes directly towards the revenue generation. While staff authority assists line authority and acts in advisory capacity. Staff and line authority have a different predispositions and goals. They have different skills and expertise. Since staff authority (managers) are in the chain of command and have a day to day access to the top boss, have a tendency to dictate terms to the line authority and usually disregard the working knowledge of the line authority. They have tendency to dominate and disregard the efforts put in by line authority managers. On the contrary staff managers have a technical know how and they are able to advice the line authority to cut down cost of production and save on wastage etc. Line authority does not like their advice at times. Staff managers get frustrated when their suggestions and ideas are not implemented by line managers and hence the cause for conflict. In the process the organizational goals are not achieved as per plans.

Role Conflict

A person in an organization has to perform various roles. Conflict arises when roles assigned to him have different expectation. *'Time'* management may cause conflict. A person may be asked to take care of an additional section in the absence of section head. Value system in an organization is also a cause for conflict. Supervisor is asked to be honest while he is dealing with sale of the product while the same person may be asked to pay commision to an official from whom a sanction is required to be obtained, thereby causing a conflict situation in the ethical value system of an individual. When an individual is line or a staff employee and also a union representative, has to perform duties of conflicting nature hence a role conflict.

CONFLICT PROCESS

Pondy developed a conflict process model, which is useful to understand how a conflict starts. He has delineated five steps that he calls as 'conflict episode'. These are ***latent conflict, perceived conflict, felt conflict manifest conflict, conflict resolution and conflict aftermath.*** The process is adopted and explained Figure 11.1 below.

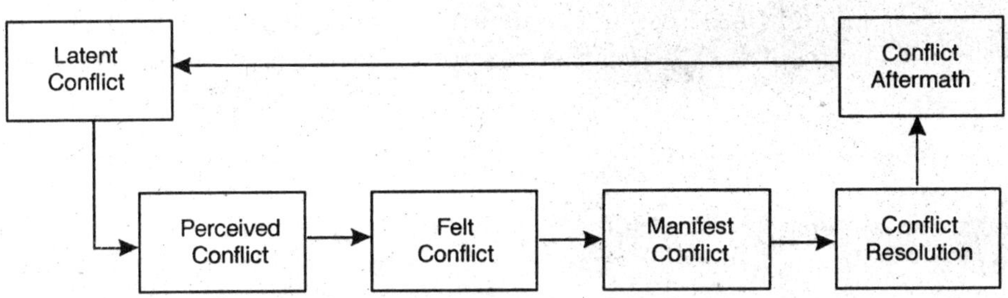

Fig. 11.1. Pondy's Conflict episode Process

Latent Conflict

It is a first stage of conflict when conflict-promoting situations appear on the scene between individuals and groups. In this stage potential conflict inducing forces exist. For example demand for various resources by departments when some may get and be satisfied and others may not get and be dissatisfied. Hence there may exist a situation between two groups. At this stage the seeds of dissatisfaction has been sown.

Perceived Conflict

When one party frustrate the design of the other party, people perceive that a confluctual conditions exist. For example sales manager may need additional budget for promotional activities which financial manager may not release. The sales manager may attribute lack of finance as potential cause for fall in sales. Thus a conflict between the two may brew. At this stage the conflict does not surface.

Felt Conflict

At this stage, the conflict is actually felt and cognised. As stated earlier, the funds are not released by the finance manager and the problem is being surfaced and there is a likelihood of confrontation.

Manifest Conflict

In this stage, there is not only recognition or acknowledgement of conflict but also manifestation of conflict by covert or overt behaviour. It is a stage of open dispute. Both parties devise their strategies to face each other. In the above example sales manager may make his point for additional funds for promotional activities especially during festival season. Finance manager may openly turn down the request since he might have allotted additional funds for procurement of better raw material for production department. Sales manager may argue that better raw material has no meaning unless the facts are brought to the notice of customers, which can only be done through promotional campaign. The debate may be unending and frustrating.

Conflict Aftermath

Once the conflict is resolved between the two parties, there is always a party, which is looser because the resolution is the outcome of win – lose or the compromise strategy, a stage is set for subsequent conflict episodes. A party, which feels defeated, may start preparations and be on the look out for the assault to take the revenge. Conflict resolution has been added as an additional box in the figure to elucidate that conflict aftermath is a direct function of the results of the conflict resolution style adopted and exercised in any given situation.

CONFLICT RESOLUTION MODEL

Conflict between parties can be resolved by five different modes. Parties involved may adopt any of the following solutions, which are explained in Figure 11.2 below.

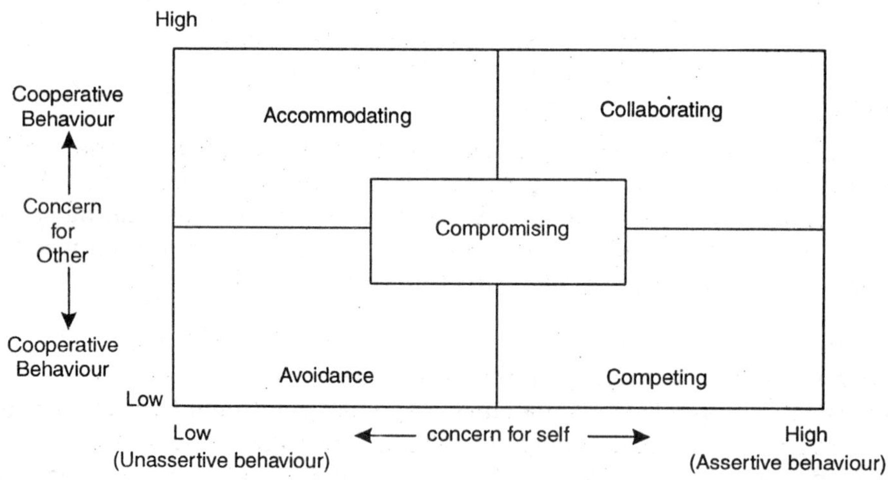

Fig. 11.2. Conflict resolution model

Avoidance

One or both parties could ***avoid*** facing the conflict. The situation pertains to un-cooperative and unassertive behaviour on the part of parties involved. A Party may avoid facing B Party. When situation reaches a point of negligence by A Party, B Party may take advantage of the situation. By avoiding, the individual might side step, postpone or even withdraw from the conflictuating situation. This strategy is useful when issues involved in conflict are of a very minor nature or when more important issues deserve attention. This strategy suits a manager whose power base is very low and there is no chance of satisfying one's own concerns. Avoidance strategy should be applied when one feels that people in the organization should cool down so that the issue can be handled at a latter date in a better psychological environment. The issue can also be postponed if additional information is required to be obtained. Avoidance is a poor strategy hence if someone else is able to handle the situation of conflict more effectively, should be allowed to do so. Managers having high score on avoidance as a strategy of conflict management, may suffer from delayed decision making and hence the loss to the organization. Those who have a low score on avoidance thereby wanting to attend to every single issue may spend lot of time on every trivial issue, hurt people's feelings and stir hostility in the organization that should be taken care of.

Competing

This strategy may be adopted when other strategies of conflict resolution are not workable. Competing is also useful in emergencies where quick decisions are required. In this strategy power must be used unilaterally as a weapon when unpopular decisions like termination, pay cuts, layoffs, cost cutting and enforcing discipline are required to be taken. This strategy is based on win-lose principle of managing conflicts. The managers who are high on power base have an added advantage in using competing strategy because people from opposite side would not dare confront a person who is so powerful. There is a tendency that managers using this strategy should be careful about 'yes' men around them. They should identify conflicting situations and take bold decisions based on win-lose strategy. On the other hand there are managers who are low on competing mode, are likely to feel powerless in many situations. Not realizing that though they have power but they are not comfortable using it. By trying to use power, one could enhance one's achievement. Another drawback in scoring low is that such individuals find it difficult to take bold stand on various issues concerning organizations. In situations when a manager is very low on 'concern for the people' may postpone vital decisions on matters pertaining to subordinates that may be detrimental to organizational effectiveness.

Collaborating

Strategy of collaboration involves attempt of one party to work with the other party in co-operative manner and find solutions to the problem for mutual benefits. The strategy involves identification of areas of disagreement, examining the issue in greater detail and a workable solution arrived at, which is for mutual benefit. This strategy signifies when two sets of solutions are important for both parties to be compromised. Hence finding integrated solution become imperative. This strategy signifies joint efforts, gain for both parties and integrated solutions arrived at by consensual decisions. Sekaran[7] concluded that when people are *high* on collaborating, they have to be concerned about how they spend their time and other organizational resources. Collaboration is time and energy consuming. Not all situations need collaborative solutions. Over use of collaboration and consensual decision-making may reflect risk aversion tendencies or an inclination to defuse responsibility. When people score *low* on collaborating, they may fail to capitalizes on situations, which would benefit immensely from joint problem solving. Also by ignoring the concerns of employees, decisions and policies may be evolved, which make the organizational members both unhappy and uncommitted to the system. The strategy attempts a win— win solutions to their goals

Accommodating

In accommodating mode a person scarifies his own interest for accommodating other person's interest. It is form of selfless generosity, obeying other person's point of view. This mode is usually adopted when other person's view is stronger, you want to achieve goodwill and indicate that you are reasonable. This strategy of conflict resolution is important when you want other person to give at a later date when it favours you. Sekaran concluded that when people are *high* on accommodating score they might be differing too much to the wishes of others and pay very little attention to their own ideas and concern even though they may realize that they are not getting the attention they deserve. This might even lower one's self esteem in addition to depriving on the influence, respect and recognition from others, since it negates the potential contribution that individuals are capable of making to the organization. While individual *low* on accommodating score, they should start thinking about whether they lack the goodwill of others and whether others perceive them as unreasonable, uncompromising, rigid and demanding.

Compromising

In conflict situation, compromising is a mode when both parties try to find out some expedient, mutually acceptable solution that sacrifies both the parties partially. In compromising, there is no clear winner or loser. None of the party is fully satisfied as they ration the object of conflict and accept the solution which is not complete to either of the parties. In compromising, there is a possibility of an atmosphere of *'gamesmanship'* in the work environment. There is also a possibility of compromising on certain principles of behaviour which is not desirable. Values, ethics, principles and long term objectives of the organization must be protected while adopting compromising. When people are tough to compromise, they find it hard to make concessions and land up in power struggle that must be avoided. Compromising policies can easily be adopted when competing or collaboration strategy fails. Research indicates that people have underlying disposition to handle conflict in certain ways. Especially individuals have preferences among the five conflict handling intensions. Their preferences tend to be relied upon quite consistently, and a persons intensions can be predicted rather well from a combination of intellectual and personality characteristics. When confronting conflict situation, some people want to win it at any cost, some wants to find an optimum solution, some want to run away, others want to be obliging, and still others want to *"split the differences"* (Robbins Stephen P.)[8].

SUMMARY

Conflict management deserves attention in present corporate environment. Conflict is a process that begins when one party perceives that another party has negatively affected something that the first party cares about. Conflict can be considered as an expression of hostility, negative attitude, aggression and gross misunderstanding. Conflict can be functional or dysfunctional. It is of three types namely task oriented conflict, behavioral conflict and structural or process oriented confllict. Traditional view of conflict (1930-40) considers conflict as harmful and synonimous to violance, distruction and irrational. Human relations era which was prevalent during the period of 1940-70 considered conflict as natural phenomenon and recommends various steps to avoid its occurance. Behavioural view on the other hand encourages conflict for creativity, higher productivity and for achieving group cohesiveness. It recommends elaborate steps to keep it as minimum as possible. Propagaters of Modern view feel that conflict is structural in nature, is inevitable and endemic to organizational milieu. It is integral to process of change.They recommend proper management of conflict as it promotes high level of competition between individuals and groups. Intra-personal conflict occurs when there is a conflict of values, that may relates to roles that an individual is required to play and decisions he has to take in the organization. Inter-personal conflict occurs due to dis-agreement over the goals of the organization. These are further aggravated due to difference of opinion. Inter- group and inter-departmental conflict take place when universality of policies, procedures and standards do not exist. Intra-organizational conflicts relates to horizontal, vertical and line and staff conflicts.

Conflict must be resolved based on the model given by Pondy. Conflict can also be resolved by displaying high co-operative behaviour. It can take various forms like avoiding, accomodating, collaborating and compromising on various issues between individuals, groups and organizations. Minimum level of conflict can keep groups vibrant, cohesive and creative.

TEXT QUESTIONS

Q. 1 Define conflict. What forms does it take in an organization?

Q. 2 Explain functional and dysfunctional conflict?

Q. 3 What are various types of conflict. Explain.

Q. 4 How has transition of conflict taken place?

Q. 5 Explain with help of diagram Pondy's conflict management process.

Q. 6 What are various causes of conflict?

Q. 7 Explain conflict resolution model?

Q. 8 Visit one of the industrial organizations in your neighbourhood and study conflict management adopted by them.

Q. 9 Conflict can be benefitial if it is kept to minimun. Explain the statemnent

Q. 10 Write shorts notes on the following:

(*a*) Latent conflict
(*b*) Perceived conflict
(*c*) Felt conflict
(*d*) Manifest conflict
(*e*) Conflict aftermath
(*f*) Behavioural conflict
(*g*) Inter-personal conflict
(*h*) What forms a conflict can take

REFERENCES

1. Thomas K.A. "***Conflict and Negotiations Process in Organizations***", Hand Book of Industrial and Organizational Psychology, 2nd edition, Volume III Palo Alto; Consulting psychologist press, 1992.
2. Austin, David L. "***Conflict: A More Professional approach***", Personal administration, Volume 21 July 1976.
3. Schein, Edgar H., "***Organizational Psychology***", Eagle wood Cliffs, NJ, Prentice Hall Inc, 1966.

4. Michael V.P ***"Organizational Behaviour and Manegerial Effectiveness"***, first edition 1989, S Chand & Co Ltd New Delhi.
5. Louis R. Pondy, ***"Organization Conflict, Concepts and Models"***, administrative science, quarterly, Sept.1969 pp 296-320."
6. Chandan Jit S. ***"Organizational Behaviour"***, 1997, Vikas publishing house (Pvt) Ltd New Delhi.
7. Uma Sekaran, ***"Organizational Behaviour"***, Text and Cases, Tata McGraw Hills Publishing Company Limited, New Delhi, Ninth Reprint, 2000.
8. Robbins Stephen P. ***"Organzational Behaviour"***, Ninth Edition, Printise Hall, India.2001.

Case Study

ESCALATION OF CONFLICT THROUGH ENDOWED CHAIR

Dr. Anant, Chairman of the department of management, and Dr. Basant, Chairman of the accountancy department, had always experienced awkwardness whenever they interacted with each other during the executive committee and other meetings. The management department had an excellent group of faculty members who were not only reputed for their research but were also first rate teachers. No other department in the entire system had such a group of profile writers in any one unit. In fact, the management department faculty and their chairman did entertain feelings of superiority even though they tried not to express it blatantly. Because of their research productivity and national reputation, the university allocated more resources to the management department – more funded trips to conferences, more Xeroxing money, more secretarial assistance, and the like.

Dr. Basant was also proud of his accountancy department faculty because the members were extremely active and successful in acquiring consulting projects and generating a lot of money for themselves and for the department. They worked with the big accounting firms and private sector organizations. These firms donated generously to the department. Because of all the money generated, the faculty had carpeted office, specialized stationery, and other status symbols. Actually, the accountancy department looked like a private company's show room, with Kashmir carpets, fancy furniture, an impressive conference room, and expensive decorative pieces.

Privately, the management department referred to the accountancy department as "the greatest show on earth", and the latter referred to the management faculty as "pen pushers". On one occasion three of the management faculty had to go to the accountancy department to obtain the tax professor's clarification on the recent budget statements made by the Finance Minister. They had to wait in the department's waiting area for the faculty member who had just stepped out of his office. Dr. Basant who happened to come out at that time remarked jokingly to the waiting members, "You must find it pleasant to sit in soft sofas after sitting on hard chairs the whole day in your offices". When Dr. Anant heard about this, he issued a memo to all his faculty that they should try to use the intercom as much as possible in the future and not bother other department faculty with personal visits to their officers. Of courses, everyone knew that the memo was the outcome of his resentment towards Dr. Basant's remarks.

Shortly after these incidents, the management department received a capital fund donation from one of its alumni, which would fetch an annual interest of Rs. 50,000. Mr. Ramesh Mehra, the donor was the President of a very prosperous, privately owned company. Mr. Ramesh Mehra, had received his M.S. degree in management 10 years ago, and had risen to the top within that time. He had always had high regard for the research – oriented faculty of the management department, and though it would be an excellent idea to fund an "Endowed Chair" for the department. This would enable the management department chairman to bring in some international scholar of repute from time to time which would further enhance the prestige of the department. Mr. Mehra was not entirely guided by philanthropy alone since he was also considering the advantages to the company by claiming the donation as a tax write-off. The management department chairman, of course, gratefully accepted the offer.

As the company's P.R. people tried to gain publicity for the donation, the management department chairman and several members of the faculty were interviewed by the press. The ceremonial award of the "Endowed Chair" by the president of the company to the department chairman was nationally televised. The company and the management department were very much in the news for several days.

When Dr. Basant met Dr. Anant in the corridor one day as all this was happening, he congratulated Anant and said with a hint of sarcasm that it must be a great feeling to receive such a donation, especially since this would be the first time that they have generated funds from outside the University system. Dr. Anant thanked Basant and said that if the accountancy department needed any assistance in getting its faculty to publish, his faculty "will be glad to share their knowledge with them on how to go about doing research and publishing". After this episode the two chairman did not even exchange greeting in the hallway. Faculty members from both departments started to make innuendos and snide remarks at each other in the classroom while lecturing to students. When all this reached the ears of the Principal of the College through the grapevine, he called the two department chairman and gave them a severe dressing down. He reminded them of their unprofessional behaviour and their deplorable conduct. In effect, he asked them to "mend or end". Though things seemed to quieter down considerably immediately after this, students still heard the management department faculty insinuating about the accountancy department and vice-versa. The Principal was not unaware of what was happing and was pondering about how to resolve the problem once and for all.

Analyse the situation above and write up the case analysis.

SKILL DEVELOPMENT EXERCISE

Understand Your Own Conflict Management Style

Instructions

Imagine that you are in situations where you do not agree with another person and try to respond to the following with that orientation.

Below, you will find several pairs of statements describing possible behavioural responses to situations. For each pair, circle the "A" or the "B" statement which is most characteristic of your own behaviour. In some cases neither the "A" nor the "B" statements would be representative of your behaviour. even so, try to select that which comes closest to what you may be likely to do.

The responses which you circle will offer you a good understanding of your conflict-handling style.

1. A. I frequently decide that I should not bother about the differences in our viewpoints.
   B. I try to get my way.
2. A. I try not to hurt the other's feelings so that our relationship can be maintained.
   B. I do all that is necessary to avoid tensions.
3. A. I get all the issues out in the open and discuss them.
   B. I try to postpone issues till I have had time to think.
4. A. I try to seek a solution which is neither totally what I want nor what the other person wants.
   B. I try to assert my viewpoint.
5. A. Many times I let the other person take on the responsibility for solving problem situations.
   B. Instead of trying to negotiate the things on which I might disagree with another, I usually emphasize the aspects on which we both agree.
6. A. I am very goal-oriented and pursue my own goals.
   B. I try to patch up so that our friendship is not spoilt.
7. A. I establish a middle ground.
   B. I do not think that I should worry about the differences.
8. A. I take a middle ground.
   B. I insist on my points being heard.
9. A. I firmly pursue my goals.
   B. I try to avoid frictions.
10. A. I usually try to find a solution which is more compromising in nature.
    B. I usually try to handle all of the other party's as well as my own concerns.
11. A. I try not to handle controversial issues.
    B. If it makes him happy, I let him have his say.
12. A. I try not to create unpleasantness for myself.
    B. I try to win my own position.
13. A. I try to be logical and show him the advantages of my position.
    B. I try to be sensitive to his wishes.
14. A. To make the other person happy, I let him have his way.
    B. I will give in some, if he will give in some.

15. A. I start working through the differences immediately.
    B. I try to see what is fair for both.
16. A. I try to deal with both persons' wishes.
    B. I let him solve the problem.
17 A. I usually search for a compromise solution.
    B. I usually let go of my own wishes so that the other person's needs are taken care of.
18. A. I try to establish a middle ground.
    B. I try to satisfy both our wishes.
19. A. I firmly stick to my point of view.
    B. I work out a solution with the other person.
20. A. If the matter is that important to him, I let him have his way.
    B. I insist on a compromise.
21. A. I usually get everyone's concerns out in the open.
    B. I usually try to give in and preserve our friendship.
22. A. While negotiating, I take the other's feelings into consideration.
    B. I deal with the issue directly, placing all the cards on the table.
23. A. I feel strongly about pursuing my goals.
    B. I feel compromise solutions are the best.
24. A. I take time to think over the issue before starting to discuss it.
    B. I give in some to gain some.
25. A. I would rather not hurt the other's feelings.
    B. I jointly work out the problem with the other person.
26. A. I try not hurt the other's feelings.
    B. I convince the other of the logic of my statement.
27. A. I express my ideas and ask for his.
    B. I try to convince him of the benefits of my ideas.
28. A. I firmly pursuer my goals.
    B. I try to get all the issues out on the table.
29. A. I generally avoid controversial situations.
    B. I pursue a policy of give and take.
30. A. I invariably work with the other person's help to come up with a solution.
    B. I try my best to do whatever is necessary to avoid tensions.

Scoring:

Circle the items below which you circled against each item of the questionnaire you have just completed.

S. No.	Competing	Collaborating	Compromising	Avoiding	Accommodating
1.	B				A
2.				A	B
3.		A		B	
4.	B		A		
5.				A	B
6.	A				B
7.			A	B	
8.	B		A		
9.	A			B	
10.		B	A		
11.				A	B
12.	A			B	
13.	A				B
14.			B		A
15.		A	B		
16.		A		B	
17.		A			B
18.		B	A		
19.	A	B			
20.			B		A
21.		A			B
22.		B			A
23.	A		B		
24.			B	A	
25.		B			A
26.	B				A
27.	B	A			
28.	A	B			
29.			B	A	
30.			A		B

Total number of items circled in each column: Highest score is your conflict resolution ability.

________	________	________	________	________
Competing	Collaborating	Compromising	Avoiding	Accommodating

CHAPTER 12

Stress Management

INTRODUCTION TO STRESS

People experience stress in private life and at work place. People have to work effectively against time and within the parameter of various rules and regulations. It is not always possible to create an organizational climate conducive to work. Various departments, groups and external environment factors affect individual behaviour. Minimal level of stress is required for organizations to operate effectively. Excessive stress is harmful for the individual as it causes mental and physical disequilibrium and subsequently leads to physical and mental disturbance. People suffer from high blood pressure, heart attack when stress is beyond control of the human beings. It is therefore necessary to identify causes of stress and modify behaviour so that the individual energy is directed towards organizational productivity and healthy organization climate is created.

Hans Selye[1], a medical researcher first used term "Stress" to describe the body's biological response mechanism. He defined stress as "the nonspecific response of the body to any demand". He views that stress is the spice of life, the absence of stress is death. Stress is usually considered to be negative and caused due to something bad. Thus stress refers to distress. Ivancevich and Matterson define stress as "the interaction of the individual with the environment" According to Beehr and Newman[2], stress is a condition arising from the interaction of people and their jobs and characterised by changes within people that force them to deviate from their normal functioning. Stress is a dynamic condition in which a person is faced with lot of constraints while functioning in the organiation. Stress causes discomfort, which leads to disequilibrium in the individual's mind set. Stress is not always negative in nature. In a broader sense it is discomfiture whether it creates problems.

Stress is also a source of inspiration. When there is a stress for any work it leads to higher performance. When stress is gravest, it reduces employee productivity. But there are example where people may get immune to stress having no negative effect on their performance. Such people do not get tense. This type of immunity is achieved through constant experience and training. John M. Ivancevich and Michael T. Matterson have defined stress as **"adoptive response, mediated by individual characteristics and/ or psychological processes, that is a consequence of any external action, situation or event that places special physical and/or psychological demands upon a person"**. As it is clear from the definition that stress is caused due to external factors, situations or events. These have adverse impact on the individual characteristics and psychological processes. These together put an additional burden or demands on individual, hence the stress. External factors may include social setting, work ethics in the organization, leadership styles, availability of resources, workload, level of technology and the work environment. The internal factors that are effected are psychological in nature and includes emotions, ego state, attitude, perception, motivational factors, need and demographics. If employees feel that external factors are of not much consequence and have no compelling effect the stress is not formed within the minds of individuals. High desire, uncertainty, result of promotion examination, unrealized ambition may cause stress to the individual.

Stress should not be confused with anxiety or nervous tension and damaging. They occur as regular features in many cases and have no long – lasting impact on the working capacities of the employees. Mishra (2003)[3] has very aptly explained that anxiety may remain purely psychological and may not cause any physical impact. Similarly, only physical impacts will not be stress unless it is felt by the mind and heart. The psychological and physical impacts are visible in the form of stress. Anxiety is the cause of stress but not stress itself. Symptoms of stress are given in Figure 12.1 below:

Symptoms of Stress

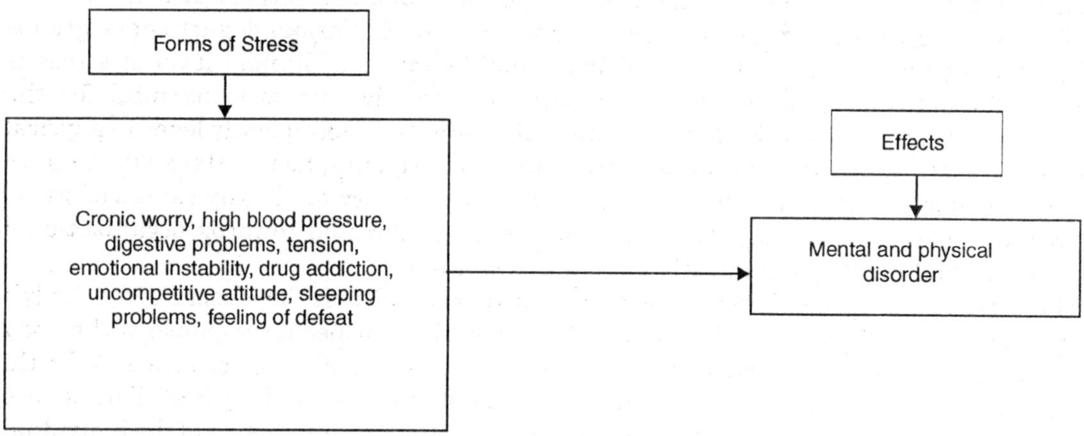

Fig. 12.1. Symptoms of stress

Stress is generally of a mild nature and one recovers from it easily. Once a person gets used to environmental factors and people with whom one generally works on a daily basis, there is no existence of stress. It is the work environment, plant, people and situations, which one is not used to, creates tension and resultant stress. The stress diminishes gradually when one get used to it. However the stress can be mild, stiff and chronic in nature. Mild stress is visible when person develops lack of appetite and high blood pressure. The stress becomes stiffer if these are not carefully countered. When stress attains a chronic stage, where a person develops instability, frustration and feel uncomfortable and can not cope up with problems. It affects physical efficiency and subsequently a psychological strength. This stage is called "**Burn out**". In this stage individual is emotionally weakened. The stage of burn-out is reached when an individual fails to achieve his objective. He exhibits irritation, errors, frustration and apathy. Executives are highly prone to burn out due to high pressure in the work environment. In such situation they resort to change the job that further adds to existing chronic burn-out situation as they are not able cope up with the changed environment. In such situation employees should resort to neuro – psycho treatment. In case of aggravation of this situation a state of "**Trauma**" is reached. Trauma is a very serious form of stress. It occurs in the organization where employees find it difficult to adjust. This may be caused due to pressure of work, late working hours, inability of employees to fulfill social obligation and poor time management. The work place trauma is carried home by employees where they develop various psychological disorder. Non adjustment in work place for a long time leads to suspension and firing of employee. Stress can be avoided by adopting an approach of co-operation, help the fellow employee in distress and social interaction with affected individuals.

General Adaptation Syndrome

The general adaptation syndrome (GAS) refers to development of individuals responses to stressful events in the form of physiological, psychological and behaviour patterns. They follow a fairly consistent pattern. These are of three types as classified by Hans Selve.

(*a*) **Alarm Stage:** This is a warning stage and occurs as first sign of stress. Many physiological and chemical reactions occur. During this stage muscle becomes tense, pupils dilate and there is a increased hormone flow. Increased pituitary adrenaline secretion, increased respiration, heart trouble and high blood pressure are major symptoms of alarm stage. Regular physically exercises and expert psychiatric treatment can prevent this phenomenon.

(*b*) **Resistance Stage:** If the alarm stage is not controlled in time, body organs develop resistance but leaves its ill effects. During the resistance stage individual is unable to rest and develops irritating nature. There is increased nervousness, tension frustration and uneasiness in the day to day work environment. Individual develops ulcer, loss of appetite and illness. Though an individual feels that he has over come the stress situation but its ill effects persist for a long time. It is therefore necessary to identify roots of stress and remove them for a permanent solution.

(*c*) **Exhaustion:** When the body, psyche is affected it is believed that the stress has reached the stage of exhaustion. During this stage individual experiences physical and mental pressures and develops ulcers and high blood pressure. Exhaustion develops moodiness, negative attitude, individual appears fatigued and displays helplessness in his behaviour. Organizations where employees suffer from exhaustion must take corrective action. Poor health of employees, negative emotions and depression reduces the organizational effectiveness to a large extent. Large number of organizations have started physical and psychological treatment of employees on a regular basis.

SOURCES OF JOB STRESS

Organization, Group and individual have impact on the performance of a job. Enviornment also effects adversely on the efficiency of the individual. It is expressed in Figure 12.2 below:

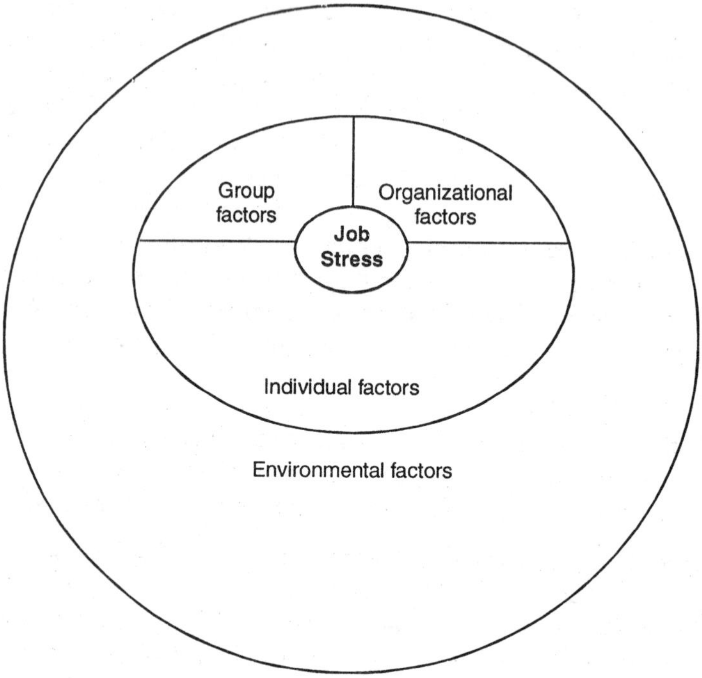

Fig. 12.2. Sources of job stress

1. Environment Factors

There are innumerable environmental factors that have caused a great deal of work stress on the employees. Ivancevich and Matterson have identified societal, economic, financial, cultural, familial and technological factors which have tremendous influence on mental health of the employees. Societal factors have forced both husband and wife to do the job to maintain a high level of life style. Government NGOs and other voluntary organizations have introduced various schemes for the welfare of the people. Though the life span in general has increased but the immunity in the body has decreased to a great level and large number of people are suffering from various disease caused by work stress. People have become more ambitious. They want their children to do well in life this causes stress. Environmental stressors like family demands and obligation, economic and financial conditions, race, caste, creed, ethnic identity, relocation due to transfer cause adverse effect on individuals. Recent communal violence around the world have changed political scenario, defence affiliations of nations have siphoned off the large resources toward defence preparedness. People are living in a fearful environment. These problems have to be solved by educating people and diverting their energies to the basic objective of the organisaion. Science and technology should be used for the development and progress of human race and not for destruction purpose. All family problems should be resolved by assisting each other and that the people should learn to live in an atmosphere of peace co-existence should be the keyword.

2. Organizational Stressors

Organizational stressors can be classified into mission statement, strategies, policies, organizational structure and design, reporting channels, communication, various processes, systems and last but not the least the working conditions. Organization mission and subsequent departmental goals have a long lasting impact on the employees. Over ambitions goals leave employees more streached for attaining the same. Good organizational polices, procedures, rules, regulations keep employees in high spirit. On the contrary, adhockism, inadequate compensation, rigid rules, ambiguous organizational policies and faulty job design cause tremendous amount of stress.

Job related policies must be sound and updated. Task design should include job autonomy, task variety so that employee derive pleasure while at work. Work place, and work environment are two very important factors. Poor hygiene in work place, inadequate space, light, lack of physical security at work place are stressors. Stress is caused by inadequate support from subordinates, conflicting job requirements, inadequate and poor performance measurement, and lack of empowerment. Managerial style, role of superior boss, command and control mechanism leave much to be desired from Indian organizations. Policies should be sound and employee participation must be ensured at each level. It must be understood that wisdom and innovativeness is widely spread in the workers, it is the ability of mangers to identify and canalize for organizational betterment.

3. Group Stressors

Hawthorne studies have established the impact of group cohesiveness, group norms and importance of group objective for attainment of organizational goals. Lack of cohesiveness creates conflict. Employees must be given full opportunities to develop themselves. People join group for social security that should be provided. Managers must ensure that job well done is recognized, omission on this account creates stress like situation in the minds of the employees. Group social events and group activities must be organized on a regular bases. Managers should form the part of group, which should not be based on rank and position. Employee morale must be kept high to avoid group stress.

4. Individual Stressors

Personal life and events of official life cannot be separated. Events of marriage, divorce, death in the family has a remarkable impact on work situation. Personal life difficulties are highly stressful.

(a) Job Security

Job and career enhancement can become a source of stress. Job security is one of the major reasons for an employee. Insecurity increases during times of recession. The prospect of losing job, specially when an employee is the sole bread earner for the entire family is very stressful. Another reason for job related stress is promotion or enhancement of appointment. A person must have a job commensurate with his qualification. Promotion must be related to efficiency and due care should be exercised in this regard. Nothing is more stressful that a junior employee being appointed as a senior to an equally competent person.

(b) Relocation

Relocation is related to transfer of a person to a different place. Transfers upsets the daily routine of individuals. The fear of working at new location with different people itself is stressful. Unpredictability about new work environment and creating new relationship cause anxiety. Transfer also creates problems for family members. It may be admission in schools, adjustment to social environment, house and may even be language. In case a person has to search a new job at a different location, the stress is even greater.

(c) Changes in life structure

Span of life has many facets. Some of these are socio-economic environment, culture, systems, religion, race, education and person's interaction with society in different roles. If all these aspects are favorable, then the stress is minimal, stress is also determined by ability of a person to cope up with it and the faith. If a person's life is stable and move with a slow pace, there are less stress and more ability to cope with stress. While a person who has great ambition and moves with fast pace is not able to cope up with stress.

(d) Stress and Behaviour

Stress is a state of mind which reflects biochemical reactions in the human body. Environmental and internal forces cause sense of anxiety, tension and depression to human being. As stress is the non specific response of the body to any demand, it is necessary to understand specific or routine activities that cause stress. There are two types of activities. Desirable activities and undesirable activities. Both these activities create stress. The stress created by desirable and successful effects is called "eustress". Eustress is a positive, healthy and developmental stress response. It leads to better performance and a more adjusted personality. In eustress situation, we learn how to deal with the situation better. It improves our capacity to deal with stressful situations. Stress created by undesirable outcomes is known "distress". It is primarily the distress form of stress which causes undesirable effects on physical and psychological well – being of the person. Highly stressful activities weakens individuals ability to cope up with various situations. Just as extremely high level of stress is harmful and damaging, extremely low level of stress is also equally harmful. It causes boredom, reduces innovativeness and ability to face challenges. Thus moderate level of stress is desirable for higher level of performance. See the diagram 12.3 below indicating the relationship between stress and performance proposed by Henry L Tossi, et al.[4]

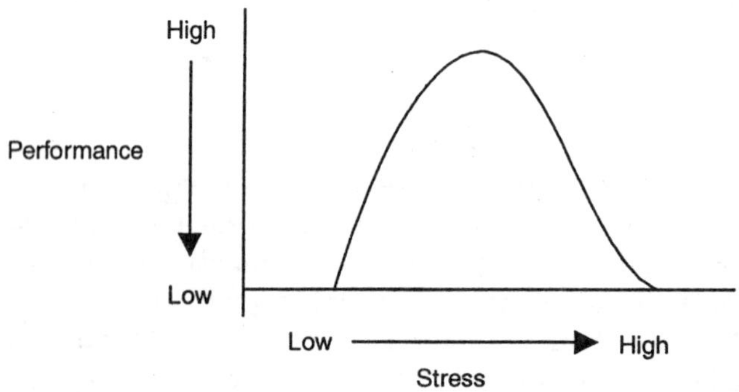

Fig. 12.3. Relationship of Stress and Performance

Physiological Response

When stress appears, immediate biochemical changes take place. Heart beat and heightening of all the body senses. Serious health problems occur as body faces stress for long period of time. Baron[5] concluded that stress could lead to breakdown of body's immune systems and may result in serious health problems such as high blood pressure, ulcer and even heart attack. High level stress can result in physical changes that threaten our health and well-being.

Psychological Response

People have different levels of handling stress. Those who are highly affected by stress tend to be depressed and display lack of self confidence. They believe that they have lost the battle in handling a situation and develop a feeling of helplessness and elicit sympathy from others. They have a greater fear of unknown, display irritating behaviour, become impatient and tend to blame others for the inefficiency. Workers who are seriously affected loose confidence in themselves and display a low productivity. To overcome this situation, individuals should be kept busy, put through promotional cadres and subjected to regular physical exercises. This reduces work stress and help individual to develop.

Behavioral Response

Chohen[6] carried out studies on the impact of stress on human-being. As per the study people under constant stress behave differently as compared to the people who are emotionally balanced. High level of stress is usually associated with smoking, increased use of alcohol and consumption of drugs. They are either defensive or offensive in their behaviour. Stress induces irrational interpersonal behaviour. They withdraw from the social environment and confine themselves to isolation.

Frustration

Frustration is a form of behaviour which occurs when a person is prevented from achieving a goal or objective. It refers to obstruction or impediment to goal oriented behaviour. Frustration is caused **firstly** due to delay in getting advancement or recognition through a promotion is insight. One even gets frustrated waiting for some one to meet at a scheduled time and date. **Secondly** non availability of various resources. A faculty member may not be able to carryout research work because he is over burdened with other responsibilities. He may get frustrated due to non – availability of time resource. The **third** cause of frustration is non attainment of goal. For example failure in the examination, non attainment of production or sales target, failure to get promotion are some of the causes of frustration which are manifested in stress.

Anxiety

Jit S Chandan[7] explains "anxiety" as a feeling of inability and helplessness in formulating appropriate responses for dealing with the anticipated negative outcome. It occurs when a decision has to be made but the outcome of the decision could have positive as well as negative consequences. Anxiety also occurs when there is situation when one does not know as to what is right. For example, an employee is serving in an organization for over ten years and fully satisfied with the organizational culture but asked to move on promotion to a different organization and to a far away place. Hammer and Organ[8] explains various causes of anxiety in the work environment. They explained that "difference in power in the organization which leave people with a feeling of vulnerability to administrative decisions adversely affecting them. These are as under:-

(*a*) Frequent changes in organizations, which make existing behaviour plans obsolete.
(*b*) Competition, which creates the inevitability that some persons lose "face", esteem and status.
(*c*) Job ambiguity (especially when it is coupled with pressure).
(*d*) Lack of job feedback, volatility in the organizations' economic environment, job insecurity and high visigibility of one's performance (success as well as failures).
(*e*) Personal problems such as physical illness, problems at home, unrealistically high personal goals and estrangement from one's colleagues or one's peer group.

Stressors Intrinsic to Job

The nature of the job will determine the level of stress it carry with it. A railway engine dreiver's job is more stressful as it does not have control over the time and attached with it is a high degree of responsibility due to number of passenger travelling in the train. The driver does not have control over the safety of passengers hence it is more stressful. High stress jobs are those in which the employees have little or no control over the operations, work under time constraints and have major responsibilities for human beings and other resources. There are high stress jobs like defence services, police, foreman, mangers, inspector, etc. On the contrary there are low stress jobs like teachers, craft worker, farm labour. Studies carried out by Karasek[9] has indicated higher risk of coronary diseases to those who work under high stress jobs. He identified two job factors that affect the level of such risk. These factors are firstly "level of psychological demand" and the "level of decision control" over the work. According to this study jobs are categorized in the following manner:

(*a*) Low psychological demand/ Low decision control. Eg. Watchman, truck driver.
(*b*) Low psychological demand/ High decision control. Eg. Mechanic, sales clerk.
(*c*) High psychological demand/ High decision control. Eg. Sales manger, bank officer.
(*d*) High psychological demand/ Low decision control. Eg. waitress, telephone operator, cook etc.

Role Ambiguity

Role of every individual must be clearly defined. According to Kahn, role is a set of activities associated with certain position in the organization or in the society. If these work activities are ill defined, then the person will not perform his duties as others expect him to do so. When there is ambiguity about role expectation, then people in the organization experience certain amount of stress. Generally, role of a person is associated with the appointment he holds and duties of various appointments are well laid down and time tested. If a person is holding station masters job, his duties are clear and there is a little scope for ambiguity. This is only possible in bureaucratic or traditional organizations. Role ambiguity is more pronounced with the organizations which are fluid in nature and subject to change with environment factors. Role ambiguity is also noticed in managerial cadre where job specifications and roles are not clearly defined because of the general nature of the job. Principle of unity of command is not followed strictly and therefore there is always a conflict about reporting channels. French and Caplan[10] in their studies concluded that role ambiguity causes

(1) Psychological strain and dissatisfaction.
(2) Leads to under utilization of human resources, and
(3) Leads to feeling of futility on how to cope with the organizational environment

Role Conflict

Role conflict occurs when individuals have a variety of expectations from another individual who is not able to meet their demands placed on him. A person may not be capable of handling two or more pressures at any one time. Employees may be demanding rise in salary, which a manger feels as genuine but he cannot recommend to the management due to the latter's pressure. Role conflict occurs when contradictory demands are simultaneously placed upon an employee. Role conflict also occurs when an individual has to play more than one role simultaneously. A manager can not permit his wife (an employee) to go home before time or he may not accept lower quality of work on one hand, but may neglect quantity on the other. There is stress due to inter – role conflict. Robert Kahn[11] and his colleagues at University of Michigan concluded that contradictory role expectations give rise to opposing role pressures (role conflict) which generally have the following effects on the emotional experience of the focal person : Intensified internal conflicts, increased tension associated with various aspect of the job, reduced satisfaction with the job and its various components, and decreased confidence in superiors and in the organization as a whole. The strain experienced by those in conflict situations leads to various coping responses like social and psychological withdrawal. "Finally the presence of conflict in one's role tends to undermine his relations with his role senders to produce weaker bonds of trust, respect and attraction. It is quite clear that role conflicts are costly for the person in emotional and interpersonal terms. They may be costly to the organization, which depends on effective coordination and collaboration, within and among its parts".

BURNOUT

Burnout is a type of existential crisis in which work is no longer a meaningful function. Workers who experience burnout may no longer view their job as meaningful. They feel work as tedious, redundant, and insignificant. They experience total fatigue which may show itself in the form of boredom, depression and a powerful sense of alienation. Work related behaviour of executives indicate very little concern for quality, creativity, enthusiasm and contribution to organizational goals.

Morely and Katherine (1982)[12] in their work on the subject have identified the pattern of behaviour burned out executives. They concluded that predictable behaviour is as under:

(*a*) Tendency to balance others in the organization for their burnout.
(*b*) To complain bitterly about aspects of work which in the past were not areas of concern.
(*c*) To miss work because of non-specific and increasingly prevalent illness.
(*d*) To daydream and sleep on the job.
(*e*) To be last to come and the first to leave.
(*f*) To bicker with co-workers or appear unco-operative and to become increasingly isolated from others.

Causes of Burnout

1. **Work Estimation:** Overwork is generally considered to be a major cause for burnout. But it not so. Burnout take place in a chaotic, unstable environment. It often happens when there is a confusion about duties and future managerial directions. Burnout takes place when there is management by crisis. Low work estimation may also cause burnout. When executives feel that there is no challenge and innovativeness in the work, burnout take place.
2. **Job Mismatch:** It has been observed that executives choose and accept jobs which has higher extrinsic reward like high salaries and power. These hygiene factors generally fail to motivate executives for a longer time. Decision to choose extrinsic reward over intrinsic rewards results in unhappiness. Job mismatch may be observed in personal value and organizational value system and autonomy provided by organization in work environment. Lack of gratification from the work generally leads to burnout.

Organizational Productivity

When executive are not able to meet organizational objective due to external environmental factors like shortage of raw material, government rules, market demand etc., they experience a burnout. They feel a sense of helplessness. Burnout may also be noticed where there is a strict bureaucratic way of doing things and very little scope for exploitation of personal skills, innovation and creativity.

Personal Problems

Personal problems like unhappy married life, financial instability, children education, job security may cause stress leading to burnout. Persons with a predisposition to burnout may be badly affected by problems unrelated to work.

Prevention of Burnout

As seen in the preceding reading, burnout emanate from organizational policy, structure, practices, nature of the work and personal characteristics of the individual. Probability of burnout increases if there is a mismatch between individual and job fit.

Preventive measures include diagnosis, prevention and treatment.

Diagnosis

It is the responsibility of all individuals to ensure that his subordinate is not subjected to burnout. This can be identified from the early warning by observing clinical signs that include the following:

(*a*) Feeling of lethargy.
(*b*) Lack of productivity.
(*c*) Lack of interest in the present job and feeling that change of job and place may change the present situation without even considering upward mobility.
(*d*) Feeling of loneliness, forced isolation and acute discomfort.
(*e*) Feeling of direction less.
(*f*) Traumatic personal problems like death in family or major accident.

Prevention

Morley and Katherine[12] have suggested the following preventive and treatment strategies:

(a) Seeking a fit between characteristics of the individual, complexity of the job and type of organizational structure.
(b) Developing programmes which help individuals cope with the causes of stress that lead to burnout.
(c) Teaching and supporting self – diagnosis and individual adaptation strategies for addressing burnout symptoms.

Treatment

(a) Evaluate and understand the cause of burnout.
(b) Determine change both personal and organizational to return to normal work – related functioning.
(c) Develop sensitivity to the signs of burnout to cope with likelihood of the same in future.
(d) Develop skills to deal with feelings and emotions to avoid burnout to fellow employees.

Role Overload / Under Load

It has been observed that organizations are resorting to promote employees to take voluntary retirement (VRS). In addition employees are being retrenched to cut down on the production cost to be able to be competitive in the market. This has led to excessive work-load to the employees. In this situation they feel that they do not have adequate time or ability to meet such requirements. When targets have to be met, employees have to work over time. At times they even have to handle more than one job to cater for absent workers. Role overload occurs when there is too much work, too little time or lack of skills.

Role underload is an opposite phenomenon to role overload. It occurs when person's skill and ability is under utilized, there is a lack of job variety or the contents of the job is so small that the person feels that his potentials are not been fully utilized. Workers who suffer from work underload experience lack of interest in the job and leads to excessive absenteeism. It ultimately results in low self-esteem and lack of job satisfaction.

Responsibility

Responsibility is a factor for work stress. People who are in finance department have to complete accounts of the organization before a scheduled date. This increases work load and stress merely because it has to be computed before a particular time. It causes a sense of burden upon an individual. Efficiency of a manager is greatly affected by the efficiency and quality of work produced by subordinates. If anything goes wrong, it is a leader who is accountable for it. This aspect causes stress upon a manger.

French and Caplin[10] state. If there is any truth to the adage that "man's greatest enemy is himself", it can be found in these data – it is the responsibility which organizational members have for other organizational members, rather than the responsibility for impersonal aspects of the organization, which constitutes the more significant organizational stress".

MANAGEMENT OF STRESS

Individual Level Strategies

Minimum level of stress is required to stimulate individuals to higher productivity. Excessive stress is harmful to both individual and organization. It is a common practice to evolve various stress reduction strategies in the organizations. Individuals must take steps to reduce stress to a acceptable level. It is clarified that every individual has different capacity to cope with individual stress. Some of the individual stress reduction strategies are as under:

1. **Define objective for Self:** Setting up of objective for self is a continuous process right from the childhood where parents generally decide as to the stream of learning, institutes and the like. When you join an organization, it is important to study organizational structure, job involved and the prospects of growth. Every person must set for himself the object vis – vis the ability and skill one possesses. It is generally observed that individuals set high objective for themselves to be achieved in short span of time. They inhibit inbuilt fear of failing. Setting up of high standard without analyzing resources available leads to stressful situation. People must modify their goals based upon various resources available, 'time' being the most important resource.
2. **Plan your life:** Work stress has an impact on personal life at home and vice – versa. It is therefore important to plan various aspects of life as is possible. This will include increasing professional competence by way of acquiring additional qualification and skill, sound financial planning, home, children education and so on. Contingency plan must also be evolved in case of uncertainty. If this is done, a person is physically and mentally prepared for events to come. Investment in insurance for children education may make you free from 'stress' if it was planned well in advance.
3. **Social Support:** A man is becoming isolated like an island in vast ocen due to breaking of joint family system, requirement of moving out of home for service purposes and thereby losing physical contacts with kith and kin. It is important to keep close rapport with relatives. At closer to work place develop friendship with fellow workers who can help in times of crisis, stress and strain. Social support can be easily built by adhering to social functions, norms and following religious activities at work place. This will enable individuals to regain sulking self confidence and build self-esteem. People have resorted to GOD in old age. Old age homes, citizens committees etc. are sings of existence of stress and evolving of stress resolution strategies. The practice of confession to a priest in the Catholic religion is nothing but a way to eliminate stress caused by some action.
4. **Physical Fitness:** Healthy body and mind are stress resistance. It has been conclusively proved that individuals who exercise and so strengthen their endurance and cardiovascular system, are much less likely to suffer from certain types of stress related illness[13]. Regular physical exercises like walking, jogging, light gymnastics exercises keep person fit and develop an ability to sustain greater level of stress. Soldiers are definitely more stress resistants as they keep themselves

physically fit. They develop an ability and mind to withstand worst of the situations. Appropriate daily diet help individual to keep good health.

5. **Biofeedback:** Biofeedback is the human ability to bring some of the bodily functions under voluntary control. It is the methodology designed to remove undesirable body responses through psychological transformation. Use of sophisticated electronics devices are designed to measure the level of stress in an individual. With subsequent relaxasation or yogic exercises the individual is brought back to normal standard situation by removing stress. The relaxation exercises are helpful to control heart attacks, acidity, brain haemorrhage, blood pressure and muscle tension etc. Changes in these deceases are caused due to high level of stress which an individual is not habitual to experience. Biofeedback takes care to control the effects of stress on voluntary basis by proper exercises.
6. **Yoga:** Yoga is a methodology to integrate body and mind and achieve a required level of harmony with the God. This is achieved by physical exercises called Asanas which stimulates various systems in the body like respiratory system, nervous system, blood circulation system etc. This brings a remarkable change into individuals physical capacity and mental ability to sustain through various stress and strain situations. Yoga is also considered as a process of attainment of ultimate peace. But for a common man, it is merely the physical exercises which are aimed at healthy body and mind to counter stress.
7. **Meditation:** Indian history is replete of examples of various saints having achieved salvation by meditation. Lord Gautam Budha had achieved 'nirwana' by meditation. Meditation involves sitting at quite place, closing eyes and concentrating on some symbol with uttering of simple world like 'OM'. It is aimed at total concentration thus forgetting routine situations. This technique also caters for syncranised breathing exercises aim being to block extraneous thoughts from one's mind. Meditation is combination of body, concentration of mind on a particular symbol, utterance of words, regulating of breathing thereby achieving a total concentration of body and mind to achieve a super natural personal power. If this is achieved a person can comfortably handle stressful situation with ease. Meditation brings peace to the mind, develops tolerance power, improves personality and ultimately leads to sainthood.
8. **Time Management:** Time management is one of the methods of reducing stress. Life has become very fast. Executives down to a common worker is pressed for time. Everybody has to play various roles in life. All the roles have to be performed in a given span of time. It is therefore necessary to plan time adequately. Time management can be for various events in life like education, marriage etc. Day to day level, it is related to planning daily routine events. Every individual must maintain a diary in which work schedule and progress should be reflected when more than one job is required to be done at a particular time, priority should be accorded to comparatively important job. It is important to keep up to the schedule of events as planned and ensure the same from the subordinates. This eases pressure on the work schedule and facilitates managing private/ personal work. It instills in an individual a habit of punctuality and a greater sense of responsibility and commitment to the organization.

9. **Live a simple Life:** It is advisable that every person should live a simple life free from cumbrances. Too much of issues being handled at any one time saps individuals energy. One should not complicate issues rather provide simple, straight forward solutions. Do not ask your subordinates to wait for any decision or action on your part. Cases must be disposed off fast without loss of time. In personal life too simplicity of behaviour help individual resolve issues in time. This reduces tension and facilitates time management.

Organizational Level Strategies

Organization play a decisive role in ensuring peaceful environment free of stress. Basically stress relates to two categories of events. First the organizational structure and policy and second relating to personal development and growth that the job can provide. Following aspects must be carefully examined and evaluated for its effectiveness and implementation.

(*a*) Organizational goals must be in realms of achievement. Too much high goals not only put the employees under undue stress but also creates unhealthy work environment.

(*b*) Organizational polices should be clearly defined with particular reference to training and development, promotion, leave, wages and salary administration, discipline, incentives, etc.

(*c*) Authority and responsibility must be clearly defined by setting up reporting channels. Principle of unity of command should be adhared to.

(*d*) Organizational structure, redesigning of jobs and improved communication reduces stress.

(*e*) Corporate policies, physical work environment should be suitable for higher productivity.

(*f*) An updated systems and processes increases efficiency.

(*g*) Management must create an healthy working environment.

(*h*) Career plan for mangers must be developed and implemented in letter and spirit. Nothing discourages employees as bad developmental programmes.

(*i*) Employees must be empowered. They should be provided with suitable time to time counselling by way of advice, reassurance, good communication, release of emotional tension and clarified thinking. Re-orientation is important to keep employees free of stress for increased productivity.

SUMMARY

Stress is non specific response of the body to any demand. Employees experience stress due to organizational climate and work environment. Excessive stress causes physical and mental disturbance. The external factors responsible for individual stress are social setting, work ethics, leadership style, availability of resources, workload, technology and work environment. Internal factors are psychological in nature and may include emotions, ego state, attitude, perception and level of motivation. These put together cause imbalance and disequilibrium and lead to stress. Hans Selve has referred to general adatation syndrome (GAS) which has three stages namely alarm stage, resistance and exhaustion stage. Ivancevich and Matterson have identified social, economic,financial, cultural, familial and technological factors which have tremendous impact on mental health of the employees.

Stress causes frustration and anxiety. The job related stress includes role ambiguity, role conflict, burnout, and role overload/underload. It is important to reduce stress so that the efficiency of the employees is improved. Stress can be managed by achieving physical fitness, biofeedback, yoga, meditation, time management, and by living a simple life. Organizations play a vital role in combating stress. The factors include among others are setting up of realistic goals, well defined organizational policy, restructuring organizational structure when needed, corporate policy update, healthy work environment and empowerment.

TEXT QUESTIONS

Q. 1 Explain stress. How does it create imbalance and disequilibrium?
Q. 2 What are various external and internal causes of stress?
Q. 3 Explain work stress, what are various steps that a manager should take to reduce stress among employees?
Q. 4 What do you understand by burnout, how can employees avoid it? What steps a manager take to prevent employees from burnout?
Q. 5 Explain stress management strategies?
Q. 6 What are various organizational strategies for management of stress?
Q. 7 Visit an organization in the vicinity of your location and study stress management adopted by them.

REFERENCES

1. Hans Selys, ***"The Stress of life"***, McGraw Hill New York, 1976.
2. Terry A. Beehr and J.E. Newman, ***"Job Stress Employee Health and Organizational Effectiveness"***, Personal Psychology, Winter, 1978.
3. Mishra M.N. ***"Organizational Behaviour"***, Vikas Publishing House Pvt. Ltd., 2003.
4. Henry L. Tossi, John R. Rizzo and Stephen J. Carroll, ***"Managing Organizational Behaviour"***, Ballinger Publishing Co. 1986.
5. Baron, R.A. ***"Behaviour in Organizations, understanding and managing the human side of work"***, Allyn and Baon, 1983.
6. Chohen, S., ***"After-effects of stress on Human Performance and Social Behaviour"***, Psychological bulletin, Vol. 88,1980.
7. Jit S. Chandan, ***"Organizational Behaviour"***, Vikas Publishing House Pvt. Ltd., 1997.
8. Hammer W.C., and D. Organ, ***"Organizational Beahviour - An applied Psychological Approach"***, Business Publications 1978.
9. Karasek, Robert A., Columbia University Department of Industrial Engineering and Operations Research. Copy Right 1983.
10. French J.R.P. and R.D. Caplan, ***"Organsiational Stress and Individual Strain"***. in A.J. Marrow (ed.), "The failure of Success", AMACOM, 1972.
11. Kahn R.L., D.M. Wolfe, R.P. Quinn, J.D. Snockand and R.A. Rosenthal, ***"Organizational Stress: Studies in Role Conflict and Ambiguity"***, John Wiley, 1964.
12. Morely D. Glickon and Katherine Janka, ***"Executive under Fire : The Burnout Syndrome"*** California Management Review, Vol. 24 No. 3, 1982.
13. Matterson, M.T. and J. Ivancevich, ***"Managing Job Stress and Health"***, The Intelligent Person's Guide", Free Press, 1982.

Case

MRS. BATRA

Mrs. Batra has been working in the administration department of a hospital in Mumbai for the last 20 years. She is highly dedicated to her job and has a very good rapport with her superiors and co-workers. About eight months ago, she was promoted into the upper ranks of management and was assigned to the supply department of the hospital as a manager. Everybody was happy for her and congratulated her on her promotion. the employees in this new department welcomed her and promised her all the cooperation. Mrs. Batra finds the job very challenging and psychologically rewarding.

She is a very good manager and an interesting person. Everyone in her department likes to come to work because Mrs. Batra makes the day interesting. Since she became the manager, absenteeism is down by over 20 per cent. She has very pleasant personality and is always available to help her subordinates. She is efficient, responsible and responds to all communication in timely manner. She attends all meetings fully prepared to discuss all issues under consideration. This is, she was, at least until last month.

During the last month, she seems to have changed considerably for the worse. Both her superiors and her subordinates find her behaviour strange. She is not as polite and amicable as she used to be. Last week she missed a very important meeting of the top administrators. She was requested to research an issue and prepare the material to present at the weekly meeting. She did not do so. She is often late to work and does not take much interest in the communication she receives from superiors and other departments and does not respond to the these memorandums in a timely manner. She has become aloof and seems tired most of the time.

The Director of the hospital, Mr. Verma, noticed this change in her behaviour early and has been covertly monitoring her behaviour for the last three weeks. Early today, Mr. Verma had a talk with one of the in-house psychiatrists explaining Mrs. Batra's changing work behaviour patterns. The psychiatrist, Dr. Rekhi suggested that perhaps she has been over-working herself and takes the job too seriously. Mr. Verma suggested to Dr. Rekhi that he should talk to Mrs. Batra and find out if there were any difficult situations at home that might be affecting her behaviour. Mrs. Batra has been married for over 20 years and has no children. Mr. Verma is concerned that Mrs. Batra ought to get help before she suffers a total collapse. Dr. Rekhi promised to do so.

QUESTIONS

1. What are some of the symptoms of overload? Does, Mrs. Batra seem to suffer from over-working conditions? Explain your reasons.
2. Given this information, do you think that there may be marital problems at her home that are affecting her work? Could it also be that her work is affecting her family life that is further affecting her work? Justify your speculations.

Based upon: Richard M. Hodgetts, Organizational Behaviour, MacMillan Publishing Company, 1991, adopted from "Organizational Behaviour", 3rd Edition, 2005. Edited by Jit S. Chandan, Published by Vikas Publishing House, New Delhi.

CHAPTER 13

The Dynamics of Communication

INTRODUCTION

Communication is the most vital element of any organization. Without communication an organization would only be an assembly of men, material and processes, which are inoperative. Organizational effectiveness depends upon the quality of communication. Managers have to communicate with subordinates and superiors. They spend more than 75% of their effective time in communicating. It is communication that gives life to organizational structure. It is a thread that holds all the units, sub units, processes, systems, culture together. If communication stops, the organization will cease to exist. Communication is vital for the very existence of the organization. Organizations have to communicate with external organizations, agencies and incorporate various inputs for survival and growth. Communication not only integrates various sub units but shifts information of value acquired from the environment to various departments, groups and individuals. An effective communication is an essence of successful managers. As the organization grows, the role of communication becomes more critical. Therefore there is a need for adjustment in the communication systems according to shape, size, performance, location and the services that the organization offers.

Effective management is an output of effective communication. Poor communication or ineffective communication is a source of frustration, interpersonal conflict and stress. It plays an important role in strengthening relationship between friends, relatives and family members since we spend nearly seventy percent of our time interacting with them by way of speaking, listening, reading and writing. Poor communication leads to unpleasant situations and breaking up of relationships. Oral and written communication is very important not only to get a job but to retain it. Oral communication is the most effective way of communication and considered to be the most important skill that an individual possesses. Effective communication is essential for management to successfully perform its functions. It is an essential ingredient in management – employee relationship. The best business plan is meaningless unless everyone is aware of it and is willing to put energy together to achieve its objectives. Communication is essential to keep entire organization functioning at optimum levels and to achieve maximum output of our greatest management resource – the people.

Management needs to take employees in confidence and make them aware of organizational policies, problems and vision. Following points need interaction with employees for successful running of an organization

(*a*) Organizations policy and future plans
(*b*) Results achieved vis-vis the industry performance
(*c*) Achievement of higher productivity
(*d*) Industrial safety, health and welfare measures
(*e*) Technical developments
(*f*) Personal growth prospects

It is the responsibility of the management to keep employees posted with latest information about the above factors by resorting to greater interaction with them.

Chester Barnard (1930) highlighted communication as a dynamic force in shaping organizational behaviour. He considered it as one of the three important elements of an organization along with common purpose and willingness to serve. He also linked communication with the concept of 'authority' which flows down through channels of communication, in a classical organization. The authority can lose its meaning if channels of communication are blocked or if the communication is misunderstood or if the strength of communication is diluted. Accordingly, he proposed seven communication factors which are indeed functions of objective authority. These are as under

(*a*) The channels of communication must be clearly set and be known to all.
(*b*) Every member of the organization should be reached by some channel of communication.
(*c*) The line of communication should be as direct as possible.
(*d*) There should be no blockage in the line of communication and formal line should be used.
(*e*) The communicator should be highly skilled in the art of communication.
(*f*) The line of communication should be constantly kept open.
(*g*) Every communication should be authenticated.

Objectives of Communication

(*a*) To keep employees abreast with external and internal environment.
(*b*) Develop understanding and cordial relationship with management.
(*c*) Development of team spirit, group task resolution and psychological bent of mind.
(*d*) Promote creativity and innovativeness.
(*e*) Develop social commitment among employees.
(*f*) Make them aware of their rights, entitlements, and responsibilities.
(*g*) Prepare employees to accept and implement change.
(*h*) Prevent mis-information and counter rumors.
(*i*) Promote participative type of leadership model.
(*j*) Motivate employees by displaying an attitude of commitment.
(*k*) Knowledge management.

COMMUNICATION PROCESS

Communication can be described as an impersonal process of sending and receiving symbols with meaning attached to them. When you make a communication there is a person called sender (source) who sends the message to another person who receives it (the receiver). The message is sent through a medium. Medium can be (*a*) written message (*b*) a verbal message (*c*) a message sent through some physical gestures or signs. When a message is sent there is an element of disturbance called 'noise'. Strictly speaking the receiver must receive a message as sender thinks he should and lastly the feedback. The communication process is shown is Figure 13.1 below:

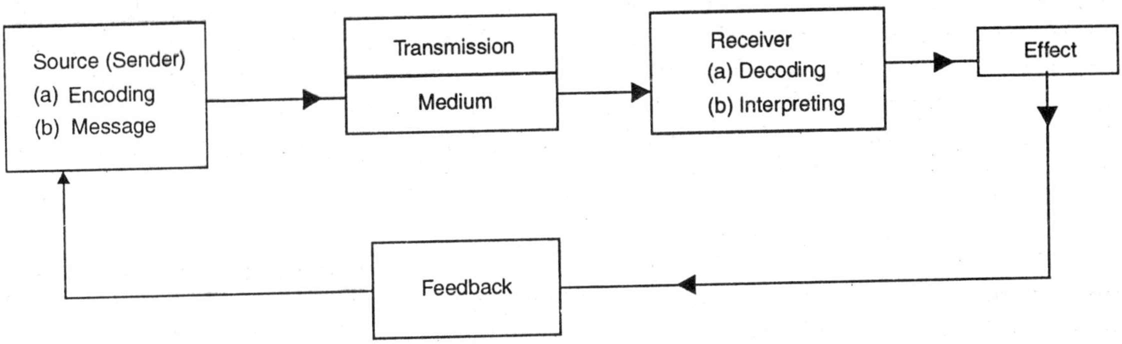

Fig. 13.1. Communucation Process

Source

Source is an initiator of a message. He may be an individual or group or even an organization. Sender is a person who represents source. When source decides to convey something – a message to the other party (receiver). Message is an item of information. Message is required to be encoded that will depend upon distance, the receiver, time available (urgency) and availability of channel.

Message

Message is an information and may be in the form of script. Message is what the communication is all about. Message may be composed of symbols like Dollar $. Encoding is a process of selecting an appropriate channel. Message had to be sent by Morse code in the Navy. That is even done today. For maintaining secrecy they can be ciphered. When such messages are received, they are decoded by the receiver. Obviously, the sender and receiver must have an identical code so that a correct meaning is assigned to the message by the receiver.

Medium

Medium is also called channels through which a message is transmitted. It is the path through which the message is physically sent to the receiver. It may be face to face communication where sender sends a message through some gestures. Telephone, tele-printer, computer network, Mobile phones and radio sets are used as medium for transmitting the messages. What is important is the compatibility of the sender and the receiver to use the medium.

Receiver

The message is received by a person called a receiver. Receiver is an individual who receives the message individually if it is meant for him or receives it on behalf of the group or organization for which he is working. Receiver is also responsible to decode the message and interpret it in an appropriate manner. He must assign correct meaning to various symbols, gestures, words as is intended by the sender.

Effect

Effect is the change in behaviour of receiver. He may pass on the message to the department who is to take action. He may ignore it. He may store the information. This will depend upon the perception, attitude and the skill of an individual. A message may contain simple information or it may affect value which will lead to a reaction or generation of a new message for sender. It must be remembered that messages are for action or for information. Action messages are acted upon and information messages are acted upon for wide circulation as information only. It is further stated that the principle of "need to know" must be kept in mind while transmitting.

Feedback

Once the message is received by the receiver, he has to either act upon it or prepare a reply message to the originator. Feedback determines that the message is clearly understood and action taken. In a real organizational situation, it may be difficult to locate the original source of a communication. A single communication may generate so many communication. It is therefore a network and a single identifiable event. It is synergistic process in which elements operate in an independent and intricately interwoven fashion. Communication generally takes the form of vertical and horizontal pattern. It is dependent on the form of organizational structure. Communication is superimposed on various appointments and related to the job. Psychological make up of the sender and the receiver is important so that positive outcome is achieved and thus organizational objectives are fulfilled.

Means of Communication

There are three primary methods of communication. These are written, verbal and non verbal form of communication. The choice as to which method to adopt would largely depend upon the location of the sender and receiver, ability, the nature of the message, urgency with which the information is required to be passed on and the cost involved in passing or receiving the information.

1. Written Communication

Written communication is generally in the form of standing orders, policy documents, orders, instructions, notes, memos, formal letters, demi official letters etc. These contain information of a permanent nature. Employees refer to these instructions as a basic document. Written communication is important to ensure the uniformity of action and future plans and it provides a permanent record for further reference. Written documents can be saved and stored. Because of the introduction of computers and other electronic equipment, information of very large size can be stored, and the required information can be retrieved in the fastest possible time. It is a great revolution. Volumes of information can just be stored in a single disc. Messages can be passed the world over in a fraction of a second with hundred percent accuracy with the help of electronic media. Written communication is lengthy, time consuming and has a high probability of leakage in respect of confidential documents.

2. Oral Communication

Oral communication is the most common form of communication. Oral communication is used when both (sender and receiver) are present. It is face to face communication. It is more effective than written communication because the receiver not only hears the contents of the message but also is influenced by the tone, pitch, gestures, speed and even volume of conversation. Oral communication is the best way of transforming an individual with particular reference to attitude, beliefs, trust and faith. Most of the education system uses oral communication in learning. Leaders use oral communication in public address system to convey their point of view. Oral communication can also be used by using electronic media like audio-visual conferencing, where people can converse with each other even while being away. It is a direct, simple form of communication which is the least expensive and yet the most effective. Feedback is spontaneous and any error in the message is corrected immediately.

Oral communication promotes better relationship due to its personalized nature. However oral communication suffers from various disadvantages like lack of records, mis-interpretation of message by the receiver, filtration, distortions and giving the meaning to the communication which suits the receiver best. Oral communication, to be effective, must be specific, short, to the point and devoid of ambiguity of any sort. "Grapevine" is also a very powerful medium of communication where messages are passed by word of month. Grapevine is an informal way of transmitting information to maximum number of employees in a minimum possible time. Grapevine travels like a wild fire. Management can use grapevine in a productive manner to convey a particular message. The greater the quantity of information that passes through the grapevine the less accurate it usually is.

3. Non Verbal Communication

Nonverbal messages are transmitted through gestures, facial expressions and through body language. It can also be expressed how one designs one's office and through official protocols. According to Tipkins and McCarter[1] facial expressions can be categorized as (1) interest – excitement, (2) enjoyment – joy, (3) surprise – startle, (4) distress – Anguish, (5) fear – terror, (6) shame – humiliation, (7) contempt – disgust, and (8) anger – rage.

Body language is known a "Kinesics". A handshake is probably the most common form of body language which conveys a lot about a persons personality. Eyes are the most expressive component of facial expressions, a glance, a stare, a smile or some provocative movement of the body conveys a lot. Facial expression can convey frustration, anger, arrogance, shyness, fear and other characteristics of a person that cannot be expressed through written or oral communication. Shrugging of shoulders expresses indifference, wink of eye an intimacy, and a palm on the forehead for forgetfulness. Knowledge of body language is very important and that should be carefully displayed. Managers should acquire adequate knowledge of non verbal communication to enable them to know their subordinates.

Structure of Communication

1. Downward Communication

Communication has a structure that is based on two things. ***First***, the organizational structure and ***second*** the purpose the communication is intended to achieve. In hierarchical structure where there are various organizational levels the communication is from top to bottom. In this pattern the communication flows from superior to subordinates. It is in the written form like policy letters, standing orders, staff regulations, handbooks, procedure, manuals and the like. When it is verbal, it pertains to passing information about day to day functioning and operations. Verbal communication is as important as written communication and should be weighed on an equal footing. The communication to be effective must be clear, simple and specific. Superior should appreciate and understand the ability of recipient and keep in mind the language and the level of perception.

2. Upward Communication

Upward communication relates to communication being made by Junior person to senior. This generally follows the reporting channel of command. The communication relates to reporting production levels, sales performance, reaction to certain orders and instructions. The communication reflects motivational condition of the employees. The flow of information from bottom to top helps the top management to know the actions, attitude, opinion and feelings of people. Upward communication indicates the reaction of employee to the policies of the organization. It is therefore necessary to ensure effective communication. Sharma (1997)[2] suggests "Research also notes the tendency, at times of subordinates or for fear of appraisals or for seeking undeserved rewards, place only that particular information before the superior which he would like. They try to check the flow of such information which goes against them or which the superior is not likely to appreciate". Organizations must provide a climate and an incentive system that encourage upward communication. Management must evolve an "Open door" system and employees should feel that their superiors are always available to share their opinion, ideas and views that can be effectively used for decision making. Effective communication promotes "We" feeling among workers.

3. Horizontal or Lateral Communication

This type of communication refers to communication across departments or between people within different departments. It does not have a superior – subordinate relationship as downward and upward communication has. It is more informal in nature and is necessary in promoting a supportive organizational climate. It provides the means by which supervisors, grass root level workers and managers organize and coordinate their activities without referring the matters to their respective seniors. Generally, people prefer accomplishment of work smoothly and therefore like to refer laterally. Production manager and marketing manager have to be in constant touch with each other to know the consumer expectations, market share vis-vis production levels. In the present liberalised market scenario lateral communication is not only restricted to the internal departments of a particular organization but spread to other organizations, government agencies who have to play a role in the business and even may extend to national and International levels.

Types of Communication

1. Formal Communication

Upward, downward and lateral communication follow the established routes of communication in the organization. Lateral communication is encouraged by organizations as it cuts down delays. Lines of such communication are formally laid down. The communication may take written or verbal form that will depend upon the relationship, time available, importance of the issue etc. This type of communication is called formal communication.

2. Informal Communication

Informal communication is not planned by the organization, hence no lines of communication exist. This type of communication takes place due to sheer desire of an individual to communicate with others. It is an outcome of social interaction. Small groups are formed and they not only communicate and discuss personal issues, but also express their candid views on other related official matters. This type of communication takes place during lunch, or coffee/tea breaks and during social gatherings. If the organizational climate is healthy, this type of communication lends speed to the organizational problem solving. When management wants to convey something to the employees and does not wish to use an official channel, it is passed on to the employees informally. This type of communication is also called "grapevine". It is important to note that there is a likelihood of roumours being spread in the organization through informal communication channels, which should be guarded against.

Evolution of Communication : In earlier era (Classicists View – An Organizational Thinking) communication was not so important. Management used to issue orders and instructions (downward communication) to various employees who used to complete their day's work. Upward communication was either non existent or discouraged. Blind obedience to orders was expected. There was break down in communication when subordinate crossed the channels of communication and narrow span of management concept of organizational structure was operative. Neo – classicists view communication as an important function of the organization. It should be aimed at need satisfaction, social interaction and a tool for participation in decision making. They recommend vertical and horizontal communication. Neo – classicists feel informal communication is as important as the formal communication as it fills the gap that may occur in formal communication. The modernists view communication as the most important function of any organization. They adopt the behavioural view. Communication must aim at ***firstly*** improvement of human relation within the units and sub-units, ***two*** obtain, store, process and shift required information for decision making and interact with various agencies that exist in the external environment so that organizations not only survive but grow. They feel overload, distortion and filtration are the basic drawbacks in the communication system that must be guarded against.

COMMUNICATION NETWORK

As stated earlier, it is the organizational structure that will, to a great extent determine the communication network. In a typical centrally controlled organization, communication generally revolves around a pivotal person. Like in a production unit, the production manager would be a pivotal person and all communication will flow down to supervisors (downward communication) and to the CEO/President/ Vice president (upward communication). Various type of communication is shown in Figure 13.2 below.

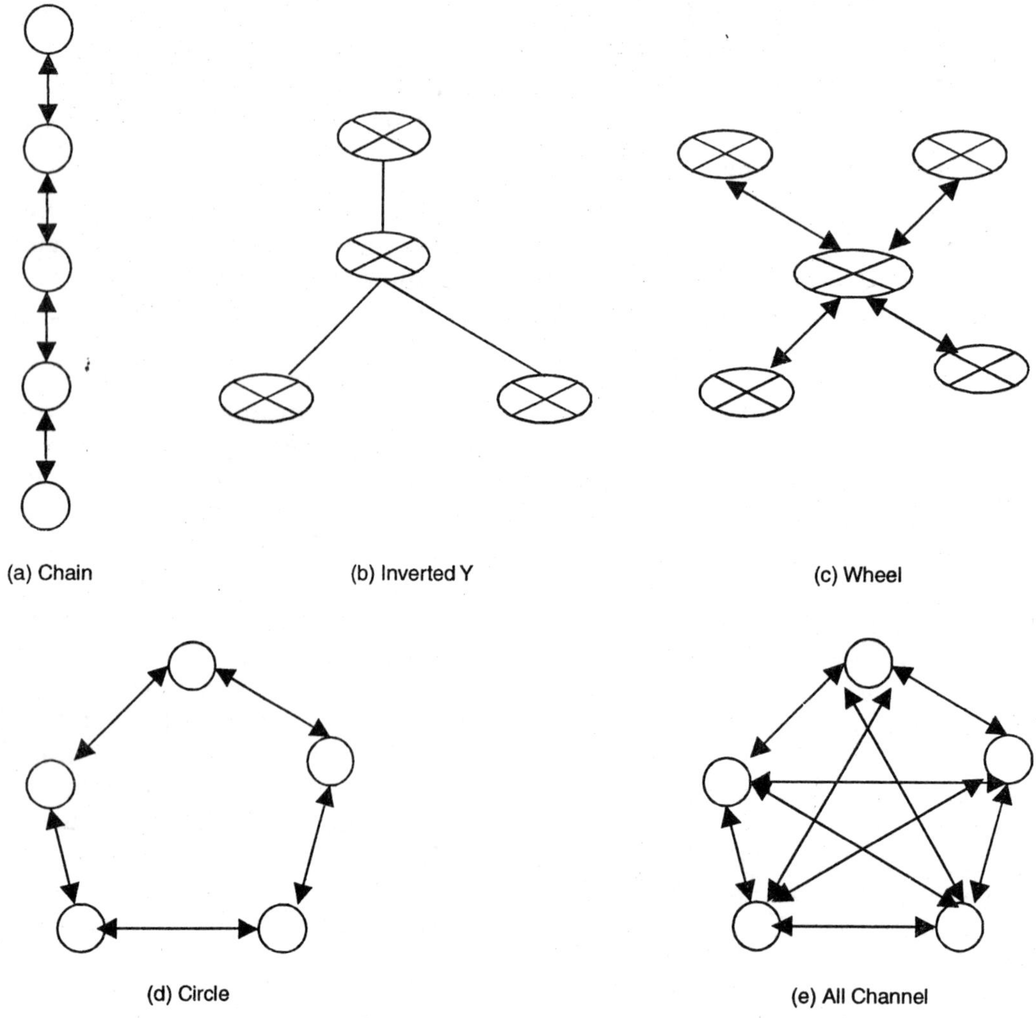

Fig. 13.2. Various types of communication

Chain, Inverted 'Y' and 'wheel' type of communication is used in centralized organization. Chain type of communication is used where information flows upward and downward in a hierarchical manner. There is no lateral communication. This type of communication is best suited for organizations where reporting is strict and jobs are well defined. Lot of written communication takes place in the form of orders, instructions, etc. Inverted Y type of communication represents one person having two subordinates. They report to the designated boss. 'Wheel' type of communication represents manager in the center having control over two superior officers. Wheel type of communication is very commonly used in most of the organization as it provides faster problem solving. This type communication displays lack of flexibility and shows lowest job satisfaction.

'Circle' type of communication is used by a member to adjoining member only. Communication is lateral. While "all channel" type of communication is used by a member to any member of the organization. There is no leader but a person may assume leadership. Members experience a greater level of satisfaction. This is prevalent in decentralized organizations. More the centralization, poorer the satisfaction of employees.

Decentralized networks are suitable to the organizations where jobs are complex and members have to interact with various departments. When the tasks are comparatively simple and of routine nature, centralized communication (Chain, Y, Wheel) is recommended.

Barriers to Effective Communication

When a communication is made by a sender, it must be received correctly by the receiver. Message must be interpreted by the receiver as has been intended by the sender. There are various problems like the message does not reach the receiver, problems of encoding and decoding, faulty selection of channel, wrong language or the interpretation of the message. The list can be long and unending. These problems are called 'Noise' in communication. These problems can be classified as various barriers such as physical distance, noise, attitude and sentiments of sender and receiver.

Physical Barrier

(*a*) **Poor Timing:** A person must evaluate the timing of sending a message. Receiver must get adequate time to implement the instruction given in the communication. If the action on the message is required to be taken in a distant future, there is a possibility that receiver may forget the content of the message. Inadequacy of timing and a last minute communication is likely to put too much pressure on the receiver. Message therefore should be sent at an appropriate time.

(*b*) **Choice of Channel:** Message can be sent in written, verbal instruction (face to face) or conveyed by electronic media, on line by telephone or using combinations. Routine messages should be passed on verbally to subordinates and boss. Important messages should be followed in writing as a confirmation to verbal conversation. Face to face communication is more effective because of the body language of sender and receiver. It provides spontaneous solutions to misunderstanding.

(*c*) **Inadequate Information:** Too much or too little information is dangerous. Information must be of value, meaningful and related to the job of the receiver. Volumes of information can be quickly sent any where around the globe. Information carries value if it is in the desired format and to the point.

(*d*) **Organizational Structure :** Every individual in the organization must know the channels of command and communication. They must also know the power centers. Authority and responsibility must be clearly defined so that the communication is directed towards the correct person and quick decision making is achieved. Information overload is dangerous. Secretary to the various managers must maintain a log book in which incoming and out going messages are recorded. Professional jealousy must not be allowed to interfere with various communication.

(*e*) **Information Overload:** Information may be passed to concerning individuals as it is needed. Excessive information causes information overload. Though lot of information now can be handled by the individual due to computers. Excessive information causes confusion and may not be required. Network breakdown may also take place due to information overload.

Interpersonal Barriers

Effective communication largely depends upon the sender and receiver and their personal bent of mind, commitment to organizational effectiveness and the relationship they enjoy. Some of the important interpersonal barriers are discussed in the succeeding paragraphs.

(*a*) **Filtration:** Filtration is a process when sender deliberately wants to withhold information from reaching the receiver. It is done by manipulating the information either because the sender believes that all the information is not required or that the receiver is better off not knowing certain aspects of the information. Filtration takes place when subordinates send information to superiors based on the liking of the latter. Boss is told what he likes to hear. Therefore the information may be far from the truth.

(*b*) **Perception:** Perceptual process that operates in a situation may heavily influence the communication process related to receiving the information from the environment and interpreting and giving meaning to such information. It is human tendency to hear what one wants to hear and ignore the information that conflicts with ones thought process. This type of communication totally distorts the intent and contents of the message. Some of the perceptual situations are as under:

(*i*) **Stereotype effect:** Manager may perceive people who belong to one category or another as stereotypes. It is general perception that old employees are not hard working, even if some of the old employees work hard. Individuals therefore must be treated distinctly as a separate individuals and their performance assessed accordingly.

(*ii*) Individuals generally assess their subordinates based on one particular trait that he likes. If an individual is punctual, he may create a favourable perception because he likes punctuality. The other employee may be efficient in his job but he is not considered favourably in his performance appraisal. It should be ensured that an individual is evaluated according to laid down standards and not based on individual liking.

(*iii*) It is human tendency that a person expects his subordinates to act, think and behave as he does. If a manager works overtime, he expects his subordinates to stay longer. This limits the manager's ability to effectively deal with different situations and individuals.

It is important for managers to evaluate situations independently and take decision on the merit of the case. The perceptual skill must be applied carefully and each individual treated separately without any perceptual bias so that the credibility of the manager is increased. One must communicate facts, keep up to commitments made and eliminate negativity in perception.

(*c*) **Semantic Barriers:** Semantic barriers refer to the interpretation of words, abbreviations and symbols used by the sender and perceived by the receiver. If a receiver is likely to misunderstand symbol of dollar,($) it is better that "dollar" is written in the script. Universally accepted symbols should generally be used in the written communication. Choice of wrong word or a comma at wrong place can change the meaning as to what is intended to be communicated and interpreted by the receiver. It is always desirable to repeat an important part of the message and ensure confirmation from the receiver.

(*d*) **Power Position:** Authority, power and status of an individual in an organization affect communication win people interacting at various levels of hierarchy. While authority makes communication more authentic but may create social distance and therefore restrict communication due to 'gap' that may be created. 'Power centres' may not allow views of lesser powerful individuals in decision making process. Thus free flow of information may not exist in the organization which is counter-productive for growth.

(*e*) **Cultural Barriers:** Cultural differences can adversely affect the communication effectiveness. Due to liberalization multinational players are operating in India. It is therefore necessary to understand ethnic backgrounds and cultures of various employees working in the organization. Religious sentiments of the employees must be protected while communicating. Norms play an important role like working on Friday for Muslims, Wearing of White clothes by Hindu women in India etc. In some countries punctuality is not considered important as long as targets are met. Accordingly the communicator must identify these barriers and identify cultural differences so that an all out effort is made to ensure effectiveness of communication.

(*f*) **Sender Credibility:** If a sender's credibility is high, the receiver will take and interpret message favourably. Conversely, if sender is not trusted receiver may try and interpret the message wrongly by deliberately giving hidden meaning to various words and may even distort the complete message. The communication of an expert is generally taken seriously and acted upon favourably. Emotions also play an important role in communication. If the receiver is happy and in a fine mood, he will receive and interpret message as intended by the sender but if the receiver is angry, frustrated and not in a pleasant mood the communication can be heavily distorted.

Feedback

Feedback completes the total communication process. Feedback is important to ascertain if the message is understood and acted upon correctly. Lack of it or wrong feedback is counter productive to effective communication. In defence services there is a procedure to repeat the message by the receiver so that the sender knows that the message is being correctly received. Wrong reception is instantaneously corrected and an acknowledgement sought. This is generally implemented when long distance weapon system is being used. Safety of own troops and maximum destruction of the enemy forces is sought. For example ground to air communication involved for guiding strike aircraft in support of ground forces.

Wofford, Gerloff and Cummins[3] point out that the greatest barrier to communication is the style of communication used by the manager. When a manager sends a message in a way that provokes defensiveness, he or she contributes to the "poor" interpersonal relationship. If relations are already strained, the chances of experiencing communication breakdown are greatly enhanced.

To conclude the message must be received with the same spirit as is being sent. The message may be vitiated in many ways. It may be distortion, omission or filtration. Distortion takes place due to motive, attitude and sentiments of both sender and receiver. Filtration takes place when message is passed on by reducing it based on the liking of receiver, or by retaining information for bargaining purpose. Omission is related to deletion of a part of a message.

Overcoming Communication Barriers

1. **Improve Listening Skills:** An individual must be a good listener. Listening is 'half' of whole communication. When one listens he also carries out concurrent mental interpretation of what he is hearing. Positive outlook goes a long way to ensure effective communication. Important points for good listener are as under:
   (*a*) Do not have preconceived ideas about a subject matter.
   (*b*) Pay full attention to what the sender is saying.
   (*c*) Think as the sender thinks.
   (*d*) Check back as to what you have received.
   (*e*) Give time to take feedback on action taken on the message received.
   (*f*) Keep the principle of "need to know" in mind to avoid information overload.
   (*g*) Do not jump to conclusions.
   (*h*) Do not have a prejudiced mind and take every message independently.
2. **Improve Written Skills:** When a message is intended to be sent, it is necessary to identify action addresses and information addresses. The text of the message should be simple and should clearly indicate as to what actions are required to be taken by the receiver. A well written communication in simple language has negligible chances of misinterpretation. Writing good message is an art and it must be practiced overtime. Basic principles of good written message are brevity, clarity and simplicity.
3. **Maintain Unity of Command Principle:** Most of communication problems arise when channels of command and control are not followed strictly. One must receive orders from a specific authority and should be answerable to the same authority. In a typical hierarchical organizations, chains of reporting are laid down and should be followed. Because of the multiplicity of organizational functions lateral and diagonal communication is necessary, the same should be undertaken on an even level. Creation of power blocks should be discouraged. The object of communication is not only to carryout assigned task but create an atmosphere of trust and understanding among all members of the organization. It is only possible when management is not only sensitive to the workers demand but keeps their promises. According to Luft[4], openness and an atmosphere of trust builds healthy relationship and closes credibility gaps thus contributing to communication effectiveness and enhancement.

SUMMARY

Effective communication is essential for the growth of the organization. Communication relates to exchange of ideas, facts, opinion and feelings. It involves two parties and a message. Message may be verbally passed or sent through a written mode. It can even be by gestures, singnals and symbols. Communication is a continuous process. It involves 1. sender 2. encoding 3. message 4. Medium of dispatch 5. decoding 6. receiver 7. action and 8. feedback. Communication should be upward, downward horizontal and diagonal. Formal communication is undertaken by superior-subordinates strictly as per the hierarchical structure of the organization. Informal communication on the other hand is predominantly an outcome of social interaction with fellow workers. Communication has different patterns namely, chain, inverted Y, wheel, circle and all channel. Communication can never be smooth, it is affected by sender's and receiver's motives, attitudes and sentiments. Apart from the above, poor timings of dispatch of communication, poor choice of media/ channel, incomplete information, organizational structure and related authority-responsibility relationship can distort communication to a large extent. Perception and motives play a vital role in interpretation of communication. Cultural diversity of employees, power position enjoyed by a person and his credibility add new dimensions to the communication effectiveness. Filtration, language, physical separation, status difference are also communication barriers. For effective communication a person must improve upon listening skill, written skill and have simplicity, brevity and clarity while interacting with people.

TEXT QUESTIONS

1. Define communication. Why is communication important to the organization?
2. Explain in detail the communication process.
3. What is 'noise' in communication?
4. What are the various communication barriers? How can they be eliminated?
5. What is communication network? Explain.
6. The key to good communication is "The principles of brevity, clarity and simplicity" explain above statement.
7. Write notes on:
   (*a*) Downward & upward examination.
   (*b*) Formal communication.
   (*c*) Informal communication.
   (*d*) Language barrier.
   (*e*) Communication channels.

REFERENCES

1. Tipkins, Silvan S., and Robert McCarter. ***"What and Where are the Primary Effects"? Some Evidence for a Theory***. Perceptual and Motor Skills, February, 1964.
2. Sharma R.A. ***"Organizational Theory and Behaviour"***, Tata McGraw Hill Publishing Company Ltd., New Delhi, Fifth reprint 1997.
3. Wofford, J.C., E.A. Gerloff and R.C. Cummins, ***"Organizational Communication"***, McGraw-Hill, N.Y., 1977.
4. Luft J. ***"Of Human Interaction"***. National Press Book, 1969.

Case

COMMUNICATION FAILURES AT BHOPAL

All the safety features had failed – that much was abundantly clear. What Warren Anderson could not find out was *why*. As CEO of Union Carbide, he needed to know exactly what had happened in Bhopal that night for a number of reasons. He knew that he would have to explain a tragic accident to employees, to government officials in both the United States and India, to the courts, and to the people. Yet he could not get answers to his own preliminary and personal questions. When telephone contact failed to yield answers. Anderson got on a plane and flew to India, where he was immediately placed under house arrest – unable to attend to the very business that had brought him there. His plant managers had also been arrested and were not allowed to talk to anyone. Indian government officials had closed the plant in order to prevent "tampering with evidence".

The basic facts that Anderson could not determine on December 3, 1984, were really quite simple. A runaway reaction had occurred in a storage tank of methylisocyanate (MIC), which was used to manufacture a pesticide. The valves on the tank had burst and a cloud of poisonous gas had escaped. Climatic conditions kept the gas from dissipating, and the winds carried it to nearby shanty towns and the populous city of Bhopal, where many people either died in their sleep or woke and died while fleeing. Those who survived suffered from burning eyes and lungs. Local medical facilities were not equipped for the disaster, and over the next few weeks thousands more died.

The Bhopal plant was operated by Union Carbide India Limited (UCIL), with the parent company, Union Carbide, owning roughly 51 per cent. After installing the plant and training its first staff, Union Carbide withdrew from the daily operation of the plant, as it was required to do by the Indian government. Union Carbide did participate in the inspections and responded to official questions and concerns, but no U.S. official of the company was on-site in Bhopal.

Before the accident, the plant had under a great deal of pressure to cut costs. Because of production problems, it was unable to run at more than 50 per cent capacity, and meeting its original profit predications had become impossible. Thus, a number of shortcuts had been taken in such matters as crew training, staffing patterns, and maintenance schedules. Although the plant had been virtually shut down for weeks for extensive maintenance and cleaning, a number of important safety features remained inoperable – and there is some doubt whether they would have been adequate even if they had been working!

Perhaps most importantly, the staff did not realize the danger of the situation – they even took a tea break after the leak had been noticed, thinking they would have plenty of time to fix it. The operator in the control room did not notify his supervisor when the temperature began to rise inside the tank, and the entire situation went unattended for at least an hour. The original procedures called for up to two years of training for employees in critical superintendent capacities, but these men had received only about a month, using classroom materials developed in the United States and printed in English.

Suggested Analysis

Obviously, Warren Anderson, the individual, faced a severe communication problem. Even more important, Union Carbide, the organization, experienced a tragic breakdown in its ability to communicate with its internal and external stakeholders – a breakdown it tried to fix while a horrified world watched the devastation on the nightly news. Ultimately, this breakdown raised questions about ethics, technical difficulties, and cultural differences, as well as Union Carbide's strategy for communicating with the Bhopal plant.

Most organizational communication problems are not this severe, of course, but the tragedy at Bhopal reminds us of how important communication is to the manager's job. Clearly, Anderson and Union Carbide had a significant communication problem. First of all, there was simply a lot of confusion over the facts. Even today, no one is clear as to exactly what sequence of events led to the disaster. Each party has a different interpretation of the "facts" that have come to light, and the resulting legal battles promise to be long. Of course, there were a number of barriers to effective communication in the immediate aftermath of the event. Various parties gave voice to differing perceptions of the "facts", and the high pitch of emotion amounted to a form of noise interfering with the communications channels.

In addition, Anderson had to communicate in multiple ways in the wake of the disaster – all of which were hampered by subsequent events and circumstances. The whole world was watching to see what Union Carbide would do. Anderson made the symbolic move of going to India to show his concern, but his subsequent arrest made any form of communication virtually impossible. Ultimately, he needed to have a policy of one-way communication in order to state what Union Carbide was going to do, but before that he needed to engage in multiple-party communication to determine exactly what had happened. Both channels of communication had been effectively shut down.

There also remained the little-publicized but important issue of Anderson's communication with other Union Carbide employees. After all, some of them worked in facilities very much like the one in Bhopal.

The Bhopal disaster is a prime example of the necessary for the pitfalls of communication. Many managers do indeed complain of "communication problems", and as Bhopal shows, the management process is subject not only to inefficiency and frustration, but even complete breakdown, if it fails to plan for effective communication. Communication consists of more than memos, phone calls, face-to-face meetings, and elaborate systems of "networking". It is a central feature of organizational culture : It concerns what we ***say*** and what we ***mean***, as well as *how* we say and mean it.

As the Bhopal story continues to unfold, it will have different meanings for a variety of groups, and perhaps there can never be one conclusive story with a hard-and-fast moral to be learned from it. There are multiple lessons to be learned from the tragic story of Bhopal – lessons about planning, organizing, leading and controlling, and the theme of communication will be among all the lessons taught in each of these management classes.

Such was the case for Union Carbide on the morning on December 3, 1984, when its pesticide plant in Bhopal leaked tons of lethal methylisocyanate gas into an overcrowded city of 700,000 people. By the time that death-toll reports reached the company's headquarters in Danbury, Connecticut, climbing first from 200 and 300 and ultimately to 2,000 with over 100,000 injured, Carbide's options for immediate reactive response had already been severely limited. There were only two telephone lines into the Bhopal area, and management in Connecticut had to rely on fragments of information funnelled out its Bombay subsidiary. The plant's supervisors had been placed under arrest, and when Carbide chairman Warren Anderson arrived to asses the situation and offer whatever resources were at the company's immediate disposal, he, too, was taken into custody. Freed on bail, Anderson was then informed that the Indian government expected Carbide to pay compensation damages that threatened to become astronomical – far beyond resources of Carbide's reported $200 million in insurance.

Carbide immediately ceased its worldwide production of methlisocyanate gas, but its problems in taking quick reactive measures were far from being under the company's managerial control. In addition to having to stem the leakage of toxic fumes with an under trained work force, Carbide found the city of Bhopal strewn with mass graves and hospitals reporting deaths at the rate of one every 60 seconds. The city's foliage withered, and the dying, writhing in pain from the inhalation of gas that swells lung tissue and drowns victims in internal fluids, scurried through shanty town streets littered with animal carcasses and teeming with flies.

The long-term outlook was no better. Carbide lost over $800 million in market value in a single week, and the company could look forward to lengthy and intensive scrutiny of its safety policies and procedures. Why, for example, had no computerized warning system been installed at the Bhopal plant? Morever, the company could expect to find itself at the center of a long and volatile debate about the practices of U.S. firms engaged in risky ventures in underdeveloped nations - a fact that will no doubt hamper Carbide's efforts to defend both its ethical practices and its financial stability among present and potential investors for some time to come. Finally, every one of the company's problems is exacerbated by public-relations issues that will have to be addressed by intricate, long-term strategies for which it had not planned.

Case adopted from the book titled "The Process of Management" by Dr. M.L. Bhasin published by Global Business Press, Abhinav Publishing Industries Pvt. Ltd, New Delhi, 1994.

CHAPTER 14

Power and Politics

INTRODUCTION

Study of power is important in the corporate environment. Power depends from person to person and its use depends upon the attitude of an individual. Power in public life is different than corporate world. While former is situational the later is object oriented. In public life, its promises may or may not work as desired. Proper use of power in organization is necessary so that the sources of power is not misused and directed towards attainment of organizational goal. It is important to understand the manager who uses power to understand employee behaviour, because methods of using power are different for different managers in the organization. It is therefore essential to allow minimum power that may be necessary to maintain peaceful environment. The study to understand how power is acquired and used for attainment of organizational goals is essential.

Power

Power is derived from the official position held by an individual in an organization. As Rosabeth Kanter says, *"power is the ability to get things done."* Those in power are able to marshal their resources in a way that helps them achieve their goals. They are able to be effective in their jobs and earn the respect of others. Having power as resource can help you gain support, information, supplies—everything and anything that is needed to be productive in your job[1]. Power is a tool and resource, a means as an end while politics represents tactics used by employees to use to manipulate power in organizational setting. Leaders use power as a means of attaining group goals. Leader use power to ensure compliance of job assigned to them. Power is also used to control various activities of individuals and groups. A purchase manager may be given power to procure raw material worth only Rs 10,000 in one transaction. This is to control his activities. A leader may use punitive power to prevent individual from restraining indisciplined activities. Manager having power to promote his subordinates uses it to attain organizational goals. Power should be used for attainment of growth of the organization and should be reward oriented in nature. Threat of power is not desirable as it has negative re-enforcement character inbuilt in it. When we discuss power, authority is associated with it. Authority is acquired from the organizational hierarchy. When we say that HR manager has an authority to employ an individual, this authority is associated with the appointment of an individual as HR manager. It is therefore legitimate. Authority relationship of various individual is contained in organizational pyramid chart, higher one goes, higher the authority. Authority and power go hand in hand. To be effective, power and authority should be equalized. Authority and power are synonymous. But in present environment it is observed that while authority remains constant there is a tendency to exercise more power. This is because of the politics played by an individual to maintain higher influence over resources. On the contrary, there may be situation when an individual does not use full potential of his authority for one reason or the other. Interpersonal and group conflicts are indicative of more influence one wants to exercise in the organizational setting. These happening are common to every layers of organizational hierarchy. Power is therefore personal and acquired. Power is an ability of a person to possess what he feels as valuable and deprive another person of the same. According to Wolfe, *power is potential ability of a person to induce forces on another person towards movement or change in a given direction within a given behaviour region, at a given time.* Cavanaugh[2] states that 'Power' is a multifaceted concept, which has been analysed from interpersonal influence process, as a commodity to be traded, as a type of causation and as an issue in the study of values and ethics.

Politics is a process whereby power is acquired and used to influence behaviour of others. It is endemic to every organization. People form groups, camps or cliques when they play politics. People playing politics for power where ethics, moral values, organizational goals are of little concern. Dalton[3] identified following six areas where politics was being played actively.

- Pressure for economy
- Co-operation of officially powerless experts with their administrative superior line and staff-relationship.
- The conflict between labour and management for interpreting agreements.
- Uncertainly about standards and strategies of promotion.
- Difficulty in linking reward with productivity
- Practicality of policies

Dalton observed that various type of alliances tend to develop among individuals, these alliances may be vertical, horizontal or mixed and are prime means of acquiring influence. This phenomenon of acquiring and exercising power seriously changes the command and control system in the organization. It forces to deviate from the established norm and process.

Bases of Power

French and Raven (1959) and Raven (1965) have put forward following six bases of power.

(*a*) **Rewards:** This power source derives from the person's control over resources, for example power to control human resources, pay and promotion. Greater the perceived value of each rewards the greater the power. These rewards can be extrinsic in nature with tangible values as well as intrinsic such as praise or recognition.

(*b*) **Coercive:** The power to punish or reward, the power to threaten and to use one's position to force others to take action. It reflects the extent to which a manager can deny desired rewards or administer punishment to control other people. For example a threat to meet given targets otherwise there would be reduction in salary.

(*c*) **Legitimate:** The power which is exercised in accordance with organizational rules. This power which is exercised with the authority of organization. Power derives from our cultural system of rights, obligations and duties, whereby position is accepted by people, i.e. right of private property.

(*d*) **Referent:** This depends on charisma or personal attraction of the individual. Interpersonal skill and emotional support from others are the sources of power for a person. Stronger the association, stronger the power. For example Mahatma Gandhi, people believed in his ideology.

(*e*) **Expert:** Power which derives from knowledge. Sometimes called sapient authority, this is power based on an acknowledgement of others expertise e.g. Physician.

(*f*) **Information:** Information about people, events or other facts assist prediction about future behaviour or events.

Power exists within two parties i.e. those exercising it and those responding to power. Power is the capacity to mobilize resources for effective use. Mobilizing capacity depends on the situation involved. For details see Figure 14.1 below:

Sources of Power	**Situational Context**	**Perceived effectiveness of power**
Reward, coercion	Capacity to mobilize sources	1. Asymmetry of Power relations
Legitimate	↕	
Referent		2. Acceptance of Legitimacy
Expert		
Information	Personality	3. Desirability of Outcome

Fig. 14.1. Source and effectiveness of power.

Capacity to exercise power depends upon the situation which provides opportunities or restrictions on the use of power and the personality of those wishing to exercise the same. Asymmetry of power refers to the perceived differences between the power of involved parties and its relationship. Personality refers to physical and psychological advantage an individual has over other persons. For example Sachin Tendulkar enjoys charisma and power related to it due to his personality. The military power relies upon the notion of legitimacy. If it is challenged the whole system will collapse.

Sources of Power

Organizational Based

1. **Knowledge as power:** Information Technology has taken a big leap in the last two decades. Information is necessary for top management to take decisions. Information is vital to carry out various operations in the business environment. Thus a person or a group holding information becomes more powerful than their counter part. Flow of information is necessary for continuous production or service operations. Persons who are in position to control the flow of information wield enormous power to influence the behaviour of others.

2. **Resource as power:** Resources are necessary for any organization. While material or tangible resources can be procured easily, it is the availability of these resources, at right time, at right place in a required quality and at a competitive price. Any person having monopoly over scares resources wield power. When project is required to be started, it is government agencies which delays the project for want of various resources, like power, water, etc. Human Resources are critical. Any person having direct or indirect control over making skilled persons available holds power. Organization cannot survive without adequate availability of various resources.
3. **Decision Making as power:** Decision making as power in organization rests with the head of the organization. Decision making is delegated to departmental heads depending upon the nature of work, ability of the departmental heads and the trust enjoyed by them. Decision making is one of the most important processes of management. Decisions are influenced, may be by subordinates, peers, friends or even family members who are psychologically close to decision maker. Therefore, both a person having decision making authority and a person who can influence decision making have power in the organization. Hiring a close relative, purchases in the organization, client selection etc. are day to day events in the organization which, indicate the power centers.
4. **Power Centers:** There exist people in the organization who desire to be more strong. They also want people dependent on them. Specialists, people with special powers deliberately delay decisions or hold resources so that they become more demanding. Power centers exist in various departments. It may in form of reservoir of power.
5. **Dependency:** Strength of power depends upon degree of dependency. Greater the dependency on the power holder greater influence will the power holder exercise over his subordinates. Dependency is directly related between power holder and those do not have it. Power holder holds power of retention to be able to increase dependency. All managers have two dimensional power base. One is the power generated by the organizational authority and the second, the personal power by virtue of personality as proposed by Whetten and Cameron[4].

Centrality: Centrality refers to activities which are central to organizations. Finance is central activity in the organization hence the finance manager holds power in excess of his authority. Finance manager further allocates funds to various departments. Department heads therefore also become powerful not because they can further allocate funds to their subordinates but because centrality of activity. Managers of various departments have power based on their departmental position. In addition they enhance their power position by virtue of opportunities they get to control activities that are central to the organization. This gives managers authority to control various units and sub-units.

Scarcity: When resources are in abundance there is no problem as everybody would get them based on their requirement. When resources become scarce, a person obtaining it will appear to be more powerful. Finance is a scares resource if a director of an institute manages to obtain additional funds from AICTE or by way of consultancy obviously he becomes more powerful in the eyes of management. Same is true of a faculty which may not be judged by efficiency of imparting knowledge but by obtaining finance for the institute from external sources.

Uncertainty: Management is related to planning for organization. It is basically related to identification of organizational objectives, evaluation of various alternatives and selection of best course of action and planning resources to put in action the course selected. Uncertainty of availability of required manpower with specific skills, raw material, finance can play havoc with the plans. There are situations when government policies change with the change of government, that further makes situation more critical. A manager who has a vision and can appreciate what is likely to happen in future and takes corrective actions in advance obviously garner additional power. According to Kanter[5] most power goes to those people, in those functions, that provide greater control over what the organization finds currently problematic. For eg. sales and marketing people when markets are competitive, production experts when materials are scares and demand is high; personnel or labour relations specialists when government regulations impinge; finance and accounting types when business is bad and money tight. There is a turning to those elements of the system that seem to have the power to create more certainty in the face of dependency, and to generate a more advantageous position for the organization.

Substitutability: Greater the value of a person in the organization, the greater the power it holds. There are some people who amass power because of their speciality. By virtue of their contribution to the organization they become indispensable. However situation changes due to marketability of a particular brand of profession. Software engineer were in great demand in the organizations. They demanded high salaries and perks. They were indispensable a few years ago. As of now they have very restricted market for them. They could not be substituted by another person. What is important is that people have a tendency to take advantage of their specialization and high demand in the market and exploit organizations by using added amassed power.

Allocation of Power

Division of Work : Work is divided in the organization based on technical and functional requirements. Though all jobs are important from the organizational point of view, yet it can not be denied that some jobs are comparatively more important than the other and persons holding those jobs holds more power irrespective of their personal leadership qualities. Division of work brings dependence hence power. There is also a smoothing effect phenomenon hidden in division of power because of distribution of power among various appointments thus leading to minimizing absolute power with a particular authority.

Organizational Power

Organization allocates power in two ways:

(*a*) **Structural power:** Organization structure has hierarchy of authority. Higher the position higher will be the legitimate authority. Mere granting of authority does not make a person powerful unless he uses it effectively. Invoking sanctions, awarding promotions or even punishments makes a manager powerful. If a leader does not use power, displays lack of interest, does not keep pace with developments, delays decisions and lacks effective communication, makes a leader ineffective and powerless.

(*b*) **Functional Power:** Functional power is related to a job a person does. By virtue of division of labour, people in organization do a very specific element of a job.

Interdependence of employees develop rather smoothly which culminates in completion of job. Any specialization in isolation does not lead to power generation, rather it diminishes its effect. Scarce skill, longer duration of a person in organization, extent of access to vital information are some of the factors that makes a person more powerful. Power comes from functional exclusiveness which can be achieved as under:-

(*i*) Devote more effort, time and energy on unbeaten, unattended fields.
(*ii*) Develop friendly work relations.
(*iii*) Share information with your subordinates and make them part of decision-making. By being seemingly sharing, one attains more power.
(*iv*) Communicate judgements rather than justifying it.
(*v*) Handle expertise carefully and yet let there be exclusiveness of skill.
(*vi*) Be available when required. Gather relevant information before decision.

POLITICS

Politics is about access to power. How organization structure promotes opportunities available or enhance access to power is therefore of considerable importance. Pfeffer[6] defines "**politics as those activities taken within organizations to acquire, develop and use power and other resources to obtain one's preferred outcome in a situation in which there is uncertainty or dissensus about choices**". He further states that power is a force, a store of potential influence through which events can be affected. Politics involves those activities or behaviours through which power is developed and used in organizational settings. Power is a property of system at rest; politics is the study of power in action. An individual, sub unit or department may have power within organizational context at some period of time; politics involves the exercise of power to get something accomplished as well as those activities which are undertaken to expand the power already possessed or the scope over which it can be exercised. Departments in organizations are dependant on each-other in varying degree. It is the degree of dependency between departments, that the power relationship is expressed. Such relationship can be collaborative or conflictual depending upon the variables. Chief among the variables is mutual task dependence. This is an incentive for collaboration, but also an occasion for conflict and the means for bargaining over inter-departmental issues. (Walton and Dutton, 1969)[7]. They have further stated that role problems cause inter-departmental friction. Blocked promotions, role ambiguity and faulty performance appraisal leads to scapegoating. Interpersonal skills plays a vital role in management of political influence. Sub-units control contingencies for one another's activities and draw power from the dependencies thereby created. A sub unit's power is related to its coping with uncertainty (which includes preventing uncertainty) to substitutability (whether there are alternative means of performing the operations) and centrality (the degree to which sub unit is linked into the organizations systems. (Crozier, M.)[8].

Organizational Politics

Political behaviour is designed and initiated to overcome opposition or resistance. If there is no opposition, there is no need for politics. Miles has identified five major reasons that have strong influence on political orientation of organizations. These are illustrated as under:

Scarscity of Resources

As discussed earlier any person or unit who has control over allocation of scarce resources yields power. Political influence plays an important part in how these resources are distributed to various departments as against the rational need.

Non programmed Decisions

Resolution of non-programmed decision is a complicated matter as there are no set solutions. These unique problem involves consideration of various factors and variables. They remain ambiguous in nature and subject to political maneuvering by those who have knowledge and techniques to solve them. Politics plays a vital role in organizations to create decisions in favour pertaining to sensitive areas like strategic planning, mergers and acquisitions, policy change and so on.

Ambiguous Goals

When setting up of organizational goals, departmental objectives and individual task are well defined. There is no room for ambiguity. However there are organizations where these are not clearly spelt out and ample room for discretion exists. In such situations people manipulate decisions and situations in their favour by playing political games intelligently.

Organizational Change

Organizational change is continuous process. People who are in position to take decision can very effectively influence the decisions. These change may include vital areas like restructuring, creating new departments, launching a new product line, appointment of key personnel at top levels and thus creating a ***lobby*** within the organization. This may prove to be counter productive and harmful for maintaining peaceful atmosphere.

External Environment

External environment is highly mobile and generally unpredictable. It is the ability of the organization to meet the challanges effectively by appropriately maneuvering internal environmental factors, technology and processes. Thus political behaviour is heightened when these are managed by interested people. Rechard (1988) states that "resources are continuously becoming scarce and competitive and the ever changing technology makes the environment more complex to handle, requiring organizations to continuously evaluate their goals and strategies. This would make most organizations political in nature so that managers in responsible positions must become sensitive to political processes and games in order to play their role in acquiring and maintaining political power[9]. Pfeffer has concluded that "In situations in which technologies are uncertain, preferences are conflicting, perceptions are selective and biased and information processing capabilities are constrained, the model of an effective politician may be appropriate one for both the individuals and for the organization in the long run".

Techniques of Political Plays

Mintzberg (1983) has suggested the following strategies to wield political power in the organizations.

1. **Cultivate right allies:** One must have alliance with right people who are rising

in the corporate ladder. It is necessary to develop friendship with upper level management. It may also be advisable to form alliance with boss's secretary or someone who is close to powerful person.

2. **Be positive towards others:** Human being wants to be appreciated and complemented for any work done. When you appreciate other people they will develop a positive outlook towards you and may be helped when situation demands.
3. **Reciprocity:** It is good to help others. Accordingly, recognize those members of the organization who will be more powerful in future. Help them so that they reciprocate the same when you need their support.
4. **Be persuasive:** It is necessary to develop a persuasive technique to get the job done. Forceful agreements when stated eloquently are often highly influencing. It improves your image and substantial pay offs in a future time.
5. **Image building:** One must build a positive image and create good impression in the organization. One must therefore be honest, sincere, attentive, sociable and display an organizational citizenship behaviour.
6. **Control information:** More the critical information and fewer the people who have access to it stronger the power base. It is therefore necessary to control and disseminate critical information when it is likely to have impact and serve self interest.

Machiavellianism (1469 - 1527)

Niccolo Machiavelli, an Italian philosopher has formulated a set of behaviour for maintaining political power. Christie and Geis have formulated an attitude scale in conformity with some basic tenets of Machiavelli. The aim of the scale is to measure the extent to which an individual follows Machiaveli views. This scale is known as "Mach Scale". The characteristics of people who measure high on Mach Scale are as follows:

- They have high esteem and self confidence and behave in their own self interest even at the expense of others.
- They are considered by others as cool and calculating and that they would not hesitate to take advantage of others.
- They tend to form alliances with people in power for the sole purpose of benefiting themselves.
- They believe that "end justify means" even if it involves lies, deceit and moral compromise.
- They manipulate others by false flatter and exaggerated praise and that they will make friends only for the purpose of using them.
- They have a very unfavourable views of human nature. They believe that "anyone who completely trusts anyone else is asking for trouble."
- They will not set others stand in the way of their personal gain.
- They are on the look out and select situations where their tactics would work most effectively such as face – to – face emotional, unstructured and ambiguous condition.
- They are able to exert control over such unclear situations.

The above attitude indicates selfish and unproductive in organizational setting. Management must identify such individuals in the organization who muster political power by adopting machiviavellian tendencies and be prepared to take measures to counter their designs. This will ensure healthy work environment.

Pettigrew (1974) has identified some behavioural patterns that executives generally use to follow to enhance the political power in organization. The catalog shown below refers to influence process between specialists and executives. Pettigrew describes the way specialists credibility is undermined by the executives in Table A below:

STRATEGIES USED BY EXECUTIVES

S. No.	*Strategies*	*Actions*
1	Strategic Rejection	If executive is self assured and powerful, rejects the report.
2	"Bottom drawer it"	Executive sends a memo praising the specialist's the technicality, and then puts it away and forgets it.
3	Mobilising political support	Executives calls it the credit's from colleagues.
4	Nitty- gritty tactics	Minor details are questioned, and mistakes in details are raised to try to discredit the whole report.
5	Emotional tactics	Relies on appeals to emotional states.
6	But in the future———	Argument that data may be historically accurate but does not consider future changes.
7	Invisible man	Avoidance, often with the support of a secretary, so no discussion can take place.
8	Further investigation is required	Specialist is sent away to collect more information, either because terms of references are changed, or to follow up the more interesting issues raise in the support
9	Scapegoat	A suitable scapegoat, who is raised as a threat to any change proposed.
10	Deflection	Discussion is deflected away from the main areas by concentrating the attention on less crucial matters.

Table A : A catalog of ploys adopted by managers : Pettigrew 1974.

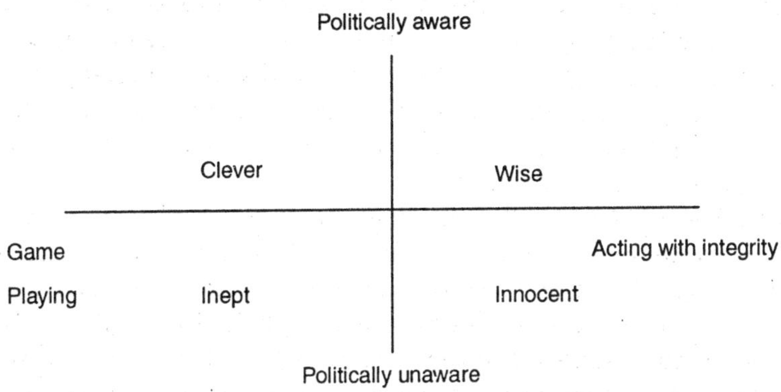

Fig. 14.2. Behavioural Model—reading political situations

Political behaviour is of two types first an ethical behaviour which is acceptable and an unethical behaviour. Baddeley and James (1990) seek to distinguish between 'politicking' and 'maneuvering'. The former refers to acting in self-defence, self oriented where people defend their ego by employing tactics which is called 'game playing'. The latter approach is distinguished by the sense of personal inequity where conscious decisions (choices) are made in different situations. The other dimension in the organization is political awareness, generally referred to the extent a person is able to understand and interpret the political behaviour in the organization. In simple word, how one is able to 'read' a political situation. Baddeley and James[10] have suggested the behaviour model of various managers as given in Figure 14.2 above:

Reading political situation

Each of the four boxes above presents behaviour – clever, inept, wise and innocent, depending upon the persons capacity to read situations and their propensity to play games or to act with integrity.

SUMMARY

Power is derieved from the official position one holds. Those in power are able to marshal resources to their advantage.

Power, authority and responsibility are inter-related. French and Raven have identified six bases of power. These are reward, coercive, legitimate, referent, expert and information power. Effectiveness of power depends upon the situation, perceived differences between the power of involved parties and its acceptance of legitimacy. Power can also be enjoyed by the people having charismatic personality. In organizational setting power base can be enhanced by using knowledge and other resources. Managers can improve their importance by delaying decision making and creating power centers. Creation of dependency, resorting to centrality of resources, creating scarcity of resources and uncertainty leads to a feeling of an enhanced authority. For efficient working, it is necessary to delegate power to subordinates, resort to division of work to the maximum extent, modify organization structure if required and give functional powers to all the individuals so that they feel empowered and develops a sense of responsibility. Politics is about access to power. Power is the property of systems at rest while politics is the study of power in action. It is the dependency between departments, the power relationship is expressed. Managers can play power to their advantage by creating scarcity of resources, resorting to non-programmed decisions, setting ambiguous goals, introducing organizational changes in vital areas and managing external environment. There are various techniques of political play. These include to cultivate right allies, being positive in dealing with others, being reciprocal and persuasive thus building a right image.

Niccolo Machiavelli (1469-1527) has formulated a set of behaviour for maintaining political power. Christie and Geis have formulated an attitude scale in conformity with Machiavelli's teaching. The scale is known as 'Mach Scale'. Machiavelli suggest that end justifies the means and that the job must be accomplished at any cost. He has suggested various techniques of manipulating power. Pettigrew has identified some behavioral patters that executive generally follow to influence management process. Among other things it includes rejection, mobilizing political support, questioning of minor details with a aim to discredit the individual. Avoidance, deflecting the main issue and making a person scapegoat if situation demands. Baddeley and James have suggested a model of reading political situations. They have classified individuals as clever, wise, inept and innocent depending upon the political awareness a person has and his ability to read situations and their propensity to play games or to act with integrity.

TEXT QUESTIONS

Q. 1 Define power. What are the various bases of power?

Q. 2 What are various organizational factors which if suitably manipulated can lead to enhance one's power base?

Q. 3 How can managers play power to their advantages to improve self-image? Are these techniques desirable in the larger interest of the organization?

Q. 4 Explain various techniques of political play.

Q. 5 Explain in detail the characteristics of people who measure high on Mach Scale. Do you recommend such attitude condusive to organizational growth?

Q. 6 What are various strategies used by executives when they interact with specialist to undermine laters credibility as suggested by Pittigrew?

Q. 7 Explain the model proposed by Baddeley and James.

REFERENCES

1. Mainiero Lisa. A and Tromley Cheryl. L ***"Developing Managerial Skills in Organizational Behaviour"***, Second Edition, Prentice Hall (P) limited New Delhi 1997.
2. Cavanaugh M.S. ***"A Typology of Social Power"***, Power politics in organizations. Chichester, John Wiley 1984.
3. Dalton M., ***"Men Who Manage"***, John Wiley and Sons, New York 1959.
4. Wetten, David A. and Kim S. Cameron, ***"Developing Managerial Skills"***, Skot Forceman, 1984.
5. Kanter, R.M. ***"Men and Women of the Corporation"***, Basic books, 1997. pp.- 170-171.
6. Pfeffer, J. ***"Power in Organizations"***, Pitman 1981.
7. Walton and Dutton, 1969.
8. Crozier, M. ***"The Bureaucratic Phenomenon"***, Chicago, University of Chicago Press.
9. Steers, Richard M. ***"Introduction to Organizational Behaviour"***, Scott Forceman and Co., Management Development Vol. 9, No. 3, 1988.
10. Baddeley S. and James, K. ***"Political Management : developing the management portfolio"*** Journal of Management Development Vol. 9, No. 3, 1990.

Case

SUDHAKER GHATE: AN ENTREPRENEUR BY CHOICE

Sudhaker Ghate, a successful entrepreneur and recipient of the 'Vijay Ratna' award, has been the chairman of Miraj Pharmaceuticals since its inception. The award is given by the International Friendship Society every year to 20 people for substantial contribution in their respective fields. Miraj Pharmaceuticals is a family managed organization that was started by Sudhaker Ghate about 23 years back. Initially starting as marketing organization, he expanded his business by adding manufacturing units to it later on.

Ghate has three sons and a daughter; two sons are Chemical Engineers and the third is a Pharmacist and all of them have obtained postgraduate degree in management. His sons joined him as Vice-Presidents after 1982. His daughter has been looking after computer operations at the Corporate Office. All of the family members including his wife are board members and most of the decisions are restricted to the top management. The sales turnover of the company in the last financial year was 12 crores and had a manpower of 600 people. The marketing network of the firm was covering almost the entire country having divisional offices at Bombay, Calcutta, Delhi and Hyderabad. The sales force of 250 medical representatives was given 'detailing training' regularly as a part of staff development activity. Apart from inculcating professional skills and capabilities, it had contributed a lot in creating an environment where interaction and information sharing could take place easily amongst executives and staff. The marketing strategy was based on review of the market through such meetings.

Ghate was born in small village in Maharashtra in the year 1934. He was the youngest in a family of nine children. His father was a farmer and was educated upto the primary level. As his father was very particular about the education of his children, Ghate went to Nagpur after high school. He did his intermediate at Nagpur and then graduation from Bombay. Being determined about progressing in life, he completed the Bachelor's degree in Pharmacy followed by a degree in law at Nagpur. During his college days he believed that he was of a different 'breed'. At that time he used to chalk out his future plans. He always wanted to do something of his own. Inspite of discouragement from his mother and elder brother, he thought of starting and managing a pharmaceutical unit when he was a student. His father was all along a source of inspiration to him. He joined a pharmaceutical company as a medical representative in 1959 and rose to the position of Deputy Sales Manager in the span of seven years. He was transferred from Nagpur to Bombay in 1966. By now he had seriously made up his mind to quit the job and start an enterprise of his own. Morally supported by his wife, he took the final decision and resigned in November 1967 from the company in which he had been working. The only financial resource available to Ghate at that time was gratuity and provident fund with which he made his initial investment of Rs. 55,000/-. His friends helped him in setting up the firm. Instead of venturing into manufacturing he thought of capturing market share first and took a loan licence with another company. He used to get two types of tablets and a capsule manufactured by the company under the formula and supervision provided by him. He encountered many difficulties while marketing the products and realized that a common product that could be prescribed to every second patient would fetch a better market than the products he was offering. At this stage he was assisted by his wife in secretarial work and two medical representatives in field work.

He knew from his experience that a particular tonic called "Metatone" was doing well in the market. He went for an agreement with the concerned pharmaceutical company and then onwards used to get the tonic manufactured by them and marketed it under his own registered brand name 'ViTL' tone'. Although he met with heavy losses during the first two financial years, he could reach the breakeven point in 1971. He applied for Government land in Bambay to start a manufacturing unit and succeeded in getting a loan of Rs. 1,98,000 from Maharashtra State.

After acquiring the land and capital for investment, he went ahead with the manufacturing as well as marketing of ViTL tone. He could achieve 100% annual growth for quite few years. Encouraged by the performance, the firm came up with four more pharmaceutical manufacturing units at Nasik, by the year 1985. As suggested by his enthusiastic and change oriented sons, ten more products were added to the product line by now. Ghate was taken aback when the firm met with heavy losses during the financial year 1986 – 1987. As it came to him as a shock, he went in for extensive market surveys, only to find that a few of his new products which were introduced in the recent past were not doing well in most of the regions. He restricted the market territories for such products and even stopped the manufacture of some of them.

The strategy worked and he started to regain his position in the market. The main product of Miraj Pharmaceuticals, i.e., 'ViTL-tone' alone achieved 26 percent line by adding one product every year and came up with a new project every second year. The firm also diversified by acquiring a sick chemical unit in 1989, which started production in September 1990. Now, Ghate was planning to enter into a joint venture by starting and running a pharmaceutical unit at U.A.E.

QUESTIONS FOR DISCUSSION

1. What were the personal characteristics of Sudhaker Ghate which helped him to become an entrepreneur ?
2. What led to heavy losses in the financial year 1986 – 87 ?
3. Does this case reveal anything about the vision of Sudhaker Ghate ?

A HUMAN RELATIONSHIP QUESTIONNAIRE

The following questions ask you about how to behave at work, what you believe about human relationships, and what value you place on them.

Each question is presented as a statement; you are asked to choose one of five possible responses:

Strongly agree: Agree : Don't know : Disagree : Strongly disagree

There are no right answers, and no wrong answers; so please be as honest as you can.

	Strongly agree	*Agree*	*Don't know*	*Disagree*	*Strongly disagree*
1. You should only tell someone the real reason for doing something if it serves a successful purpose	[ ]	[ ]	[ ]	[ ]	[ ]
2. People who lead upright and respectable lives will get on in the world	[ ]	[ ]	[ ]	[ ]	[ ]
3. Braveness is inherent in most people	[ ]	[ ]	[ ]	[ ]	[ ]

(Contd.)

	Strongly agree	*Agree*	*Don't know*	*Disagree*	*Strongly disagree*
4. You should always assume that people can be villainous and that this will appeal if given a chance	[ ]	[ ]	[ ]	[ ]	[ ]
5. Telling people what they want to hear is the best way to deal with them	[ ]	[ ]	[ ]	[ ]	[ ]
6. The old saying that 'there's one born every minute', is not true	[ ]	[ ]	[ ]	[ ]	[ ]
7. Laying to other people cannot be forgiven	[ ]	[ ]	[ ]	[ ]	[ ]
8. Giving the actual reason rather than ones which may carry more weight is the way to behave when asking someone to do something for you	[ ]	[ ]	[ ]	[ ]	[ ]
9. It is sensible to pander to important people	[ ]	[ ]	[ ]	[ ]	[ ]
10. It is hard to be successful in an organization without cutting comers	[ ]	[ ]	[ ]	[ ]	[ ]
11. What differentiates criminals from other people is that they are foolish enough to get caught	[ ]	[ ]	[ ]	[ ]	[ ]
12. Euthanasia should be a choice for those having an incurable disease	[ ]	[ ]	[ ]	[ ]	[ ]
13. In the final analysis, most people are good and well meaning	[ ]	[ ]	[ ]	[ ]	[ ]
14. You should only act when it is morally defensible	[ ]	[ ]	[ ]	[ ]	[ ]
15. Humility coupled with honestly is a better combination than dishonesty and self importance	[ ]	[ ]	[ ]	[ ]	[ ]
16. Unless forced to work hard, most people will not stretch themselves	[ ]	[ ]	[ ]	[ ]	[ ]
17. Being good in all respects is quite possible	[ ]	[ ]	[ ]	[ ]	[ ]
18. The death of a parent is more easily forgotten by most people than the loss of a piece of property	[ ]	[ ]	[ ]	[ ]	[ ]
19. It is simply asking for trouble to completely trust someone else	[ ]	[ ]	[ ]	[ ]	[ ]
20. It is best always to be honest	[ ]	[ ]	[ ]	[ ]	[ ]

Table 4.2: Scoring key for human relationships questionnaire

Question No.	*Strongly disagree*	*Agree*	*Don't know*	*Disagree*	*Strongly agree*
1	5	4	3	2	1
2	1	2	3	4	5
3	1	2	3	4	5
4	5	4	3	2	1
5	5	4	3	2	1
6	1	2	3	4	5
7	1	2	3	4	5
8	1	2	3	4	5
9	5	4	3	2	1
10	5	4	3	2	1
11	5	4	3	2	1
12	5	4	3	2	1
13	1	2	3	4	5
14	1	2	3	4	5
15	1	2	3	4	5
16	5	4	3	2	1
17	1	2	3	4	5
18	5	4	3	2	1
19	5	4	3	2	1
20	1	2	3	4	5

Calculate your over all total score: ___________

Analysis

Score	**Comment**
20-38	Goodness shines through you. How do you survive ?
39-54	No is not an impossible word to say, you only think it is.
55-69	An honest cynic; at least relatively honest.
70-85	Congratulations – you could be an honorary member of the Borgia family.
85-100	You might even be able to teach Machiavelli something ('Never give a sucker an even break' – W. C. Fields).

CHAPTER 15

Leadership

INTRODUCTION

Leadership is one of the most important aspects of studies of human behaviour in organization. It is the leader who creates working environment. The success of an organization depends upon the efficiency of the leader. It is the attributes, positive approach and the ability to solve problems that make a person leader. Leader should be able to turn the hopeless situation in favour. In the environment of tough competition in the market where it is undergoing financial recession, lay offs is the order of the day, market is facing poor demand for product because every body has enough and poor or no growth situation persists. In this situation leader should not loose his balance but turn the situation in his favour. He should be able to evolve techniques and lead the organization to win-win strategy. Leader should be able to motivate employees. All leaders are not managers as they have to work in non-organized sectors while the managers work in the organized sectors. All managers should be leaders so that they are able to work efficiently. Warren and Benin have identified certain criteria between manager and a leader. The same is given below.

Manager characteristics		*Leader characteristics*
Administers	-	Innovates
Copy	-	An original
Maintains	–	Develops
Focuses on systems and structure	-	Focuses on people
Short-range view	-	Long-range view
Relies on controls	-	Inspires trust
Asks how and when	-	Asks what and why
Eyes on the bottom line	-	Eye on the horizon
Imitates	–	Originates
Accepts the status quo	-	Challenges
Classic	-	Own person
Does a thing right	-	Does right things

Source: Warren and Benin's" Managing the dream. Leadership in 21st century, Journal of Organizational Change Management Vol 2, No. 1 1989.

Definition

Although many definitions of leadership could be cited, the most would depend on the theoretical orientation taken. Besides influence, leadership has been defined in terms of group processes, personality, and compliance particular behaviour, persuasion, power, goal achievement, and interaction, role differentiation, initiation of structure, and combination of two or more of these (Bernard 1990)[1] leader has an ability to lead effectively. He is visionary and accomplishes objective by using discretion (authority). It is generally seen that good leader achieves willing obedience of their subordinates. They follow the leader unquestioned because he fulfills their desires, wants and needs.

Leadership can be defined as influence, that is, the area or process of influencing people so that they will strive willingly and enthusiastically towards achievement of group goals[2].

People should be brought to such a pitch of their devotion to duty that they not only work willingly, but also work with utmost zeal. The leaders are like front line captain, who not only inspires his soldiers by physical presence but also brings down accurate fire from supporting weapons (utilizing skills) and displays high degree of bravery and is not perturbed by danger of enemy fire. Leader instills values of honesty, takes calculated risk and displays concern for employees and customers. They do not stand and wait to see in despair things taking shape.

Ingredients of Leadership

Every group in the organization has a leader. A successful leader has within him the following ingredients.

1. **The ability to use power effectively:** A leader inherits power by virtue of his appointment. Known as the legitimate power apart from the above he achieves willing obedience by using one or more of power bases like expert power, referent power, reward and coercive power. Line authority also facilitates to influence subordinate.
2. **An ability to comprehend:** Human beings have different motivational needs at different times and situations. The ability to comprehend relates to understanding people, their needs, expectations and what a leader has been doing to satisfy them. This is a continuous process that gives a leader the understanding of his subordinates and an ability to explore the situation to his advantage to get the organizational goal achieved.
3. **Ability to inspire:** Inspiration is best judged when subordinates work with zeal in hopeless situation. Leader must identify each individual's capabilities, skill and inspire them. Inspiration emanates from a leader who may have charm, an appeal, devotion to duty, which subordinates further want to enhance them by loyally obeying the leader willfully. Inspirations also come from charismatic personality of the leader. Subordinates promote what leader desires.
4. **Leadership style:** Leadership style is ***firstly*** the ability of a leader to act in a manner that will develop a climate conducive to the response from the led and ***secondly*** arouse motivation among the employees, leader must design and maintain an environment for efficient performance. He should identify motivational needs, desires of the subordinates and work out a plan that fulfills motivational

needs and aspirations of the employees. Organizations practices must include appropriate reward system, freedom of action in work environment, recognition, open communication system and very informal and cordial behaviour pattern among various layers of organizational structure. Leaders must be participative, face the same problems as his subordinates, work in the identical environment and not show the signs of tiredness. He must be loyal to his subordinates and follow an appropriate leadership style taking into consideration the organizational climate and the environment he has to work. His approach must be reconciliatory.

Theories of Leadership

Trait Theory of Leadership

Not all managers are effective leaders and not all leaders are effective managers. It is therefore difficult to identify effective managers and leaders. Early studies of leaders defined them by traits they were supposed to exhibit. Sometimes it was also called "attributes" that the leader possesses. The theory therefore was called "trait theory" or attribute theory of leadership. It is also known as "great man's" theory. A leader might be described as loyal, brave, trustworthy or companionate. But all these qualities may not be found in a successful leader. Therefore long list of unending traits may be listed as desirable for a leader. Despite these difficulties, Davis[3] has identified four characteristics that leader tends to have. They are more likely to be present in middle and upper-level managers than in those who hold lower-level supervisory positions. Their characteristics are as under:-

1. ***Intelligence:*** leaders tend to have higher degree of intelligence than their followers.
2. ***Social maturity and breadth:*** leaders have a tendency to be emotionally mature and to have a broad range of interests. They are members of some what exclusive social club.
3. ***Inner motivation and achievement drives:*** leaders want to accomplish things, when they achieve one goal they seek out another. They are inner motivated and do not depend on outside forces for their motivation.
4. ***Human relations attitude*:** Leaders are able to work effectively with other persons. They understand that to accomplish any task they must be considerate of others.

Many studies of traits have been undertaken. Ralph. M.stogdill[4] found following traits in a effective leader:

Physical Traits such as Energy, appearance, height, intelligence, ability and **personality traits** such as adaptability, aggressiveness, enthusiasm and self-confidence. They also have **task related characteristics** such as achievement drive, persistence and initiative and **social drive** like cooperativeness, interpersonal skills and administrative ability.

Not all leaders possess all the traits. Trait theory of leadership gives no guidance as to how much of any trait a leader should have. The theory is not conclusive. Most of the traits identified in successful leaders are actually the pattern of behaviour.

Leadership Skills and Style

Another way of analyzing leadership behaviour in terms of skill possessed by the leader. There are three types of skills, which are required to be used appropriately at different levels of management. These are shown in Figure 15.1 below:

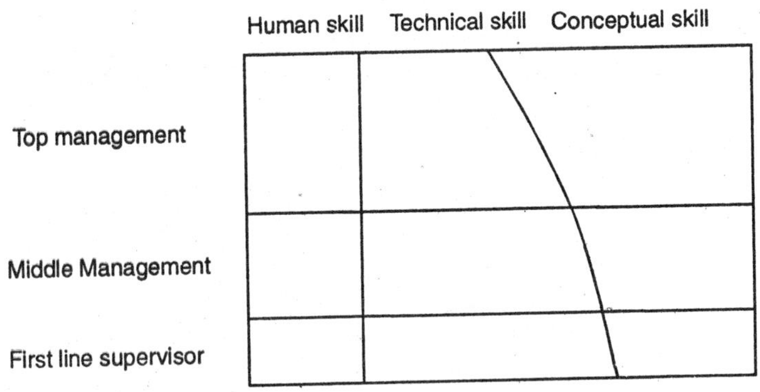

Fig. 15.1. Proportions of Skill Required

Human skills are important for all the levels of management. They are concerned with interpersonal relationship between managers and other persons who come in contact with the leader. The leaders apply internal motivation to the employees so that their willing obedience and cooperation is obtained. ***Technical skill*** involves the ability of employees to know the technical aspect and operation and maintenance of machine, tools and allied fixture they work with. Lower level managers who are in close contact with workers have to know it in greater details as compared to higher managerial cadre. The former spends considerable time on utilization of technical skills. ***Conceptual skill*** involves the ability to view the organization in strategic term. It is most important for top level management where long term planning and futuristic thinking is required. As managers move to higher position in the organization they must develop and utilize the conceptual skill increasingly. But at times managers are found wanting of this skill. Training, development and exposure to various situations would make the managers to cope up with higher responsibility, based on skill, maturity and understanding.

Leadership styles and behaviour. In this chapter fallowing leadership theories are discussed.

1. Leadership based on authority
2. Likert's four system of management
3. Managerial grid
4. Leadership styles based on power and influence
5. Contingency or situational leadership
6. Path-goal theory of leadership
7. Charismatic Leadership
8. Transformational leadership.

LEADERSHIP STYLES BASED ON AUTHORITY

Autocratic leadership: This type of leadership is practiced by the managers concentrating on power and authority within themselves. Leader expects high degree of compliance by subordinates. he is dogmatic and positive in his approach. Manager exhibiting this type of style has the ability and enforces decision by use of rewards and fear of punishment. Communication tends to be primarily in one direction from manager to follower. Some autocratic leaders are seen as "benevolent autocrat." Though they listen considerably to their followers' opinion before making any decision, the decision remains to be their own. They seemingly consider their subordinate's ideas but when it comes to decision making they are more autocratic than benevolent. An advantage of autocratic leadership is the speed of decision-making, as the leader does not have to obtain group members approval. However there appears to be a low morale syndrome on the group members because their

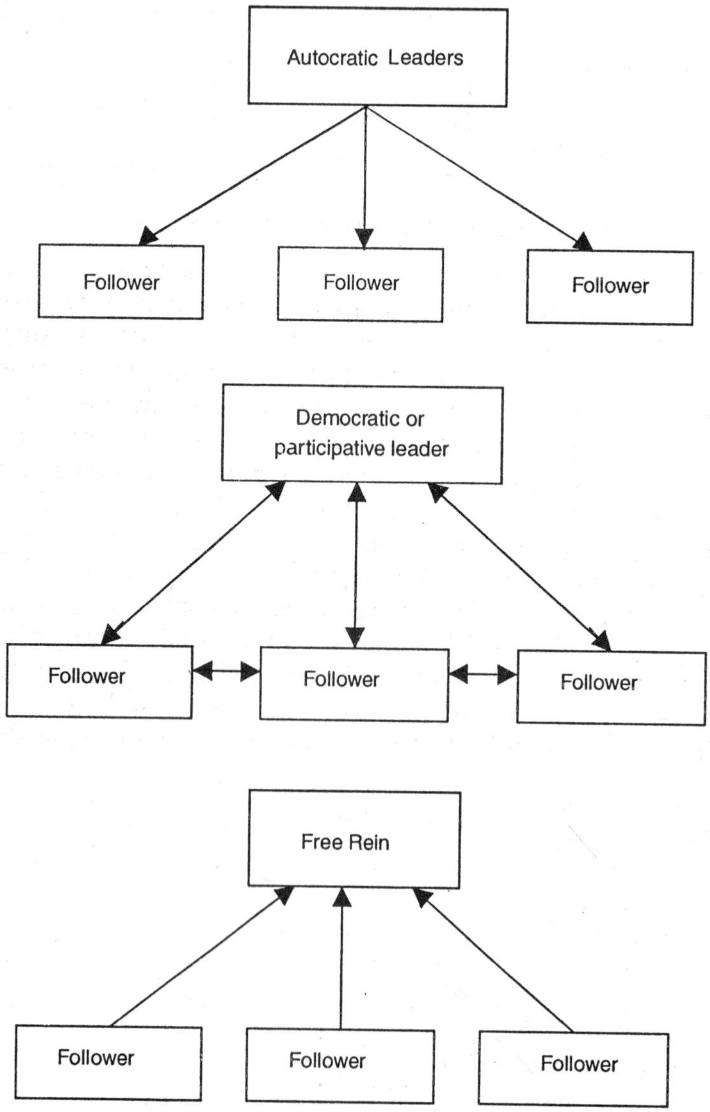

Fig. 15.2. Flow of Communication and Influence.

views are not given due consideration and may resent the decision and support the same as little as possible. The pattern of communication with subordinates and influence exercised over them in various leadership styles is given in Figure 15.2.

Democratic or Participative Leadership

In contrast to autocratic leadership, democratic or participative leader consults subordinates, encourages participation in decision-making. In the process of interaction with subordinates, democratic leader suggest actions or decisions and obtains views of those under him. He has respect for subordinates views and does not act without their concurrence. The leader is supportive. This style of leadership has various advantages, which include high morale and support of subordinates, smooth implementation due to subordinates being party to decision making. Because of the participation of subordinates, the quality of decisions is better as compared to the autocratic leader. Disadvantages include slower decision, lack of accountability for decisions per se and possible compromise in the process of trying to please majority of the people involved in decision-making.

Laissez-faire Leadership

A leader who practices laissez-faire leadership is also called "free rein" leader who uses his power very little giving subordinates full freedom of action and independence for setting their goals and means of achieving them. This type of leaders depends heavily on subordinates and see their role as one of aiding the operation of followers by furnishing required information when asked for and acts only as contact between various departments and outside agencies (external environment). Here the leader attempts to exercise very little control or influence over the group members. Such type of leadership style promotes individual growth and freedom of action for goal setting. However, the loose control by the leader over the group may lead to lack of group cohesiveness and unity of purposes toward organizational objective. This may ultimately lead to inefficiency and even worse to chaos.

Which leadership style is best? Mc Murry[5] argued for what he called "Benevolent autocracy" by managers towards their employees. This compassionate but dictatorial approach was based on the fallowing premises:

Benevolent Autocracy

1. Most top managers have hard driving, autocratic personalities. Therefore they find participative management difficult to accept.
2. Significant decisions affecting firm must be made by top management because of the potential damage that could result from a poor decision.
3. Many members of large bureaucracies are in reality security seekers who do not wish to share in the decision-making process.
4. Participation may be interpreted by employees as their right to veto managerial decisions and to generally become lax in their work behaviour.

The use of any style will depend on the situation. Managers may be highly autocratic in emergency or when they are custodian of a particular solution. The same leader may be participative when he wishes to find alternative solutions to the problem. Model discussions are carried out in the Defense Services to arrive at a solution to operational problems by involving as many subordinates as possible. In Research and Development organization the leadership style may even be of free-rein where problem has been defined and subordinates are left to themselves to arrive at a solution and minimum involvement of a manager is expected. Deference between autocratic, democratic and laissez-faire leadership styles is given below in a diagramatic form below:

	Autocratic	*Democratic*	*Laissez-faire*
1.	Determination of policy by the leader.	Policies are decided by the group assisted by the leader.	Complete freedom. Decision by individual/group.
2.	Techniques and activity dictated by manager. One at a time, future course not known.	Techniques, processes decided during group discussion. Technical advice sought from managers. Courses two or more suggested by managers. The group makes a choice.	Material supplied by leader. No part in discussion decision of techniques processes by individuals.
3.	Dictates tasks and forms group by selecting individuals by himself	Members can work with whomsoever they want to.	No part is played by leader in determining task and who is to accomplish that.
4.	Leader is "personal" in praise and criticism. Keeps away.	Leader is objective and tries to be group member.	No praise no comments. Act as defunked leader. He fills the vacancy no personal contribution.

Likert's four Systems of Management

Prof Rensis Likert carried out studies relating to patterns and styles of leadership in the university of Michigan for almost 30 years. He has developed a model called likerts four system relating to leadership styles. His ideas and approaches are important for understanding of human behaviour in the organizations. Likerts four systems of management are as under

System-1 Exploitive-authoritative

Managers practising exploitive–authoritative system of management are highly autocratic, have no trust in subordinates and put a finger everywhere. They believe in motivating people through fear and punishment and occasionally reward them. They engage in down ward communication and limit decision-making at top level of management only.

System-2 Benevolent-authoritative

Managers practicing benevolent-authoritative type of leadership displays full trust and confidence in their subordinates. They motivate the employees by giving occasional rewards but maintain fear amongst subordinates and awards punishments wherever it is required.They believe in minimum upward communication and invites some ideas relating to issue in hand. Managers permit certain decision-making and delegates authority to a limited measure. They exercise close control policy in leading their subordinates.

System-3 Consultative

Managers practicing consultative type of management have substantial but not full confidence and trust in their subordinates. Usually they make use of ideas and opinion of subordinates. They believe in upward and downward communication when dealing with subordinates. To motivate, the managers issue rewards but occasional punishment is also awarded. They lay down broad policy and keeps decision making on important policy matters to top level. However, specific decision-making is left to subordinates which may relate to day to day functions within the policy parameter laid down.

System-4 Participative-group

Likert's fourth management system is called participative-group leadership. In this system managers have complete confidence and full trust in subordinates on all matters of organization. They always get ideas from subordinates and use them constructively. They give economic rewards for participation and involvement in goal setting. Manager practicing participative-group system of management encourages decision making by subordinates and merge themselves in the group and carryout task without any differentiation. They believe and encourage communication with subordinates, superiors and with the peer group. As name suggests, managers participate in-group activities throughout the organization.

In series of studies on morale and productivity among workers, Likert concluded that the most effective supervisors are employees centered. "Supervisors with the best record of performance focus their primary attention on the human aspect of their subordinates' problems and on endeavouring to build effective work-groups with high performance goals. (Likert 1961)[6]. Likert's findings suggest that a democratic orientation towards leadership with support and encouragement offered by the leader tend to improve the chances for long term high productivity. The task of the leader is seen as building a highly cohesive and mutually supportive work group. Likert is aware that job centered, autocratic and supervision can produce short-run gains in productivity. But long run effects of this approach would harm the organization by 'liquidating its human assets'. By decreasing morale and encouraging absenteeism and turnover, which is typical of autocratic way of management that would damage the organization. Likert carried this idea forward by recommending that human resource valuation be included as a part of organizations accounting statements[7].

MANAGERIAL GRID

"Managerial Grid" style of leadership was developed by Robert Blake and Jane mouton (1969). The managerial grid model explains concern of a manager for production and people. Blake and mouton's model helps to measure a managers relative concern for people and task and reflects bi-directional nature of leadership. The managerial grid shown at figure-15.3 identifies a range of management behaviour based on the various ways that the task oriented and employee oriented styles, which have been explained as a continuum on a scale of 1 to 9 as Figure 15.3 on the next page.

Blake and mouton have very clearly emphasized the concern for people and production. Concern for people includes such elements as degree of personal commitment towards goal achievement, maintenance of self-esteem of people, assigning task based on trust, provision of good working conditions and maintenance of good inter-personal relationship. When a manager has concern for people, he is more worried about fulfillment of various need factors that are included in hygiene factors of McGregor in his motivational style. As far as the leadership style that displays concern for production includes elements like output of the workers, work efficiency, quality of policy decisions, various processes and procedures that are followed during the production line. It also includes creativity, research and development undertaken, quality of product produced and last but not the least services provided by the staff. Let us now study four styles of leadership.

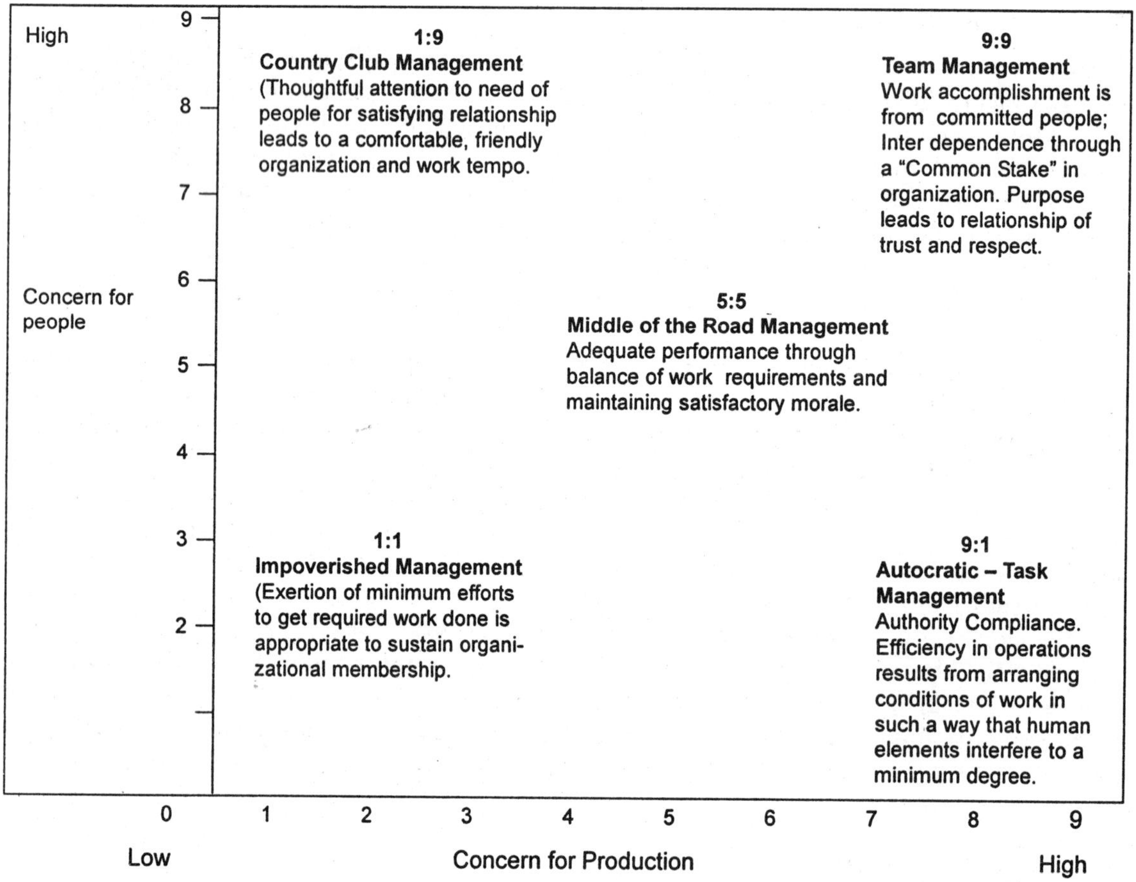

Fig. 15.3. Managerial Grid

Impoverished Management 1:1

Under this style (as shown in the figure-left bottom corner,) is referred to as impoverished management or Laissze-faire type of management. Managers do not involve themselves with the work or people, they only mark time and have abandoned their job. They act as messenger to pass information from superiors to subordinates. They neither display any concern for people nor for the production. They display minimum involvement in the job they are assigned to. This amounts to exertion of minimum efforts on the part of leader to get required work done is appropriate to sustain organizational membership.

Team Management 9:9

At the extreme opposite is team management style of leadership where managers mesh interest of people and production needs in the balanced manner. Their involvement is total. They are real team leaders who have full knowledge, skill and aptitude for job and also concern for the welfare of workers. Blake and Mouton argue strongly that style 9:9 is the most effective management style. They believe, this leadership approach will, in all situations, result in improved performance, low absenteeism, and turnover and high job satisfaction.

Country Club Management 1:9

Leaders who follow this style of leadership display very high concern for people and very little interest for production. They create a very relaxed and friendly environment. There are no organizational goals and leader exibits very loose style of functioning. The working evironment is workers welfare oriented.

Autocratic-task Oriented 9:1

This leadership style concentrates on setting of organizational goals, development of effective operations systems, utilization of organizational resources, achievement of objectives and stress on quality of work and production. The leader functions in an autocratic way with no or very little concern for people.

Middle of the Road Management 5:5

Managers have both concern for people and production. They set moderate production goals and achieve them. They have equal concern for people and work. They achieve reasonably satisfactory results and maintain high morale of workers and meet production requirements.

The managerial grid is widely used model for training and development of managers. The model cannot determine a particular style of a leader because leadership is influenced by personality traits, skills, attitude of the leader and the followers. Apart from the above situational factors in work environment and the organizational culture affects the leadership style to a great extent.

CONTINGENCY APPROACH TO LEADERSHIP

As studied earlier, Trait Theory is not conclusive and behavioural approach to leadership depends largely to the nature and content of the work and prevailing organizational culture. Researchers therefore began trying to identify those factors in each situation that influence the effectiveness of a particular leadership style. Contingency approach to leadership is therefore important. The theory focuses on the following factors.

(*a*) Task requirements
(*b*) Peer's expectations and behaviour
(*c*) Employees characteristics, expectations and behaviour
(*d*) Organizational culture and policies

HERSEY AND BLANCHARD'S SITUATIONAL LEADERSHIP MODEL

One of the major contingency approach to leadership is Paul Hersey and Kenneth H. Blanchard's ***Situational Leadership model***. The model emphasis on the following points:

1. The most effective leadership style varies with ***"readiness"*** of employees. ***The readiness is defined as the desire for achievement, willingness to accept responsibility, and task related skill, ability and experience.***
2. Goals and knowledge of followers.

To understand the model, it is necessary to understand task and relationship behaviour.

Task Behaviour

Task behaviour is defined as "the extent to which the leader engages in spelling out the duties and responsibilities of an individual and group. These behaviours telling people what to do, how to do it, when to do it, where to do it, and who is to do it." (Paul Hersey and Kenneth H. Blanchard and Dewey E. Johnson)[8]. Task behaviour is characterized by one-way communication from leader to follower. The leader is not concerned with the feeling of follower but he is concerned as to how to help the follower to achieve the set goal.

Relationship Behaviour

Relationship behaviour is defined as "the extent to which the leader engages in two way or multi way communication, The behaviours include listening, facilitating and supportive behaviour." (Refer Paul Hersey and Kenneth H. Blanchard and Dewey E. Johnson)[9].

Hersey and Blanchard believe that the relationship between a manager and follower moves through four different stages. See Figure 15.4 below:

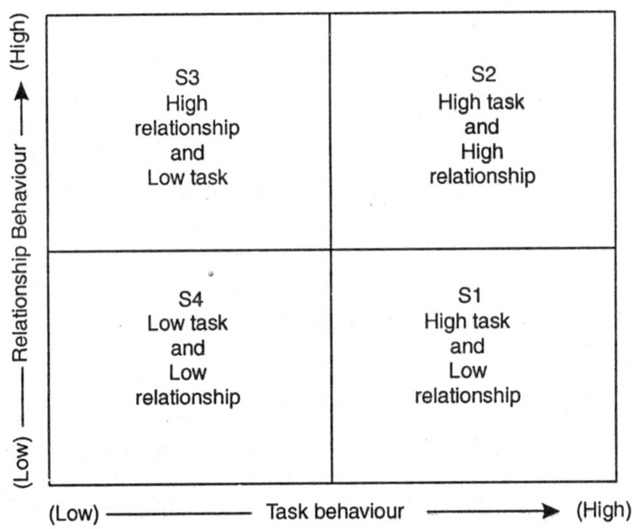

Fig. 15.4. Relationship between a Manager and Follower

(Adapted from Paul Hersey and Kenneth H. Blanchard, Management of Organizational Behaviour—Utilising Human Resources, 5th Edition.)

Style-S1 This relationship style is characterized by above average amounts of task behaviour and below average amount of relationship behaviour.

Style-S2 This relationship style is characterized by above average amount of both task and relationship behaviour.

Style-S3 This style is characterized by above average amount of relationship behaviour and below average amount of task behaviour.

Style-S4 This style is characterized by below average amount of both relationship and task behaviour.

In the initial stage of readiness (S1 situation) a leader is required to guide the follower about the task. In this situation leader shows least concern for their welfare, and personal relationship. As the situation improves (S2 situation) the leader's trust in his employees increases as the leader becomes part of the group and wishes to encourage them to accomplish the task. In this situation the employees have to work within the framework of the task structure hence the leader has to maintain an highest degree of commitment to task relationship. In S3 situation the employees develop high degree of work ability and achievement orientation (motivation) begin to surface as they seek greater responsibility hence very close relationship is required to be maintained. In S4 situation follower no longer need direction as they become more confident and experienced.

Motivation, ability and experience of the subordinates must be continuously assessed to determine which style is appropriate at a particular moment. This model of leadership is considered ideal as it is dynamic and flexible. The model assists in maintaining close relationship of leader and the led, facilitates professional development of subordinates and in doing so improves motivational level of followers. A leader must however remain alert and change to suitable leadership style in different situations and at different levels of progression.

BEHAVIROURAL APPROACH TO LEADERSHIP
(Leadership Styles-Robert Tannenbaum and Warren H Schmidt-a model)

Every leader has to undertake two major functions in any organization ie *one* task related functions and *two* functions that will promote group effectiveness (maintenance). Managers who have task-oriented style of leadership will closely supervise employees as far as the progress of the work is concerned. Getting the job done is given more emphasis than employee growth. On the contrary managers who have employee oriented style of leadership will put more emphasis on employee motivation rather than controlling subordinates. Managers seek friendly, cooperative, trusting relationship with employees. It may be noted that no manager is either task oriented or employee oriented. Every manager uses little of each style.

Robert Tannenbaum and Warren H.Schmidt were among the first theorist to describe various factors that influence leadership style. They have developed a leadership continuum on which various styles of leadership have been shown ranging from highly boss centered to highly subordinate centered. The same has been shown in figure 15.5 below. The most important element that may influence managers' style can be seen along the continuum. These are explained in following paragraph.

1. **Leader:** The forces that operate while leading subordinates are the managers personality, skill, ability and attitude towards the work, employees and the organization he is serving. Confidence in subordinates and his personal inclination towards leadership style which play a dominating role in selecting a particular style of leadership.

2. **Subordinate:** According to Tannenbaum and Schmitt, a manager can allow greater participation and freedom when employees crave independence and freedom of action, want to have decision – making responsibility, identify with the organization's goals and are experienced enough to deal with a problem efficiently. They should possess experience that lead to "*participative management.*" When these conditions are non existent, the managers initially can have tight control and use authoritarian type of leadership. They can later modify the style as employees develop skill, confidence and organizational commitment.
3. **Situation:** The forces of situation play a decisive role in selecting leadership style. They include organizational value system, tradition, delegation of authority, group cohesiveness and time management. The level of organizational effectiveness is an important factor to be considered.

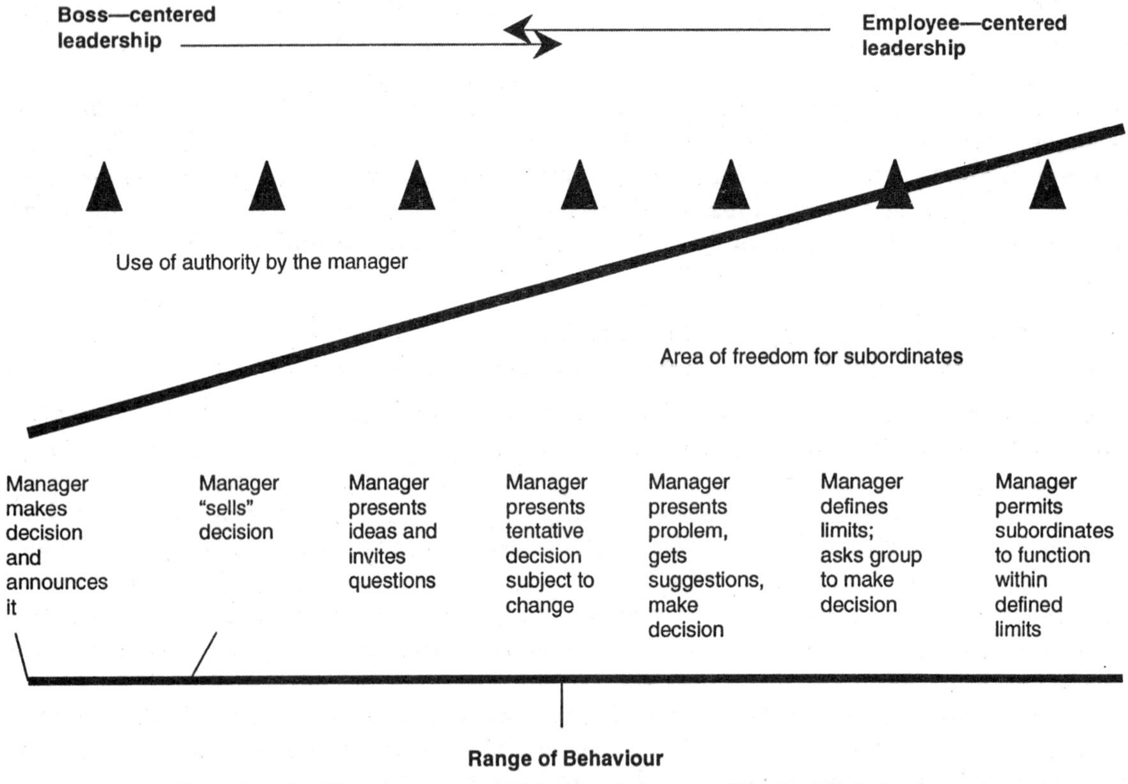

Fig. 15.5. The Tannenbaum and Schmidt continuum of leadership behaviour.

Weihrich and Koonz have stated that in reviewing their continuum model in 1973 (it was originally formulated in 1958).Tannenbaum and Schmidt placed circles around the model, as shown in the figure indicated above to represent the influence on style imposed by both the orgasnisational environment and the social environment. This was done to emphasise the open system nature of leadership styles and the various impacts of the organizational environment and of the social environment outside the enterprise. In their 1973 commentary, they put increased stress on the interdependency of leadership style and environmental forces such as labour unions, greater pressure for social responsibility, the civil rights movement, and the ecology and consumer movement that challenge the rights of managers to make decisions or handle their subordinates without considering interests outside the organization (Heinz Weihrich and Herold Koonz[10]).

FIEDLER'S CONTINGENCY APPROACH TO LEADERSHIP

Fiedler carried out intensive work on leadership. He believes that most of the leaders are inflexible and try to fit in every situation they face. If they succeed they are considered good leaders. Fiedler feels that matching the managerial style with the situation or changing the situation to match the manager's leadership style can achieve effective group performance. The research is based on the leadership styles similar to the employee oriented leader or the task oriented leader studied earlier. What differentiates Fiedler's model is the measuring instrument he used in his research work. Fiedler measured leadership style on the scale that indicated the degree to which a person described favourably or unfavorably. He coined the concept of ***Least preferred co-worker*** (LPC) –The employee with whom the person could work least well. As per Fiedler's findings: *One,* a person who describes his least preferred co-worker in a relatively favorable manner (high LPC rating) tend to be permissive, human relations oriented and considerate of the feelings of his men. But a person who describes his least preferred co-worker (LPC) in an unfavorable manner-(low LPC rating) tends to be managing, task oriented and less concerned with the human relations aspect of the job. *Two,* the scores on the Assumed Similarity between Opposites (ASO) Scale-ratings based on then degree to which leader see group members as being themselves. (Fred. E. Fiedler)*[11]. High LPC managers are employee oriented and want to

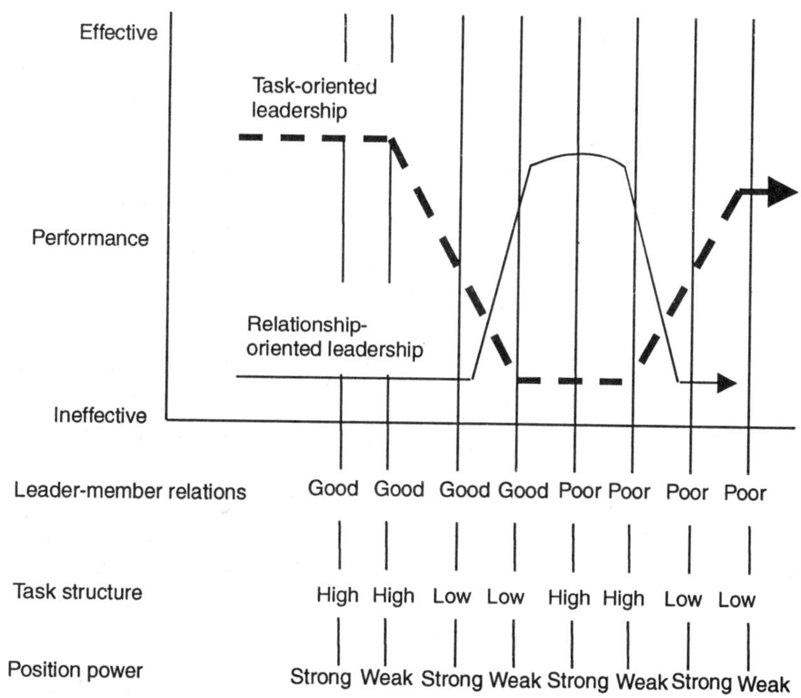

Fig. 15.6. Fiedler's model of leadership

maintain a good interpersonal relationship with their co-workers. They regard their close ties with employees important for their efficiency. While managers having low LPC are task oriented. They display lower priority for employees than the level of productivity. Fiedler identified three variables to determine the ideal leadership style as given in Figure 15.6.

(*a*) **Leader-Member Relationship:** If a manager is able to establish good relations with his workers based on personality, skill and knowledge he may be successful leader and does not have to depend on power and authority. Leader-member relations were measured on LPC scale, either they were good or bad depending upon the degree of cohesion, co-operation and the level of conflict prevailing between the leader and the led.

(*b*) **Task Structure:** High task structure is related to a task where all actions required to be taken are explained in sequential manner and employees understand and anticipate what is coming next. On the contrary when a task is unstructured, the employees do not know as to how to handle the work and group-member's role become ambiguous.

(*c*) **Position Power:** In this situation power derieved by the leader from his formal position and other power bases are not considered. Fiedler feels that a leader having a strong power position can obtain (wield) followership more easily than a leader not having a formal power base. The position of power is determined by the amount of control which the leader has over allocation of resources, determination of salaries, rewards, punishments and hiring of people.

LPC Score

										Scoring
Pleasant	8	7	6	5	4	3	2	1	Unpleasant	—
Friendly	8	7	6	5	4	3	2	1	Unfriendly	—
Rejecting	1	2	3	4	5	6	7	8	Accepting	—
Tense	1	2	3	4	5	6	7	8	Relaxed	—
Distant	1	2	3	4	5	6	7	8	Close	—
Cold	1	2	3	4	5	6	7	8	Warm	—
Supportive	8	7	6	5	4	3	2	1	Hostile	—
Boring	1	2	3	4	5	6	7	8	Interesting	—
Quarrelsome	1	2	3	4	5	6	7	8	Harmonious	—
Gloomy	1	2	3	4	5	6	7	8	Cheerful	—
Open	8	7	6	5	4	3	2	1	Guarded	—
Backbiting	1	2	3	4	5	6	7	8	Loyal	—
Untrustworthy	1	2	3	4	5	6	7	8	Trust worthy	—
Considerate	8	7	6	5	4	3	2	1	Inconsiderate	—
Nasty	1	2	3	4	5	6	7	8	Pleasing	—
Agreeable	8	7	6	5	4	3	2	1	Disagreeable	—
Insincere	1	2	3	4	5	6	7	8	Sincere	—
Kind	8	7	6	5	4	3	2	1	Unkind	—
									Total	

Fig. 15.7. LPC Score

Fiedler then went on to specify eight possible combinations on the above three variables. Leader-member relations may be good or poor, task may be structured or unstructured and lastly the position power may be strong or weak. He then measured the performance of a leader under *favourable, moderate and unfavorable situations.*

Least Preferred Co-worker (LPC) Scale

Describe the person on the scale that follows by placing an "X" in the appropriate space. Look at the words at both ends of the line before you mark "X". There are no right or wrong answers. Work rapidly; your first answer is likely to be the best. Do not omit any item and mark each item only once. Now describe the person with whom you can work least well. Enter the score in the column provided. LPC Score method is explained in Figure 15.7.

Determine your LPC score and its implied leadership style by adding the numbers recorded in the right-hand column. Mark this total in the space provided.

If your score is 64 or higher, Fiedler considers you to be a high LPC person. The high LPC person essentially says of his or her least preferred co-worker, "Even if I can't work with you, you may still be an okay person". Because of this sensitivity for relationships with others, the high LPC person is considered to be "relationship-motivated" as a leader.

If your score is 57 or lower, you are a low LPC leader. A low LPC person describes the least preferred co-worker in very negative terms. Essentially he or she says, "Work is extremely important to me, therefore, if you are a poor co-worker and prevent me in my efforts to get things done, then I can't accept you in other respects either." This low LPC individual is termed "task motivated" as a leader.

A score of 58 to 63 indicates a possible mix of motivation and goals. If you fall in this range, Fiedler argues that you need to decide for yourself where you fit between task and relationship motivations.

Fiedler, in his research concluded that The task oriented leadership style would be ideal for favourable and unfavourable situations. In favorable situations when Leader-Member relations are good, the task is structured and position power is strong , the task oriented leader will be effective. On the other hand, under unfavorable situation, when leader-member relations are poor, task is unstructured and position power is weak, task oriented style of leadership will be good. However when the situation is *moderate* (moderately favourable or unfavourable) the human relations–oriented leader will be most effective.

Analysis of the model: There is however, some criticism. One of the major criticisms is that the model is simplest. Early research relied heavily on correlation findings, cause and effect conclusions. Indeed, as we have mentioned earlier, it may well be that the LPC scale is a better measure of the personality of the individual than it is a description of leadership behaviour through motivation. There is another aspect to the correlations. There are some people who would utterly reject them on the basis that they do not always reach conventional levels of statistical significance. Perhaps the most damaging criticism, however, is the LPC scale itself. (Tyson Shaun and Jackson Tony)[12].

PATH-GOAL THEORY OF LEADERSHIP

Path-Goal theory of leadership was proposed by Martin Evans and Robert House in 1970-

71. The theory is an amalgamation of Contingency approach of leadership and Expectancy theory of motivation. The theory is based on situation factors that includes ***firstly,*** subordinate attributes like ability and the locus (internal and external locus of control). ***Secondly,*** the work setting attributes like task, formal authority system prevailing in the organization, cohesiveness of the work group and the like. Robert House states that leader has to set the goals for subordinates based on their ability, identify various courses of action to achieve the organizational goals and select the best course open, taking into consideration the situational factors. Both the theorist further stated that reward system and relationship with co-workers are very important factors. These factors are shown in Figure 15.8 below:

Leadership styles
- Supportive
- Directive
- Participative
- Achievement oriented

Situational factors
- Subordinate attributes
- Ability
- Locus of control

Work setting attributes
- task
- formal authority system
- primary work group

OUTPUT
- Job satisfaction
- Acceptance of a leader by the group
- Motivational behaviour

Expectancy
- Efforts would lead to performance
- Performance would lead to reward

Fig. 15.8. Path Goal Theory of Leadership

Based on the above attributes leadership can be of following four types:

1. Directive Leadership

Directive leadership is the style of leadership in which the leader provides guidance and methodology to accomplish the task. This is required when the task is not structured. The leader sets the goals for group/teams/individuals, depending upon the nature of the work, allocates them, exercises strict control, gives the detailed directions to accomplish the same and also provides continuous support to his subordinates. He ensures that all the resources are made available to them and keeps a very close watch over the progress of the work.

2. Supportive Leadership

This type of leadership gives consideration to the needs of subordinates, shows concern for their well-being and creates a conducive work environment. It has a great impact on the performance of the subordinates. In this style, leader attempts to get the feed back on the decisions he has made. He invites suggestions from subordinates but the control over decision making remains with the leader.

3. Participative Leadership

The leader solicits subordinates' suggestions. He allows and encourages subordinates in decision-making. This approach improves motivational level of subordinates as they feel that they are the part the decision-making and therefore committed to the implementation of the task.

4. Achievement-oriented Leadership

Setting challenging goals, seeking improved performance, seeking trust of continued efficiency of the subordinates are the main factors of this style of leadership. The style is highly effective for those who have clear cut and non repetitive assignments and have an urge to satisfy higher level of motivational needs.

The theory propagates that any of the four leadership styles can be practiced by a leader depending upon situational factors such as subordinates characteristics and the attributes of work setting. If there is an ideal fit between the leadership style and situational factors in work-setting then subordinates will have high job satisfaction. They will be highly motivated that will transform their energies into high productivity leading to high rewards. The logic behind the model is that the leader can help subordinates to achieve their goals by advising them from time to time and removing hurdles from the path so that the goals are achieved by the subordinates. High performance is attempted by the employees because they are convinced that it would lead to high rewards (expectancy theory of motivation). Leader can apply various patterns of theories based on the situations. If employees seek higher level of job satisfaction they can be given challenging work by the leader so that their self-actualization need is fulfilled. If the employees have good skills and desire to contribute to the achievement of organizational goal then the participative type of leadership style can be practiced.

CHARISMATIC LEADERSHIP

A new theory of leadership is taking a large dimension in the organization. It has been seen that charismatic leader aims to get willing followers to attain organizational goals. Charismatic leader have following characteristics that make them stand out as successful leaders

(*a*) **Vision:** Charismatic leader has vision. He sees an organization from futuristic point of view and has a great foresight to preempt problems and seek solution and therefore he is ahead of his competitors and sails in safe waters.

(*b*) **Risk takers:** Charismatic leaders take great amount of risk to accomplish the vision. Indira Gandhi the erstwhile prime minister of India took a risk by launching its defense forces into East Pakistan to liberate it. She also displayed a high degree of risk while nationalizing banks and taking away privy purse privilege from Indian kings.

(*c*) **Sensitivity to environment constraints and follower need:** Charismatic leaders display a high degree of knowledge and its applicability to practical problems likely to face, may be shortage of raw material, competitors strategy, trend in market and likely pattern that may emerge. They believe the subordinates contribution and hence the importance to their needs.

(*d*) **Distinct Behavioral pattern:** Charismatic leaders are sympathetic towards subordinates and hence a soft corner for them. They are supportive and employee oriented. They behave differently in different situation and do not have a brand.

Charismatic leader influences subordinates by articulating an appealing vision. This vision provides a sense of continuity for followers by linking the present with better future for organization. The leader then communicates high performance expectations and expresses confidence that followers can attain them. This enhances follower self-esteem and self-confidence. Next, leader conveys through words and actions, a new set of values and by his or her behaviour, sets a example for followers to imitate. Finally the charismatic leaders makes self sacrifices and engages in unconventional behaviour to demonstrate courage and convictions about the vision (B Shamir, R J House and M B Arthur)[13]. Charismatic leadership is more pronounced when there is a high degree of uncertainty and leader is able to come out successfully.

TRANSFORMATIONAL LEADERSHIP

This type of leaders guide their subordinates by establishing goals which can be achieved by role identity and task requirement. Transactional leader use reward system very effectively to achieve organizational goals and set new standards. Transformational leadership follows various leadership models. Transformational leadership is practiced when leader intellectually stimulates the subordinates, excites, arouses and inspires them to perform beyond their expectations. By providing a new vision, the transformational leader transform the followers into people who want to self-actualize. Leader by inspiration have won wars by voluntarily demanding highest sacrifices of soldiers in the battlefields. History is replete of various examples of valour and sacrifices. Transformational leadership is beyond the charismatic leadership. Field Marshall S H F J Manekshaw, the then COAS of Indian Army provided transformational leadership which won 1971 war by Indian Army.

SUMMARY

Leadership is an art of leading subordinates. Leaders are visionary and by sheer nature achieve willing obedience of their subordinates. They take calculated risk and display devotion to duty and concern for employees. Leadership is about influencing subordinates to act willingly towards achievement of organizational goals. A successful leader should have an ability to use power successfully. They should be able to identify human needs and inspire them even in hopeless situation. A good leader should arouse motivation among employees and create a climate conducive to work.

There are various leadership theories. Traits Theory of leadership is is also called "great man's theory". The theory suggests that to be leader, a person must possess certain traits. Davis has identified that a good leader should have intelligence, social maturity, inner motivation, achievement, orientatation and lastly the human relation's attitude. As far as the study of human skills is concerned, every leader has human skill, technical skill and conceptual skill in varying degree. There are various leadership styles based on authority. These are autocratic leadership style, democratic leadership style, free rein or laisse-faire leadership style. There is no one best style. It will depend upon the prevailing situation in the organization.

Likert carried out research on leadership styles. He concluded that there are following four systems of leadership.

System 1 Exploitative—authoritative

System 2 Benevolent—authoritative
System 3 Consultative
System 4 Participative—group

Robert Blake and Mouton developed a leadership model commonly known as "Managerial Grid". The model is based on bi-dimensions. The scientist believe that every leader has concern for people and production in varying degree. Based on this premise Blake and Mouton have identified following leadership styles.

(*a*) Impoverished Management—Leader is having no concern for people or task.
(*b*) Team Management—Managers combine interest of people and production in a balanced manner.
(*c*) Country Club Management—Leader displays very high concern for people and low concern for the task.
(*d*) Autocratic Task—Leader displays very high concern for the task and very little concern for the people.
(*e*) Middle of the road Management—A manager who has an equal concern for people and the task.

Since trait theory was proved to be inconclusive, a contingency approach to leadership was evolved. The theory focuses on (*a*) task requirement (*b*) Peer expectations and behaviour (*c*) employee characteristics, expectations and behaviour, organizational culture and policies. Hersey and Blanchard propagated situational approach. They superimposed employee readiness on Blake and Mouton model of leadership. Robert Tannenbaum and Warren H. Schmidt proposed a behavioural approach to leadership. The factors that influence leadership style are the leader, subordinates and the situation. The leader leads his team based on his personality, skills, ability and attitude towards work, employees and the organization he is serving. Leader can use participative or authoriatarian type of leadership depending upon the situation employees create. Situation plays a decisive role in adoption of leadership style. Situation encompasses factors like human rights, ecology, social responsibility apart from other environmental factors that have a bearing on the quality of decision a manager may make.

Fiedler's Contingency approach deals with LPC score in relation to contingency/situational variables He identified three variables namely leader-member relations that could be good or poor, task structure which could be structured or unstructured and position of power which may be strong or weak. Using these eight type of situations with high LPC or low LPC leader score, a leader could modify his leadership style.

Path-Goal Theory is an amalgamation of contingency theory and expectancy theory of leadership. Based on subordinate attributes and work setting attributes, Martin and Robert have suggested four types of leadership styles. These are *one*, supportive leadership, *two*, participative leadership, *three*, directive leadership and *lastly* the achievement oriented leadership.

Charismatic leadership is a unique type of leadership style. A leader who practices this type of leadership has following characteristics namely 1. leader has a vision. 2.he is a risk taker. 3. he displays sensitivity to environmental factors and follower needs. 4. He displays distinct behavioural pattern based on situation. 5. The charismatic leader makes self sacrifices and engages in unconventional behaviour.

Transformational leadership is based on stimulating follower to achieve organizational goals by inspiring them. The individuals are so motivated that they can sacifies themselves to protect honour, dignity and value system.

TEXT QUESTIONS

Q. 1 Define Leadership. What are various ingredients a leader should possess.

Q. 2 Leadership is a corner stone of managing an organization. Discuss

Q. 3 What do you think of universalistic theories of leadership ? Critically examine Likert's four systems of leadership. Which of the systems, you feel is ideal. Give reasons.

Q. 4 Explain "managerial Grid" with the help of diagram.

Q. 5 Explain Fiedler's Contingency approach to leadership.

Q. 6 Path-Goal theory of leadership is an amalgamation of contingency theory and expectancy theory of leadership. Explain the above statement.

Q. 7 Explain various skills. How are they distributed in organizational hierarchy. Explain with the help of appropriate diagram.

Q. 8 Charismatic leaders have different charisteristics, that make them stand out as successful leader. Explain.

Q. 9 Draw out a leadership skech of a charismatic leader you have known.

Q. 10 Explain Transformational leadership. This type of leadership style has come to stay. Express your views.

REFERENCES

1. Bernard, M.bass, Bass and Stogdill's ***"Hand Book of Leadership"*** 3rd edition, Free Press, New York, 1990.
2. Heinz Weihrich and Harold Koontz ***"Management"***, Mc Graw Hills International Edition, 1994.
3. Keith Davis, ***"Human Behaviour at Work"***, 4th Edition Mc Grow Hills, New York, 1972.
4. Ralph. M.stogdill, ***"Handbook of Leadership"***, A Survey of Theory and Research, New York, Free Press 1974.
5. Robert N. Murry, ***"The Case for Benevolent Autocracy."*** Harvard Business Review Jan-Feb 1958.
6. Rinses Likert, ***"New Patterns of Management"***, McGraw Hills, New York, 1961.
7. ***A New Twist to People Accounting*** Business Week, Oct 21, 1972.
8. Paul Hersey and Kenneth H. Blanchard and Dewey E. Johnson. ***"Management of Organizational Behaviour—Utilising Human Resources"***, Seventh Edition 1998, Prentice - Hall, India."
9. Paul Hersey and Kenneth H. Blanchard, ***"Management of Organizational Behaviour"***, Utilising Human Resources, 5th Edition.
10. Heinz Weihrich and Herold Koonz ***Management – A Global Perspective***. Tenth Edition, Mc Graw Hills.
11. Fred. E. Fiedler, ***Engineer the Job to Fit the Manager***, Harvard Business Review 43 No 5 (1965).
12. Tyson Shaun and Jackson Tony, ***"The Essence of Organizational Behaviour"***, 1997, Prentice-Hall of India, New Delhi, India.
13. B Shamir, R J House and M B Arthur, ***"The Motivational Effects of Charismatic Leadership, a Self Concept Theory"***, Organization Science Nov 1993.

LEADERSHIP EFFECTIVENESS AND STYLE ADAPABILITY

NAME:______________________________ GROUP:__________________

DIRECTIONS: Assume YOU are involved in each of the following twelve situations. Each situation has four alternative actions you might initiate. READ each item carefully THINK about what YOU would do in each circumstances. Then CIRCLE the letter of the alternative action choice which you think would most closely describe YOUR behaviour in the situation presented. CIRCLE only one choice.

SITUTATION	ALTERNATIVE ACTIONS
1. Your subordinates are not responding lately to your friendly conversation and obvious concern for their welfare. Their performance is declining rapidly.	A. Emphasise the use of uniform procedures and the necessary for task accomplishment. B. Make Yourself available for discussion but don't push your involvement. C. Talk with subordinates and then set goals. D. Intentionally do not intervene.
SITUTATION	**ALTERNATIVE ACTIONS**
2. The observable performance of your team is increasing. You have been making sure that all members were aware of their responsibilities and expected standards of performance.	A. Engage in friendly interaction but continue to make sure that all members are aware of their responsibilities and expected standards of performance. B. Take no definite action. C. Do what you can to make the group feel important and involved. D. Emphasis the important of deadlines and tasks.
SITUTATION	**ALTERNATIVE ACTIONS**
3. Members of your group are unable to solve a problem themselves. You have normally left them alone. Group performance and interpersonal relations have been good.	A. Work with the group and together engage in problem solving. B. Let the group work it out. C. Act quickly and firmly to correct and redirect. D. Encourage group to work on problems and be supportive of their efforts.
SITUTATION	**ALTERNATIVE ACTIONS**
4. You are considering a major change.Your subordinates have a fine record of accomplishment. They respect the need of change.	A. Allow group involvement in developing the change but don't be too directive. B. Announce changes and then implement with close supervision. C. Allow group to formulate it's own direction. D. Incorporate group recommendations but you direct the change.

SITUTATION	ALTERNATIVE ACTIONS
5. The performance of your group has been dropping during the last few month. Members have been unconcerned with meeting objectives. Redefining roles and responsibilities has helped in the past. They have continually needed reminding to have their tasks done on time	A. Allow group to formulate it's own direction. B. Incorporate group recommendations but see that objectives are met. C. Redefine roles and responsibilities and supervise carefully. D. Allow group involvement in determining roles and responsibilities but don't be too directive.
SITUTATION	**ALTERNATIVE ACTIONS**
6. You stepped in to an efficiently run organization. The pervious administrator tightly controlled the situation. You want to maintain a productive situation but would like to begin humanizing the environment.	A. Do what you can to make the group feel important and involved. B. Emphasis the importance of deadlines and tasks. C. Intentionally do not intervene. D. Get group involved in decision making, but see that objectives are met.
SITUTATION	**ALTERNATIVE ACTIONS**
7. You are considering changing to a structure that will be new to your group. Members of the group have made suggestions about needed change. The group has been productive and demonstrated flexibility in it's operations.	A. Define the change and supervise carefully. B. Participate with the group in developing the change but allow members to organize the implementation. C. Be willing to make the changes as recommended but maintain control of implementation. D. Avoid confrontation, leave things alone.
SITUTATION	**ALTERNATIVE ACTIONS**
8. Group performance and interpersonal relations are good. You feel some what unsure about your lack of direction of the group	A. Leave the group alone. B. Discuss the situation with the group and then you initiate necessary changes. C. Take steps to direct subordinates towards working in a well defined manner. D. Be supportive in discussing the situation with the group but not to be directive.
SITUTATION	**ALTERNATIVE ACTIONS**
9. Your subordinates, usually able to take responsibility are not responding to your recent redefining standards.	A. Allow group involvement in redefining standards, but don't take control. B. Redefine standards and supervise carefully. C. Avoid confrontation by not applying pressure, leave situation alone. D. Incorporate group recommendations but see that the new standards are met.

SITUTATION	ALTERNATIVE ACTIONS
10. You have been promoted to a new position. The previous was uninvolved in the affaires of the group. The group has adequately has handled it's task and direction. Group inter-relation are good.	A. Take steps to direct subordinates towards working in a well-defined manner. B. Involve subordinates in decision-making and reinforce good contribution. C. Discuss past performance with group and then you examine the need for new practice. D. Continue to leave group alone.
SITUTATION	**ALTERNATIVE ACTIONS**
11. Recent information indicates some internal difficulties among subordinates. The group has remarkable record of accomplishments. Members have effectively maintained long range goals. They have worked in harmony for the past year. All are well qualified for the task.	A. Try out your solution with subordinates and examine the need for new practices. B. Allow group members to work it out themselves. C. Act quickly and firmly to correct and redirect. D. Participate in problem discussions while providing support for subordinates.
SITUTATION	**ALTERNATIVE ACTIONS**
12. Recent information indicates some internal difficulties among subordinates. The group has remarkable record of accomplishments. Members have effectively maintained long range goals. They have worked in harmony for the past year. Al are well qualified for the task.	A. Try out your solution with subordinates and examine the need for new practises. B. Allow group members to work it out themselves. C. Act quickly and firmly to correct and redirect. D. Participate in problem discussions while providing support for subordinates.

DETERMINE YOUR LEADERSHIP STYLE AND STYLE RANGE

In the questionnaire are in effect asked how would you exercise leadership over your group in each of the twelve situations given. The questionnaire seeks to identify two things. First, your current style of leadership, (Fig. 1 and 2) second, your effectiveness as a leader (Fig. 3 and 4).

1. **Determine Leadership Style (A)** Using figure 1 below draw a circle around the letter of the alternative action or response you chose for each situation.

Fig. 1

		ALTERNATIVE ACTIONS			
SITUATION	1	A	C	B	D
	2	D	A	C	B
	3	C	A	D	B
	4	B	D	A	C
	5	C	B	D	A
	6	B	D	A	C
	7	A	C	B	D
	8	C	B	D	A
	9	C	B	D	A
	10	B	D	A	C
	11	A	C	B	D
	12	C	A	D	B
Quadrant Scores		Quadrant 1	Quadrant 2	Quadrant 3	Quadrant 4

BASIC LEADERSHIP BEHAVIOUR STYLES

(B) Now the total number of circle you have for each column write down these totals in the spaces provided (Quadrant Scores).

Now transfer these quadrant scores to the appropriate boxes in Figure 2.

(Low) Relationship Behaviour (High)		
	Quadrant 3 [ ] High Relationship and Low Task	**Quadrant 2** [ ] HighTask and High Relationship
	Quadrant 4 [ ] Low Relationship and Low Task	**Quadrant 1** [ ] HighTask and Low Relationship

(Low) ← Task Behaviour → (High)

Fig. 2

DETERMINE YOUR LEADERSHIP STYLE ADAPTABILITY AND EFFECTIVENESS

Your dominant leadership style is then the quadrant with the highest number. This is the style that you use the most often. Other quadrants with lower numbers, but having at least two responses, comprise your supporting style (or styles) this is the style (s) that you use on occasion.

2 Determining Leadership Effectiveness

Now that you know your style (s) of leadership, let us now see how effective you are as a leader – manager.

Using Figure 3 below, draw a circle around the number (+2, –2,+1, or –1) that falls under the letter (A,B,C, or D) that you chose as your answer for each of the twelve situations.

Fig. 3. ALTERNATIVE ACTIONS

		A	B	C	D
	1	+2	-1	+1	-2
	2	+2	-2	+1	-1
S	3	+1	-1	-2	+2
I	4	+1	-2	+2	-1
T	5	-2	+1	+2	-1
U	6	-1	+1	-2	+2
A	7	-2	+2	-1	+1
T	8	+2	-1	-2	+1
I	9	-2	+1	+2	-1
O	10	+1	-2	-1	+2
N	11	-2	+2	-1	+1
	12	-1	+2	-2	+1
		Quadrant 1	Quadrant 2	Quadrant 3	Quadrant 4
Quadrant Scores					

Fig. 4. LEARDERSHIP EFFECTIVENESS SCALE

Now add algebraically all the encircled numbers for each column and enter the sub totals in the spaces provided. Finally add the subtotals at the Total Value.

Below is a scale ranging from –24 to +24.

Locate your score on the scale and see if your leadership style is effective or ineffective.

-24 -22 -20 -18 -16 -14 -12 -10 -8 -6 -4 -2 0 2 4 6 8 10 12 14 16 18 20 22 24

Case 1

COOL PRODUCTS*

Mr. Vasudev is a general Manager of Cool Products, a company dealing in production and distribution of packed condiments in the state of Madhya Pradesh. The Co. was established in the year 2000 and has been performing well. Over the past five years the Co. has introduced excellent production processes, quality control, established its own distribution network, and has been able to achieve good consumer response for the products they manufacture and distribute. The company is a market leader in the state of M.P. Seeing the success of the business, the management has decided to expand the same in the state of Rajastan. They have identified Kota as the place for establishing production unit. The head of the unit will hold the rank of GM. The post is tenable by marketing or production manager since the job involves skill of productivity and marketing. The management has invited you to select a person to head Kota unit. The management have handed over to you profiles of two managers. Mr. Varun is production manager, and Mr Avinash is the marketing manager. Both are working with Cool Products since its inception. You as a consultant, required to select one of them. You do not have personal knowledge about them and have to take the decision based of their write-ups only. The write up of the managers are as under.

Mr. Varun Tyagi

Mr Varun is a mechanical engineer passed out from MACT Bhopal (now MANIT). He has about 10 years of service in food preservation industry. Prior to this appointment he was working with 'Pare Masala' a famous condiment manufacturer of Pune. Varun is hard working, sincere, honest and a dependable engineer. He is foresighted, technically sound and can work independently under stress and strain. He had been able to handle employee grievances in the present organization successfully to the satisfaction of employees and management has been critical about the decision he had taken on their behalf. He enjoys good rapport in the Industry and has been consultant to couple of industries in the state of MP and Maharashtra. He is straight forward and goes by the rule of law when in difficulty. He has a pleasant personality and workers fall back on him when in difficulty. Varsha-his wife is a nursing graduate and works in one of the private nursing homes. Families of employees, very frequently consult her and she therefore enjoys personal influence over the families of 'Cool Products'. Mr Varun has been able to complete his targets of production every year and has been contributory factor for the growth of the Co.

Mr. Avinash

Mr. Avinash Kale belongs to Nagpur and comes from farmers family. His father was a poor man and taught his only son with a great difficulty. Avinash has done MBA from IMS Indore in the year 1996. His performance in academics has been excellent. He stood first in IMS among the marketing boys that year. Mr Avinash is very calculative and thinks ten times before taking any decision. He evaluates the pros and cons of the issue at hand before proceeding further. He is very professional and keeps his sales team on the tender hooks and ensures monthly sales at any costs. He is hard task master as it relates to his

* Case prepared by Prof. V.G. Kondalkar, HOD, VNS Institute of Management, Bhopal (M.P.)

job and can bend either way if situation so demands. He is very obedient and keeps the tag of management move, their daily schedule and any important event that is likely to take place. People in Cool Products say that Avinash knows everything in the organization before it is formally announced. He is considered to be a management man. He implements instructions of the management in letter and sprit. He maintains distance from workers and is not interested beyond the task he is supposed to do. But the task he does well and therefore he is liked by higher ups. One may say he is a task oriented leader. He is a smooth sailer, a diehard salesman, visionary, opportunist, a soft spoken executive who never hurts anyone in his dealings, a tight rope walker. He has good communication skills. He has been recently married to a lady who is employed as Assistant Sale Tax Officer in Bhopal. She belongs to state provincial services cadre. She also has a bright career as she is a topper in her batch.

Q. 1 Read the case carefully and carryout analysis. In the light of various theories you have studied, what type of leadership style Mr. Varun Possesses.

Q. 2 What type of leadership style Mr. Avinash has. What are the strength of his personality.

Q. 3 As a consultant would you like to meet them before you take a decision, if so why.

Q. 4 Who is your Choice as a GM of Cool Products, Kota?

PART FOUR

Dynamics of Organization

CHAPTER 16

Organizational Structure

INTRODUCTION

Organizational mission is expressed in terms of organizational goals. These goals have to be attained by combined efforts of various resources, which involves division of labour on one hand and grouping of various activities on the other. Organizational structure plays an important role in attaining these goals. Any organization when it starts has a small structure and it takes a mega form as it develops. The development is both ***vertical*** and ***horizontal.*** Vertical structure indicates the line authority and reporting channel. Horizontal structure indicates the division of work and specialization. Tiers of organizational structure are indicative of power structure, positions and its inter-se relationship, roles, channels of reporting, delegation and accountability. Organizational structure to be effective must be continuously reviewed, modified especially in the present scenario where cost cutting is the order of the day if an organization has to be competitive. It has been observed that the formation of organizational structure is subject to influence of various people who have a say in the organization and therefore there exist a divergence between planned and operating organizational structure.

DEFINITION

According to Sheldon[1] *Organization is the process of combining the work, which individuals and groups have to perform with the facilities necessary for its execution, that the duties so performed provide the best channels for the efficient, systematic, positive and coordinated application of the available efforts.*

Koontz and Donnel have defined organizational structure as *'the establishment of authority relationships with provision for coordination between them, both vertically and horizontally in the enterprise structure'.*

Good organizational structure indicates the following:

- The structure must lay down formal reporting hierarchy right from the lowest level of worker to the highest level of board of directors/MD as the case may be.
- Grouping of identical activities in one department so that equipment, machines, processes and expertise can be developed at one place under the guidance of one departmental head. If the department grows unwieldy then the identical

organization of two or more departments can be structured with formal reporting policy laid down.

- Coordination of various activities be laid down and coordinating authority specified.
- Individual, group and departmental goals should be laid down with specific time frame. Monitoring of goals is essential.
- Seniority between the departmental heads is generally the point of organizational conflict hence the lateral and vertical relationship with particular reference to seniority must be laid down in the policy or the standing orders for the organization.
- Standing orders, policies, procedures, drills, rules and regulations should exit in an organization. These are required to be laid down in details. Duties of each and every appointment reduces operating problems.

Operating structure of any organization differs from the formal structure because of *social systems* and *power blocks*. Formal structure only represents the technical part of the functional organization. Human behaviour, attitude, value system and culture play a dominant role in execution of assigned task when interaction between various work groups and departments are involved. It is necessary to promote organizational culture which starts from top management level down to the lower levels. There are basically two forms of organizational structure:-

FORMS OF ORGANIZATION STRUCTURE

(a) ***Mechanistic form of organizational structure***. An organizational structure based on formalized system that is relatively rigid in nature. This is generally applicable to those organizations that are not influenced by technological, product, market changes and generally maintains a constant pattern. In mechanistic form of organizational structure, authority is centralized at the top level of management and has a rigid hierarchy of authority. Decision making is generally reserved at the top level. The tasks are well defined so that the goals set by the top level management are attained smoothly. The structure is characterized by plenty of written orders and instructions.

(*b*) ***Organic form of organizational structure***. Organizations those are subject to change due to environmental factors like technology, market changes and product development generally adopt organic form of organizational structure. For example software industry. In such structures authority is delegated to various functional levels/individuals. Decentralised decision making is practised that allows people to make their own decisions based on the environment and that they do not have to look over their shoulders. There are very few levels of organizational hierarchy and existence of flexible reporting system. Jobs are fairly well defined with few orders and instructions. These days organic form of organizational structure is related to work groups and teams working independently on a particular project that report directly to top management. They are self-supervised, self-directed and self-controlled sub units that are self-accounted for their performance and attainment of organizational goals. The structure is more loose and subject to changes very frequently to adopt to the environmental changes. It is highly flexible.

Bureaucracy

Max Weber, a German Sociologist has introduced a mechanistic form of organizational structure. He envisaged bureaucracy as an ideal form of organizational structure. The system is based on the logic, of delegation of authority. He felt that the bureaucratic system was far better that other forms of organizational structure that functioned on the whims and fancies of a leader like charismatic leadership or the structure based on precedence (history). Weber felt that ideal bureaucracy is based on the principles of equity and rationality. In bureaucratic model every individual has an equal chance of personal growth based on performance. The system has detailed policy, rules, regulations and charter of duties of various appointments inbuilt in it. Weber's bureaucracy has been widely criticized since it has following dysfunctional characteristics.

(*a*) The model is highly rigid, that creates inflexibility in the organization. In the present scenario situational aspects has a higher chance of success.

(*b*) Weber's model emphasises on rules and regulations that tend to become an end in itself. This promotes delays and has a tendency to promote red tapism.

(*c*) Bureaucracy promotes politics in an organization. This system tends to serve interests of few elite personalities.

(*d*) Specialisation has been recommended in the bureaucracy model. Specialists have self-serving tendencies. This at times overlooks the general interests of the common employee in the organization.

(*e*) The model is detrimental to personal growth due to high demands on an individual to conform to the system, which is rigid.

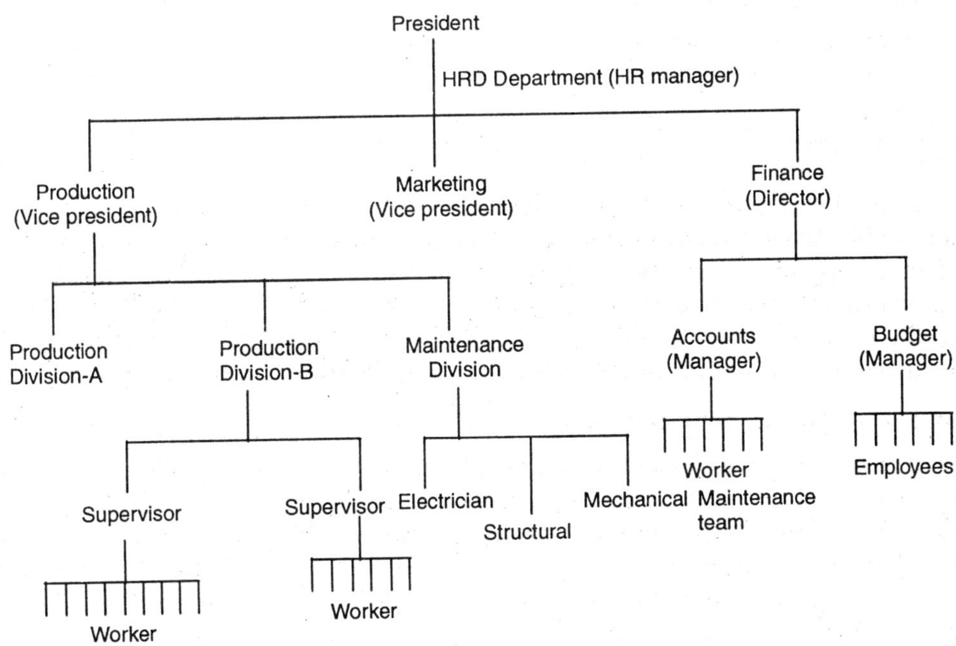

Fig. 16.1. Mechanistic form of organizational structure.

(*f*) The model is impersonal, mechanical in nature. It promotes self-perpetuation. It promotes blind faith in rules. It is suitable only to large organization where changes are slow. The model cannot visualize individual needs and therefore cannot exploit full potential of individual.

(*g*) There is no consideration for inter personal and mutual relations. It is highly bureaucratic.

It has been observed that most people structure their organizations on bureaucratic model, building on its strengths and minimizing dysfunctional features of the system. A diagrammatic layout of mechanistic form of organizational structure is given in Figure 16.1 above.

Comparative evaluation of mechanistic and organic form of organizational structures is given as under:

Mechanistic system	*Organic system*
• Centralized work culture	• Decentralised work structure
• Highly formalized (exhaustive written orders)	• Formalisation is very low(very few written instructions)
• High specialization	• Low level of specialization (team work)
• Standardised job structure	• Fluctuation in work culture
• Narrow span of management	• Wide span of management
• Tall organizational structure with number of organizational tiers	• Flat organizational structure with few tiers
• Centralised decision making	• Decentralised decision making

CONCEPTS OF ORGANIZATIONAL STRUCTURE

Organizational structure must necessarily be formed taking in to consideration the organizational objectives it has to achieve. Vertical organizational structure indicates among other factors the line authority and unity of command principle of management. Horizontal organizational structure could be simple or complex. It will depend upon the complexity and the nature of work level and intensity of integration. Let us therefore study some of the important concepts that are related to organizational structure.

Centralisation and Decentralisation

Centralisation refers to reservation of authority for decision making at top level of management. Lower levels are responsible for implementing the decisions. They are operators or implementers. Generally speaking, the authority is not delegated to the lower levels. Subordinates carry out work to accomplish their assigned task. If there is a block, hurdle or operation is halted due to some reason, then the matter is referred to an appropriate authority who has the power to take appropriate decision to resolve the problem. Level of authority for any decision-making is generally spelt out in organization's standing orders. Centralisation is more pre-dominant to financial transaction. For example, in the banking services, authority to sanction loan for projects etc is reposed in a particular authority, may be general manager of the bank and subordinates are only responsible to project the case after due investigation and ability of an individual/firm to repay. Centralisation of authority for small organization is more prevalent where the management wants to have a tight control over the activities of subordinates. Centralisation is found where the organization structure do not have many layers and it is relatively flat. It is found where subordinates are not trained to handle higher jobs, where there is a lack of trust in subordinates and the intricacy or the magnitude of work that demands centralized control.

Decentralisation on the other hand refers to authority being delegated to various levels of organization for making appropriate decisions. Centralisation and decentralization is not opposite to each other but two ends of continuum as under

Centralisation ______________________________ Decentralisation

When we say that the organization is decentralized, what it means is that the authority for the decision making has been vested in appropriate levels, depending upon the ability of the individual. In decentralized organizations, individuals at lower levels are authorized to make decisions pertaining to their jobs that give them autonomy. Authority does not flow with the same rate to each of the levels of the organization. It is important to understand that each level is having appropriate authority for decision making when need arises and that one does not have to wait for upper level to take decisions for you. Decentralisation, commensurate with the need, ability of the individual to shoulder the higher responsibilities is necessary. It helps managers to take risk and to develop skills to achieve higher objectives. It motivates junior level managers if they have been vested with an authority to take decisions pertaining to various operations. Manager on the spot knows the local problems and therefore is better suited to take decisions. Flat organizational structure is ideal to have a decentralized command and control especially in the present environment where specialization, information technology, competencies, work teams , work group culture and systems prevail. It develops sense of responsibility among employees, cuts down time, improves productivity, team sprit, motivation and bring 'we' feeling among work groups. Greater decentralization offers employees higher level of job satisfaction as they feel that they have work autonomy. They can respond to a particular situation quickly. It must be remembered that delegation of authority to lower levels does not absolve the delegater the responsibility or the consequences of the actions of their subordinates. This is one reason why managers do not delegate authority to their subordinates.

Charlisle[2] suggested the following guidelines to determine whether there should be centralization or decentralization.

(*a*) ***Mission, goals and objectives of the organization.*** Certain organizations which have a democratic power sharing set up should be decentralized. Small organizations have a centralized structure.

(*b*) ***Size of the organization and complexity of the work***. Large organizations with diverse production lines and conglomerates with companies involved in different fields should be decentralized.

(*c*) ***Geographical location of customers***: Organizations which cater for customers which are geographically located far apart should have decentralized organizational structure.

(*d*) ***Competency***: If the top management is highly skilled, knowledgeable and experienced and has the capacity to handle more activities at one time, then the centralization is recommended. When subordinates are skilled, experienced and have high level of efficiency, decentralization is appropriate. If on the other hand employees are not adequately trained, centralization is suitable.

(*e*) ***Communication***: If the communication between the management and employees is efficient, then the decentralization is recommended. This will enable problem solving and accord a sence of autonomy amongst workers.

(*f*) ***Timeframe***: If the work nature is such that the production is based on time schedule, then the decentralization is recommended as it involves self supervision.

Formalisation

Organizational structure is formed and displayed by various ways. Organizational charts are generally used for providing a picture of organization at a glance. They are indicative of level of authority, relationship (as it is related to each other's duties and responsibilities). These could be depicted in various forms

(*a*) Skeleton form, expressed only by lines.

(*b*) Function wise for each appointment.

(*c*) Indicating names along with designation.

Depiction of organizational charts are important. What is more important is the process of functioning, duties that each of the individuals is required to perform in the organization. These are contained in ***'standing orders'*** of the organization. Standing orders are extensively written instructions in defence organizations. Standing orders for peace and war are written separately and gives full detail of authority, responsibility, duties to be performed by each of the individuals from junior most level to the highest rank and file in the organization. They are also related to various operations of war and terrain in which they are operating**.** ***Policies*** are general guidelines which are required to be considered by a manager while performing his work. Since these are guidelines, they are changeable considering the situation at a particular time. For example there may be a policy in an organization where every individual is required to undergo a refresher training for a duration of four weeks in a year. But the duration could be cut down or may be enhanced if the situation so demands. Policies lay down broad parameters under which the job is undertaken by individuals to attain the over all organizational goals**.** ***Rules*** on the other hand are prescribed code of conduct, which is required to be followed by every individual in the organization. They are rigid form of instructions like leave rules. If an individual avails more number of days of leave than prescribed, he will be subjected to penal deductions. There are no discretionary powers with manager when rules are required to be implemented. ***Procedures*** are written instructions as to how a work is to be done, what does it involve and the sequence to be undertaken**.** Assembly line procedure or grievance handling procedure are some of the important examples which are laid down by organization. It may be noted that standing orders, policies, rules and procedures must be drafted carefully taking into consideration the work culture in the organization. It would be desirable if these are provided into shortened form to the employees preferably in the language they understand. This will assist in smooth functioning of the organization. These are necessary so that the managers can concentrate on the planning without wasting time on routine matters. These help managers to manage by exception. Too much of instructions in the form of standing orders, policies, rules and procedures may lead to false perception by employees as they may feel that the managers are functioning in impersonal and rigid way that may be suitably guarded against. Bureaucratic organizational structures are more formalized by way of detailed and exhaustive policy, rules and regulation enactment.

Standardization

Standardization involves repetitive and routine jobs. Jobs are formalized so that every individual can undertake such standardised jobs without additional training. A bit of briefing/explaining may be required. In manufacturing organizations manufacturing of various standard parts is a common phenomenon. In recent times standardisation of process has become important. For example "induction training", where standard package of instructions are imparted to new entrants in the organization. Such a process takes a form of Standard Operating Procedures (SOPs). SOP relates to a standard approach towards a particular job, may be reception procedure or send off procedure for an employee. SOPs also lay down who is to officiate in case permanent incumbent proceeds on long leave, course or on a permanent posting. No fresh instructions are required in case of established, tried out time tested SOPs. These cover administrative and all other departmental activities.

Specialisation

When all related activities are put together in particular departments, division of work takes place. Every department attempts to specialise in the work assigned to them. Individual achieves expertise when he performs same job over and over again. Principle of unity of direction must be achieved when jobs are broken down in tiny compartments to achieve specialization. Individual doing a same job over a long period of time is likely to achieve boredom, that must be avoided by rotating him within the department on identical jobs. Variety is required to be achieved for higher job satisfaction. In research and development department, jobs are not well defined. Though there is specialist earmarked to do the job, it is not adequately defined, as it cannot be broken down in pre-determined manner. Division of labour principle therefore is not applicable in R and D department to a desired extent.

Stratification

Stratification is related to culture and power distance index between various levels of organization, work groups or in the hierarchy. In bureaucratic organization, levels of command and control is well defined, interaction between staff in minimal and restricted to one up or one down levels. It is equally applicable to line personnel. In highly stratified organizations, office accommodation, cafeteria is separately earmarked for managers, supervisors and workers. This leads to minimum level of communication and reduced interaction between various levels of organization. Apart from leading to ego infatuations, it inhibits free flow of information, supervisor-subordinate interaction. When such stratification culture penetrates deep into work setting, it prohibits growth, creativity and innovation. A wide gap is created that is marked by 'we-they' feeling. This phenomenon is not good for development of organization. In high power distance, organizations decision making is concentrated in highest authority and there is little delegation of authority. Subordinates have to be dependent on their superior even for the minor decisions. In organic form of organization stratification is minimal and therefore high growth prospects and cordial relationship among various levels of management exist. This type of organizations are marked with low power index ratio. Due to social change that is taking place so fast, organic type of organizations are preferable where free flow of communication, delegation of authority and freedom of work culture is prominently practiced.

Formal Organization

Formal organization has a mechanistic hierarchical structure. In such type of structure position, authority, responsibility and accountability is well defined. Formal organizations have well-defined lines of command and control, delegation of authority and a system where effective coordination can be carried out. Detailed policies, procedures, and standing orders are laid down for various departments so that everybody is aware of his duties and obligations towards the organization. In a formal organization goals are set and individual tasks are assigned. Supervisors exercise strict supervision and control.

Informal Organization

Informal organization comes into existence due to social interactions and exists out side the formal authority without any rules. Informal organization may consist of various groups, which are generally based upon socio-psychological support. Members of the informal group enjoy freedom and interaction within the group. Their existence depends on development of social contacts within and outside the organization. The bond of friendship among members is very strong and they display sense of belonging and to-getherness. The informal organization develops in shadow of formal organizational structure and may have its own structure. Informal organization has group goals, social roles to play, leader-follower relationship, unwritten behaviour pattern and code of conduct. It serves as a parallel communication channel for the organization. The informal organization is a powerful instrument and runs parallel to formal organizational structure. The leader of the informal organization train subordinates, assist them when needed and ensures welfare. Promotional, financial, social, and religious obligations are fulfilled by the management. The power of the informal organizations is immense. Some times it means failure or a success of an organization that must be understood by the management.

Span of Management

In a classical organization, effectiveness and efficiency is determined by number of people a manager can handle effectively. This depends upon the relationship a manager enjoys with his subordinates. Span of management is also known as span of control. The basic principle of span of management is an ability of a manager to effectively supervise a finite number of people. It has been established that at higher levels a manager can control four to eight people while at lower levels eight to fifteen people can be supervised. There is a limit to the number of people a manager can effectively supervise as mentioned above, but the impact of effectiveness will depend upon individual situation, issues that consumes time in handling superior –subordinate relationship and identification of devices that reduces the time pressure. Span of management is of two types:

(a) ***Wide Span***: Wide span of management is suitable where work is delegated to work groups and teams and there is near autonomy in work environment. Clear policies are laid down and subordinates display a high degree of sense of responsibility. However, tendency to overload superiors to decision making and danger of superiors to loose control over the events must be evaluated. This can be achieved by employing high quality managers having successful track record.

(b) ***Narrow Span***: Organizations having narrow span can achieve fast communication, close command and control and keep track on the pulse on the progress of the work. In narrow span there are number of organizational layers and each of the individual is accountable to his leader. This type of structure is too costly. There is no freedom of work as supervisor's tend to get too much involved in the job of subordinates. Because of the excessive distance between lowest level and top level, danger of filtering of information should be guarded against.

Evaluation

Division of activities into departments, hierarchical nature of organization and creation of multiple levels are not desirable as they are not economical. On the contrary levels complicate communication planning and control. Urwick[3] concluded, "No executive should attempt to supervise directly the work of more than five or at the most six direct subordinates whose work interlocks". This is considered as an ideal because too wide a span would put a heavy burdon on manager in effective guidance and control and too narrow a span would mean under-utilisation of managerial capacity, ability and resources.

DESIGNING OF ORGANISATIONAL STRUCTURE

Sheldon[4] suggested – "Organization is the process of so combining the work, which individuals or groups have to perform with the facilities necessary for its execution, that the duties so performed provide the best channels for the efficient, systematic, positive and coordinated application of the available efforts".

Good organizational structure facilitates the following:

(a) Every individual has to perform certain activities in the organization. He is responsible to accomplish the same and therefore certain amount of power and authority is given to him. Individual must also know his power position, seniority and official relationship in an organization so that he can perform his duties effectively. It is therefore necessary that an ideal structure is formed that will facilitate accomplishment of organizational objectives.

(b) Identical activities are grouped together in order to facilitate efficient functioning and achievement of results. Organizational structure is therefore needed for integration of diversed activities.

(c) It is necessary that idle machine time is avoided, capacity is fully utilized and operations of production in particular and other functions are regulated to achieve utilization of resources. Bottlenecks are avoided and smooth flow of activities is achieved. This is possible once a well thought out organizational structure is formed with specific functions allotted to each of the employees in the organization.

Steps in Formation of Organizational Structure

1. ***Determination of organizational goals and identification of related activities:*** Organizational goals must be well defined and clearly spelt out. Based on the goals all activities that are required should be identified and broken down into smallest possible sub activities that may be assigned as a task or a job to the worker. This is applicable to both managerial as well as operational functions in the organization.
2. ***Grouping of activities:*** All identical activities should be grouped keeping in mind formation of various departments or divisions. Set of activities could further be sub-divided and assigned to a particular section of a department. For example, in an automobile industry, activities relating to manufacturing of body of a vehicle could be grouped and assigned to a department responsible for it. Activities relating to manufacturing of chassis could be sub-divided and allotted to chassis manufacturing section and the like. This process will lead to formation of department and sections. It will also indicate the workload, human resource requirement, skills that may be necessary, the composition and layout of various facilities. Hence the progression in forming an ideal organizational structure.
3. ***Delegation of authority:*** A person can not perform his duties unless he has been given adequate authority to accomplish the assigned task. He can not be made responsible and accountable if requisite authority has not been given. Authority, responsibility and accountability are tied together. An individual employee can not be held responsible without authority. Production manager can not be held responsible for shortfall in production if he has not been authorised to hire additional workers if required to meet the production targets. It is therefore necessary to adopt the following process:

   (*a*) Determination of course of action to meet the organizational objectives.
   (*b*) Division of various activities into appropriate segments to be handled by individuals appropriate to their skills.
   (*c*) Assignment of tasks to individuals delegating necessary powers and resources.
   (*d*) Coordination to ensure that resources are adequately utilized and that there is no overlap or gap in task accomplishment.

When jobs, activities are classified, divided and grouped under executives at various levels, it would give birth to a rough skeleton on which an organizational structure is established. Formulating an organizational structure on the basis of the content of the job and subsequently making placements of various people is generally carried out. However first assigning a job and later shaping an organizational structure can also happen. Some thinkers are of the opinion that beginning to allot the task should be made at the top level coming down to the bottom level. The others feel that the bottom level tasks should be allotted at the beginning and gradually moving up the ladder and making allocations. It is not important as to which approach is taken in making an organizational structure, what is important is grouping of jobs and activities, delegation of authority and utilization of resources to its full capacity. It is also important to keep in mind that each job is confined to single person and adequate care is taken for narrow specialization within the structure of the organization.

Determinants of Organizational Structure

Line Organization

Line organization is the simplest and very commonly used organizational structure. The basic form of the organizational structure is departments, sections and individuals working within. Superimposed on it is the organizational, departmental, sectional goals and allotment of individual tasks. In line organization authority, responsibility and accountability is clearly spelt out between various levels. The structure is hierarchical in nature. Instructions emanating from President at the top level passes through the departments down to the workers. There is a unity of command and reporting channels are clearly spelt out. Because of systematic demarcation of duties, roles and functions, adequate command and control mechanism exist between managers, managers and supervisors and supervisors and employees. Line personnel are directly involved in achieving the objectives of the organization. They are the ones who earn revenue for the organization. The organizational structure is explained in Figure 16.2 below:

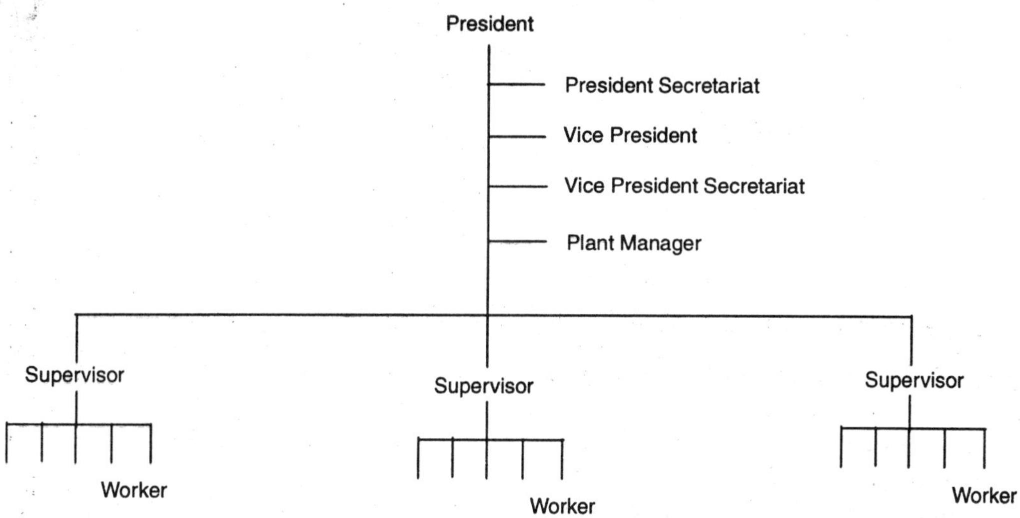

Fig. 16.2. Organizational structure

Because of the small size and compact nature of organization, it is easy to develop organizational culture in the organization. The sense of belonging and close knit relations are generally developed. The value system and the organizational climate further spills over in family life too. There are certain drawbacks in line organization. These are generally rigid in nature and there is little scope for creativity, there is no scope for specialized work which is so essential for organizational growth.

Departmentation

Departmentation refers to grouping of individuals and/or functions by units of activities. Departmentalisation maintains that activities should be grouped so as to combine homogenous activities within the same organizational unit or sub unit. Homogeneity may be based on similarity of purpose, place and activity. Departmentation may take following forms.

TYPES OF ORGANIZATIONAL STRUCTURE

1. Departmentation by Functions

One of the most popular ways to group activities is by functions performed by the organization. Traditional functions are human resources, marketing, finance, R&D and information technology departments. Each of the departments is known by the principle activities performed by the group of people. These departments could be further divided into functional groups like marketing department may further be sub-divided into sales, advertising, publicity and promotion departments and headed by manager/supervisor depending upon the work load, size of the organization and quantum of the work involved. A typical organization based on functions is given in Figure 16.3 below:

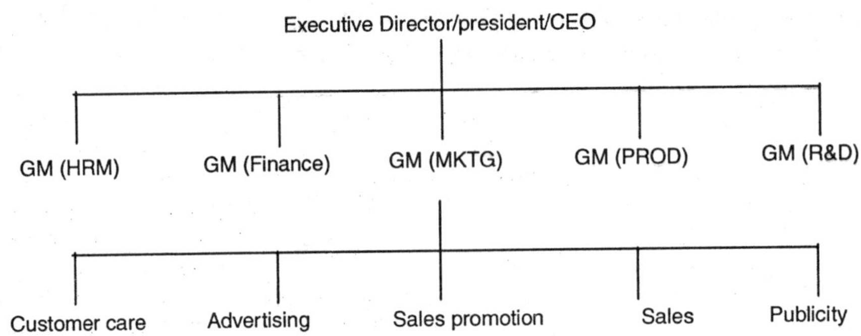

Fig. 16.3. Organization structure based on functions

This type of grouping has the following characteristics:

(*a*) Jurisdiction of particular department is clearly defined. In good organizations standing orders are written down for each of the departments in which detailed functions and duties of each of the members are outlined. Interference in the functioning of other departments are avoided.

(*b*) Since roles of the each of the department is outlined, supervision becomes easy. All the employees work within the parameter of their respective jurisdiction. Activities are easily managed by supervisors in terms of coordination and control. Each functional area develops its own guidelines for compliance.

(*c*) It is easy to organize training and development activities. Employee's skill is further enhanced if employees are subjected to seminars, workshops and conferences. It is the responsibility of the departmental heads to ensure that the staff has updated knowledge in their areas of operations.

(*d*) There is healthy competition between various departments. Each of the departments develop their culture over a period of time. This type of departmentation is easy for command and control.

2. Departmentation by Place

Territory or geography is used as the base to depart-mentalise activities in the organization. Geographical departmentalization takes place when an enterprise is large and has number of divisions located in different areas. It may be dispersed within a nation or may even be spread world wide. Enterprises divide their activities into zones or divisions. These are independent profit earning centers and work under local environment. Life Insurance Corporation of India is one such example where organizational policy is same but the nature of operation vary depending upon the local geographic, social and cultural disparities. Life Insurance Corporation of India is a classical example of organization based on place.

Geographic departmentation has following characteristics:

(*a*) Product and services can be taken as close to customers as possible.
(*b*) Local talent and resources can be exploited to the best of advantage.
(*c*) Departmentation by place reduces the cost of material. It has been observed that organizations open their units as close as possible to the vendors and suppliers.
(*d*) It reduces the cost of marketing the products and services.
(*e*) Local talent can be put to optimum use especially in rural development /handicrafts manufacturing units.
(*f*) Due to geographic dispersion, control by the head office becomes difficult. A situation may arise where goal of those who manage the unit become more important than the corporate goals. This may lead to empire building.
(*g*) There is competition for acquiring of resources from the corporate exchequer.
(*h*) Employees resist transfer to another unit

3. Departmentation by Product and Services

An organization may produce single product or multiple products. In the later case the unit becomes large that can not be managed easily due to multiplicity of products, services and processes. For example the Tata Group which has number of products being manufactured and sold under one umbrella like steel, finance services, hospitality, publishing, power, automobile and telecommunication etc. If these are grouped under one unit, it does not make a sense. These are to be independently managed because losses in one unit can be offset by profits in the rest of the units. An organization of a unit having departmentation by product/service is given at Figure 16.4 below:

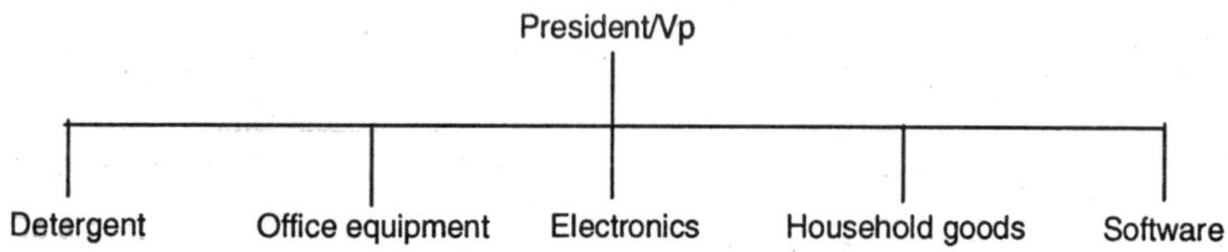

Fig. 16.4. Organization based on product/services

The characteristics of organization built around product/serices are as under:

(*a*) One of the most important characteristics of units that are structured based on departmentation by product/services is coordinating intra unit and inter unit activities to achieve organizational goals.
(*b*) These units have been termed as independent profit earning centers. These have to function independently and contribute towards corporate earnings.
(*c*) Competition by units.

(*d*) Since units are independent, it becomes necessary to set up all the functional areas and employ a large number of employees at the cost of high expenses. This leads to duplication of efforts.

(*e*) Corporate office should exercise its control and discourage empire building tendencies and one-upmanship.

4. Departmentation by Time

Hospitals and other public utility organizations like telephones, railways, hotels that work round the clock are departmentalized on the basis of shifts. For example hospital may have day shift, evening shift and night shift. Production units may also have this type of organizational structure when the load of production is adequate that makes organization to adopt such organizational structure.

5. Departmentation by Matrix

Where technological and product changes occur at a fast rate and co-ordination between functional and product department become critical, matrix system is recommended. In matrix system attention is paid towards co-ordination of various functional activities including product innovation. Matrix system is depicted in Figure 16.5 where every matrix has three sets of positions and role relationship.

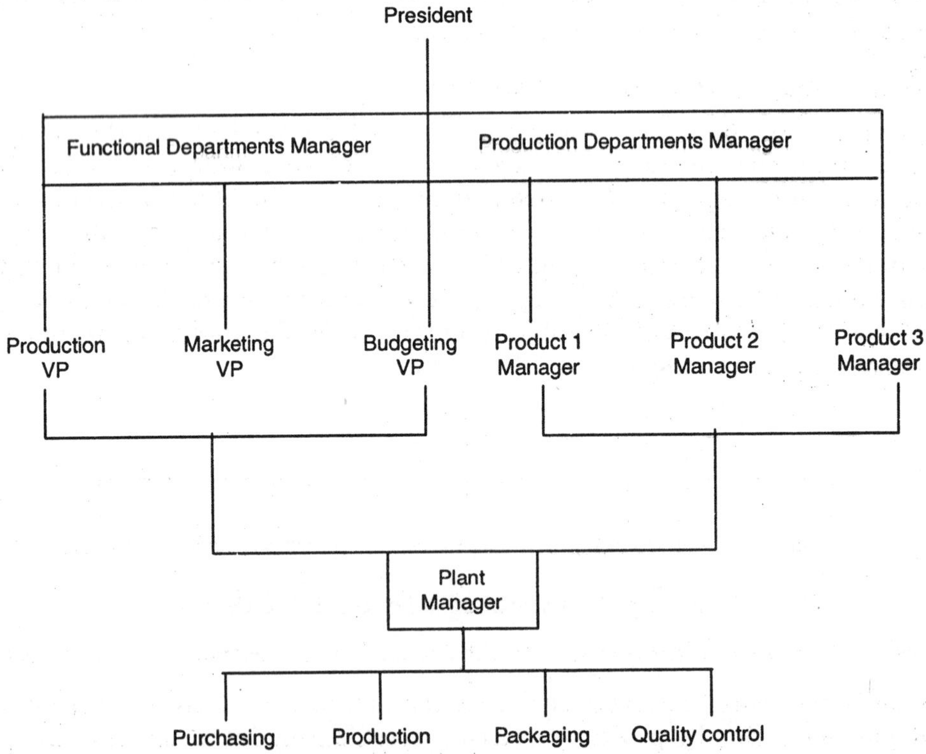

Fig. 16.5. Layout showing Matrix type of Organizational structure (Adopted from S.M Davis and P.R. Lawrence, 1977)

President heads the operation balancing dual chain of command; The functional and product managers who have equal authority and status, have the same subordinates reporting to them. Finally the lower level managers and skilled specialists report to both functional and product managers. A unique characteristic of the matrix structure is the dual reporting system due to dual hierarchy that often creates problems and tensions for employees. The violation of unity of command principle is a weakness of this system. Projects of specific periods also function under the matrix system. The project managers are generally responsible for over all direction and integration of activities and resources related to the project. They are responsible for completing the project within time frame and resources. They are also responsible for integrating the efforts of the functional managers to accomplish the project and directing and evaluating project activities. The functional managers are concerned with the operational aspect as under:

(*a*) Providing technical guidance.
(*b*) Providing functional staff which should be highly skilled and specialized.
(*c*) Completing the project based on qualitative requirement and technical specification
(*d*) Hiring technical persons, processes and sub letting the work if required by time and technical constraints.

Greiner[5] sees matrix organizations, in which cross functional teams are used, as a response to growing complexity associated with the organizational growth. These complexities, both internal (size and technology) as well as external (markets and competitors) create problems of information processing and communication that are best dwelt by matrix type of organizations. Stephen Robbins has emphasized that most of the business schools adopt this type of organizational structure where director of various schools superimpose additional programmes like faculty development programme on the existing infrastructure and utilize faculty and other teaching resources, which pays rich dividends. The merits of this type of organizational structure is as under:

(*a*) greater coordination and control exercised by the project manager (both horizontal and vertical).
(*b*) Optimum utilization of resources is achieved because of the utilization of resources for various projects going on at the same time. Utilisation of human resources is also achieved. No duplication of efforts and optimum use of various skills.
(*c*) Faster response to organizational changes and interdisciplinary work environment is created. Autonomy of work is achieved.
(*d*) Personnel development and employee motivation is achieved.
(*e*) Delegation of authority is the key element of matrix system, this enables top management to devote maximum time and energy for planning.

Hybrid Structure

When organizations expand, there is a need of striking a balance in exercising command and control yet giving organizations a freedom of action so that the productivity is enhanced. Hybrid organizational structure is therefore adopted. This helps to capitalize on the strength of both forms (functional and product based structures). While avoiding disadvantages of both. Here, functions that are critical and central for each product or market are decentralized, but functions like legal services, employee welfare are centralized. An example of hybrid structure is given at Figure 16.6.

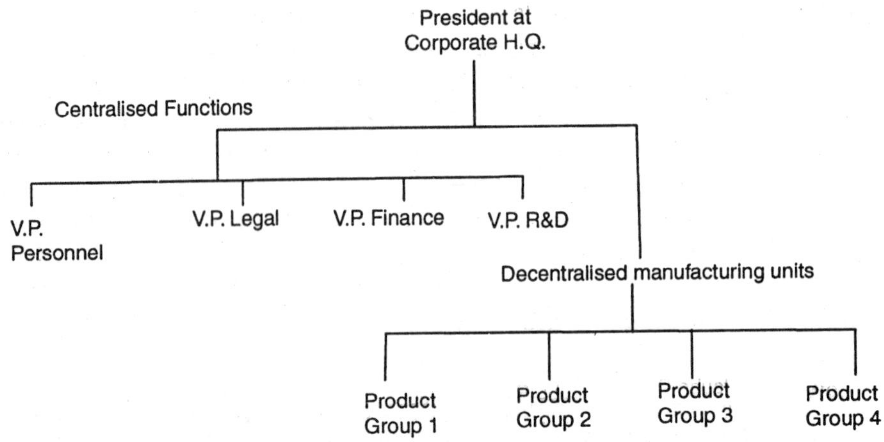

Fig. 16.6. Hybrid Structure

SUMMARY

Organizational structure takes into consideration division of work and grouping of activities. It indicates the formal authority and the reporting channels. Horizontal structure indicates division of labour while vertical structure indicates the line authority and unity of command. Formal structure and the operating structure may be different due to social system and power blocks. There are various concepts of organizational structure. These are centralization, decentralization, formalisation, specialization, stratification and standardisation. Max Weber has suggested a concept of bureaucracy where maximum stress is laid on the written orders, instructions, policy formulation, rules, and regulations. This type of concept is strict and employees are bound by formal rules in their day to day functioning. Bureaucracy is highly rigid and has a tendency to promote politics and power blocks. Organizational structure may be mechanistic or organic. Mechanic organizational structure is generally adopted by those organizations which are not influenced by technological, product or market changes and generally maintain a constant pattern. It is like the bureaucratic model of organizational structure. On the other hand organic structure is flexible and prone to frequent changes due to technological, market or product change. Delegation of authority to various levels, autonomy in work environment and decentralization are the hallmarks of such organizational structure. When an organization is planned to be started, a micro level centralized organizational structure is recommended.

Informal organizations develop within the framework of formal organizational structure. They have their own structure, norms, leadership and working ethics. The formal structure can be either flat or narrow, depending upon the number of subordinates a manager is capable of handling. It is also known as span of management. It has been proposed by Lyndll that for achieving optimum efficiency, the number of subordinates under one manager should not be more than five/six. But this may not be true in present environment because of tremendous progress in information technology and communication. The type of organizational structure is a function of the micro-environment of business, the size of the organization, technology used, philosophy and the strategy adopted by the organization. A large organization using sophisticated technology lends itself to organic type of structure.

Various types of organizational structures include line structure that is very simple and hierarchical in nature where employees are involved in production of goods and services. The second type of organizational structure could be based on line and staff where specialists are added to assist the line. Then there is a functional structure that permits a specialist in a given area to enforce his directive within the clearly defined area. A matrix structure is a combination of project and functional structures in which cross functional teams are used. Both functional managers and project managers are specialists and are jointly responsible for operation and completion of the tasks.

Departmentation is most important aspect of the organizational structure. Organizations are formed based on the following parameters:

(*a*) Departmentation by functions
(*b*) Departmentation by place or geography
(*c*) Departmentation by product and services
(*d*) Departmentation by matrix
(*e*) Hybrid structure of organization

TEXT QUESTIONS

Q. 1 Define organizational structure and explain various implications that are associated with the organizational structure.

Q. 2 What are various concepts of organizational structure.

Q. 3 Explain various steps involved in formation of organizational structure. Give example of an organization.

Q. 4 Differentiate between mechanistic and organic structure. Under what circumstances would each type of structure be more beneficial in achieving organizational goals.

Q. 5 Explain centralized and decentralized authority. What are various variables taken into consideration in order to determine whether centralized or decentralized structure would be more effective.

Q. 6 Differentiate between formal and informal organization. How important are informal groups within over all concepts of formal organization.

Q. 7 Explain the concepts of span of management. What factors are considered while deciding whether to have a narrow span or wide span. Give merits and demerits of each of the types of span of management.

Q. 8 What are various determinants of organizational structure. Visit an organization in your neighbourhood and study the organizational structure it has adopted. Evaluate the same and give your comments/modification to the existing structure.

Q. 9 What are various types departmentation. Explain the same with the help of diagram.

Q. 10 How does matrix organization differ from functional and project organization. How can matrix organizational structure be more effective in a brick type of work involved.

Q. 11 Explain the following concepts in detail

(*a*) Line organization
(*b*) Line and Staff organization
(*c*) Project and functional organization
(*d*) Line and staff Conflicts
(*e*) Impact of technology on formation of organizational structure.

REFERENCES

1. Sheldon Oliver, ***"The Philosophy of Management"***, John Wiley and Sons. 1930.
2. Howard, M.Charlisle, ***"Contingency Approach to Decentralisation"***. Advance Management Journal, July 1974.
3. Urwick, Lyndall F., ***"Scientific Principles of Organizations"***. American Management Association, New York, 1938.
4. Sheldon, Oliver. ***"The Philosophy of Management"***. John Wiley and Sons. 1930.
5. Grenier, L.E. ***"Evolutions and Revolutions as Organizations Grow"***. Harvard Business Review, vol 50 No 4.

Case

GHANDI MEDICAL CENTRE

Ghandi Medical University Centre is engaged in full time teaching and medical research for a medical college, dental college, nursing college and other health related professions. It is attached to university which enrolls approximately 2,000 students. It has about 800 beds in medical, surgical and psychiatric wings. It is funded by state government. It is widely recognized as top institution in the provision of medical services in the state. However, the medical center faced consistent financial problems, especially the teaching is unable to break-even.

The state government has brought Dr. Rao, previously Director of a large private hospital by offering lucrative salary and perks. Lured by an excellent salary, favourable climate and the opportunity to test his abilities, Dr. Rao accepted the post of Director of the center.

In the post of Director, Dr. Rao holds control of administration of the teaching, hospital and the college of health related professions. He is accountable for both its management and its budget. While Dr. Rao enjoys free hand in the internal affairs of the university, all long range plans and budgets are approved by state legislature and university. The medical center is expected to obtain approval for major programs from both the university and state it is subject to their rules, regulations and priorities. While the state favours expenditure on health care, the university prefers a budget structure supporting teaching and research.

This being the external intricacies, Dr. Rao found that the teaching and health care personnel directly reporting to him have conflicting priorities. While the former group emphasizes teaching and research, latter stresses on health care. A sluggish bureaucracy entrenched in the organization, most of the important people respect it as it provides necessary resources. However, many individuals within the bureaucracy flap well-conceived plans because they lack initiative or have no interest in the effective management of the institution.

In this back drop, Dr. Rao found Mr. Das was handling all procurements, a unique personality, he being a retired military person. While purchasing, he buys exactly what every physician orders with no regard to cost. Many of his purchases are dictated by state specifications. This frequently resulted in running out of budget allocation within eight or nine months, contributing to deficit. This forced the center to borrow supplies from local hospitals. Mr. Das, it seems neither made an attempt to change state specifications nor persuaded physician and teaching staff to order less expensive items of equal quality. However, he is not violating the rules, but discharging his duties perfectly with the bureaucracy. Dr. Rao recognized that he is not only an exception in the center.

QUESTIONS

1. What are the specific problems of Dr. Rao? How do you eliminate them?
2. How could you redesign the organization? Construct a chart.
3. Dr. Rao is not strong believer of bureaucracy. As such what type of leadership styles are appropriative in this case?

(The Case extracted from the book titled "The Process of Management" edited by Dr. M.L. Bhasin published by Global Business Press, Abhinav Publishing Industries Pvt. Ltd., Delhi, 1st Ed. 1994.)

CHAPTER 17

Job Design

INTRODUCTION

In an era of industrial revolution products were manufactured centrally and distributed to the consumers. The products were sold easily because demand was more and the competition did not exist. One of the major characteristics of industrial revolution was specialisation. Adam Smith was pioneer to introduce division of labour and specialization. In this system a worker is assigned a small unit of job so that he produces the same efficiently, and over a period of time he becomes specialist in that job. Specialisation led to higher efficiency and productivity. Henry Fayol later introduced a new set of management principles based on primacy of administration. He laid stress on doing job in a scientific way. Fredrick W. Taylor latter introduced scientific management and is considered as father of scientific management. In his work, he emphasized that the work design must take into consideration specialization, standardization and simplification to ensure optimum productivity. He emphasized that the job is divided into basic components and that one of the components of job be assigned to a worker thereby achieving specialization. Principles proposed by Adm Smit, Henry Fayol and Taylor have led to jobs becoming over simplified. This has resulted in jobs becoming monotonous, routine and boring. It also led to workers becoming unimaginative and lacking challenges and innovation. This had an adverse effect on productivity. Peter Ducker stated that restrictive work rules "forbid workers moving from one job to another, thus restricting them to narrow repetitive tasks." Elton Mayo, therefore proposed a behavioural approach to management that established production and managerial efficiency through understanding of human relations. Maslow also tried to identify the need hierarchy and formulated a motivational model based on satisfaction of human needs in a systematic manner. This did not solve the problem and basic nature of the job remained static. Herzberg introduced a concept of work design. He concluded that workers were happier on their jobs based on intrinsic value of the job itself. Such as personal growth, higher responsibility sense of achievement and recognition. He stressed that work motivation and higher productivity can be achieved if appropriate changes are incorporated in the job design.

Job Enrichment

(*a*) **Enhanced Responsibility:** Employees should be assigned a properly defined job. They should be given higher responsibility for the accomplishment of assigned job and made accountable. This would bring sense of commitment to the organization, increased work performance, greater satisfaction and a sense of achievement and growth.

(b) **Greater Control Over Resources:** This factor is related to according greater autonomy to the employees in decision making. Workers should be permitted to manage their own time. Greater freedom in adopting methods and procedures should be given to employees within the framework of organizational culture.

Personal Growth & Achievement

(a) **Innovation:** A job should be growth oriented. Once a person achieves a reasonable level of expertise in the job he is doing he should be worth (fit) for consideration to the next higher job. Job must also lead to a feeling of accomplishment and recognition. Managers should ensure a positive reinforcement to the employees. He should encourage innovation and evolve new procedure, systems, methods and sequence of doing the job.

(b) **Feedback:** Nothing gives more joy to employees than the feedback on good performance. It is the duty of each appointment in the ladder to apprise their subordinates about their performance so that appropriate modification can be carried out. Performance feed back is an essential part of managing work force. Supervisors have the responsibility to provide immediate feedback directly to the employees. Performance may be communicated verbally, in written form as it has direct bearing on employee promotion. Feedback should be corrective in nature and conveyed as such. It at times assumes a connotation of criticism which must be taken care off.

(c) **Job Redesign:** The recent changes in technology have seen a progressive use of technical devices and increasing dependence on technology. This has led to decrease in and erosion of the human component. To keep the morale high and simultaneously meet the organizational objective, redesign of work is necessary. Redesign aims at higher productivity, optimum utilization of skills and experience of employees. Various benefits of redesign are as under:-

(i) *Relationship Between People and Job:* Job redesign alters the relationship of people and the job assigned to him. Every job must be interesting, challenging and accord happiness to the worker. Job has an ever lasting influence on employee motivation. The job must provide intrinsic value to the employees for which they must be proud of. Certain component of job that needs modification should be altered keeping in mind the employee job satisfaction.

(ii) *Job and human behaviour is directly related to each other:* While redesigning a job, it must be kept in mind that the employee who is likely to be assigned the job should have positive attitude and therefore display a creative and favourable approach towards the group in which he is working. When job contents are not favourable, employee is likely to display resistance. Stress symptoms lead to conflict situation that is more dangerous to the organization. It should be borne in mind that employee behaviour is more important in an organization than any other elements of management.

(iii) Work redesign open avenues and enhanced opportunities to the employees in various departments in the organization they are serving. It is likely to invite changes in various areas of operation. Work redesign exercise must ensure workers participation so that the change is accepted by them willingly. The process can be enlarged to cover other areas.

(*iv*) Management of resources, processes and keeping work force satisfied are the major responsibilities of manager. Former two aspects can be easily handled by an experienced manager. However creating an enhanced level of satisfaction among the employees is a crutial job. Work redesign brings among people a feeling of worth, facilitates personal growth and make them psychologically and technically fit to handle higher responsibilities. Organizational policies should cater for training and development that brings every individual capable of holding higher responsibilities.

Job Design

Job design is related to deliberately structuring technical, social and human aspect of a job. It is related to organizing (assembling) the components of job to enable participation by all group members to accomplish the same. Jobs can be highly complex or very simple in terms of use of employee skills. Once a job is designed, it must give satisfaction to the worker and he should be able to experience 'Worth' in doing the same. Various job design techniques are as under:

(*a*) **Job Simplification:** In this technique, jobs are broken down into very small parts where a fragment called "task" is repeatedly done over and over again by the same individual. Thus the worker achieves high level of proficiency. Quality of the product and high volume is produced in a limited time frame. Employee therefore is paid higher rewards. On the organizational side, the productivity is high. Since the individual is doing the job repeatedly, he achieves proficiency and training cost to the organization is practically negligible. However there are certain disadvantages also. Because of the repetitive nature of the task, a worker is likely to get bored and remain absent frequently. Quality and quantity may suffer in the long run due to frustration. Organization may have to attract workers by offering higher wages.

(*b*) **Job Enlargement:** Job Enlargement means where two or more simple tasks are combined and allotted to an employee. As in the case of vehicle driver, apart from driving he can undertake the job of maintenance of the vehicle. In this situation it adds more tasks to a job so that the worker has variety of simple tasks to perform. The advantage of this method is more variety in a job and acquiring additional proficiency. Dissatisfaction of employees can not be avoided after a long period due to boredom.

(*c*) **Job Rotation:** Job rotation refers to a technique where the employee is periodically rotated from one job to another within the work design. It involves moving employees among different jobs over a period of time. In this system workers do not get bored and problem of job enlargement is automatically taken care of. In job rotation workers get opportunities to do different jobs within a span of few weeks / months as he is rotated from one job to another. Thus company achieves specialization among the work force. However, people who desire challenging jobs are likely to develop frustration as rotation involves very restricted exposure on job variety.

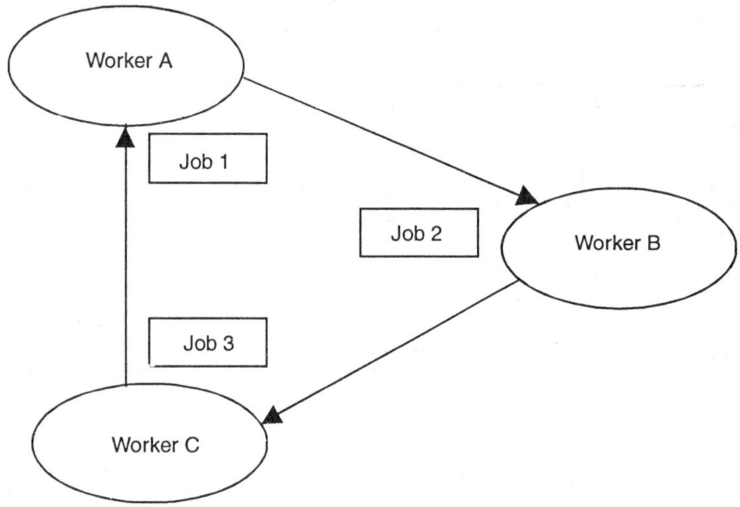

Fig. 17.1. Job Rotation

In the Figure 17.1 above worker A, B and C are performing different jobs within a specific period of time.

(*d*) **Job Enrichment:** Job enrichment refers to the technique of job design in which variety of skills are required to be possessed by the individual. Job enrichment entails skills development and a challenge. It entails inbuilt motivation, absolute control over the job and opportunities for growth and learning. Enriched jobs offer an intrinsic value to the worker and promotes motivation among the individuals doing the job.

THE JOB DIAGNOSTIC SURVEY

Hackman and Oldham (1976)[1] developed the Job Diagnostic Survey (JDS) which provides measures for some job related variables. The study provides certain guidelines and analysis of independent variables like core job Characteristics, intervening factors based on psychological states of people and consideration of dependant variable in terms of outcome that provides high intrinsic value to the worker. The JDS model is given in Figure 17.2.

Job characteristics (Core Factors)

1. Skill Variety

It denotes the degree to which a job requires utilization of variety of skills, abilities and talent of an individual doing the job. If the job is enriched, obviously the worker will achieve job satisfaction as it entails challenges in accomplishment of the same.

2. Task Identity

It is degree to which the job requires completion of "Whole" identifiable unit of work. The job requires involvement of an individual from beginning to the completion of a piece of work. This gives an individual a sense of pride, job satisfaction and desire to improve upon the present standards. Job identity gives an individual an identity in the group he belongs to and provides him an intrinsic reward.

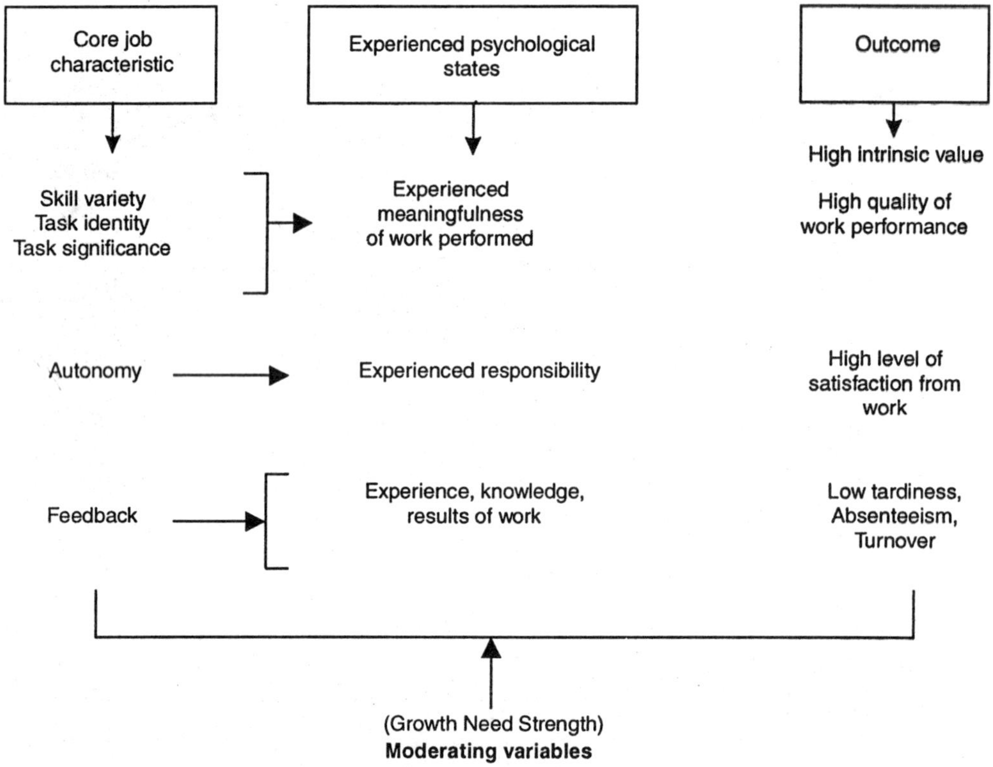

Fig. 17.2. Job design model of Hackman & Oldham

3. Task Significance

It refers to the meaningfulness or significance of the impact on the lives of people both inside and outside the organization. In Defence Research and Development Organization (DRDO) where Tanks are being assembled, the manager states that a worker is putting nuts and bolts on a tank that will defend the territorial integrity of our nation. The task significant in this case is of a very high order than putting nuts and bolts on a car though the skills requirement for both the jobs are the same. It is this part that motivates the employees. Managers should ensure that the people are doing worthwhile and significant jobs, which are beneficial to the society.

4. Autonomy

Autonomy reflects the extent to which job provides an individual, freedom of work, independence in decision making and full discretion in scheduling and execution. If the job content caters for the above factors, obviously an individual will take pride in completing the same. Greater the degree of autonomy more the person feels "in control" of the work in hand. In such situations people are motivated and display a great sense of belonging and job satisfaction.

5. Feedback

It is a core dimension of achieving direct feedback from the work itself as to how well a person is performing. Are the things going in the right directions? This is a conscious phenomenon, a person experiences while doing a job. If you are painting, one would definitely get to know if the paints are reflecting the image one desires, are the colours being mixed appropriately. This will indicate performance standard of the individual.

Experienced Psychological States: (Intervening Variables)

While doing a job, individual is likely the experience three Psychological States. These states basically determine the degree to which the core characteristics of a job (mentioned above) affect and enhance the employee's responses to the job itself. These are briefly explained below:

1. Experienced Meaningfulness

It is the extent to which the individual experiences and perceives his work as meaningful, valuable and worthwhile. It results from using a number of skills (skill variety principle), doing and identifiable piece of work (skill identity principle) and engaging oneself in a job that has significant impact on the society or group (task significance principle).

2. Experience Responsibility

It is degree to which an individual feels fully responsible for the job he is doing. This is achieved by feeling independence (job autonomy principle).

3. Experience, Knowledge and Results of the Work

In this psychological experience, individual perceives as to how well he is working? This feedback is not provided by supervisors but by the job itself.

Growth, Need Strength (Moderating Variables)

Growth and need strength refer to the need people have to develop, learn and achieve growth on the job. Everybody do not have high growth need strength. Some people feel happy wherever they are. Higher growth need is an intrinsic motivator. Employee having "high" growth need strength will experience the critical psychological states of experience meaningfulness, experienced responsibility and experienced knowledge of results. They may be able to achieve positive results when core characteristics are embedded in their work and they experience positive psychological experience. Those employees who do not have high growth need strength will not be affected by core job characteristics. Hackman and Oldham State that the outcome of the model are intrinsic motivation, work performance, job satisfaction, job involvement and Low absenteeism and turnover. Growth need strength is a moderator in this model.

Motivation Potential Score (MPS)

Hackman and Oldham (1975) came up with a formula for motivation potential score. This formula is used to measure the propensity of each job to be motivating. It can be assesssed by using the following formula

$$\text{MPS} = \frac{(\text{Skill Variety} + \text{Task Identity} + \text{Task Significance})}{3} \times \text{autonomy} + \text{feedback}$$

Autonomy and feedback are important in the above model. If they are non existant in the job design, the job may not have motivation potential. It is therefore necessary to design the job that caters for autonomy and feedback.

Managerial Implications for Job Design

Based on core dimensions of the job and MPS score, it is necessary to redesign each job so that workers are intrinsically motivated to undertake the same. Redesign involves the following:-

(a) *Forming natural work units:* Though specialization involves division of work, yet formation of 'whole' job is important because it gives performer an identity and association with completed work. The job must be identifiable and individual made responsible and accountable with the job with appropriate authority. For example an accountant in an office should be given an independent job instead of flittering his energy on various trivial jobs. He should be able to produce balance sheet, reconciliation with the bank, transaction with bank and account for receipts and payments, so that he experiences an autonomy in the work. This way the employee will view his work as meaningful and important rather than irrelevant and boring. This contributes towards the principle of task identity and task significance.

(b) *Combine tasks:* Managers must view division of labour and specialization scientifically. Attention must be paid to combine small jobs or part of job in a whole job so that workers performing it, feel proud of producing item and thus achieve task identity. Workers in automobile industry for example should be assigned a job as a group so that they develop a sense of group identity and achieve skill variety.

(c) *Establish client identity:* While producing product or creating services, worker does not have direct contact with the user of product or services. If the managers can achieve this contact, the workers will be able to get a first hand feedback from the client regarding customer choice. He may also be able to modify product or services as per the requirement of the ultimate user and achieve autonomy and develop skill variety while producing. This principle is very important and needs vision on the part of managers.

(d) *Expand job vertically:* Taylor in his scientific management has suggested separation of planning and doing a job. This has led to workers doing a particular job which has been planned by the managers with very little or no involvement of workers. Planning, execution and control therefore, need to be unified and gap between doing and controlling needs to be reduced. This phenomenon is called "vertical loading". In typical fractionalized organizations, responsibilities and control that formerly was reserved for higher level of management are now added to the job itself. This increases workers autonomy in performance of job. Expansion of the job can be achieved by workers by scheduling, work methods, quality controls, prioritizing the work, exercising financial controls and making appropriate decisions within the parameter of work schedule. This will provide the worker the sense of 'self worth' and intrinsic motivation that will lead to higher productivity.

(e) *Feedback:* Feedback is an important aspect of employee performance assessment. Feedback about on-going work should be given to the worker on line as he proceeds with the job. Negative feedback should be avoided and given in the form of suggestion and be corrective in nature. Positive feedback is like re-enforcement which builds up morale, positive attitude and propels individual to higher performance.

The above dimensions are presented diagrammatically in Figure 17.3 below:

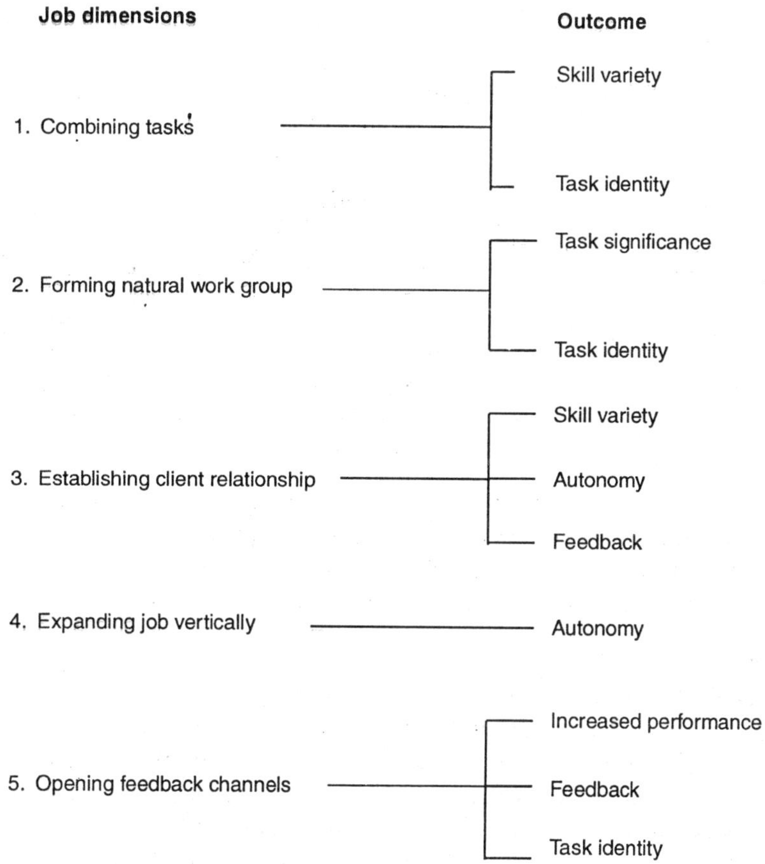

Fig. 17.3. Core job dimensions and its outcome.

Options for Job Design

We have already discussed in detail the core job characteristics for improving the individual and group performance. These are skill variety, task identity, task significance, autonomy and feedback. There are various other methods which can be considered to make jobs more interesting and satisfactory. These aspects are discussed below :

1. Job Sharing

Job sharing is related to two persons sharing one full time job with sharing rewards and responsibility for its completion. This method is ideal when two persons can do part time job on day to day basis for a limited time. This method is suitable for working mothers, doctors, and other professionals who can gainfully utilize their available time.

2. Flexitime

This method allows workers more freedom to select work schedule within the general guidelines laid down by the organization. Flexitime stipulates that all workers must be present during the core time so that interpersonal and inter departmental activities can take place smoothly. Flexitime system is shown in the figure below:

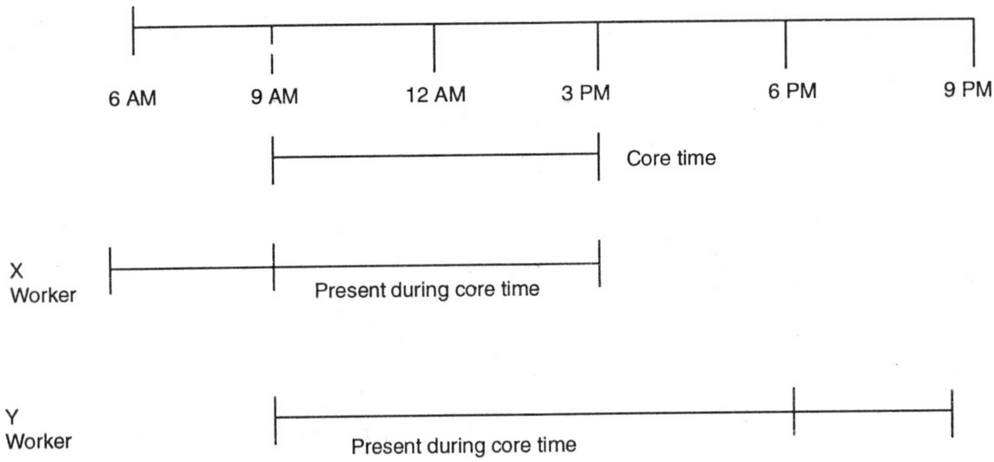

From the above figure it will be seen that employees can choose timings of work which are convenient to them. Flexitime method is beneficial to both as individual has freedom to select own time of work and the organization can attract talented workers.

3. Telecommuting

With the increased capabilities and sophistication of personal computers all sorts of jobs can be undertaken by an individual at any place. Jobs having financial implications like billing, accounting, telemarketing, e-commerce, graphics, media can be done at home for global organizations. This method is also known as flexiplace. It provides comfort, convenience and ease of work but isolates employee from team work and personal physical supervision. Managers need attitude change to incorporate such system in organizational setting.

4. Compressed Work Week

An individual is required to work eight hours a day, and six days a week, making it 48 hours a week. This work hours can be compressed into five or even four days a week with long hours of daily work with two or three days free at the week end. This system gives worker more leisure and higher productivity. Five days a week is a popular concept in India. This system ensures less absenteeism, more time available for maintenance of machines & equipment. It suffers from a disadvantage of high fatigue and boredom due to extended work days.

5. Quality Circles

Quality circles is one of the recent concepts of group job design. It consists of a group of 7 – 10 employees from a unit or across units who have volunteered to meet together regularly and analyse, make proposals about product quality, investigate causes and suggest corrective actions. The recommendations of quality circles are later forwarded to coordinating or steering committee. Meetings of quality circles are held once in a week or when need arises and are chaired by supervisors or any of the group members. Leaders are encouraged for a high degree participation within the group. Group members are trained in group communication skills, product quality and problem solving techniques. This concept promotes a sense of belonging, boosts employee morale, accords job security and develops 'we' feeling among group members and enrich organizational culture.

Job Design and Quality of Work Life

Quality of work life refers to high level of satisfaction an employee enjoys by virtue of job design. Quality of work life is measured by factors like job involvement, job satisfaction, competence, job performance and productivity. People must ensure that the job they are doing is central to individual's life and they display maximum involvement. Studies indicate that challenging jobs that have skill variety, influence employees to get involved in their jobs. Correlation of job involvement are such personality characteristics as n Achievement and high work ethics (Ref. Sekaran 1981 Robinowiz and Hall, 1977.)[2]

Job Satisfaction

Job satisfaction indicates the positive and affective responses of employees to their job environment. More specifically, job satisfaction indicates employees satisfaction with

1. Nature of work they do.
2. Quality of supervision they receive.
3. Co-workers.
4. Pay and
5. Promotional opportunities. Job satisfaction is correlated to job characteristics (skill variety, autonomy etc) and to job involvement. Sekaran (1977) in his work indicated that job stress decreases job satisfaction. Job stress could result from role ambiguity, role conflict, role overload or role difficulty.

Sense of Competence

Competence involves knowledge, skill and ability. When an individual attains competence he is more involved in his job because he is intrinsically motivated. By greater involvement the individual achieves higher degree of competence. Hence greater the involvement greater is competence. Thus competence and involvement re-enforces each other. Sekaran has given a model depicting relationship among job characteristics, motivation, sense of competence and job satisfaction. It is explained in Figure17.4.

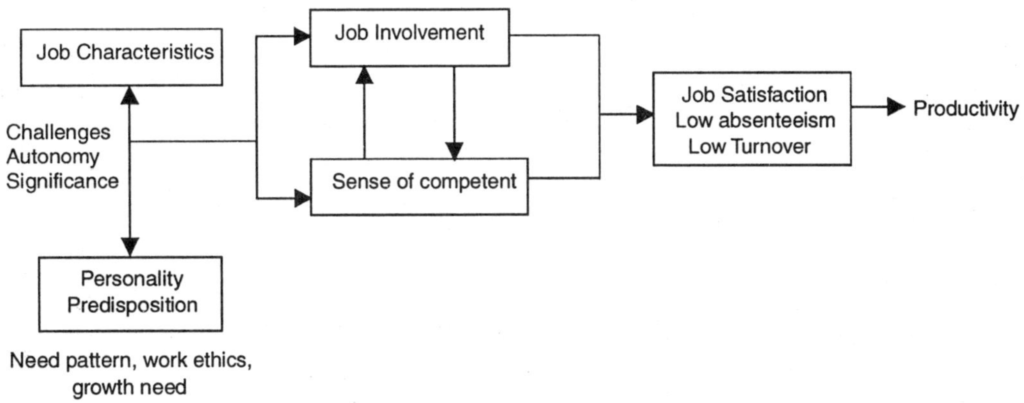

Fig.17.4. Sense of competence

Job Performance

Job performance increase with the increase in Job satisfaction, Job involvement and job competence. Job performance and Job satisfaction are inter-related.

Productivity

Productivity increases when there is a perfect fit of personality predisposition and the job itself. All the core factors of job design, predisposition of the individual give rise to productivity and quantum of output which is for the social good. It is therefore safe to conclude that job design is singularly responsible for growth, quality of work life of employees and the society. It is therefore important that managers pay attention to job design. Organization culture is sum total of ethical value demonstrated by employees. Job design, the urge for self-growth, intrinsic motivation and value system of the individual and group enhance the quality of work life in an organization.

SUMMARY

Division of labour, specialization, standardization and simplification lead to improvement in productivity. This phenomenon leads to jobs becoming monotonous, routine and boring. To achieve innovation and creativity among employees, it is necessary to introduce the concept of work design and promote intrinsic value of the job so that personal growth, recognition and sense of achievement is experienced by the employees. This can be achieved by giving employees enhanced responsibilities, greater autonomy, higher control over the resources, assuring them of personal growth and achievement. Positive feedback is important in the growth of workforce. Job should be designed properly and evaluated continuously so that it could be redesigned to meet the environmental changes. Job design can be achieved by job simplification, job enlargement, job rotation and job enrichment. Job redesign is necessary to ensure high employee morale, improved organizational productivity and job motivation. Work redesign improves human behaviour and opens awareness and enhanced job opportunities in the organization. It achieves job satisfaction and a feeling of worth. Hackman and Oldham developed "Job Dignoistic Survey (JDS). The work identifies core job characteristics that will provide higher intrinsic value to the employees. Psychological state of employees also play a decisive role in achieving greater employee satisfaction. The core characteristics (independent variables) that have been identified are skill variety, task identity, task significance, autonomy and feedback. The outcome (dependant variables) is higher intrinsic value, higher quality of work performance, high level of satisfaction and low tardiness, absenteeism and turnover. The intervening variables identified are related to the psychological state of employees that includes meaningfulness of work performed, responsibility for work results and the knowledge of the work. Later they came up with new model in 1975. The model is called Motivation Potential Score (MPS). The scientists have found out that the MPS of any employee can be worked out by a formula as under:

$$\text{MPS} = \frac{(\text{skill variety} + \text{task identity} + \text{task significane})}{3} \times \text{Autonomy} + \text{feedback}$$

It is a challenging task for manager to design an appropriate job keeping the foregoing factors in mind. This can be achieved by combining various tasks keeping (forming) a natural work units, combining tasks, establishing clients identity, expanding job vertically and feedback. Job can be made more interesting by job sharing, introduction of flexitime, tele commuting and by introduction of compressed work week. The aim of job design is to achieve an improved quality of work life. This can be measured by involvement, job satisfaction, developing a sense of competence, job performance and increased productivity.

TEXT QUESTIONS

1. What are various factors that achieve job enrichment?
2. Discuss various job design techniques.
3. Discuss Job diagnostic survey (JDS) model proposed by Hackman and Oldham.
4. How is Motivation Potential Score (MPS) used to determine propensity of job? Discuss various managerial implication to design the job.
5. What are other options to design the job apart from core dimentions?
6. Visit any organization in the vicinity of your location. Discuss quality of work life in that organization.

REFERENCES

1. Hackman, J.R. and C.R. Oldham, ***"Motivation Through Design of Work"***, Test of a Theroy. Organizational Behaviour and Human Performance, Vol. 16, 1976.
2. Sekaran 1981 Robinowiz and Hall, 1977.

Case

CONTINUOUS IMPROVEMENT AT KANCHAN AND COMPANY LIMITED

Kanchan and Company Limited was one of the leading manufactures of pumps for the domestic, agriculture, and industrial use. It had its corporate office at Delhi. One of its plants was located at Faridabad, the industrial town of Haryana which is only 30 km away from Delhi. The plant at Faridabad manufactured nearly 200 different types of pumps categorized as, the mini domestic pump, jet pump, four inch submersible pump, single phase monoblock pump, three phase monoblock pump, end suction pump and pumps for special use. Target customers for these products were household units, farmers, urbans (municipal corporation, civil contractors etc.), industrial houses etc.

Until 1995, the company was one of the major players in all the market segments without having any threat from its counterpart competitors. With the process of liberalization and globalisation, a number of competing companies entered in the business of manufacturing pumps. Some of the major competitors were Taximo in the agricultural segment, KSB and Kalama the submersible segment, Sharp in the domestic segment and Crompton in almost all the segments. Because of the stiff competition, the company had lost its market share in all the segments. Also the financial performance of the company had deteriorated as indicated by EBIT and PBT as shown in Annexure–I. To counter the competition and to get international acceptance for its products, the company pursued to get ISO 9000 and obtained the ISO 9001 certification in the year 1994. For its social acceptability, the company obtained ISO 14001 in the year 1997, and to retain this certification, the company started incorporating continuous improvements in all the areas of its operations. Until 1995-96, the focus was on maximum capacity utilization of man and machine and the bargain parts were manufactured continuously without analyzing their actual requirements resulting in the high inventory level of some parts and stock out in others. This resulted in the higher cost of manufacturing in two ways i.e., production stoppages because of the unavailability of parts and higher inventory cost of part which were not required. To have maximum utilization of machines, and to meet the market demand, the unit was working in three shifts. Since machines were used 24 hours a day, the organization needed hitech machines with low maintenance requirements resulting in short life span of the machines. The organization was able to meet seventy percent of the market demand in all categories of the product. With the increasing competition, the company had to face declining market share in some product categories. The company formed inhouse team to identify the areas in which the unit was facing problems. The team identified that the high inventory in all the areas, high rejection rate of the parts manufactured inhouse, low worker morale, high absenteeism, high cost of manufacturing, high level of wastages and scrap, lower customer satisfaction and unsatisfied demand in some product categories were some of the major reasons contributing to the poor performance of the unit. The problems were discussed by the management and the consultancy services of Tata Institute of Social Sciences were hired to look into the problems in the area of human resources. The other areas were investigated by inhouse teams. On the basis of the suggestions received from the consulting team from TISS and the inhouse teams, following changes were introduced.

- Overall manufacturing system was reoriented from the push system to the pull system, i.e., the different products were manufactured according to the market demand. Machining center to the manufacturing facility and part of the foundary section was converted to a synchronous manufacturing system.
- The plant layout was changed from the process based layout to group technology (Cellular layout) resulting in multi-skilled work requirement instead of a single skilled work requirement. The organization provided training to the existing workers to acquire the skills in the additional areas. This also resulted in the team approach towards the same objective.
- A system of the Joint Development Council (JDC) consisting of three tier organization, viz. functional council, cross functional council and the apex council, having equal representatives from the management and the union was evolved. There were three functional councils for the three functional areas, the foundary department, the service department and manufacturing department. The functional councils were responsible and accountable for absorbing the latest organizational methods and processes for the day to day operations to achieve the company goals of growth and profitability. The cross – functional council was responsible and accountable for making recommendations for the development / improvement, which would help to achieve the annual operating plans through the quarterly / monthly plans. This council was also responsible for resolving issues pertaining to the operations and maintenance of the manufacturing standards, quality standards, capacity utilization and resource mobilization. It also helped the apex council in taking final decisions in these matters. The apex council was responsible and accountable for resolving the issues that would arise in the operationalisation of

the various developmental / improvement schemes and also looked after the overall well being of the workmen besides addressing itself to achieving the company goals. Meetings of all the three councils of the joint development council system were conducted every fortnight, every month and on each quarter.

- The company introduced various programs for the development of its workforce like,

  (*a*) A cadre system by which the company offered grades to the employees purely on the basis of their merit and work experience. In order to asses the knowledge, skills and behaviour inventory of the workers, the system of conducting theory and practical examination followed by an interview was evolved. In earlier system, the workers carried out simple functions based on the skills and the scales were also fixed based on the type of work carried out by the workers, resulting in the disparity in the scales of workers working on the same product and having similar experience.

  (*b*) Continous Performance Improvement Scheme (CPIS): This scheme was developed to focus on ensuring the meeting of customer needs, zeroed rejections at the various operations, zeroed breakdown of the machines, maximize the capacity utilizations and developing the workers' pride in the ownership. For these objects, the selected parameters of the CPIS were, the quality of operations, upkeeping of the machines etc., availability of workmen and the capacity utilization. And therefore, the daily earning of the direct workmen under the CPIS were computed based on reducing the internal and the external rejections, increasing the availability of manpower and machines and improving the capacity utilization. In order to calculate the daily earnings of the direct workers under CPIS, following formula was developed :

  $$Ed = \{(EQ\,1 + EQ\,2 + EA\,1 + EA\,2 + EC) * N/n\} * \{Aa/An\}$$

  (For details on the CPIS see Annexure - II)

Efforts for System Improvement

- Broad production norms were developed.
- Cell owners concept was introduced.
- Integrated quality control system was introduced.
- Integrated productive maintenance system was introduced.
- Single digit minute die – exchange time was achieved in seventy percent of the cases.
- Rapid exchange of tool / dies was achieved in twenty to thirty percent of the cases.
- First out time was introduced to reduce inventory at the casting and finish stores.
- Focus was shifted from machines to shops.
- A number of managers and workers were removed / withdrawn from the number of activities.
- Shift from the individual incentive scheme to the group incentive scheme.

Despite all these efforts, the organization was still facing teething problems in a number of areas :

1. The organization had reduced the raw material and the finished goods inventories but still it was on the higher.
2. Process improvements had been carried out only in parts because of high investment requirements.
3. The workers were apprehensive and suspicious about the way the CPIS was introduced.
4. The organization had not done the cost benefit analysis of the changes they had made.
5. Tools and die replacement time had been considerably reduced but still needed improvement.
6. Synchronised manufacturing system had been introduced only in a few parts of the manufacturing unit.
7. To cater to the changing demand, the organization had assigned higher man power than required, leading to some idle man hours during normal demand periods.
8. Power supply constraints forced the company to use the age old method of manufacturing instead of the new technology.
9. Bilateral settlement had been signed with the recognized union however, there were more than one union having their representation amongst the workers.
10. Rejection level of the casings had come down from 12.5% to 12.2%.
11. With the measure taken by the company, the financial position had improved as indicated by the EBIT and the PBT.

The apex body during its last meeting appointed a committee to review the progress made by the different department under the continuous improvement program. Ramchanderan was appointed the chairman of the committee. Ramchandran after completing his preliminary investigation, forwarded the preliminary report to the management. The General Manager of the unit, Harish Narayan, noted that the unit had made a lot of progress through continuous improvement program but still the unit was not in a comfortable position in relation to its competitors. He was worried as to what the organization should do to speed up the process of continuous improvement.

QUESTIONS FOR DISCUSSION

1. Did Kanchan and Company Limited adopt the right strategy in improving the overall performance of the organization?
2. Was it right to use a complex system for determining the workers' incentives?
3. Which areas still needed improvement?
4. If you were the head of the unit, what steps would you have taken to remove the problems which were still persisting.
5. What should the company do to maintain and improve its market position?

Source: Continuous Improvement at Kanchan and Company Limited. Upinder Dhar, Santosh Dhar and Richa Agrawal (Eds.), Cases in Management – An Indian Prespective: PIMR Monograph Series, 2001, 81-85.

ANNEXURE I

Operating profit and PBT value (All figures are in Crore Rs.)

	1996 – 97	1997 – 98	1998 – 99	1999 – 2000	2000 – 2001
PBDIT	55.9	51	31	68.03	119.98
OP	48.3	49.5	21.5	68.46	112.38
PBT	-5.2	-5.2	-19.5	16.31	61.9

* The figures are projected.

ANNEXURE II

Calculation under CPIS

Ed = {EQ1 + EQ2 +EA1 + EA2 +Ec]*N/n} *{Aa/An}

Where,

Ed = Daily earnings of the direct workman through CPS.

EQ1 = Daily earnings by reducing the internal rejection.

EQ2 = Daily earnings by reducing the external rejection.

EA1 = Daily earnings by increasing the availability of manpower.

EA2 = Daily earnings by increasing the availability of machine.

Aa = Present hours in the shift of the workman.

An = Working hours in the shift of the workman.

N = Desired equivalent numbers of workers of a group.

n = Actual equivalent numbers of workers of a group.

*EQ1, EA1, EA2 and EC to be calculated on a daily basis.

*EQ2 will be calculated on daily/ weekly basis for each direct workman.

EXERCISE IN JOB DESIGN

Below are 20 questions which ask you to rate this course in terms of certain core characteristics. First responds to each item by *circling* the number that you personally feel is the appropriate response to the question, using the scale below.

Strongly Agree	*Agree*	*Slightly Agree*	*Neutral*	*Slightly Disagree*	*Disagree*	*Strongly Disagree*
StA	*A*	*SA*	*N*	*DS*	*D*	*StD*
S7	*6*	*5*	*4*	*3*	*2*	*1*

Sr. No.	*Statements*	*StA*	*A*	*SA*	*N*	*DS*	*D*	*StD*
1	Most of the things I have to do seem useless or trivial.	7	6	5	4	3	2	1
2.	I usually know whether or not the work I do is satisfactory.	7	6	5	4	3	2	1
3.	My course work requires the use of all the knowledge and skills I possess.	7	6	5	4	3	2	1
4.	I have the opportunity to do challenging things for this course.	7	6	5	4	3	2	1
5.	The course requires me to keep learning new things.	7	6	5	4	3	2	1
6.	The work I do for this course is very meaningful to me.	7	6	5	4	3	2	1
7.	I often have trouble figuring out whether I am doing poorly or well in this course.	7	6	5	4	3	2	1
8.	I use a wide range of abilities in this course.	7	6	5	4	3	2	1

(Contd.)

Sr. No.	*Statements*	*StA*	*A*	*SA*	*N*	*DS*	*D*	*StD*
9.	My course work can be done well by a person working alone without talking or checking with others to find if he/she is on the right track.	7	6	5	4	3	2	1
10.	There is no opportunity to use my own special abilities in this course.	7	6	5	4	3	2	1
11.	I can continually learn something worthwhile in this course.	7	6	5	4	3	2	1
12.	The course requires me to use a number of complex or high level skills.	7	6	5	4	3	2	1
13.	The work for this course provides me the chance to completely finish a piece of work which I can identify.	7	6	5	4	3	2	1
14.	The course itself is not very significant or important in the broader scheme of things.	7	6	5	4	3	2	1
15.	The course work gives me considerable opportunity for independence and freedom in how I do the assignments.	7	6	5	4	3	2	1
16.	The course denies me the chance to complete the work I start.	7	6	5	4	3	2	1

(Contd.)

Sr. No.	*Statements*	*StA*	*A*	*SA*	*N*	*DS*	*D*	*StD*
17.	I wish I could do the assignments without instructions from the professor in this course.	7	6	5	4	3	2	1
18.	I have no idea how all the pieces fall together in this course.	7	6	5	4	3	2	1
19.	I wish I had more freedom to do the assigned work my own way in this course.	7	6	5	4	3	2	1
20.	This course seems to be a waste of time.	7	6	5	4	3	2	1

The 20 questions tap the dimensions of Variety, Identity, Significance, Autonomy, Feedback, and Challenge, Now, score your responses following the steps below.

First, reverse the scores for items, 1,7,10,14 and 16 to 20. That is, if you strongly agreed on these 9 items, you would score them as a 1 instead, a 7, and if you agreed you would score them as 2 instead of 6, so on; this means that if you strongly disagreed on these items, you would score them as 7 instead of 1. Put your corrected responses for these items on the sheet itself.

Next add up your scores for the items listed below to asses the extent of your perceived core characteristics for this course.

Characteristics	*Actual Scores on Items #s*	*Your Score*
Variety	3 + 8 + 10 + 11 + 12 = (/5)	=
Identity	13 + 16 +18 = (/3)	=
Significance	1 + 6 + 14 + 20 = (/4)	=
Autonomy	15 + 17 + 19 = (/3)	=
Feedback	2 + 7 + 9 = (/3)	=
Challenge	4 + 5 + 11 = (/3)	=

Now calculate the MPS for this course.

Get into groups of four and see to what extent your scores agree. Based on your discussions, redesign this course if necessary.

CHAPTER 18

Management of Change

INTRODUCTION

Change is inevitable. Nothing is permanent except the change. It is the duty of the management to manage change properly. Organizations must keep a close watch on the environment and incorporate suitable changes if the situation so demands. Change is a continuous phenomenon. Organizations must be proactive in affecting change. Even in most stable organizations change is necessary just to keep the level of stability. The majoı environmental forces, which make the change necessary are technology, market forces and socio-economic factors. Resistance to change is not desirable. It is counter productive for growth and destructive in nature. Managers must evolve policies to affect change. According to Barney and Griffin, "the primary reason cited for organizational problems is the failure by managers to properly anticipate or respond to forces for change."[1]

UNDERSTANDING CHANGE

Change refers to any alteration, which occurs in over all work environment of an organization. It may relate to change in technology, organizational structure, working processes, work environment, organizational policy and even the roles people play. Introduction of change in one part in an organization forces change in other part. If the change is beneficial people accept it willingly. If it is not desirable, there is great resistance. If it is of no consequence to the people, they may adopt an attitude of indifference. If they consider the change detrimental to their growth and prosperity, they may resist through counter pressure. This reaction is based not necessarily on the reality or facts but on their perception. The change therefore should be sufficiently strong enough to overcome the counter pressure. Due to advancement of technology and social environment, change has become a necessity. If the change takes place, a balance or equilibrium is achieved by the organization. Thus people learn to expect various environment relationship within the organization. They learn adaptation. The essence is when people feel that there is need to change, and when they change, they actually are adjusting to changed situation thus an equilibrium is achieved with the changed environment. This process carries on and is never ending because change takes place continuously.

Organizational Growth as a Kind of Change

Grainier has evolved a theory of change by considering 'growth' as a factor for change. He has identified various problems at each stage of evolution. The solution to the problem brings about the change. To illustrate, he quotes an organization that desires to achieve 'growth'. Initially growth is achieved through creativity of founders who are usually entrepreneurial oriented but that creates a problem of leadership. To tie over the problem of leadership, management hires top class managerial personnel who take charge of the situation. Over a period of time it comes to the notice that excessive leadership creates a situation of concentration of power in the organization. With the effect the subordinates have to wait for the decision on a trivial issue. Therefore a change is necessitated and that leads to delegation of authority to subordinates. This leads to another problem based on autonomy at group level and control becomes difficult. Since the organization has already changed from concentration to delegation a new change is envisaged to exercise adequate control over the group. The change is in the form of issuing fresh orders and detailed instructions on each of the perceivable issue so that while individual enjoys autonomy in work culture, he still has to work within the framework of rules and regulations. It was later noticed that excessive rules and regulations brought with it the redtapeism. This problem leads to change of philosophy to collaboration. In this changed situation job is performed by individual employee, work teams and work groups. It will be seen that for

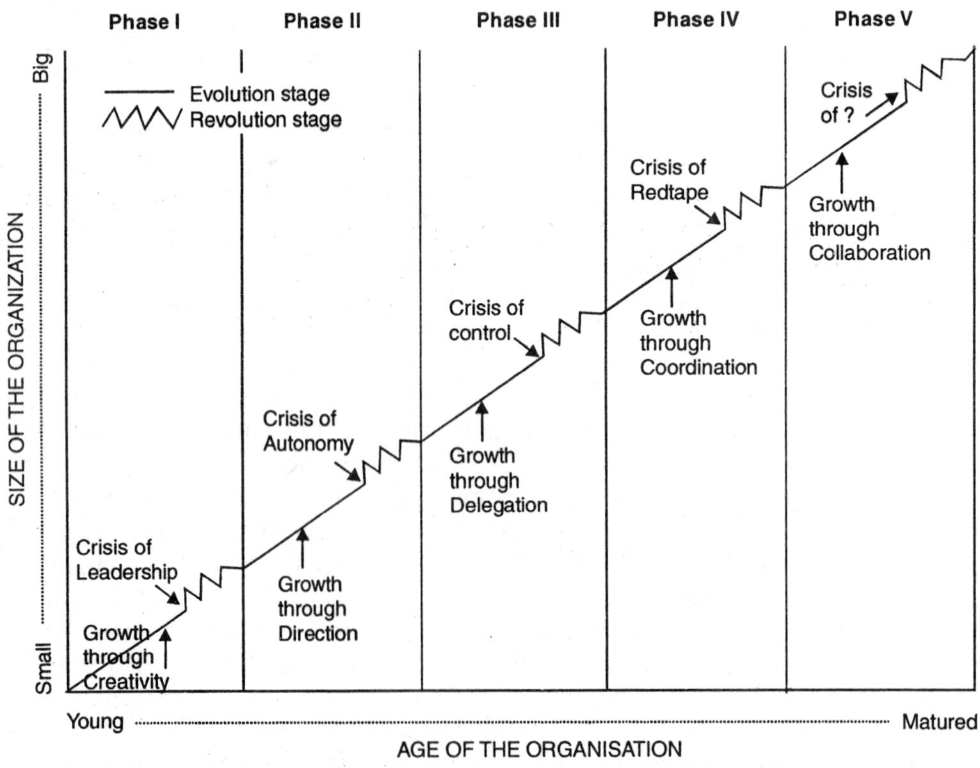

Fig. 18.1. Greiner's Model of Organizational Growth

achievement of organizational growth, the organization has to change its strategy beginning from entrepreneurship, leadership – delegation – autonomy of work groups—collaboration leading to the current strategy of self control, self discipline and individual work ethics. It is important to understand that each change that takes place is associated with unforeseeable problems. It will also be seen that change is necessary at every stage. If that was not implemented the organization will not be able to achieve growth. Greiner's model is explained in Figure 18.1 above.

Greiner's (1972) model shows various stages through which an organization is likely to pass during its growth period. The potential issues and problems between various stages are highlighted. The major problem should also be seen as one of managerial behaviour: that is, what managers have to do in order to overcome these crisis in relation to time span.

FORCES OF CHANGE

An organization is an open system which has to interact with environment and is solely dependant on it. Any change in environment makes it necessary for the organization to incorporate change in the internal systems, sub-systems and processes. This change has a chain reaction on the other internal elements of organization. For example any change in consumer preferences, may change product feature, cost, technology, marketing strategy and the like. Organization must interact with external environment in order to survive. Organization gets input from environment (men, material, process, finance, information etc.) Transform it and export output (product and services) to environment. Organization take what environment gives and in the process passes on what the environment wants. Thus organizations are responding to the social requirements. If the response is positive, then the change takes place and growth is achieved. If on the contrary response is negative it will adversely affect the growth. So there are various factors that must be considered to implement change.

(*a*) External Forces of Change

Technology is a major external force which calls for change. In the recent times information technology has made a remarkable impact on the ability of managers to use information to arrive at a decision. Storage, retrival of information and its utilization is important part of technology. Where human being can not operate, robbot has been replaced to work for and on behalf of human beings. Financial decisions, operations, product features, new product development, market potential and marketing strategies are changing at a fast speed and organizations must carry out appropriate change in time otherwise one will be left behind in the race. Because of liberalization market has become one entity. Organizations have to be highly sensitive to the changes in the external environment. External environment is task related and general in nature. Task related environment has a direct influence on the health of the organization. It consists of customers, competitions, suppliers, labour and stakeholders. All these factors induce change in the organization. General environment consists of political, legal, economic, socio-cultural and technological forces. Change in government polices or fiscal policies have a direct impact on the organization. Changes in needs, expectation and desires of society for housing has changed a financial sectors outlook and loans are easily available to all sections of society.

(b) Internal Forces of Change

Once the organizations adapt to the external change, the mangers have to take appropriate steps as far as internal systems are concerned. Change of process, modification to human behaviour, training and development of work force based on new technology and adopting new polices, which are beneficial to the organization. Due to current social changes where women are taking jobs in greater numbers, child care, more and frequent rest periods, flextime may be necessary. Workers are more educated and are aware of their duties and rights. This may necessitate change in corporate policies towards wage and salary implementation, promotion policy and management's obligation towards them. Changes in internal environment may be brought about by customers, shareholders, board of directors and employees. These however, have to be in line with the external factors and not arbitory. Change which is deliberately designed and implemented is a 'planned change'. This is carried out to counter threats and encash opportunities. "Reactive changes" are unknown and cause as a response to sudden surprises like change in price of a particular product etc. It is therefore necessary that the management must be '**proactive**' in incorporating change with fewer surprises.

Force Field Analysis: When a decision to implement change has been taken, it is necessary to identify and understand as to what forces are likely to push change and what forces are likely to restrain it. The process of identifying the number and strength of driving and restraining force is called the force field analysis. If the analysis indicated that the restraining force is strong, steps may be required to reduce their strength or increase the strength of the driving force. This may be carried out by briefing sessions, meetings and conveying a point informally. The communication must be appropriately modulated. It is the responsibility of the leader to select appropriate leadership style to incorporate change. Knowledge of organizational climate in general and group behaviour and attitude in particular is essential for implementing change. If the subordinates are not communicative among group members, participative style of leadership may be necessary. If the pattern of communication permits mutual consultations among subordinates, the Autocratic style may mar the prospects of change. Modification may be required not only to the style of leadership but also to the 'change' itself. The implementation may start by introducing readiness of the group to proposed change and later introduce the required change. It is a gradual process and emotions, value, feelings, attitudes of employees need study in depth. Implementation of change in defence services is comparatively easier because people are customized to change and have achieved a higher degree of readiness to change by virtue of their professional climate.

CHANGE PROCESS

Kurt Lewin[2] proposed Three Stage Model of the change process for moving the organization from present position to the changed position. This is as under:
Stage 1: Unfreezing : Creating motivation and rediness to change through

(a) Disconfirmation or lack of confirmation.
(b) Creation of gulit or anxiety.
(c) Ensure subordinates of psychological safety.

Stage 2: Changing through cognitive restructuring : Helping the client to see things, judges things, feel things differently based on new point of view obtained through.

(*a*) Identifying with a new role model, mentor, etc.
(*b*) Scanning the environment for new relevant information.

Stage 3: Refreezing: Helping the client to integrate the new point of view into

(*a*) The total personality and self – concept.
(*b*) Significant relationship.

1. **Unfreezing:** Process of unfreezing makes individuals ready for change. Lewin believes that employees must be informed in advance of impending change and that they should not be surprised. Unfreezing entails unfreezing the old behaviour or situation. Edgar Schein[3] took this excellent idea propagated by Lewin and improved by specifying psychological mechanism involved in each stage of the model. Unfreezing involves creating motivation and readiness to change by creating an environment of disconfirmation of existing psychological safety in the changed pattern of behaviour. This can be achieved by making announcements, meetings and promoting the idea throughout the organization through bulletin, boards, personal contacts and group conferences. The unfreezing process basically cleans the slate so that fresh behavioural patterns, customs, traditions can be imprinted which can then become a new way of doing things.
2. **Moving:** Once unfreezing process is completed, moving takes place. Moving is incorporating change. Persons undergo cognitive restructuring. The process is carried out by the following three methods as proposed by Kelman.[4]
   - **Compliance:** Compliance is achieved by introducing rewards and punishments. It has been established that individual accepts change if he is rewarded or punished. This is a behaviour modification tool.
   - **Identification:** Members are psychologically impressed upon to select their role model and modify behaviour. If a leader can act as a role model the change is easier.
   - **Internalization:** Internalization involves internal changing of individual's thought processes in order to adjust to a new environment. Members are advised to carry out soul searching and adopt a new behaviour.
3. **Refreezing:** It is related to integrate the new behaviours into the person's personality and attitude. It is referred to stabilization. The change behaviour must necessarily fit into the social surroundings. Refreezing takes place when the new behaviour is adopted in a normal way of life. New behaviour must replace the old on a permanent basis. New behaviours must be re-enforced continuously so that it does not diminish. Change process is not a one time process but it is continuous hence unfreezing, change and refreezing must also be continuous.

Another 'change model' was proposed by Ronald Lippitt, Jeanne Watson and Bruce Westley. They expanded the original Lewin's (3 stage) model into seven stage model.

Phase 1: The development of need for change.
Phase 2: The establishment of change relationship (establishment of 'Client' and 'Change agent' relationship).

Phase 3: Diagnosis of client system's problems.
Phase 4: The examination of alternative routes and goals; Establishing goals and intentions of action.
Phase 5: The Transformation of moving intentions into actual change efforts.
Phase 6: The generalization and refreezing stabilization of change.
Phase 7: Achieving a Terminal relationship with client – change agent.

LEVELS OF CHANGE

Hersey and Blanchard[5] identified four levels of change. These are ***knowledge change, attitudinal change, individual behaviour change and group or organizational performance change.*** The objective is to bring about change in the organization. It is possible through knowledge change which in turn changes attitude of the individual. Knowledge change is simple as one can improve the level of knowledge by reading or listening. Bringing attitudinal change is difficult, because it is difficult to change the individual and his perception. Change in individual is related to personality traits. A manager may believe that empowering subordinates is essential for organizational growth yet he may not empower them because of his upbringing. Changes in group and organization is even more complicated than implementing individual level change as it involves change in group norms, customs, and traditions. Change in group level involves change in organizational culture. This is a long term process, which must be continuous with active involvement of top management.

1. **Knowledge Change:** Change in knowledge can bring change in individual and group behaviour. It is related to the leadership style, Hersey and Blanchard refer to it as participative or democratic change cycle and autocratic or directive change cycle.

   (*a*) Participative leadership style in bringing change in group or organization is largely based on the style of leadership. Change in knowledge of workforce coupled with participative leadership style can transform an individual in his outlook. It can bring change in his attitude and an individual can be more committed towards the organization. He can be more responsible towards his duties and obligations. New methods and techniques can be implemented to bring change in he group in desired direction. Assistance from like minded leaders having democratic outlook can help mangers to implement desired change. Once this is achieved, organizational change may be effected by getting other people to begin to pattern their behaviour on the lines of successful leaders. Thus the change cycle works through change in knowledge, attitude, individual behaviour, group behaviour and organizational change.

   (*b*) There are autocratic leaders in the organization. This type of leadership announces the desired change all of a sudden. This type of process of change may result in whole hearted acceptance of change or the group may resist the change totally. What is expected in the autocratic change cycle is organizational change, group level change, knowledge change and through this cycle, to implement individual behaviour change. Since this approach is opposite of participative cycle change, it is difficult to implement and individuals are not ready to accept change in first place. Secondly, the change may not be of a permanent nature. Participative change is ideal when the employees are achievement oriented having task relevance and willing to accept responsibilities. It has deeper and longer lasting impact. Autocratic change cycle has fast speed and revolutionary in nature. It is sustainable where people are not willing and certain amount of force is required. This change cycles are complimentary to each other and therefore may be used according to the situations.

2. **Attitudinal Level Change:** It is difficult to bring attitudinal change. Attitudes are formed and conditioned by feelings. The way one feels about change will determine how one is likely to behave. Attitude is formed in early childhood based on social surroundings. When you are part of a group, an attitude is greatly influenced by group norms, expectations of the group members and behavioural code a group adopts. Further the work environment influences the attitudes. Due to complex nature of situations, there is either positive or negative impact on individual behaviour. Often actions or reactions of individual are effects of group-think. It often happens that the workers join the strike to show togetherness of the group or the organization. Individual may not be able to justify a particular behaviour but he does it merely because all others are engaged in a particular behaviour. We are not able to explain our emotions largely that make us behave in a particular manner. These feelings as Davis[6] explains are not a matter of logic. They are neither logical nor illogical; rather they are non-logical hence, logic alone is not enough to modify the feelings in modern times. It is however necessary to effect change in individual attitude. It is possible by way of delegation of authority and empowering employees in their work. Making work more pleasant and interesting by way of providing the workers wherewithal necessary for its accomplishment, creating autonomy in work and introducing management by objective concept in the organization. Cultural change is important. Organizational culture must conform to majority of workers culture and they must feel at home while working. Attitude of leaders also play a vital role in attitude change of subordinates. Participative leadership culture go a long way in obtaining willing obedience of employees. It must be borne in mind that it is a continuous process and all the members must sub-conscientiously attempt to improve work culture in the organization for attitudinal change.
3. **The Group Level Change:** Group plays variety of roles in bringing about change in the organization: The group as medium of change, the group as the target of change and the group as an agent of change. Cartwright[7] has developed the following principles in this regard.

   (*a*) **The group as a medium of change:**

   (*i*) If group is to be used effectively as a medium of change, those people who are to be changed and those who are to exert influence for change must have a strong sense of belonging to the same group.

   (*ii*) The more attractive the group is to its members, the greater is the influence that the group can exert on its members.

   (*iii*) In attempts to change attitudes, values, or behaviour the more relevant they are to the basis of attraction to the group, the greater will be the influence that the group can exert upon them.

(*iv*) The greater the prestige of a group member in the eyes of the other members, the greater the influence he can exert.

(*v*) Efforts to change individuals or sub-parts of a group which, if successful, would have the result of making them deviate from the norms of the group that will encounter strong resistance.

(*b*) **The group as a Target of change**

(*i*) Strong pressure for change in the group can be established by creating a shared perception by members of the need for change, thus making the source of pressure for change lay within the group.

(*ii*) Information relating to the need for change, plans for change, and consequences of change must be shared by all relevant people in the group.

(*iii*) Changes in one part of a group produce strain in other related parts which can be reduced only by eliminating the change or by bringing about readjustments in the related parts.

4. **Organizational-wide Change:** Organizational change is of a mega nature. It starts at the bottom level and acquires a very huge dimension. In defence services if a person is promoted at the top level, there is a chain reaction upward for promotion and resultant placement, transfers etc. If an organization is attempting to change the job of an individual, his role-set is also likely to change which may distrusts the self – concept of the individual. Thus any action for change may also have chain reaction. It is therefore necessary to plan for change carefully. Allen has suggested following steps:

(*a*) Development of clean objectives
(*b*) Analysis of existing organizations
(*c*) Preparation of an ideal plan
(*d*) Trying out the plan
(*e*) Establishment of uniform nomenclature
(*f*) Overcoming resistance to change

In the fast developing world today, there are pressures on the human resources. Due care must be taken to ensure that employees are not disturbed physiologically and psychologically. Careful review of the situation to identify the gaps must be carried out. Change costs money and therefore it is advisable to undertake a pilot project before a universal change is implemented. Status system, titles and appellations attached to it must be protected by introducing uniform nomenclature, designation etc. People must be educated about the impending change so that they are not taken by surprise. Benefits of change must be highlighted. Automation of systems in organization have proved fruitful and cost effective for which it had initial resistance.

'Change Management' has already emerged as a discipline. It requires proper planning, programming, evolving appropriate procedures and systems. An organization must modify polices, procedures, rules and regulations based on changed objectives. Behavioural science plays an important role by way of ensuring that revised system is in tune with the time.

TYPES OF CHANGE

(1) **Strategic Change:** Strategic change requires when mission is changed. A single mission of defence forces participating under UNO banner may require changes in use of weapon system, co-operation at international level, serving under a person not of an Indian origion and the very thought of employing various strategic and tactical doctrines. The multinational companies have to adapt to the culture of the nation where they are providing product and services. Various cultural factors, have to be considered in this regard. This is generally carried out as 'planned change'.

(2) **Structural Change:** Decentralization of authority and introducing flatter organizational structure enable employee to experience a sense of autonomy in work environment. Decentialisation leads to empowerment of lower level employees to take appropriate decisions pertaining to their job parameters. It has major impact on the social climate of the organization on one hand and development of team spirit on the other. Structural changes promote acquision of new skills and improves ability of subordinates to take on the spot decisions even in critical situation.

(3) **Process-oriented Change:** Process changes are necessary to keep pace with the development in technology, automation, information technology, free market environment and availability of trained manpower. The organization must take advantages of these processes. This however needs heavy investment and entails various operational changes but cuts down time and energy. This would bring about change in work environment, organizational culture and modify behaviour pattern of employees.

(4) **Cultural Change:** Due to electrifying changes in communication, an individual is exposed to social changes. This has necessitated to introduce a right culture in the organization. It is the responsibility of the top management to ensure proper organizational philosophy, instill culture and value system among employees and practice ethical approach in business. These are important inputs for improved performance, group cohesion, devotion to duty and for development of 'we' feeling in the organization. This can be achieved by close interaction, training in behavioural sciences and building a sense of belonging to the organization. These changes are people – oriented and therefore have to be continuous for achievement of organizational mission.

STEPS IN MANAGING CHANGE

Organizations must plan to implement change in a systematic manner. It must identify the field in which the change is required whether it is strategic, structural, process – oriented or cultural change. Changes can also be affected in all the areas concurrently, but it must be managed appropriately so that there is no bottleneck effect. Once the need for change is identified and the area in which it is to be implemented, the following steps have been suggested by Greiner.[8]

(*a*) **Develop new goals and objectives:** Objectives and goals are derived out of mission statements, objects may need revision due to change in external or internal forces.

(*b*) **Select an agent for change:** It is the responsibility of the management to entrust execution of change to appropriate authority. A manager may be given this responsibility. Outside Change Agent can also be employed for the purpose. A specialist or a consultant can be brought in to suggest change and monitor implementation. He is also called a facilitator.

(*c*) **Diagnose the problem:** Diagnosis is the first step to implement change. If an organization has a large number of employee turnover then the data must be collected and made available to the consultant so that the reasons for turnover can be identified and appropriate corrective measures taken. The process of identification of problem is not simple as it appears. This itself may need a research.

(*d*) **Select Methodology:** It is comparatively easy to implement material change as a part of change of a system. What is important is to protect the emotions employees must be made party to select methods so that it is easier to implement at a later stage.

(*e*) **Develop Plan:** If the organization wants to reduce employee turn over, it may like to carry out comparative study of other organizations in respect of job content, reward system, employee performance, appraisal system, promotion criteria, training & development and the strategy adopted by the organization for its growth. Based on examination of these factors, consultant would be able to develop a plan for change. It may require to introduce a new training and development policy that may reduce employee turnover. While developing a plan, various other factors must also be reviewed. Plan should not be finalized in isolation. All departmental heads must be co-opted in the exercise.

(*f*) **Strategy for implementation:** Timings of implementation of change is very crucial. A deliberate decision must be taken in this regard like hike in price of a product, the decision to implement the change is critical. If the change is related to internal employees, it must be communicated at an appropriate time so that there is no resistance to planned change.

(*g*) **Implementation of Plan :** Once the decision to implement the plan and communication through which the plan is to be implemented is decided, it is the responsibility of the various departments to implement the same. This may need notification, briefing sessions or in-house seminars so as to ensure the acceptance by all the members of the organizations, specially those who are likely to get affected. Implementation may be for a short duration as one time change of the system or process but its aftermath is of great value. Employee reactions in attitudes, aspirations, emotions and behaviour must be canalized in positive directions due to change.

(*h*) **Evaluation & Feedback :** The result of the change must be evaluated and suitable feed back obtained. If modification to training & development causes decrease in employee turnover, the objective of the change would deem to have been achieved. If the results are contrary to the expectation, then a new change may be required to diagnose cause.

CHANGE AGENTS

Change agent are factors that are responsible for the change in individual behaviour. Other changes like change in organization structure, organizational strategy, process, policy and the like can always be introduced in the organization with proper consultations of the employees so that they are accepted by them. Change in human behaviour is a complex phenomenon that may require a number of strategies to make desirable change. These are called change agents. They may either be initiator of change or serve as catalysts for such change. Four types of change agents have been identified (Tichy, N.)[9]

(*a*) **Outside Pressures :** External environment like fiscal policy, government policy, technology and social change bring change into the organization. Change is generally executed by the organizations itself. Government may also indulge and help organizations to adopt to new policy like controlling strike in the organizations.

(*b*) **Changes from Top Management :** The organizational change may come from the top management. It may be in the form of structural, strategic or institutions changes that may be beneficial to the organization with particular reference to employees.

(*c*) **Internal Organizational Development :** Organizational objectives must be reviewed from time to time. This is necessitated because of the environmental changes. Areas where organizational development can be carried out are work design, delegation of authority, team building, empowerment, autonomy, job enrichment , job rotation etc.

(*d*) **Individual level Change :** Individual level change refers to change in attitude, skills and behaviour. Management by objective (MBO) encompasses self decision making, setting objective for self, evaluating whether those have been met and resultant modification to work. If such development processes are introduced, individuals are likely to be more responsible and accountable for the work they are assigned. It is therefore necessary to introduce development processes / models in the organization.

RESISTANCE TO CHANGE

Change is a constant phenomenon. Dynamic forces are always at play and therefore individuals must adjust to it and carryout change. If the change in not implemented, society will be stagnant and become hopeless. Individuals accept change in the technical field but resist the other as it has far reaching consequences for the social change. Change no matter how beneficial, is generally resented and is always difficult to implement. It must be emphasised that change brings with it new challenges, new experiences, spirit and associated rewards and therefore it should be welcomed and implemented with positiveness and full support. However, there are certain factors that resist change; these are given in Figure 18.2.

Job Security

One of the major reasons for change is job security. In recent times there has been the trend for down sizing the organization as a measure of cost cutting. Introduction of modern technology and systems should lead to the growth in productivity of the organization and should not lead to employee turnover.

Lack of Communication

Different people will see different meanings in the proposed change. Management must communicate in advance the need for change, process to adopt for implementation of change. Employees should be co-opted right from the beginning in the process of change so that they are party to change and resistance is reduced to a great extent.

Reasons for Resistance	*Management of Change*
– Job security	– Participation & Involvement
– Lack of communication	– Communication & Education
– Rapidity and Extent of Change	– Leadership
– Group resistance	– Negotiations & Agreement
– Emotional turmoil	– Willingness for sake of group
– Loss of power & Control	– Timing of Change
– Technology	
– New practices	– Participation
(*a*) Acquisitions and mergers	
(*b*) Woman Power	

Fig. 18.2. Reasons for Resistance and Solutions

Rapidity and Extent of Change

Autocratic leader has a tendency to introduce change abruptly with speed. Resistance therefore may be expected to the degree that the persons influenced by the change have pressure put upon them to make it happen. If the change is of a minor nature and involves routine operations, the resistance would be minimal. If on the contrary the change is major and involves large number of employees there could be tremendous resistance to it. For example when Balco was privatised all employees resisted it.

Group Phenomenon

Individual on occasions resist change because group wants it that way. Importance of group cohesion, group norms, code of conduct and the security group provides to individuals play a dominant role in individual behaviour that makes them to resist change.

Emotions

Resistance can be expected when those influenced are caught in a jam between forces of change and forces of resistance. Resistance may be expected if the change is made on personal ground and past history of change of identical emotions. If the experience has been pleasant, then the resistance would be negligible. Workers willingly accept technical change if it does not have adverse effect on social fiber of the group. Resistance can be expected if the nature of the people who are going to be influenced by the change. Resistance may also be expected if the change ignores already established institutions in the group with particular reference to customs and group norms. It is therefore necessary that due care must be taken to protect the emotions of people.

Loss of Power

Downsizing of department or posting of an executive to different department, where there is a reduction of power base will be resisted by the affected individuals though it may be of overall interest to the organization. For example superintendent of police of a district will resist positing as an instructor to the police-training academy.

Technology

Technology changes are required for the growth of organization. People have now realized to be competitive. Latest technology, which improves the human skills must be introduced in the organization. It is important to consider that no human resources should be replaced by these changes. Certain amount of displacement should be taken in stride. Introduction of technology that causes economic loss and disturb social relationship are generally resisted.

New Practices

Due to advent of technology and education, more and more female employees are joining organizations. Some of them are serving in the position of top decision-making. Women domination is not liked by the people and is therefore resisted. For survival, organizations have to adopt the strategy of acquisitions and mergers, which is also resisted by the employees.

Managing Resistance to Change

Change ultimately affects people in the organization. It is always better to explain to them why change is necessary, what benefits are likely to accrue as a result of change and how these benefits are to be shared by employees and the organization. Free flow of information and two-way communication is necessary. If proper communication is not maintained negative attitudes are likely to be formed while change is being implemented. There is a general impression that benefits from change accrue to the organization and management at the cost of workers. This is a false impression and must be corrected by appropriate authority. It must be remembered that without full cooperation of workers, no change can be planned, implemented and the benefits, enjoyed. No growth of the organization can take place unless workers bring it about. Management must understand that workers are the key element of any organization and that they must be involved from planning stage of change. This will result in increased productivity of the organization. Participation should not be simply a mechanical act of calling upon employees to "Participate". It should be clearly understood that there is no one simple panacea to be used in all situations. Participation is not being universally followed. The different combinations of different methods, techniques and procedures may have to be tried. There may be need for the counselling and training of people. If the situation so warrants, the plan even may have to be dropped. Conscious efforts must be made by the leader to remove the fears of employees. Participation should be a part of total treatment of change. Such participation of workers would ensure commitment to implementation of change. Individual involvement right from the planning stage of the change is essential to ensure total commitment. It should ultimately appear that the employees require the change and management is implementing it at their behest. It has been observed that management is regarded as the instigator of change and unions are considered as forestaller of change. It is therefore for management to take labour leaders in confidence so that they are able to convince the members of the need and utility of change. It is important to make the workers feel that they can discuss the modalities of change and understand the nature of fears they may have, know for themselves that there is no danger or a trap in the change being planned and that the change is for the benefit of workers and organization. Coch and French's[10] study showed that the group which was not only informed of change and why it was to occur, but also participated in helping to design and plan the new jobs as well as retaining programmes, demonstrated more successful adaptation to change than the other two groups. These included: 1) group which had no orientation to change other than a short announcement by management that the change would be made. 2) group which was informed by management of the need for change and its implications and the workers were asked to select representatives to help devise the necessary retaining programmes. The results were much better in the second group involving all of them, than the first group in which only an announcement regarding change was made.

SUMMARY

Change is a permanent phenomenon. It is necessary due to external forces like technology, systems, and social changes interacting with the internal variables of the organization. To implement change Kurt Lewin's model of unfreezing the situation, implementing a change and refreezing must be implemented. Individual, group and organizational changes takes place continuously. Individual change refers to change in attitude, perception and also acquiring new skills to cope up with external environment. Group is the important unit of organization. In the present scenario group undertakes work. It is successfully completed because of group norms and groupthink. Organizational level changes can be implemented by clearly defining objectives and plans for change. Driving forces and restraining forces must be evaluated while implementing change. Change is structured when planned and unstructured when change is implemented as a reaction to some situation. There is great resistance to change because of the fear of unknown. Workers in the organization, therefore must be educated, trained, made party to change and benefit of change must be divided between the employees and the organization. It is handling of employee emotions and making them psychologically ready to implement change that will ultimately work. The fear must be removed from the minds of people. Change must be taken in the positive manner for the growth of the organization. It is difficult to predict which strategy will succeed in implementing the change. Efficient communication, educating the people about impending change, participation, and active involvement and last but not the least sharing benefits of change with people is the essential requirement for overcoming resistance to change.

TEXT QUESTIONS

Q. 1 Explain meaning of change, indicate whether all changes are beneficial.
Q. 2 Explain external and internal forces that induce change in the organization.
Q. 3 Describe the process of organizational change.
Q. 4 Discuss Lewin's model of change.
Q. 5 Discuss the functions of change in organizational viability. Why does an organization so often fails to make the necessary changes.
Q. 6 Explain the levels of change. How will you bring changes in individual behaviour.

Q. 7 Under what conditions does resistance to change develop ? Does it show lack of awareness in those who resist.

Q. 8 Why is organizational change often resisted by individuals and groups. Suggest strategies to prevent such resistance.

Q. 9 How will you use group as a medium of change if change is to be affected.

REFERENCES

1. Barney, J.B. and Ricky. W. Griffin, ***"The Management of Organizations: Structure, strategy and behaviour"***. Haughton Miffling Publishing , 1992.
2. Lewin Kurt, ***"Field Theory in Social Science"***. Harper and Row, 1951.
3. Edgar H. Schein. ***"Organizational psychology"***. Prentice Hall, 1970. P. 120.
4. Kelman H.C. ***"Compliance, Identification and Three processes of Attitude change"*** Conflict Resolution 1958.
5. Hersey, P. and Balnchard, ***"Management of Organizational Behaviour: Utilising Human Resources"***, Prentice Hall of India, New Delhi, 1977.
6. Divis, K. ***"Human Behaviour at Work"***, Tata McGraw – Hill Publishing Co. Ltd., New Delhi, 1977.
7. Cartwright Dorwin, ***"Achieving changes in people: Some Applications of group Dynamits Theory"***, Human Relations, Vol. 4, No.4, 1951.
8. Greiner, Larry E., ***"Patterns of Organizational Change"***. Harward Business Review, 1967.
9. Tichy, N. and H. Hoernstein, ***"Stand when your number is called : An Empirical attempt to Classify Types of Social Change Agents"***. Human Relations, Vol. 29, No. 10.
10. Coch, L. and J.R.P. French, Jr., ***"Overcoming Resistance to Change"***, Reading in Social Psychology, Holt, Rinehart and Winston, Inc., New York, 1952.

Case 1

MAGIC KINGDOM

One of the most popular tourist attractions in America is Disney World at Orlando in the State of Florida. It is a theme park with numerous attractions and a visit to America is not considered complete without the visit to Disney World. Prior to the opening of Disney World at Orlando, there was a similar theme park near Los Angeles in the State of California, known as Disneyland. Disneyland was a creation of Walt Disney, a famous family movie maker who had produced such movie hits as Fantasia and Snow White. Disneyland is a family entertainment phenomenon and is also known as **magic kingdom.**

Following Walt Disney's death, the magic kingdom hit a downward trend. The management rested on the past laurels of its success and the organization stagnated into its status quo. It shunned innovation and stayed in its ivory tower away from the pulse of the audience. It become fearful to change and by all accounts, it was not fully utilizing its potential or its resources and considering the demand for its products and services, it was under charging for its licensing of cartoon characters and admission to its theme parks.

Michael Eisner, the head of the Disney organization felt that he had to become more like Walt Disney, an innovator and a risk taker who encouraged creativity and who had built the Disney Empire. After analysing the situation carefully, he devised a plan that would encourage oppennes to change, and culture of strong creativity, that was always a hallmark of Disney's success.

Eisner himself came up with a number of new and creative ideas including new health food restaurants and he encouraged an induced creativity among others and creativity became one of his top priorites. His idea of creating a Euro Disneyland in Paris came into high focus. He met with 12 of the Worlds most respected architects in a widely creative session to bring out as best design for the theme park as possible. He encouraged and rewarded new ideas, opened the channels of communication and took the members into confidence by sharing with them his strategic plans and ambitious growth strategies.

One change that came into being was the renovation and expansion of its hotel chains. He ordered an ambitious $ 1.0 Billion hotel expansion plan that doubled its room capacity to 20,000 and came at par with the well known Ritz Carlton chain of hotels.

The movie business that had practically come to a stand still and was hardly reaching break-even point, got a boost of creativity. By tightening budget without sacrificing quality and working with adventurous scripts and unknown but talented actors, it became a dominant force in the American movie industry and produced such hit films as Beauty and the Beast, Pretty Woman, Ruthless People and so on.

Michael Eisner's creativity, openness, innovation and team sprit has not been without its rewards. From 1984 to 1990, Disney's sales increased from $ 1.7 billion to almost $ 6.00 billion. Dianey has expanded his family entertainment business to include book publishing and records and has opened a theme park in Japan.

Michael Eisner made a dramatic turnaround of Disney fortune in 1980s. He is even more ambitious during the 1990s and calls it The Disney Decade. He has surrounded himself with ambitious, energetic and creative staff and he expects a period of extensive growth for Disney operations around the Globe. With the fall of close societies and advent of instant communications and emphasis on internationalization, he is very optimistic that Disney will become a household name around the World, as it did in America.

QUESTIONS

1. Why do you think that the Disney organization, once a highly successful and growing organization become stagnant after the death of its founder Walt Disney? Discribe as many reasons as possible.
2. How important is Michael Eisner's role in the process of turn around of the Co-fortunes? Does it mean that the success of the entire organization depends upon the philosophy of its CEOs? Give reasons.
3. List and explain the internal and external forces that necessitated the change in the outlook of Disney operations.
4. Can you identify the change agents that were at work in changing the behaviour of the organizational members?
5. If you were hired as a consultant to the organization, what changes would you suggest, if any, to bring Disney organizationinto the global limelight?

Case adapted from Courtland L. Bovee et al., Management, MacGraw Hill, 1993, pp 361-362.

Case 2

TRADITIONAL MANAGEMENT OR PROFESSIONAL? R. MURLIDHARAN

Neo Labs, a medium sized Bombay based pharmaceutical concern in the private sector, was in the business of manufacturing basic drugs and formulations. Through to line among the top concerns in the field, yet it had achieved a considerable amount of success in North. It has not been able to make much headway in the South though.

Neo Labs Private Limited (NLPL) was governed by a Board of Directors, consisting of three Khanna brothers . Mr. Ajit Khanna, the founder member, as well as the eldest brother was the head of the marketing team, with a number of people spread all over India, under his command. Starting life as salesman for a pharmaceutical concern, he set up his own factory within one year and worked hard to spread it's activities all over India. He controlled all the marketing operations, whereas his brothers used to look after production and finance.

Mr. Ajit Khanna did not believe in recruiting managers from outside. Rather, he believed in promoting his old employees from within to the ranks of managers. Despite the advice of friends to bring in professional managers, in order to compete effectively, he would not change his mind. He would say. "I do not want to give my money to people who only talk about working. I want people who can really work".

Future plans for expansion, widening market activities, increased work load and above all, poor sales turnover ultimately forced Mr. Khanna to appoint Mr. Kalra, a professionally trained manager with ten years of experience, as Marketing Manager.

While assuring desired result within a reasonable amount of time, Mr. Kalra put forth his own precondition that there should be no interference whatsoever from Mr. Khanna in the marketing operations and that he (Mr. Kalra) should be given a free hand. This was accepted.

After carefully analyzing the company culture, environment and the operations, Mr. Kalra came to the following conclusions:

1. The management lacked professionalism and failed to make the manager s responsible for results.
2. Too much stress was placed on personal loyalty of employees to the Managing Director and personal considerations came in the way of managerial functioning.
3. Many managers, in connivance with the field people under them, compromised on the quality of the job performed.
4. Majority of the managers lacked professional skills. Mr. Khanna had promoted them, relying more on their personal loyalty and experience in the company rather their professional competence. Training facilities were inadequate.
5. There was a lack of coordination between the production and the marketing department hampering sales, leading to losses.

Within a short time of taking over as the Chief of Marketing, Mr. Kalra took certain drastic steps. He enhanced the salary and allowances of the marketing force to make it at par with other good concerns. He weeded out dishonest, inefficient and unproductive managers. This included some of the loyalists who had been with the company since its inception. Initially, Mr. Khanna was against this decision but since the charges against them were irrefutable, he had to concede.

Mr. Kalra made some important changes in the product mix and its promotion also. Many of the products which could be sold better through prescription demand by promotion with doctors were in continuous deal offer, benefiting the retail chemists more. Mr. Khanna, with his excellent personal contacts with chemists had relied more on their goodwill initially, and this practice followed even after Neo Labs became an all-India concern. Mr. Kalra set things straight by making suitable changes in the product promotion, laying emphasis on creating genuine prescription demand for the products. NLPL recruited an efficient product manager, displacing the old one, at his initiation.

Another aspect which Mr. Kalra felt needed toning up immediately was the communication. Reports were sent and filed more as rituals and no follow-up work was done. Mr. Kalra implemented certain very effective and concise formats for managers which reflected the daily activities and worth of the managers.

The older employees, habituated to an easy life, found it difficult to cope up with the stringent changes. However, Mr. Kalra used to openly declare in the meetings that, "Those who find the job tough may better opt out before it is too late". There were also a few young managers who appreciated these moves initiated by Mr. Kalra for toning up the system.

In the meantime, Mr. Ajit Khanna started getting personal letters from some of his trusted managers complaining about the authoritarian functioning of Mr. Kalra. He ignored them at first, but started taking notice after some of the managers personally met him and talked to him. Further, the sales increase that he had expected vis-a-vis the investment made based on Mr. Kalra's decisions (like enhancement of salary of field force, new appointments to senior managerial posts, expenses on training and development, etc.) was not commensurate.

Mr.Khanna invited Mr. Kalra for discussion and had a long discussion on the following issues:

1. General restlessness and resentment of the managers against him and the effect it had on the morale of the team.
2. Decline in the sales of some of the products which were doing well earlier under the lucrative deal offer.
3. The high expenses incurred on training, sales meetings and other sales promotion activities.
4. Reasons for not achieving Rs. 10 crore sales that Mr. Kalra had envisaged in a year's time, an increase of nearly 30% growth over the previous year.

Mr. Kalra gave valid reasons for the deficit. He pointed out that two or three products which had picked up well suffered due to short supply.

Heated discussion followed and a disgusted Mr. Kalra told his Managing Director curtly, "I throught Neo Labs was a marketing organization but now I realize that it is still a trading house".

Mr. Ajit Khanna reviewed the whole situation once again. True, he realized that Mr. Kalra had done something to improve the image of the company but this was not enough. He tried to take an objective view but failed. All along, Mr. Khanna had the satisfaction of virtually running the organization but now he felt things were slipping. And things are no better now, or probably worse. At the back of his mind was what one of his senior managers wrote to him, "NLPL will never be the same again unless you are back in your seat again".

Shortly Mr. Kalra received a letter from his Managing Director relieving him of his services together with a cheque for salary and allowances for three months as per the terms of employment.

QUESTIONS

1. What is your assessment of the situation?
2. How far was Mr. Khanna right in his attitude of promoting people only from within?
3. Given the fact that Mr. Kalra could not achieve the target set for himself, would you say that Mr. Khanna's management of men and matter is more effective than Mr. Kalra's in this case?
4. Was Mr. Khanna justified in sacking Mr. Kalra?

The case has been appended from the book "The Proces of Management Edited by Dr M.L. Bhasin,. Published by Global Business Press, Abhinav Publishing Industries Delhi.

CHAPTER 19

Organizational Developement

INTRODUCTION

Organizational transformation, organizational development is a buzz word in successful and growth oriental organizations. Information technology revolution and other technology adoption has made tremendous dent into structure, functioning, systems, process and speed with which change takes place in the organizations. Cycle time of production and delivery of products to customer has improved and cycle time reduction is a continuous phenomenon. As the boundaries of markets have increased with free market concepts, the competitiveness has also increased. Technological change and social revolution that the individual is facing these days, he is experiencing a distinct pressure. It has a sequential impact on life style. It is therefore, essential for organizations to improve organizational culture, redefine and redesign jobs, accord full freedom of work and empower the employees so that the organizational productivity is improved and the employees carry at home the pleasant memories of workplace so that their social life is pleasant and enjoyable. Organizations are at work constantly to improve the job satisfaction of employees through organizational development. Organizations have to keep pace with the external environment to enable internal processes and systems updated. Organization development relates to development of individual, group and introduction of such systems in the organization so that the productivity is increased. Organizational development is about people and the organizations and how they function.

Definitions

Organizational development is a planned process of change in an organization's culture through utilisation of behavioural science technologies.

"Organizational development is a long term efforts, led and supported by top management to improve an organization's visioning, empowerment, learning and problem solving processes, through an ongoing, collaborative management or organization culture – with special emphasis on the culture of intact work teams and other team configurations – utilising the consultant – facilitator role and the theory and technology of applied behavioral science, including action research[1]."

Features of Organizational Development

(a) **Long term effort:** Organization development can not be completed in short span of time. As French and Cecil state that it is not a quick fix. It takes several years or even decades to achieve a change. A manager must set very high goals and achieve the same in stages.

(*b*) **Organization development must be initiated, led and supported by top management:** Any change to be effective must be planned at the highest level, initiated and supported throughout its journey. Organization development is a serious issue and top management should not loose sight of it even in the worst of the situations. They must encourage subordinates to introduce change leading to development.

(*c*) **OD is a visioning process:** Visioning means creating a picture of the desired future that includes salient features of the human side of the organization and then working together to make that picture a reality. It is important, therefore, for the members of the organization to anticipate customer preferences, develop a viable plan to design and produce product and services, which delight them. Application of conceptual skills is important for visioning.

(*d*) **OD is an empowerment process:** Empowerment is not meant to be a delegation of authority. It is much more than that. Empowerment invisages identification of leadership qualities and human behaviour practices. It envisages setting up of organizational goals, which promotes individual growth, involving each of the individuals in organizational processes, formulating suitable strategies and attaining organizational empowerment that deals with freedom of action in work environment. It involves job redesign, structural modifications and attainment of goals.

(*e*) **Learning process:** Peter Senge describes learning organizations as "Organizations where people continually expand their capacity to create the results they truly desire, where new and expansive patterns of thinking are nurtured, where collective aspirations is set free, and where people are continually learning how to learn together"[2]. Organization development is interaction of individuals, teams and groups functioning within the parameter of various systems and organization processes with the aim of sharing knowledge and achieving environment leading to growth.

(*f*) **Organization development is a problem solving process:** Problem solving is a collective process in which individual creativity, commitment, vitality is chanalised to diagnose the problem and solve it. The aim of problem solving is achievement of organizational purpose. Collectively organizational environment plays a vital role in problem solving. If internal environment is ideal, problems ease. Contribution of members for a common cause even makes it easier.

(*g*) **An ideal culture is mandatory for Organization Development to be successful:** Organizational processes, systems, visioning, empowerment can be successful if all the members share the common cultural values in the organization. These are ways how organization development can be achieved. Organization culture is something like a fertile land. It consists of basic assumptions, values and norms of behaviour which are perceived as correct. Culture is bedrock of organizational behaviour. The culture is passed on to the new employees. Organizational culture and processes are central to organizational development. Processes are how things are done. For organizational development, it is necessary to enrich organizational culture and update processes to cope with changing environment.

(*h*) **Team based and applied science:** Organizational development revolve around teams, the work assigned to them, the process they adopt and ultimately the output. Team is central to organization. They are building blocks of the organization, when team functions well, the whole organization functions well. Teams are usually independent and task oriented. They are self-directed and take full responsibility of job right from planning to executing. Team takes full responsibility of its success and failure. Complex job is undertaken by cross functional teams who assemble for a purpose and when it is achieved they disband for another mission. Organizational development is applied in nature. It relates to people and their behaviour in a particular situation. Models of psychology, social sciences, economics and other interactive fields are necessary for any organizational development efforts to be successful.

Organizational development focuses on culture and process. Individual group operates under a particular process and develop social relationship. Decision making and problem solving is at all levels. Organizational development relies on action research and focuses on total system change on a long term basis. Organizational development relies on continuous change and development of individual employee and organization as a whole.

Organization development **"is a long term philosophy based on collective commitment, vision, empowerment, problem solving and employee welfare where latest technology and organizational processes are used to create quality of work life to achieve organizational effectiveness and transformation into a vibrant, competitive and growth oriented learned organization.**"

Objective of Organizational Development Programme

1. Individual and group development.
2. Development of organizational culture and processes by constant interaction between members irrespective of levels of hierarchy.
3. Inculcating team spirit.
4. Empowerment of social side of employees.
5. Focus of value development.
6. Employee participation and problem solving and decision making at various levels.
7. Evaluate present systems and introduction of new systems thereby achieving total system change if required.
8. Transformation and achievement of competitive edge of the organization.
9. Achieve organizational growth by total human inputs by way of research and development, innovations, creativity and exploiting human talent.

Quality of Work Life

Objective of quality of work life (QWL) is to improve the general working environment of the organization so that the employees enjoy working because they feel pleasant experience interacting with each other. Lawler (1975) suggest that one of the ways of measuring QWL is to focus on the behavioural outcomes such as rate of turnover, absenteeism, drug abuse, alcoholism, and mental and physical illness resulting from psychologically harmful jobs.

Dubin (1975) points out that job involvement or the self investment of individuals at work is a good index of QWL experienced at work. Uma Sekaran has explained QWL encompassing the extent of job involvement or self-investment at work, their sense of competence (i.e., the extent of their confidence in their own competence at work), the job satisfaction or the satisfaction they derive from the various facets of their work such as from the nature of the job itself, the supervision, co-workers, pay, promotional oppourtunities, growth and development on the job, and other aspects of work environment. Mental health of the employees is also an important factor to measure QWL. Uma Sekaram has carried out research studies in this respect and developed a model of mental health. He has considered individual, job, organization and other network factors as independent variables. Job involvement, sense of competence and job satisfaction as intervening variables and mental health as dependant variable which is an ultimate indicator of QWL. The model is explained in Figure 19.1 below:.

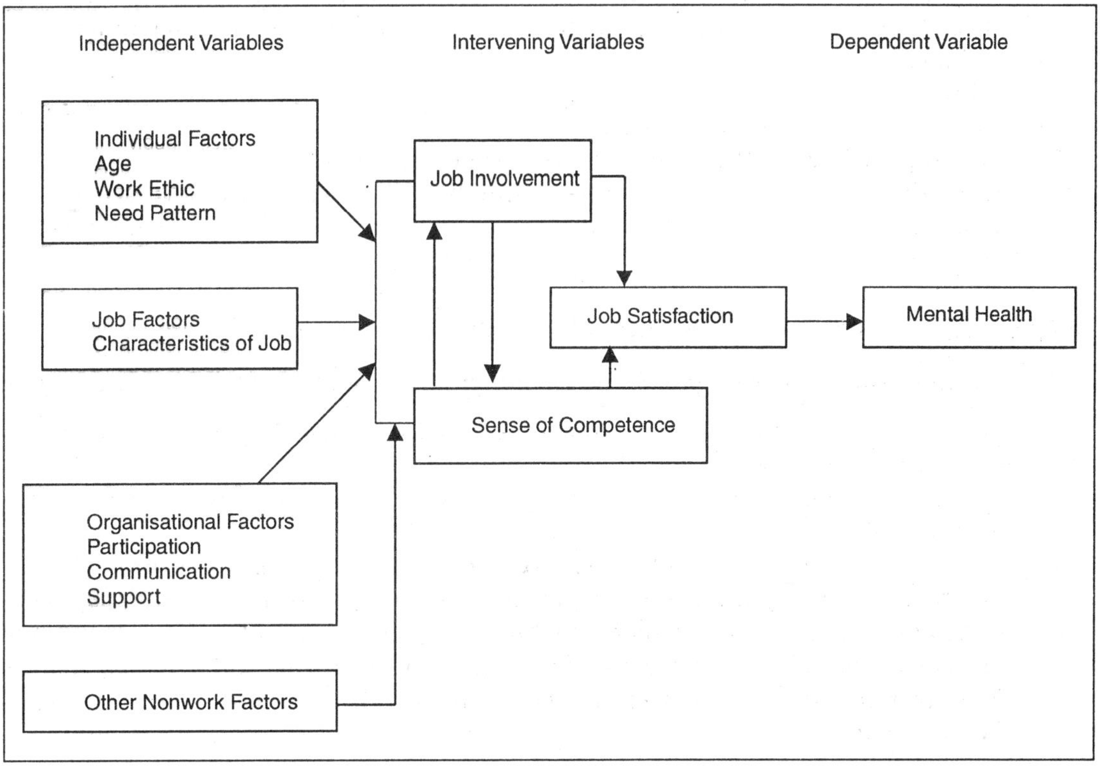

Fig. 19.1. Paths to the Mental Health of Employees

QWL, apart from employee point of view, is also considered from organizational point of view that includes factors that measure organizational growth and effectiveness. These include profits, market share, customer satisfaction, product quality, product innovativeness, services after sales and the image they carry. Social aspect of the QWL measures factors like ecology maintenance, pollution control, generating additional employment, social responsiveness etc. QWL is therefore measured by combined impact of individuals delight, organizational growth and societal gains.

Features of Quality of Work Life

Quality of work life is a concept evolved to solve problems and achieve organizational development. Some of the feature of QWL are as under:

1. Team building and voluntary participation of employees in organizational developmental programme.
2. Training of employees in team problem solving.
3. An understanding of no loss of job in the event of loss caused due to implementation of QWL programmes.
4. Training and development of employees.
5. Use of quality circles and organization for periodic meetings to review the progress of quality of products and to study the problems affecting employee performance at the plant level and general work environment.
6. Organization of meetings, brain storming sessions to discuss on the matters of customer welfare, quality, safety, customer care and production schedules.
7. Job designing.
8. Skill training.
9. Autonomy in work implementation.
10. Evolving various methods to promote responsiveness of workers.
11. Any other issue which promotes employee autonomy, problem solving and improvement of work culture within the overall umbrella of development of organization.

ORAGANIZATIONAL DEVELOPMENT INTERVENTION STRATEGIES

Study of organizational development can be carried out on four different fronts as under:

(*a*) People side or organization which includes personal counselling and career planning at intra personal level.
(*b*) Problem solving, interpersonal communication and interpersonal relationship at dyadic level.
(*c*) Group goal achievement and aspects related to group dynamics at group level.
(*d*) Societal level, organizational development intervention may include assisting people to resolve their personal problems like housing, education, induction programmes and social acceptance especially for those who are new to the organization. Organizational development strategies can be broadly classified in Figure 19.2 on the next page.

Organizational Strategies for Personal Concern

1. Sensitivity Training

Sensitivity training was first introduced by Kurt Lewin in 1945. Sensitivity training is also known as T-groups or Lab training. The method is used to train teams with an ultimate objective of organizational development. Sensitivity training envisages formation of unstructured small groups. Members of the group interact with each other and learn from various situations. Kurt Lewin was a prolific theorist, researcher and practioner of inter-personal and inter group dynamics and a strong propagator of community relationship

OD Strategies for personal concern	Job related OD interventions
Sensitively training	Work flow
Transactional analysis	Job redesigning
Process consultations	
Team building interventions	
Third party interventions	
Individual counseling	
Life and career planning	
Role playing	

Social-technical intervention	Structural interventions
System analysis	Change in physical setting
Flexible work hours	Formalisation
Job sharing facilities	Organizational mirroring
Job evaluation and role analysis techniques	

Fig. 19.2. Diagram showing Intervention Strategies

as an approach to overall organizational development. T group developed various models of role playing, learning, change and transactional nature of human beings. Team building dynamics was the major contribution of T group. Sensitivity training also involved organizational topic like deadlines, study pertaining to duties and responsibilities, policy, procedures and inter organizational group relationship.

Lewin carried out sensitivity training by field theory, group dynamics, evolving change processes and action research that was of profound importance to people involved in development. The method helped individual to change attitude, understand human nature, modify behaviour to suit a particular situation and be a useful member of the team.

2. Team Building Interventions

Teams: Team is a small number of people with complimentary skills who are committed to a common purpose, set of performance goals, and an approach for which they hold, themselves mutually accountable. (Katzenbach and Douglas Smith) Teams have emerged as the most important group phenonenon in various organizations. Joseph Juran first tried to adopt "team approach to problem solving". Today, teams have become increasingly popular as a result of advanced information technology and concern for total quality management and organizational learning processes. Organizational development has shifted from a reliance on individual managers and workers to inter-functional management teams and work teams that focus on complex problems and tasks. Teams can be formed for any purpose. They can go beyond traditional formal work group by having a collective synergistic effect. Production teams, teams for rendering advice in the form of board and review panels are generally formed. Teams can also be formed for completion of the specific task like research and development, engineering work etc. Action teams for sports, entertainment, expedition, surgery and negotiation are also formed. The objective of such teams are to plan, implement and receive feedback of the job done. However Quality Circles and Self Managed Teams are very common in most of the organizations.

Teams and Work-groups: "Team" is frequently used for any group, especially to get them to work to-gether and to motivate them. Jon and Douglas differenciated team and work-group. A work-group's performance is a function of what its members do as individuals. A team's performance includes both individual results and what we call "Collective work products". A collective work products is what two or more members must work to-gether. It reflects the joint, real contribution of team members. Comparative understanding of teams and the work-group is given below:

Teams	Work-group
1. Plays a shared leadership role.	1. The workgroup has strong, clearly focused leader.
2. Team has individual as well as mutual accountability.	2. Individual accountability for the part of work he is doing.
3. Team has a specific purpose.It is a specific part of organizational purpose.	3. Its purpose is the same that of the organization.
4. Collective work products.	4. Work group has individual work products.
5. Encourages open ended, active Problem-solving meetings.	5. Work group runs effective meetings.
6. It measures performance directly by assessing collective work products.	6. Work group measures effectiveness directly (for example, financial performance of overall business).
7. The team discusses, decides, and Real work together.	7. It discusses, decides, and work together.

Fig. 19.3. Comparision of team and work group

(Reference Jon R.Kazenback and Douglas K. Smith, "The Discipline Teams" Havard Sussiness Review)

Quality Circles and Self-managed Teams

Quality circles are made up of volunteers from the lower levels of operations in manufacturing and offer advice to management on improving quality and productivity. On the contrary, self-managed teams, sometimes called autonomous work teams, are formally designated by management and can be made up of employees from all levels. Self-managed teams may make decisions and do the real work of the organization. These teams have no appointed manager. They do their own managerial functions.

Development of Self-managed Teams: Self-managed teams can be developed to a great extent. These teams should be made up of dedicated people who enjoy working together, who maintains high standards and demonstrate high productivity. These teams should be monitered on a regular basis and evaluated in the following areas:

(*a*) Team mission
(*b*) Goal achievement

(*c*) Empowerment
(*d*) Open and honest communication
(*e*) Positive role and norms

By controlling such key functions, self-managed teams can be effective and contribute to the performance goals of the organization[4]. Effectiveness of the team can be achieved by considering following points:

(*a*) A proper training and development schedule should be planned well in advance.
(*b*) A facilitator (trainer) must be co-opted with the team right from the beginning. Team members and facilitator should develop rapport. Facilitator should create an environment where individual member can clear his doubts without hesitation.
(*c*) Group goals should be set up in advance and required resources made available to the team. Processes should be well established.
(*d*) Decision making, delegation of authority and extent of empowerment be clearly spelt out by the organization. Members should experience autonomy in the work environment.
(*e*) The group should be trained in various methods of group decision making, intra group relations and have an adequate knowledge of various group functions
(*f*) Intra-group procedures involving setting up of meeting format, involving taking down of minutes of conference and progressing each point should be known to each of the members of the group.
(*g*) Team members should be so trained that they are self-managed.

3. Transactional Analysis

We have already studied transactional analysis in Chapter 9. TA was first introduced by Eric Berne in 1964. He stated that every individual has three ego states in varying degree. Person acts and reacts depending upon situation and the ego state displayed by the person with whom one is interacting.

(*a*) Parent ego state represents feelings of superiority, authority, being judgemental and so on.
(*b*) Adult ego state represents maturity, objectivity, logic and rationality in communication.
(*c*) Child ego state indicates dependant, impulsive and rebellious nature of behaviour. Most of us have one dominant ego state. Any communication between two people is called transaction. The transaction can be analysed in terms of ego state from which each of the transactions can be complimentary, crossed and ulterior. Complimentary transaction are those transactions where two people communicate verbally from a compatible ego state. For example adult to adult communication. Crossed transaction occur when a message from one ego state is responded in a incompatible ego state. An adult to child communication falls in this category. Such type of communications are not good and it produces anger, resentment and frustration between the two individuals involved in the communication. An ulterior transactions take place when two parties involve themselves in communication where main issue is circumvented.

(*d*) TA ia a useful technique to understand people, their attitude and behaviour. Communication should preferably be from adult-adult ego state. This will lead to better understanding and logical approach to the problem. Crossed and ulterior communication should be avoided while interacting with each other. TA helps to quickly identify and untangle crossed transactions. By understanding the extent to which ulterior transactions occur in organizations, efforts can be made, if necessary to minimize them since avoiding authentic encounters adversely affects the organizational effectiveness. It is therefore necessary for the employees to identify individual ego state, situations under which one is working, organizational stress and its effect on individual behaviour and transact accordingly. By practice, interpersonal problems can be reduced to a great extent and organizsational growth is achieved.

4. Process Consultation

Process consultation requires combination of skills in establishing helping relationship, knowing what kinds of processes to look for in organizations and intervening in ways to improve organizational processes (Schein, 1969). The essence of process consultation is that a skilled consultant (facilitator) works with managers, groups and individuals with the object of developing their process skills. It involves diagnosing, understanding and solving process related problems. There are various processes in the organizations like enrolment process, administrative process having various sub-processes within it. The managers have to evolve a particular process and see to it that it is implemented by all the employees. For example communication process. In this process manager must ensure free flow of vertical, horizontal and diagonal information flow and that no work should suffer for want of required information in required format. Should there be any problem an outsider consultant is employed to examine the process, identify problem areas, suggest solutions, implement and obtain feedback. It involves ascertaining solutions to various issues in the organization. Major processes that are generally evaluated are as under:

(*a*) Organizational structure and organizational design modification
(*b*) Dynamics of inter-personal relationship
(*c*) Nature and scope of communication
(*d*) Issues relating to leadership style that are followed by various leaders
(*e*) Group problem solving on organizational, social and domestic issues
(*f*) Decision making process
(*g*) Welfare measures
(*h*) Training and development
(*i*) Issues of production, Quality control leading to product modification and thereby achieving organizational effectiveness.

The process consultation sensitizes the individuals who are directly or indirectly involved in above processes. Phenomenon is observed in the organizational systems where individual display their voluntary commitment to develop organizational processes and assist each other to resolve issues irrespective of their departmental boundry.

5. Third Party Peacemaking Interventions

Third party interventions are used by a facilitator to resolve conflict in the organization.

Walton (1969) suggests that a fundamental aspect of third party peacemaking is for the consultant to make two disagreeing parties to confront and agree that the conflict does exist which is leading to situation where organizational development is hampering. The problem generally relates to emotional disagreement by conflicting parties. The facilitator resolves the issue by creating congenial atmosphere by way of selecting a place, mode and appropriate agenda for the meeting. During the conduct of meeting, he evolves such techniques that both parties do agree that there exist a conflict between them. The facilitator identifies the problem and suggest remedial methods. If the problem is of structural nature like sharing scares resources, then the problem solving strategies are implemented. If the problem is of emotional nature like anger, distrust, fear the consultant has to adopt strategies for behaviour modification. This will take a reasonably longer time and efforts to resolve the problem.

6. *Individual Counselling*

Counselling refers to the process of advising an employee or preferably in most cases, listening to the statement of his problem and enabling him to form his own thinking and taking a solution for it (Harrel)[5]. Counselling relates to understanding and helping people. As counselling involves discussion, it forms a process of communication. Effective counselling is a function of communication skills by which an individual tends to share his emotions with another individual. Counselling deals with resolving emotional difficulties of individuals which excludes mental illness. Although the emotional problems may not appear to be very significant to others, they are important to the individual who has them and thus whose productive efficiency is affected by them. The problems may relate to stagnation in promotion, job insecurity, feeling inappropriate handling by superiors, job stress and the like. Apart from emotional imbalance, need for counselling may arise from varied on-and-off the job conditions such as dissatisfaction, resistance to change, alienation, frustration, stress and conflict. Counselling provides to solve employee problems so that they develop self-confidence, self-worth, understanding and ability to work effectively. Various functions therefore of counselling are to advice, reassurance, communication, release of emotional tension, clarified thinking and re-orientation (Keat Devis)[6]. While performing the above functions, counselling may have several accomplishments. (Maier) indicates seven such accomplishments of counselling. These are

(*a*) Identification of attitudes and values.
(*b*) Reduction of frustration
(*c*) Location and acceptance of true problems
(*d*) Stimulation of problem solving
(*e*) Development of responsibility
(*f*) Conformity of solution with value system
(*g*) Availability of expert knowledge

Counselling is of two types:

(*a*) **Directive Counselling:** Directive counselling is process of listening to employees emotional problems and advising them. Advice is not preferred as compared to listening. Facilitator may develop mutual understanding with the individual so that the later may be free to release his tension and thus modify self behaviour.

The advice and assurance provided by the counsellor during the counselling process may be worthwhile if the employee has faith in the counsellor. It is more of matter of trust and belief between the two.

(*b*) **Non-directive Counselling:** Roger's, the founder of non-directive counselling states as, "within the client reside constructive forces whose strength and uniformity have been either entirely unrecognized or grossly underestimated. In most of us, if not all, individuals there exits growth forces, tendencies towards self-actualization. The individual has the capacity and the strength to devise, quite unguided, the steps which will lead him to a more mature and more comfortable relationship to his reality. All of his capacities are realized in the individual if a suitable psychological environment is provided (Rogers)[7]. This non-directive counselling is instrumental in the release of dynamic forces within the individual and resolving emotional problems.

7. Life and Career Planning

Life has become very fast because of automation, Social changes, technological leap. Expectation of individual have therefore grown out of proportion. In a family both husband and wife are earning members and they desire growth and social recognition. It is the responsibility of the organization to plan growth of each of the officer/ managerial cadre. This will enhance organization culture, growth and develop sense of belonging. This will also facilitate succession in the family run organizations. At supervisor and workers level, training and development is essential. It is the responsibility of the line managers to organize periodic cadres, refresher courses, promotion cadres and ensure that the work force is kept updated. Career Manning Cell should be established in large organization, whose sole responsibility should be to plan, organize and conduct career planning courses in consultation with HR department, training institutes, government agencies and NGOs. One of the drawbacks of career planning is constant turnover of employees for various reasons. If career planning is effective, the employee turnover will reduce drastically. Career planning is one the important functions of the organization which should be taken seriously.

8. Role Playing

Role playing is a spontenious acting of a realistic situation. Real life situations are used to teach the trainees. When role is played by few individuals, the others observe and criticize at the end of the session. Role playing is a substitute for experience. It emphasizes techniques of observation, participation, copy and discussion. Trainees try to enrich by trying different approaches of role playing. Role playing as a tool of organizational development is an important instrument. It should be carried out under an expert so as to derive maximum advantage.

JOB RELATED INTERVENTIONS

1. Workflow

In highly technological environment, every job has to be reviewed periodically to ensure the job has the following attributes:

(a) **Task identity:** As far as possible a job must identify **"whole"** from its inception to its completion. It is necessary because a worker identifies himself with the job and derieves a greater satisfaction.

(b) **Meaningfulness:** While designing a job due care should be taken that every job should involve skill variety. The job should encompass use of abilities of individuals. The job should not be of routine nature.

(c) **Task Significance:** Employees will derieve maximum satisfaction if the job they are doing is of a great significance. For example manufacturing of a firing mechanism in a petrol vehicle is of great significance.

(d) **Autonomy:** Employees should enjoy autonomy while they are performing. Freedom of action, decision making and discretion in scheduling a job adds to the organizational development efforts. autonomy envisages the content, structure and organization of job in such a way that individuals or groups performing those jobs can plan, regulate and control their own work. Autonomy implies use of individual skills effectively so that the contribution to accomplishment of job is meaningful. It regulates the individual. Autonomy is self governance.

2. Job Evaluation

Wendell French defines job evaluation as "a process of determining the relative worth of the various jobs within the organization, so that differential wages may be paid to jobs of different worth. Relative worth of a job means relative value produced." The variables which are assumed to be related to value produced are such factors as responsibility, skill, efforts and working conditions. It is important to note that job evaluation is ranking of job, not the job holder. Job holders are rated through performance appraisal. Job evaluation provides basis for developing job hierarchy and fixing structure. It must be remembered that job evaluation is about relationship, and not absolute. That is why job evaluation cannot be sole determining factor for deciding pay structure. Various external factors like technological changes, labour market, collective bargaining capacity of the workers, political and economic factors affect the level of wages. It is important to note that regular review of various jobs should be done by the organization and suitable modification to pay structure made. Employees have a positive impact on personal development. It is at the work place that the individual derive their satisfaction and further leads to organizational development in a long run.

3. Job Redesign Strategies

Job design refers to the study of jobs, tasks and constellations of tasks. It includes job enrichment, job enlargement, job characteristics models and social information processing perspectives. The traditional approach involved fitting people to job. A more recent approach to designing jobs incorporates both objectively gathered descriptions of the jobs and the perceived requirements and relationships of job holders. Since Hertzberg's work on job enrichment, a great deal of interest has been aroused in job redesigning, apart from collecting data pertaining to the job and work, a great deal of emphasis on human values have been added. Davis proposed the concept of job design as "the organization (structuring) of a job to satisfy the technical – organizational requirements of the work to be accomplished and the human requirements of the person performing the work". Job designs change as job holder needs and work requirement change. Job redesign strategies seek to address these changes. Job redesign approaches aimed at enhancing productivity and employee motivation include job enlargement. Scópe of the job, variety, activities, number of processes and required skills to accomplish work. Job extension, (doing more of the same work), is a form of job enlargement.

Socio-Technical Interventions

1. Systems Analysis

An organization should study environment both external and internal, analyse the socio-economic factors like prevailing standard of living, social demands on employees, aspirations of children and the ability of the individual to fulfill the same. Demographic factors also play a dominant role in the organizational development paradigm. Based on the above factors an organization should design its reward system so that the employee is able to live in a desired level and meet its social obligation. This is important because the systems so evolved would be able to generate enthusiasm and desire to excel in the job that will being growth to the organization. Contingency approach should be adopted by the managers in this respect and aspirations of the employees be met. Off late the individual has started comparing his status vis-vis the status of the workers world over. Certain amount of parity is required to be adopted by the organizations. In the light of the above discussion following system needs attention:

(*a*) Recruitment system
(*b*) Reward system
(*c*) Appraisal system
(*d*) Training and development
(*e*) Organizational mission with particular reference to growth potential
(*f*) Technical upgradation
(*g*) Social recognition
(*h*) Ability and will of the organization to plan for the growth of children of the employees to enable them to be competitive in the present social scenario.

2. Flexible Work Hours

Organization should plan working based on brick pattern. The responsibility to produce is assigned to teams and work groups. The work should be assigned to them based on timings. All the resources are made available and no interference be made by the senior members thereby providing them the total autonomy. Concept of flexi hours has been discussed in greater details in Job Design chapter. Flexible work hours are necessary for dual career families. For instance, dual career members, who are now trying to combine their family and work lives, face problems managing their work – family interface. Workshop conducted for both spouses on time management, childcare, stress management, and management of the overlaps among the work and family boundaries will be immensely helpful for the members. Uma Sekaran concluded that spending organizational resources for such workshops increase the productivity for the organization[8].

3. Job Sharing Facilities

Organizations should create job-sharing facilities within the organization and may also have tie-ups with other organization for sharing the job. This is particularly required for research and development branch of any organization. Job sharing creates additional facility without any monetary burden on the organization and optimum utilization of resources is achieved. If the facilities are available for performing the work, employees can meet the dead line of their tasks.

4. Job Evaluation and Role Analysis Techniques

An individual should be trained in handling more than one job so that, should there be need, he could be gainfully employed in a different role (job). Individual has to play different roles in the organization. He should be made self-sufficient so that he can fulfill his obligation. It is important that an individual should be satisfied on the job he is performing. Job redesign, job rotation, job simplification, job automation is some of the methods where organizational development takes place.

Structural Interventions

1. Change in Physical Setting

Physical setting and its importance on productivity is a subject on which lot of work has been done. The objective of ideal physical setting of machinery is to reduce physical fatigue to the worker and afford his maximum physical convenience in doing the job. This involves layout of the machinery, position of the operator, availability of tools and raw material. This also involves the supervision that is required to be carried out by the superiors. For example you would see the layout in the banks or in a bottling plant. There are standard layouts available and the organizations can adopt them with suitable modification. The objective is to improve productivity. Taylor has done the pioneering work on the subject in early twentieth century when management concepts were in evolutionary stage.

2. Formalization

Formalization refers to the extent to which policies, procedures, rules, regulation exists in the organization. Policies are basic guideline and principles based on which the organizational objectives are to be fulfilled. Policies are laid down with great thought and deliberation and are indicative of the culture, the organization wants to follow. Policies are mandatory requirements of any system. Policies are general in nature and gives basic guidelines to the manager how to operate. For example recruitment policy or training and development policy for managers. While rules and regulations are strict in nature and individuals have to obey those. There is no scope for deviation. These are prescribed codes of conduct that needs to be strictly followed. Procedures are methods which are practical in nature to carryout any work and the steps involved in it. These are generally stated in the standing orders for an organization. These are necessary to relieve managers of any necessity of directing, so that he can concentrate on the job exclusively. There are certain situations that are not covered in the policy of the organization. Under such situation manager has to interpret the event/situation and give his decision. This phenomenon is called "management by exception". Thus formalization of rules regulations, policies and procedures help managers to focus on the primary managerial functions. Too much of formalization is not advisable as it reduces the personal contact between employees and managers. It also gives the feeling of too much of bureaucracy and lack of operational freedom. For creativity and innovation minimum formalization is recommended. For organizational development, it is therefore necessary to ensure mix of both formalization and work autonomy to the employees.

3. Organizational Mirroring

Organizational mirroring is an intervention technique to assess and improve organization's effectiveness by obtaining feedback from the organizations it is interacting. When an organization experiences difficulties working with other organizations, it can seek assistance from these organizations. The process of organization mirroring is as under:

(*i*) Representative from outside organizations like suppliers, government organizations with whom host organization is facing problems are invited for mirroring or reflect back their perception.

(*ii*) Consultant generally interviews the people attending the meeting in advance of the scheduled meeting.

(*iii*) Consultant in the interview identifies the magnitude of the problem the host organization is facing.

(*iv*) Meeting continues in which groups/sub-groups identifies problems faced by the host organization and suggest solutions.

(*v*) Host organization should be genuine in wanting to resolve problems it is facing with the external organizations, and then only, the organizational mirroring can be of use.

(*vi*) Host organization should implement the action plan developed during the meeting.

LEARNING ORGANIZATIONS

Major work towards learning organization was done by Frederick W. Taylor by introduction of scientific management. However, use of term learning organization is usually attributed to seminal work of Chris Argyris and his colleagues, who made the distinction first – order or "single – loop" and second – order or "double loop" learning[9].

1. Single – loop Learning

It involves improving the organization's capacity to achieve known objectives. It is associated with routine and behavioural learning. Under single – loop, the organization is learning without significant change in basic assumptions.

2. Double – loop Learning

It re-evaluates the nature of the organizations objective and the values and belief surrounding them. This type of learning involves changing of the organization's culture. Single – loop and double – loop learning organization made a drastic change in the present times, in which adoptive learning, generally based on change in basic assumptions like cultural, value and structural change was introduced. The system faced several difficulties. The more important generative learning was needed. Generative learning involves creativity and innovations. Generative process leads to a total reframing of an orgnisation's experiences and learning from that process. Generative learning was propagated by Senge. Based on the above factors, characteristics of the learning organiztation is given in Figure 19.4.

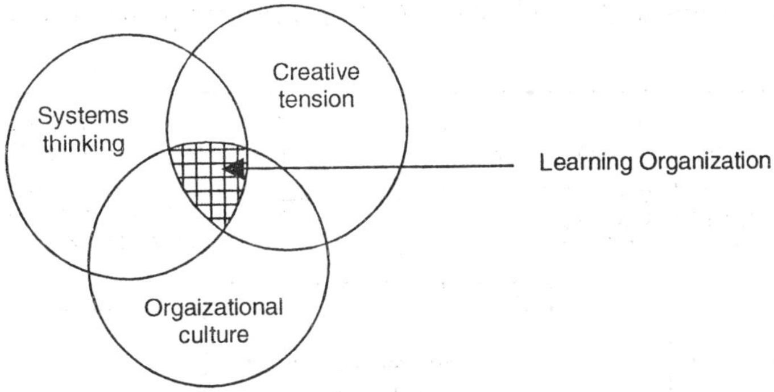

Fig. 19.4. Learning Organization (Source – Luthans)

Figure 19.4 shows the three major dimensions or characteristics of learning organizations. The presence of tension – Senge calls it **"Creative tension"** – serves as a catalyst or motivational need to learn. This tension stems from the gap between the organization's vision and reality and suggests the learning organizations continually questioning and challenging the status quo. The second circle – **"systems thinking"** refers to the ability of learning organizations to recognize the shared vision of employees throughout the whole organization and the openness to new ideas and the external environment. The third major characteristics is the **"organizational culture"**. It must place a high value to learning and setting up of a mechanism for suggestions, teams, empowerment and empathy. The factor of empathy reflects the genuine concern and interest in employee suggestions and innovations that can be backed up by reward system. The congruence of the three circles thus formed can be called as truly a learning organization.

Innovation

Innovation is the process of creating new ideas and putting them into practice. It is the means by which creative ideas find their way into everyday practices, ideally practices that contribute to improved customer service or organizational productivity. Product innovation result in the introduction of new or improved goods or services to better meet customer needs. Process innovations result in the introduction of new and better work methods and operations.

Innovation Process

New product development can be carried out by innovative ideas. The process of innovation takes the following four steps:

1. **Idea Generation:** To create an idea through spontaneous creativity, ingenuity, and information processing.
2. **Initial Experimentation:** To establish the idea's potential value and application.
3. **Feasibility Determination:** To identity anticipated costs and benefits.
4. **Final Application:** To produce and market a new product or services, or to implement a new approach to operations.

The innovation process is not complete until final application has been achieved. A new idea – even a great one – is not enough, In any organization, the idea must pass through all stages of innovation and reach the point of final application before its value can be realized.

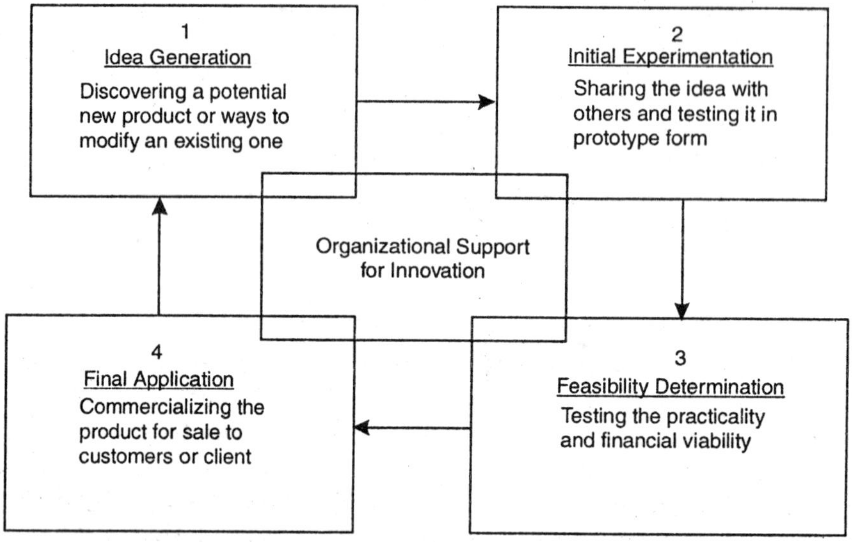

Fig. 19.5. Innovation Process: New Product Development.

Features of Innovative Organization:

(*a*) Highly innovative organizations have strategies and cultures that are build around a commitment to innovation.
(*b*) Tolerance to mistakes and respect for well – intentioned ideas.
(*c*) Highly innovative organizations have structures that support innovation.
(*d*) Emphasise creativity through team work and cross functional integration.
(*e*) Innovative organizations practice decentralisation and empowerment.
(*f*) Plan and staff organization with clear commitment to innovation.
(*g*) Innovative organizations pay special attention to critical innovation roles of idea generators, information gatekeepers, product champions and project leaders.
(*h*) Innovative organizations benefit from top – management support.

Creativity

Creativity generates unique and noval responses to problems. Individual decisions are made by one individual on behalf of a group. In a dynamic environment full of non routine problems, creativity in crafting decisions often determines how well people and organizations do in response to complex challenges[10]. We have examined in chapter on group dynamics that the group, as an important resource for improving creativity in decision making. Indeed,making good use of such traditional techniques as brain storming, nominal groups,and the Delphy techniques can greatly expand the creative potential of people and organizations. MIS, DSS and otheer computer based techniques futher enhance decision making ability of individuals.

Stages of Creative Thinking: Creative thinking is carried out in five stages as under:[11]

(a) ***Preparation:*** In this stage people engage in the active learning and day to day sensing required to deal successfully with complex environment.

(b) ***Concentration:*** Actual problems are defined and framed so that alternatives can be considered for dealing with them.

(c) ***Incubation:*** People look at the problems in diverse ways that permit the consideration of unusual alternatives, avoiding tendencices towards purely linear and systematic problem solving.

(d) ***Illumination:*** In this stage people respond to flashes of insight and recognize the problem.

(e) ***Verification:*** Refers to proceeds with logical analysis to confirm that good problem-solving decisions have been made.

All these stages of creativity need support and encouragement in the organizational environment. However creative thinking in decision making can be limited by number of factors. These are 1. Judgemental heuristics can limit the search for number of alternatives. 2. When attractive options are left unconsidered. 3. Cultural and environment blocks.

Creativity Model

The rational decision maker needs creativity: this is the ability to produce novel and useful ideas. Most people have creative potential that they can use when confronted with decision making problem. But to unleash that potential, they have to get out of the psychological ruts most of us get into and learn how to think about a problem in divergent ways.

Three Component Model of Creativity

This model is based on the extensive work done by T.M.Ambabile on the subject. This model proposes that individual creativity essentially requires expertise, creative-thinking skills, and intrinsic task motivation. The model is shown in Figure 19.6 below:

Three components of Creativity

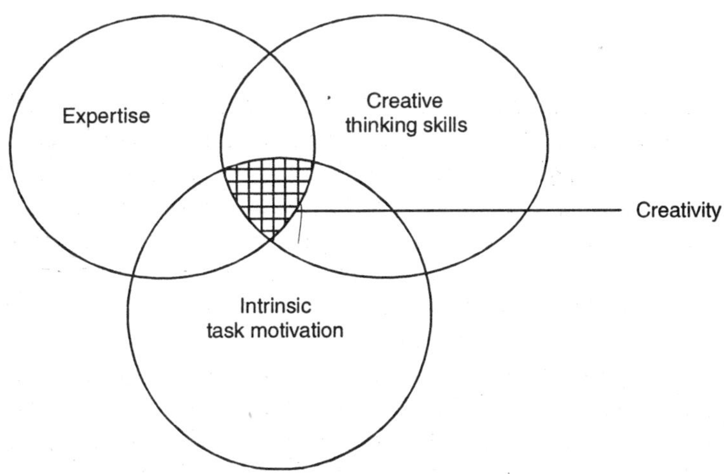

(*Source:* T.M. Ambabile "Motivating of Creativity in organizations". California Management Review 1997)

Fig. 19.6. Creativity Model

1. Expertise

Expertise is the foundation of all creative work. Aryabhatta had an expertise hence he was creative in Mathematics. Dr. Bhaba's knowledge of Physics made him creative in nuclear sciences. The potential for creativity is enhanced when individuals have ability, knowledge and proficiencies.

2. Creative Thinking Skills

This encompasses personality characteristics associated with creativity, the ability to use analogies, as well as the talent to see the familiar in a different light. For instance, the following individual traits have been found to be associated with the development of creative ideas: intelligence, independence, self-confidence, risk taking, an internal locus of control, tolerance for ambiguity and perseverance in the face of frustration[12]. Introduction of telephone has been possible to use analogy of ear drum.

3. Intrinsic Task Motivation

This is desire to work on something because it is interesting, involving, exciting, satisfying or personally challenging. This motivational component is what turns creativity potential into actual creative ideas. It determines the extent to which individuals fully engage their expertise and creative skills. Creative people often love their work. An individual's work environment can have a significant effect on intrinsic motivation. Specially, five organizational factors have been found that can impede your creativity: 1. expected evaluation-focussing on how your work is going to be evaluated; 2. Surveillance – being watched while you are working; 3 external motivators-emphazing external, tangible rewards; 4. competition-facing win-loose situation with peers; 5. constrained choice-being given limits on how you can do your work[13]. It is therefore necessary to objectively study and lay down evaluation systems. Installation of cameras for boss to observe what workers are doing is a bygone method of supervision as it kills creativity. For enhancement of creativity healthy competition and autonomy in work environment is necessary.

SUMMARY

Growth oriented organizations have to study the internal and external environment and make suitable changes. Introduction of information technology, knowledge revolution, technology advancement, competition due to global market scenario, high expectations of customers due to social revolution, and last but not the least the work pressure an employee is facing has made it necessary to carry out organizational development in a planned way. It is imperative to improve organizational culture, redesign and redefine jobs and accord full freedom of action and autonomy to workers so that the organization is always a learning organization. Organization development therefore is a planned process of change in an organization's culture through utilization of behavioral science technologies. Organizational development has following features 1. It is long term 2. organizational development must be initiated, led and supported by top management. 3. It is visionary in nature. 4. It is an empowerment process. 5. A learning process. 6. A problem solving process. 7. An ideal culture is necessary for organizational development. 8. It is team based and applied science.

Basic organizational development objectives are indivisual, group deveopment that involves cultural transformation, social change, improvement of processes, and achieving growth and competitive edge by human inputs.

Organizational development assumptions need to be studied before worthwhile change programme is initiated. Study of individual behaviour is necessary. Achievement of quality of work life is important as it propells the individual towards self investment. Organizational development is classified into four categories 1. Strategies which are related to individuals. 2. Job related interventions. 3. Socio-technical interventions and 4. Structural interventions.

Creativity and innovation is concurrent in nature and management should promote their employees in this aspect. No investment is large for this purpose as it pays rich devidants in the long run. Organization should always train their employees, adopt latest technology and processes, be alert and scan the environment carefully and be pro-active to implement the changes so that you are ahead of the rest and be competitive. Organization development is a continuous process and management support is prerequisite.

TEXT QUESTIONS

Q. 1 Explain the concept of organizational development. What are various inputs that are required for organizational development to be of any value.

Q. 2 What are various objectives of organizational development programme. Why it is said that the programme is to be carried out by human inputs, explain.

Q. 3 List out various organizational development assumptions.

Q. 4 Explain the concept of quality of work life. Does this concept exist in your organization.

Q. 5 What are various strategies relating to personal concern that are carried out by organizations for its development.

Q. 6 Explain job evaluation and how can the job be re-designed. Explain the concept after visiting an organization in close vicinity of your work place.

Q. 7 Evaluate the present environment of the organization and apply socio- technical intervention.

Q. 8 Change in physical setting improves the organization. Explain.

Q. 9 Write detailed notes on the following topics

(*a*) Organization mirroring

(*b*) Organizational culture

(*c*) Work groups

(*d*) Systems analysis

Q. 10 Visit an organization and carryout a study of various methods adopted by them for organizational development.

REFERENCES

1. Wendell L. French and Cecil H. Bell, Jr., ***"Organization Development,"*** Prentice Hall, Fifth Edition 1996.
2. Peter M.Senge, ***"The fifth discipline. The art and practice of Learning Organization"*** (New York: Doubleday/ Currency, 1990.
3. Jon R.Kazenback and Douglas K. Smith, ***"The Discipline of Teams"*** Havard Sussiness Review).

4. Reference.Victoria A.Hovemeyer, ***"How Effective is your Team?"*** Training and Development, Sept 1993. P 68).
5. Harrell T.W: ***"Industrial Psychology"*** New Delhi: Oxford and IBH Publishing Co. 1964.
6. Devis K; ***"Human Behaviour at Work,"*** Tata McGraw Hills New Delhi 1977).
7. Rogers C.R.: ***"Significant aspects of Client-centered therapy,"*** American Psychologist.1946.
8. Uma Sekaran, ***"Organizational Behaviour, Text and cases,"*** Tata Mc Graw Hills Ltd New Delhi, 9 the reprint, 1989.
9. Chris Argyris and Donald Schon, ***"Organizational Learning,"*** Addison – Wesley, Reading, Mass, 1978 and Chris Argyris, ***"Overcoming Organizational Defence,"*** Allyn & Bacon, Needham Heights, Mass, 1990.
10. Bakabanoff and J.R. Rossiter, ***" Recent Developments in Applied Creativity"*** International Review of Industrial and Organizational Psychology 1994).
11. Comeron M.Ford and Dennis A. Gioia. ***"Creative Actions in Organizations."*** Thousand Oaks, CA: Sage Publications 1995).
12. R.W. Woodman, J.F. Sawyer, and Griffin, ***"Towards a Theory of Organizational Creativity"*** Academy of Management Review April 1993.
13. T. Stevens, ***"Creativity Killers"*** Industry week, 23 Jan 1995.

Case

PROBLEM OF RABINDER INDUSTRIES

As an entrepreneur, Mr. Rabinder Bandhopadhyay was fairly successful. He had established his enterprise nearly eight years ago as a small commission agent for a toy manufacturer. Today, he was considered as a major factor in Calcutta for toys, kitchen-aids and presentation articles. He ascribed his success to three principal reasons:

(*a*) Representing only firms that produced well-fashioned quality products;
(*b*) Rendering a courteous and efficient service; and
(*c*) Operating at the most competitive prices.

Not only had he managed to secure the customer of some of Calcutta's discerning and leading retailers, but had also won the business of the medium-sized and the smaller corner-shop operators in and around Calcutta.

As his business grew, he started supplying goods to stockiest all over West Bengal and also to several parts of Assam, Orissa and Bihar. He managed this through a central warehouse and three sub-depots located in Calcutta and another three warehouses, each located in cities in the neighboring states. His present turnover exceeded Rs. 25 million per annum and his enterprise realized a net profit of around 19.5 per cent.

In order to remain competitive, he had designed and operated a differential pricing policy. This was done by issuing his clientele with different colour identify cards, each colour representing a specific trade discount. This enabled him to differentiate between large and small, and the regular and not so regular customer. Also, in order to serve his warehouses and customers efficiently, he maintained and operated his own fleet of lorries, mini-vans and three wheelers.

The nerve center of his business was his headquarter office, located in a four-storied building in the heart of the business center of Calcutta. He was assisted in running the organization by functional and staff managers, who were, for the most part, his relatives and close associates. They were: Finance Manager, Purchase Manager, Sales Manager, Quality Controller, Personnel Manager, Administrative Manager, Logistics Manager, Credit Controller, Stock Controller and Warehouse Managers.

The entire organization comprised of 248 employees, who worked on an average 42 hours per week as follows: Monday to Friday: 0900 to 1730 hours with a 45 minute break for lunch between 1300 and 1345 hours. Saturday: 0900 to 1215 hours.

He considered himself to be an enlightened and progressive employer who operated a 42 hours working week as opposed to the 48-hour week, which was the prevailing custom in most other offices. He also provided his employees with bright, clean, well-ventilated and spacious offices. Further, the employees enjoyed a 70% subsidy on all items provided through the canteen.

Recently, Mr. Bandhopadhyay started feeling uneasy and perturbed. He felt his long-term strategies for further expansion and diversification, especially in the areas of manufacturing, would have to wait until his immediate problems were overcome. A major problem concerned the crisis that was brewing in his liquidity position. Lately, he had been having quite a few arguments with his Bank Manager, concerning his overdraft.

Bank overdraft was quite high. His efficiency was slipping. He was living from crisis to crisis. He was now worried about the reality of the situation that both the warehouse side and the sales side presented. Warehouse complained of delayed deliveries, suppliers not willing to send goods due to outstanding not having been settled and generally poor stock control. Similarly, the Credit Controller complained of delayed collections. When he had contacted the clients to remind them for payments due, he was surprised to learn that some of them had not even received the invoice whilst others said, "give us a chance. Your invoice arrived here only two days ago". Investigating the supplies side of the business, he found there had been delays in sending out orders for fresh supplies. These were, in turn, blamed on the Stock Controllers, who had not raised the requisition on time. Lately, even Quality Control was proving to be a bottleneck area. And finally, to make matters worse, he found his customers complaining of incorrect billing.

When each of the departmental heads investigated his section, they had to admit that efficiency indeed was slipping. All probes indicated that the malady was due to the slackness in the generation, movement and execution of paperwork, which triggered all actions.

This made Mr. Bandhopahyay wonder: "Is my staff incompetent? Am I understaffed?" His Administrative Manager suggested that it was, in great part, due to the uncontrolled late arrival and early departure of staff. On the latter's advice. Mr. Bandhopadhyay addressed a personal memo to all Managers to ensure that their staff should give full 42-hour work output per week. Each Manager devised his own means of communicating this message downwards and took steps he deemed correct.

Each one emphasised that late arrival and early departures would no longer be permitted. Others insisted that the staff would have to put in as much unpaid overtime as the job demanded so as to ensure that no work was kept pending. The result of this was not a happy one. Staff resented the manner in which the Managers tried to pull up their men.

One day, Mr. Mukherjee, who had known Mr. Bandhopadhyay fairly well and had been with the organization from the start, excitedly walked into Mr. Bandhopadhyay's office: "What are you trying to do through your Managers? Incite our staff to take industrial action? Both you and I know the primary reason for this decrease in volume of work output. We cannot escape the fact that on an average each one of us gives only approximately 30 hours of work per week. Over the years, Calcutta's transport has deteriorated and even the most willing amongst us, cannot report on time. Many of us may be one hour late, even after having left our homes fairly early. Naturally, efficiency will suffer. And why do you bring us here on a Saturday? It is a non-starter. You can write if off completely".

For the first time Mr. Bandhopadhyay felt helpless. He realized that what Mr. Mukherjee said was perfectly true. Managing the individual's time to the organization's advantage in the present environment, was going to be a formidable task. He decided it was time to think this over very carefully, he invited two of his Senior Managers, Mr. Mukherjee and two other staff members to spend a week-end with him in the country-side just to discuss the situation in detail.

Place yourself in Mr. Bandhopadhyay's shoes and outline the possible strategies that he may consider adopting, after having carefully considered the opinions of his senior managers, Mr. Mukherjee and the two other staff members.

(The case has been adopted from the book titled "The Process of Management" By Dr. M.L. Bhasin. Published by Global Business Press, G.T. Road Delhi.110095).

CHAPTER 20

Organizational Culture and Climate

Achieving and maintaining quality of product and customer satisfaction are two most important factors of successful organization. To achieve these twin objectives, an organization has to marshal various resources, plan its use over a period of time and produce a product or service, which meets the consumer needs, desire and aspirations. For an entrepreneur, the most important and difficult task is to manage human resource. The task becomes more pronounced if the employees are from different geographical areas having different culture. In such situations, manager should evolve a technique where a strong organizational culture is established. Culture is invisible power of any organization. When thinking and actions of employees are institutionalized, an organizational culture is deemed to have taken birth. It guides the employees. Edgar Schein defined culture as **"A pattern of basic assumptions invented, discovered or developed by given group as it learns to cope with its problems of external adoption and internal integration worked well enough to be considered valuable and therefore, to be taught to new members as a correct way to perceive, think and feel, in relation to those problems."** Wagner III and Hollenbeck have defined organizational culture as **"the shared attitude and perceptions in an organization that are based on a set of fundamental norms and values and help members understand the organization."** Organizational culture is not inborn. It has to be invented and later developed over a period of time. It enables employees to perform within the framework of the organization's culture. Environment plays a dominant role in developing the culture and so does demographic factors. That is why we generally refer to Japanese culture or Indian culture. It is therefore environment specific in nature. On examination it reveals that the organization's culture is informal in nature and relates to shared way of living. It is a common binding factor in the organization. Organization culture help develop professionalism among its employees. Value system is the corner stone of the organization culture. It promotes standardization in various systems and sub-systems, which reduce role conflict to a great extent. Once the culture is developed, it virtually becomes a people's organization from a functional point of view that promotes risk-taking among managerial cadre and generates novel ideas. It promotes communication that improves productivity and job satisfaction. India is a multi-religious, multi-lingual multi-cultural society. Organization culture promotes equality and work culture. The corporate culture ***"consists of norms, values and unwritten rules of conduct of an organization as well as management styles, priorities, belief and interpersonal behaviours that prevail. Together they create climate that influences how well people communicate, plan and make decisions"*** [1]

Organizational culture originates from the founders of the organization based on value system held by them. It is further passed on, down the line. Organizational culture is also a function of the nature of work and goals of the organization. It is visible from the organizational structure. Centralized command and control, strict hierarchy and fixed communication are indicative of formal culture with little freedom of action and with scant attention to innovation and creativity. While decentralized work culture will promote autonomy that will lead to greater job satisfaction. Peters and Waterman state, "Without exception, the dominance and coherence of culture proved to be an essential quality of the excellent companies. Moreover, the stronger the culture and more it was directed towards the market place, the less need was there for policy manuals, organization charts and detailed procedures and rules. In these companies, people, way down the line know what they are supposed to do in most situations because the handful of guiding values is crystal clear.[2]

FUNCTIONS OF ORGANIZATIONAL CULTURE

(*a*) ***It gives members an organizational identity***: Sharing norms, values and perceptions gives people a sense of togetherness that helps promote a feeling of common purpose. Culture provides shared pattern of cognitive perceptions or understanding about the values or beliefs held by the organization. This enables the organizational members how to think and behave as expected of them.

(*b*) ***It facilitates collective commitment.*** The common purpose that grows out of shared culture tends to elicit strong commitment from all those who accept the culture as their own. It provides shared – pattern of feelings to the organizational members to make them know what they are expected to value and feel.

(*c*) ***It promotes systems stability.*** By encouraging a shared sense of identity and commitment, culture encourages lasting integration and cooperation among the members of an organization. It enhances social stability by holding the organizational members together by providing them appropriate standards for which the members should stand for.

(*d*) ***It shapes behaviour by helping members make sense of their surroundings.*** An organization culture serves as a source of shared meaning that explains why things occur the way they do. Organizational culture is not fully visible but felt. At less visible level culture reflects the value shared by organizational members.

(*e*) ***It provides a boundary:*** Culture creates distinction between one organization and the other. Such boundary – defining helps identify members and non-members of the organization. Culture facilitates the generation of commitment to something larger them one's individual self-interest. It serves as a control mechanism that guides and shapes the attitude and behaviour of organizational members.

(*f*) It helps organizational members stick to conformity and expected mode of behaviour. Culture ensures that everyone thinks and behaves in a prescribed manner.

MANAGING ORGANIZATIONAL CULTURE

Once the culture is formed, it is the duty of the organization to enrich it. Management of organizational culture is explained below in Figure 20.1.

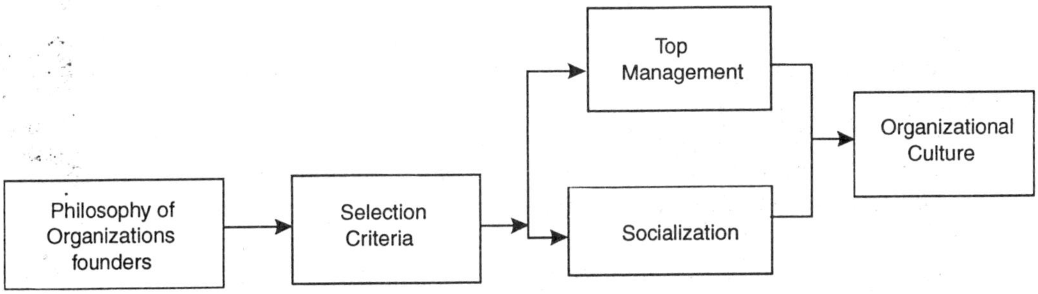

Fig. 20.1. Management of Organizational culture

(*a*) **Philosophy of Organization's Founders:** Culture is valuable for the organization because it enhances organizational commitment. It guides employees towards right direction. Culture is also marked by dysfunctional aspect as well when shared values conflict with the aspects of organizational effectiveness. Such situations take place in dynamic organizational environment where organization do not change with changed environmental factors. Early traditions are the basis of culture in the organization. The vision of founders and various functions of the organization create culture. The ideology and customs are bedrock of any organizational culture. The mission and vision of founder members, hard work, competitive spirit and the way of life is important as it establishes cultural value of any organization. The vision of Ratanji Tata has created a Tata culture. Luthans has suggested following two steps in creation of culture.

1. A single person (founder) has an idea for a new enterprise.
2. The founder brings in one or more other key people and creates a core group that shares a common vision with the founder. That is, all in the core group believe that the idea is good one, is workable, is worth running some risk for.

LEVELS OF CULTURE

According to Edgar Schein, there are three levels of culture, these are discussed in the succeeding paragraphs.

(*a*) ***Observable artifacts of culture:*** These are the symbols of culture in the physical and social work environment. These are visible and most accessible. They include *organizational heroes.* As mentioned earlier, organizational culture originates from the top management and their leadership styles. These leaders become the role model. Employees would like to copy their behaviour, work ethics and represent what an organization stands for. ***Modelled behaviour*** is a powerful tool and organization should continuously learn. They should re-inforce organizational value system. ***Rites and rituals*** are recurring activities that are used at special times to influence the behaviour and understanding of organizational members. For example taking out **Colours** when oath ceremony is underway in the defence services. Colours remind soldiers of the excellent work done by their predecessors and the sacrifices they have made. Presentations of certificates and convocation ceremony in the university. ***Rituals are systems of rites*** like departmental song, colours, and company picnic or retirement dinners. "***Cultural symbols*** are an object, act, or event that serves to transmit cultural meaning". Corporate uniform, tie, buttons etc are the examples. ***Saga is a heroic account of accomplishments.*** Sagas are important because they are being used to tell new members the real mission of the organization, how the organization operates, and how individual can fit into the organizational settings. A saga of valour and sacrifices in the regimental history is a good example of organizational culture. It communicates organizational culture. Certain dress logo can reflect its value and orientation. Many people wear buttons on the uniform suggesting that they are members of golf club or rotary club thus reflecting a sense of value. Some of the material artifacts are reserve parking, air conditioned office, luxury automobiles given to senior members of the organization. These carry with it the value system prevailing in an organization.

(*b*) ***Shared values.*** In earlier chapter we have studied two types of values, i.e. terminal values that reflects end state of existence and instrumental values. Instrumental values are means to achieve terminal values. Being hard working (instrumental value) may lead to achieve solace (Terminal value). Shared value resides at the very heart of the organizational culture. It helps turn routine activities into valuable, important actions, tie the corporation to important value of society, that may provide a very distinctive source of competitive advantage. Employees should be taken into confidence and good work done by them should be recognized so that other workers are motivated to work harder for the organization. Values should be linked with work. A person should feel that he is producing an umbrella that keeps health of the society. He is not merely working for material gain but for good of society. Organizations should therefore develop a **"dominant and coherent set of shared values"** so that individual behaves in a graduated manner in line with the organizational philosophy.

(*c*) ***Common Assumptions.*** Common assumptions are fallout of shared value system and observable artifacts of culture. Employees, over a period of time form within themselves a common culture. In Bajaj Automobiles, everybody comes in time to the plant. Punctuality is therefore a common assumption that is embedded in their organizational culture. In Maruti Udhog, safety is accorded a high priority. Workers health and safety in plant therefore is assumed a common assumption. The cultural artifacts develop cohesiveness that leads to operational productivity. Indians believes in truth and non-violence. Therefore it is a common assumption of our national culture.

MANAGEMENT PHILOSOPHY

Every organization exists for fulfillment of social objective whatever it may be. Automobile industry is there to fulfill the social need of transportation (movement). Organization therefore should spell out their mission and objectives. This will reflect the management philosophy of the organization. It is necessary because 1) it establishes boundaries of operations for each member. 2) It provides the way that situations can be effectively handled and 3) it provides unity of thoughts and known path towards success. Management philosophy should be documented. To promote management philosophy / corporate culture following actions are recommended:

1. Slogan should be prominently displayed indicating organizational mission.
2. Policies, rules, procedures, regulations should be made known to all employees.
3. Recognition of heroes.
4. Belief that rituals and ceremonies would be observed for unity of employees.
5. Informal set of behaviours.
6. Sharing of information and free flow of communication.
7. Adherence to all social, religious norms.
8. Reaching beyond organizational boundaries to dependants of employees and other connected organizations, which can directly/indirectly assist parent organization.
9. Belief in value system and adherence to business ethics.
10. Faith that workers hand would be held in difficult situation.

Myths

Unproven and often unstated beliefs that are accepted by employees. For example 'Safe plant is an efficient plant'. 'Safety over rides every other process in nuclear power plant.' In spite of that there are plants where accidents have taken place. Therefore 'safety is a myth'.

Sub-culture

There is typical and unique dominant culture within each organization. There is usually a sub-culture within a particular group or department with its own pattern of values and philosophy that is not inconsistent with the values of the larger culture of the organization itself.[3] In an organization, finance department may have its own sub-culture that may be part of larger culture of the organization. It is typical of R and D departments to have its own sub-culture in which every individual enjoys a comparatively greater freedom of action. These sub-cultures co-exist with and enhance the overall organizational culture. This is especially true in functionally structured organizations.

Counter Culture

Countercultures have a pattern of values and beliefs that sharply contracts the dominant social norms, values and behaviour patterns. This counterculture tends to emerge when individuals or group strongly feel that the existing organizational culture is too rigid and does not support their creativity or the style of operation. Countercultures are distinctly visible in the organizations that have been merged or acquisitioned. In Balco, there is an original culture when it was a government undertaking. Counterculture has probably emerged after it has been privatized. Both type of culture are coexisting in the organization. In relation to dominant organizational culture, the counterculture groups usually engage in three types of dissent. 1) Direct opposition to organization's dominant values. 2) Opposition to the dominant culture's power base. 3) Oppositions to the methods of interaction with dominate culture. (Yinger, J.M.)

Top Management

Organizational culture is an important aspect of organization success. Once the organizational culture is established, it is the duty of managers to ensure that all workers respect the organizational culture and run the organization as per its philosophy. It is the duty of the management to lay down organizational mission, which is achievable. Too much of ambitious mission is likely to fail resulting in low morale of the employees. It is therefore important that managers play a significant role in keeping values, behaviors and opinions of the organizational members under control and guide them appropriately. Leaders should pay continuous attention to maintaining the established standards and send clear signals to all the members as to what is expected of them. Some of the important points are as under:

(*a*) **Selection.** Standardized procedure should be used to hire right people for right job. Experts should interview the candidates and try to screen out those whose value system does not conflict with that of the organization. Additionally, the selection process provide to the applicants, information about the organizational culture. Should they do not match, the applicants should be given freedom to join other organization. It is important that organizations lay down detailed process of selection criteria and selects a team who can employ right people for right jobs. Personality – job fit must be carefully worked out without any bias. People who are qualified and experienced must be appointed ignoring those with pull and push. The vision, mission, and policy of a sound organization must not be bypassed while selecting the people for work performance. People who do not have core values of an organization must not be appointed because one day they might destroy the very foundation of value system in an organization. Once this happens the whole organization is likely to collapse and suffer losses. In India some of the public sector undertakings have survived because of correct selection process not heeding to political pulls and pushes. While others have discredited because they have fallen pray to whims and fancies of people who have destroyed cultural and value system.

(*b*) **Socialization.** Employees should be properly inducted in the organization. Organization policy should lay down procedure in this respect. Individual employee should be briefed on the organization structure, his department and the immediate superior to whom he is to report. On the job training would go a long way for the growth of an employee. Induction also involves lying down career path for managerial cadre. Training and development programmes, promotional cadres should be planned on a regular basis so that an appropriate message is passed on to the employees. As stated earlier it is the duty of the senior managers to ensure that organizational culture is enriched by their way of handling things under stress and strain where emotions have to be controlled and canalized in the desired direction. It is here that the employees receive a positive signal of the level of organizational culture. Less productive workers should be encouraged and not treated as second-class citizens of the organization. Good managers are able to support and reinforce existing organizational culture by being strong role models and by handling situation that may result deviation with skill and diplomacy.

Newly recruited employees are put through adaptation process called socialization. Socialization starts once an individual is selected. A proper brief of the organization is sent to him at his home. Individual or group of individuals are received at railway, bus stations or at air terminus. They are taken around to various departments and introduced to key appointments. They are later put through the culture of an organization through intensive training program. Special attention is paid to each of the individuals who are put through all the activities of the organization. The aim being to make him aware of the problems and difficulties envisaged. The importance of doing a minor job and its contribution towards a 'whole' job is also an important consideration. The training programme is scheduled in such a fashion that 'on the job training' is given to an individual along with making him aware of organizational culture. The organizational culture is maintained not only in work functions but also in dining, dressing and other developmental activities. Employees on their part prove their commitment with the organization. In case employees fail to adapt to the organization's culture are called 'non conformist' and are further put through an intensive training programme as under.

(*i*) **Pre-arrival Stage:** The values, attitude, personality and learning aptitude is assessed to drive the individual towards organizational culture. It is diagnosis stage, which identifies, in an individual the possibilities of socialization (adaptation) of the organization's culture. Psychologists and behavioral scientists are invited to smoothen individual values to suit the organizational requirement.

(*ii*) **Encounter Stage:** It is an induction stage where a recruit joins an organization and is put through the job. He compares his expectations and image that he has formed with the organizational set up. If the expectations are far from reality, they are expected to learn and follow organizational value system. Those who modify and learn are taken into the mainstream of the organization. Those who resist have to quit the organization being misfit.

(*iii*) **Metamorphosis Stage:** It is a consolidation stage where individual learn the values, norms, culture of the organization. They are made to familiarize with various individuals, and adapt to various prevailing organizational systems and processes. It is voluntary process where an individual is put under a facilitator for learning process. Individual masters skills required for job performance, he adopts new role and adjust himself to changed life style. This becomes a stepping-stone to be an effective member of the team. It is "refreeze stage" of change process.

In the defense services socialization has a great importance where leaders are born and made. Socialization is called 'regimentation'. An individual officer is required to follow daily routine that soldiers follow. In initial stages he has to go through the duties and responsibilities of a soldier by physically doing it. An officer even has to eat the food prepared for troops, share the same barracks for sleep. The aim of the exercise is to make him aware of the criticality and knowing each function from grass route level. This also enables his troops to understand him and his commitment towards them in exercise of command. This type of induction has paid rich dividends.

An officer is taken into the fold of the regiment who sacrifices for cause when time comes and obtains willing obedience and ultimate sacrifice of his subordinates. They live like a family for whole life (duration of service). This exercise continues for about six month to a year. During this period an officers masters skills of handling solders, he knows regimental customs and traditions. He commits himself to the regiment he serves and becomes part of the organization that cannot be detached. Organizational commitment, and commitment to troops you command is total. In Chetwood hall at Indian Military Academy from where the commission is sought, there exist and advice to officer cadets **"Welfare and dignity of my country comes first always and every time, welfare and dignity of troops I command comes second always and every time. Welfare of self comes last always and every time."** That is the socialization (regimentation) all about.

(*c*) Following additional points contribute to enrich the organizational culture

(*i*) Carryout job analysis periodically
(*ii*) Encourage an individual in public for good work done
(*iii*) Define clearly the job requirements
(*iv*) Celebrate festivals that employees greatly value
(*v*) Publicize stories, encourage hero worship
(*vi*) Organize social functions
(*vii*) Ensure quality decisions
(*viii*) Show concern to all employees
(*ix*) Encourage innovative ideas and reward them
(*x*) Lay down promotion policy; create a healthy and competitive work environment
(*xi*) Ensure quality of work life

ORGANIZATIONAL CLIMATE

According to Bowditch and Buono[4] **"Organizational culture is with the nature of belief and expectations about organizational life, while climate is an indicator of whether those beliefs and expectations are being fulfilled."** Employees in the organization keep studying the management philosophy and various actions they take to deal with organizational factors that are of a routine nature. These include the following:

(*a*) Selection Process of the employees.
(*b*) Leadership style and approach to solve problems of the employees.
(*c*) Wage administration.
(*d*) Attitude to implement change and incorporate latest technology.
(*e*) Job description.
(*f*) Organizational structure and frequency to modify the same based on need.
(*g*) Performance evaluation.
(*h*) Promotion policy and its implementation.
(*i*) Efforts involved in promoting creativity and innovations.
(*j*) Availability of resources for research and development.
(*k*) Organizational values and promotion of culture.

Richard M. Hodgetts[5] has classified organizational climate into two factors as under:

(*a*) **Overt Factors**
- Hierarchy
- Goals of the organization
- Financial resources
- Skills and abilities of employees
- Technological state of the organization
- Performance standards adopted
- Efficiency measurement

(*b*) **Covert Factors**
- Values
- Attitude
- Norms
- Feelings
- Interaction
- Supportiveness
- Satisfaction

Overt factors can be measured and fair assessment can therefore be made about the intentions of the management and efforts they are putting in to build an appropriate organizational climate. While on the other hand covert factors can not be quantified being of subjective nature. To measure the level of organizational climate a questionnaire is prepared and feedback is obtained from the employees on the five points scale

(*a*) Strongly agree	5 points
(*b*) Moderately disagree	4 points
(*c*) Neutral	3 points
(*d*) Moderately disagree	2 points
(*e*) Strongly disagree	1 points

Likert[6] has carried out studies on organizational climate by isolating six different variables namely decision making, leadership style, motivation, goal setting, communication and control. Each variable was then evaluated on four diamensions. Each of the dimensions can then be studied on the five-point scale enumerated above. Based on the inputs so received on the specific study of a particular variable an appropriate conclusion of the prevailing organizational climate can be drawn. Suitable remedial measures then can be initiated to modify the climate to desired level.

SUMMARY

Achieving required quality of product and managing customer satisfaction are important factors in running a growth oriented organization. While all the resources can be managed, it is difficult to manage human resource especially when globalisation is the order of the day in all facet of our life. Therefore culture plays a decisive role in running of an organization smoothly. Culture is an invisible power of any organization. When the thinking and actions of employees are institutionalized, an organizational culture is deemed to have been formed. Organizational culture is a pattern of basic assumptions invented or discovered by the people of the organization. Organization culture deemed to have been born when people have learned to cope up with problems of exernal adoption of various systems, processes and technology. Organizational culture is required to be passed on to new members as correct way of thinking, perceiving and behaving. Organizational culture is not inborn, it has to be invented over a period of time and nurtured by all members of the organization. The corporate culture consist of values, norms, unwritten rules of conduct and the the style of governance. Following are functions of organizational culture: (*a*) It gives members an organizational identity. (*b*) It facilitates collective commitment. (*c*) It promotes systems stability. (*d*) It shapes behaviour by helping members make sense of their surrounding. (*e*) organizational culture help develop professionalism among its employees.

Edgar Schein who has carried out indepth study on the subject has identified three levels of culture. They are observable artifacts of culture and include organizational heroes, rites and rituals, dress and logo. These are organizational symbols of culture in the physical and social work enviornment. They are visible and most accessible. Second is shared values and the third level of culture is common assumptions that actually fall out of shared value system. Myth may also be considered as one of the cultural aspect as the indians are having faith in these type of happenings. Every organizarion has a dominant culture and and each of the group of workers or department may have its sub-culture.It is the responsibility of the management to evolve, initiate and promote its own philosophy. It is necessary because 1) it establishes boundaries of operations for each member. 2) It provides the way that situations can be effectively handled and 3) it provides unity of thoughts and known path towards success. Management must pay proper attention to selection and socialization of employees. While carrying out social adaptation activity a newly recruited indivisual passes through pre-arrival stage, encounter stage and metamorphasis stage.

"Organizational culture is with the nature of belief and expectations about organizational life, while climate is an indicator of whether those beliefs and expectations are being fulfilled". Richard M. Hodgetts has classsified organizational climate into two factors. 1) overt factors which can be analysed. 2) covert factors that can not be analysed being subjective in nature. Likert has carried out studies on organizational climate by isolating six different variables namely decision making, leadership style, motivation, goal setting communication and control. Each variable was then evaluated on four diamensions. Each of the dimensions can then be studied on the five-point scale as explained in text of the chapter.

TEXT QUESTIONS

Q. 1 Define organizational culture. How does it differ from social culture?

Q. 2 Organizational culture generally reflects the belief and ideologies of the founder. Do you agree with the above statement? Give reasons.

Q. 3 As a manager of an organization having 400 employees, how will you promote organizational culture?

Q. 4 What are various levels of culture? Explain in details.

Q. 5 What are various functions of organizational culture? Give examples.

Q. 6 How do subculture and counter cultures within the dominant organizational culture exist? Should the management tolerate the counterculture? If so, give your views.

Q. 7 Briefly explain two factors of organizational climate. Visit an organization in your neighbor-hood and carry out detailed study of organization climate it possesses.

REFERENCES

1. Sinn, larry, ***"Corporate Culture"*** - in Readings in Management and Organizations, Edited by Moniqe A. Pelletier Kendall – Hund publishing, 1991, P. 378).
2. Peters Thomas J. and Robert H. Waterman, ***"In Search of excellence"*** Harper and Row, 1982).
3. Martin, J. and C. Siehl, ***"Organizational Culture and Counterculture: An uneasy Symbiosis",*** Organizational Dynamics, Vol 12, No. 2, 1983, pp 52-64)
4. Bowdwitch, J.L. and A.F. Buono, ***"A Primer on Organizational Behaviour",*** John Wiley & Sons, 1990, p 247.
5. Godgetts, Richards M. ***"Organizational Behaviour: Theory and Practice",*** Macmillan Publishing, 1991
6. Likert, Rensis, ***"The Human Organization",*** McGraw Hill, 1967.

Case

ESPRIT DE CORPORTE

(Economic Times dated 14 March 2006)

> The Indian army can teach corporations a things or two about managing their most important resource : human beings. Nikhil Menon finds out what makes the Indian army probably the best – run organization in the country

If you thought that the size of your company presented a mammoth HR management challenge, you might want to think again. In comparison, the Indian army, consisting of over a million men, equipment and infrastructure should be an operational and logistic nightmare. But it isn't. in fact, the army is known for being an institution in a class of its own. Compare it with an organization – any organization - and admittedly the similarities are many. There are hierarchies and functions, leaders and followers, teams, meetings and strategy sessions, very high emphasis on 'delivering the goods' and above all, a sense of organizational social responsibility that makes it our most reliable asset during times of crisis. Perhaps the only differentiator between the armed forces and corporations, then, is the ***raison d'etre***. The objective of the armed forces is task orientation instead of profit-orientation. The attitude is to do 'whatever-it-takes'. "The army's rules and procedures are rigid," admits (retd.) Maj Gen. Satur. adding, "But the rules in the corporate world are bent at the drop of a hat".

However, it's neither possible to run an organization in the same way as the army nor can companies put employees through the same grueling degree of training and spit-and-polish regimentation. However, here are a few things to be learnt by every corporation that wants to create a battle-ready organization that runs smoothly on the back of a loyal and motivated workforce.

Finesse under fire: Soldiers learn to maintain their mental calm and respond instinctively to extreme provocation. "It is a very high pressure job," says Col. Mathew Abraham, HR head, Oberoi Flight and Airport Services, adding, "We ask from them the supreme sacrifice: their lives. But their training and the institutional culture of the army ensures that their physical standards, mentally robustness and professional competence see them through even the biggest crises." Abraham, who has seen the best of both worlds, says that the army's high standards ensure that only the fittest get in at the entry level. The filtering that is subsequently done ensures that it is only the best that make it into the forces and are eligible for higher office.

Lesson to be learnt

Recruiting a candidate is extremely crucial. You have to be sure he/she can handle duress, and actually relish it to an extent.

Take charge

"I sometimes see people grumbling and saying, 'why should I do it? It's not my job," says Abraham. The military's way to get things done is to put your back into the task until it gets done. Sometimes people are not keen to take risks, lest their plans backfire. The support of one's superiors and the knowledge that mistakes are all right as long as they lead to further learning can do wonders for anybody. When in the armed forces, split-second decisions have to be taken and risks are inevitable. "Remember that those under your command are constantly watching you," says Col CPS Waraich, GM-Personnel, Admin and HR, Supermax. "You have to take your role seriously and keep your own conduct above reproach. You cannot afford to wash your hands off a problem," he adds.

Lesson to be learnt

Responsibilities shouldn't prevent you from going out of your way to do something that needs to be done. Also, put your people in the job that best suit them. If you have an energetic young executive on your hands, give him a position that best utilizes his energy. Don't forbid mistakes, it only encourages quick-fixes and shoddy work.

Learning lasts a lifetime

The army is a staunch believer in continuous training and learning. It begins with the military training administered at the beginning of a candidate's entry into the armed forces, then regimental training and then examinations and further regimental training and then examinations and further training at the time of entry into higher levels of authority. Officers are routinely sent for refresher courses and higher studies to improve their skills and knowledge. The Indian army today sends some of its people to the IIMs and other institutes for six-month management courses. Says Col S. Khare, a consultant with an Indian MNC, "There is need – based skill enrichment. Training is not a one-time affair... Like you see in organizations or even the civil services. Soldiers receive training even for retirement."

Lesson to be learnt

Specialization and continuous practice is the key. People wonder what the army does during peace time. The answer is, train harder, improve learning to ensure that people and equipment don't fail when the hour of reckoning comes.

Take pride in your regiment

"The feeling of ownership comes naturally in the army," says Col.Waraish, "You have to create a situation where a person is proud of his company and his battalion." The awe-inspiring image that the army has built up over decades, creates a feeling of belonging that is intensely powerful. Sports and other competitive events build pride in one's own regiment. Officers and their men also intermingle freely at parties, during celebrations, and in the camp. The communication between a CO (commanding officer) and a soldier takes place on a very personal level too. Adds Col. Waraich, "For the first year or so, officers are told to be seen and not heard. This ensures that they observe and understand their environment and comrades closely before they become mature enough to form opinions about them."

Maj. Gen Satur says, "Any jawan has the right to approach the general and get his grievances dealt with. It doesn't work like that in the corporate world. If I don't like your face, I just might remove you and bring someone else in!"

Lesson to be learnt

Reinforce pride in the organization through fair and equal treatment. It is important for the administration to reach every person, instead of the other way round. Only then would he or she want to work with you.

Organisations have always borrowed heavily from the military's strategies and management models. But somehow they haven't been able to attain the same level of discipline that is so essential for the military to function and deliver beyond all expectations. "Perhaps the difference is that the army corporatises the individual, while civilian organization individualise the corporation," theorises Col Khare. Add to that a scenario where different strata and echelons of employees rarely interact with each other and watertight responsibilities that confine individuals to a series of tasks instead of aligning them with the eventual all-important objective, and you begin to see why companies are still entrenched in their old ways, while the army marches on towards dizzying heights of organizational excellence.

QUESTIONS BY THE AUTHOR

Q. 1 Draw a sketch of organizational culture of the Army.

Q. 2 How will you design and implement training and development in your organization.

Q. 3 In Army interpersonal communication has been the key for developing awareness. How will you promote the same in your organization.

Q. 4 Visit one of the Army units in your neighborhood and write an essay on regimentation.

Index

N

O

P